CADMUS'
OPERATIONAL
AUDITING

THE WILEY/RONALD-INSTITUTE OF INTERNAL AUDITORS
PROFESSIONAL BOOK SERIES

Gil Courtemanche • The New Internal Auditing
Philip Kropatkin • Management and the Audit Network
David S. Kowalczyk • Cadmus' Operational Auditing

CADMUS' OPERATIONAL AUDITING

David S. Kowalczyk, CIA, CISA

JOHN WILEY & SONS

New York • Chichester • Brisbane • Toronto • Singapore

P. 93 *Principles and Standards of Purchasing Practice*
used with the permission of the National Association of
Purchasing Management.

P. 405–407 Copyright © by The Institute of Internal
Auditors, Inc., 249 Maitland Avenue, Altamonte Springs,
Florida 32701, USA. Reprinted with permission.

Library of Congress Cataloging in Publication Data:

Kowalczyk, David S., 1946–
    Cadmus' operational auditing / David S. Kowalczyk.
        p.   cm.—(The Wiley/Ronald-Institute of Internal
    Auditors professional book series)
        Bibliography: p
        ISBN 0-471-82660-X
        1. Auditing, Internal. 2. Auditing I. Title.
    II. Title: Operational auditing.   III. Series.
    HF5668.25.K696   1987
    657'.458—dc19   87–23267
                                                    CIP

Printed in the United States of America

10 9 8 7 6 5 4 3 2 1

Preface

Operational Auditing is a term that goes in and out of vogue as the years change. It means many things in many different corporations. Call it what you may, but it is a methodology, a way of thinking. To me, it is internal auditing.

Chapter 1 introduces the subject of operational auditing. The next chapter introduces Manufacturing Resource Planning (MRP II), and gives detailed discussions of day-to-day activities as well as common responsibilities and controls performed in functional areas within a manufacturing environment. The topics covered apply to other industries as well, but are addressed and organized from a manufacturing viewpoint.

Chapters 3–11 address important administrative areas that can give auditors high payback for the effort expended if they use operational audit techniques. The topics covered are not unique nor are they "unauditable." With a little research and a multitude of questions, you can achieve a notable audit in any of these areas.

Finally, Chapter 12 discusses the future of operational auditing with two appendices containing relevant codes and standards for the internal auditor.

I hope this book inspires others to venture into audit areas not previously reviewed. Hopefully readers will be motivated to research and understand other (new) functional areas. The result should be a better, more well-rounded internal auditor and audit group who better understands the corporate environment in which he or she works.

DAVID S. KOWALCZYK

Parsippany, New Jersey
November 1987

Acknowledgments

This books is truly a labor of love. For many years, I contemplated working on *Cadmus' Operational Auditing*. This edition is dedicated to the man who gave me (and many others) the knowledge and information on which to base a profession. His writing style is an inspiration and a challenge to maintain. My thanks also to a mutual friend, Dr. Frederic E. Mints, with whom I have enjoyed many years of friendship; and a man who bridges the generation between Bradford Cadmus and myself.

My appreciation to Paul Heeschen for his many hours of work reviewing, editing, and generally keeping me on track. Paul's editing comments were invaluable. My appreciation also to Paul Sanfilippo, my brother-in-law, for his assistance with the Insurance chapter. Many thanks to my current and prior employers who gave me the latitude and opportunity to experience working in all the areas covered within the covers of this book. To my fellow staff members and other employees over the years, thanks for your contributions may they have been large or small.

However, I give most of my appreciation and all my love to my wife, Linda, and my daughters, Karen and Lori. They are the ones who "lost me" during my travels and many thousands of hours of isolation in "the computer room" while I worked on this book. (But I can't really complain; they do still recognize me when I do walk in the door!)

Contents

CHAPTER 1

Nature of Operational Auditing

OPERATIONAL AUDITING

The term *Operational Auditing* was first used by progressive internal auditors in the 1950s to describe the work they were doing to improve the operations being audited. The constructive approach, the techniques, and the positive results that characterize operational auditing were first used in manufacturing and merchandising but are equally applicable to governmental activities, financial institutions, thrifts, service organizations, or any organization of sufficient size to maintain internal auditing as a separate function.

Operational auditing is characterized by the approach and the state of mind of the auditor—not by distinctive methods. It can be an extension of normal internal audit activities, that is, financial or cycle reviews. Operational audits apply the talents, backgrounds, and techniques of the individual internal auditors to the specific operating controls that exist in the business. Common sense and a good businessperson's view of activities are primary assets in a good operational auditor. This book is concerned with the operational approach that has characterized good modern internal auditing.

Definition

The logic and the reality of the extension of the scope of internal auditing into operations was first recognized when the Institute of Internal Auditors' (IIA) *Statement of Responsibilities of the Internal Auditor* was revised in 1957. This revision described the nature and objectives as follows:

> Internal auditing is an independent appraisal activity within an organization for the review of accounting, financial and other operations as a basis for service to management. It is a managerial control, which functions by measuring and evaluating the effectiveness of other controls. The over-all objective of internal auditing is to assist all members of management in the effective discharge of their responsibilities, by furnishing them with objective analyses, appraisals, recommendations, and pertinent comments concerning the activities reviewed. The internal auditor therefore should be concerned with any phase of business activity wherein he can be of service to management. [The most recent and complete Statement is given in Appendix A.]

The definition in the Statement gives an adequate description of the nature of operational auditing. If this definition is accepted by management and the board of directors, the auditor will have a broad scope for audit activities—as evidenced by the phrases *other operations, assist all members of management,* and *any phase of business activity wherein he can be of service to management.*

EVOLUTION OF OPERATIONAL AUDITING

The extension of the internal auditor's responsibility into operations is a logical evolution from the initial delegation of responsibility to the auditor for the protection of the interests of the company. Protective internal auditing is a function that exists in any business larger than a sole proprietorship. For example, in a shop where two clerks work, the owner will be continually alert to how the clerks are performing their duties. The owner will, almost involuntarily, keep watch to see that sales are properly handled, sales slips are prepared on charge sales, cash sales are rung up on the cash register, merchandise on shelves is neatly arranged, customers are well treated by the clerks; in short, that all that is done by these clerks facilitates the profitable operation of the shop. When watching the cash register, the owner is doing "protective" internal auditing; when observing how customers are being treated, the owner is in the realm of "operational" auditing.

When a business grows to the point where the owner can no longer keep personal watch over everything, he delegates some of these auditing functions to subordinates. The first delegation is apt to be that of responsibility for enforcing the controls that protect the business against fraud, waste, and loss—the protective controls. This is logical because these controls can be definitely established and enforced with little need for judgment in determining how well they have been applied. For example, assume that established procedures call for registering cash sales on a cash register. If they are so registered, as determined by observation, that is "right." If not registered, that is "wrong." Little judgment or business sense is required to verify and appraise in this situation. However, as the size and complexity of business operations increases, the internal auditor moves far beyond the simple situations where appraisals can be based on a clear or obvious right or wrong.

The usual business organization includes a range of operating and service departments designed to mesh together to produce and sell the products or services that make a profit for the business. Governmental and not-for-profit activities are similarly organized with the objective of providing effective service to the country or community. From a control standpoint, one of the advantages of increased size and departmentalization is the opportunity for increased specialization in operating activities. Such specialization enables the utilization of organizational checks and balances for protection against fraud and loss. For example, in a small office the work volume may be so low that a single employee can handle incoming cash receipts, maintain the customers' ledger, and prepare bank deposits. This essentially poor control situation requires considerable detailed protective attention through internal audit or other secondary controls. In a larger office, different employees will be assigned to each of the operations performed by the single employee of the small office. With duties segregated, much less detailed audit work is required. The auditor's attention can and is focused on compliance with procedures and on the effectiveness of how the audit can contribute to the betterment of the unit audited—and to the welfare of the entire business.

Coupled with the specialization of work by personnel in operating departments is specialization in the responsibilities of the work of the different departments. With each department performing its assigned task to the best of its abilities, that task is only one part of the total job. As a result, it is sometimes difficult for any one department or manager to have an objective view of his or her responsible operation in proper perspective to the whole business. The executive will be almost entirely concerned with managing his or her assigned area of the business—even though it may be that more effective operation would be possible through better coordination and communication with other operating departments.

To illustrate, a sales campaign may call for a special advertising program (the responsibility of the sales promotion department) and adequate stocks of merchandise in stores (the responsibility of the marketing services and sales departments). Failure of any one of these departments to do its assigned job at the proper time will affect the success of the entire campaign.

Successful business operation is a team effort. The internal auditor is the member of the team who examines the controls that general and departmental management has established over its operations. The auditor appraises the manner in which these controls combine to permit the most effective and profitable team operation. In short, the auditor's job is to assure management that the controls governing the operations are soundly conceived and effectively administered, and that they help the business operate profitably. If this assurance cannot be given, the auditor must recommend corrective measures where his capabilities permit. If the situation is beyond the auditor's experience and competence, the findings should be reported and further study of the problem recommended.

NATURE OF OPERATIONAL AUDITING

The nature of operational auditing is well illustrated by the viewpoints expressed by senior executives of two large companies who were addressing meetings of their audit staffs.

One said: "I want you to assume that you are the owner of this business, that the business and all of its profits belong to you. Before you recommend a change, before you criticize an operation, ask yourself whether you would do this if the business was yours."

The other said: "I want you auditors to regard your job as that of doing the things for management that the managers would be doing for themselves if they had time to do them."

Both of these views feature the same point: The auditor should be thinking as a general manager thinks. As discussed later in this book, management has only a secondary interest in protective control. Management's main interest lies in line activities; the auditor's observation and appraisal of these activities and the related controls is the essence of operational auditing.

As was previously stated, operational auditing should be considered as an attitude—a manner of approach, analysis, and thought—not as a distinct and separate type of auditing that is characterized by special programs and techniques. A common misconception of some internal auditors is that a clear-cut distinction exists between operational auditing and financial auditing. Auditors look for special manuals that will tell them how to make operational audits when all that is really necessary is a change in their own manner of approach and analysis. Traditional internal auditing was largely directed to protective analysis and appraisal, often to some set of dogmatic standards of financial control. Operational auditing begins with familiarization with actual operations and operating problems, followed by analysis and appraisal of the controls to assure they are adequate to protect the business. This, however, is only the beginning of the audit. The internal auditor is always concerned with the answers to such questions as:

1. Is this control helpful to the management of the operation being audited?
2. Is the cost of maintaining the control justified?
3. Is work being done in one location and duplicated in another? If so, where is the better place to do the work?
4. Are duplicate controls maintained in different locations?
5. Are both good and bad situations brought to management's attention as the basis for management action?

NATURE OF INTERNAL CONTROLS

The IIA's *Statement of the Responsibilities of the Internal Auditor* (see Appendix A) states that internal auditing "is a control which functions by examining and evaluating the adequacy and effectiveness of other controls." This means that the auditor must be concerned with all forms of control that may be established or administered by general and departmental management. The auditor must be familiar with the elements of control as a basis for studying the operations that the controls are intended to govern. Only with this background is the auditor able to identify situations (1) where overcontrol may exist, (2) where controls are inadequate or lacking, (3) where controls are satisfactory, or (4) where improvement or economy in operation is required.

Virtually any organization begins with management developing objectives, plans, policies, and procedures. These decision statements are developed for such matters as product lines and services to be offered, methods of distribution, and organizational responsibility. All of these decisions, while influenced by surveys, studies, and forecasts, are based upon business judgment.

These initial decisions on objectives and policies, and the placing of plans in operation, are the beginning of the duties of management. Beyond these, there is both the necessity and the responsibility for establishing and maintaining a functional structure that will implement and promote the attainment of the objectives. The group of functions designed to accomplish these objectives has come to be known as internal control.

ELEMENTS OF CONTROL

The elements that comprise the structure of internal control are:

1. *Organization.* Adequate organizational control requires that all employees know clearly what their place in the organization is, and exactly what authority, responsibility, and accountability have been assigned to them. Only when this condition is met is it possible to gauge the effectiveness of each employee within an assigned sphere. Additionally, organizational control requires adequate checks and balances. This may entail separation of operation responsibility and accountability so that the same individual is not charged both with the authorization and the performance of a task and also with responsibility for recording and reporting on how that task has been accomplished.

2. *Policies and Procedures.* Policies establish the top level guidelines within which an organization operates. Policies enable operations personnel to make decisions in recurring situations with assurance that decisions will be consistent with the objectives of the business. In brief, policies tell what has to be done; procedures tell how. Control through procedures entails the division and assignment of the total work to be done among the employees of the established organization. Properly designed procedures, within the limits of organizational checks and balances, divide tasks into logical, understandable sections that specify the work and responsibility of each employee. When procedures are not in writing, there is danger of misunderstanding and of considerable variation between procedures and actual operation.

3. *Accounting and Other Historic Records.* The results of the operations must be documented promptly, accurately, and completely, and in conformity with operating responsibilities. Accounting and other records provide the means by which prior results are retained and are available for information and reports.

4. *Standards of Performance.* For reports to be of maximum usefulness, standards of performance are necessary to compare actuals with what was planned or with what happened in some previous period. Budget standards covering departmental expenses and standard unit production costs are examples of standards of performance in common use. It is imperative that standards be attainable and acceptable to those to whom they apply.

5. *Reports.* Reports (usually relating accounting and other measures of activity to standards of performance) are a major means of management control. Inadequate reporting can lead to unwise decisions or ill-considered action. As with records, reports must be prompt,

accurate, concise, and complete. Additionally, they should be (a) impartial in presenting a fair picture of what has been done in comparison with standards and prior periods, and (b) usable in administration to fit the pattern of organizational responsibility.

6. *Internal Auditing.* Internal auditing is responsible for measuring and evaluating the appropriateness and effectiveness of the other elements of control that have been described; and appraising compliance with those control systems.

EVALUATION OF CONTROL

In a given situation, the operational controls will vary under the influence of such factors as:

1. Size and type of operation
2. Cost of particular control measures
3. Organization structure
4. Dominant executives
5. Abilities of incumbent personnel

Because of this variation, each control situation must be individually appraised. Appraisal, by definition, means to estimate worth. Such estimation implies a comparison with some established standard. Thus, the appraisal of internal control requires setting standards of control with which to compare actual operations.

A customary standard of control may not be practical in a particular situation, because of some factor such as has been mentioned. When this occurs, control may still be maintained through intensification of other means of control. For example, in a small, decentralized office, a single purchasing employee would have responsibility for originating requisitions for certain items, placing orders, approving receipt of material, and approving payment to the vendor. The volume of work might not justify any other procedure, despite the manifest control weaknesses. In this case, control might be maintained through such measures as the review of purchasing transactions by another supervisor and a more detailed internal audit program. However, a more detailed audit would not relieve the supervisor of an ongoing responsibility for properly evaluating the work of the purchasing agent.

A subsequent chapter considers various functions of procurement and outlines standards of control in certain instances. These are intended not as axiomatic principles but only as a means of bringing out those situations that may require further study or application of other control measures. Operating controls can seldom be judged on an absolute right or wrong basis. The auditor's initial examination and findings in many situations may do no more than point a way to further study, which will then lead to specific evaluation and recommendation.

INTERNAL AUDITOR'S RESPONSIBILITY

The application of this philosophy of the evaluation of control brings us to the general areas of responsibility of the auditor when reviewing a department or function. The internal auditor is responsible for examination, appraisal, and recommendation of such matters as:

1. *Organization structure,* to see that this gives due consideration to effective operation and protective control.
2. *Policies and procedures,* to determine if they are effective, adequate, economical, understood, and followed.
3. *Records and reports,* to see that they are providing adequate information for both operating personnel and management and that they reveal favorable and unfavorable exceptions from the normal pattern.

Beyond this, the auditor is responsible for examining and reporting on the operation of established policies. This may or may not bring the auditor outside his or her assigned area of prior experience, training, or competence. When it does, the auditor's responsibility is to see that the facts are brought to light, with initiative and action then passing to those receiving the reports. This may be better understood by example. Assume that management policy is to make all purchases of a specified item that is used in a number of locations from local suppliers. In the course of the examination, the auditor notes that one location is able to purchase the specified item at a price considerably lower than any other. In this situation, the auditor should report the effect of the prescribed purchasing policy in effect, supporting the finding by a schedule showing the cost to the company, and suggesting the present policy be reviewed. However, unless assigned this project as a special study, the auditor may not be in a position to make a definite recommendation. The primary responsibility is fulfilled when the auditor has brought the results of the policy to management's attention through the audit report, which should present the facts so the situation may not be overlooked or dismissed without adequate review at an appropriate management level.

When an audit covers an individual department, the internal auditor should be alert to matters that may require further study in other departments. For example, an auditor might note that extensive and expensive changes were authorized by a department after an original purchase order had been placed by the purchasing department. Here, the situation requires the auditor to make sure that the facts are understood and brought to the attention of those responsible for purchasing and for approval of the expenditure, and that the records reveal the additional cost.

Where a departmental audit indicates possible gaps or overlapping in responsibility and activities, management may decide that further study on a broad functional basis is desirable.

Internal auditors in many companies plan functional audits on a regular basis. For example, an audit of materials management might cover requisitioning, purchasing, receiving, incoming inspection, expediting, production and inventory control, storerooms, and issuing product to production. Such an audit avoids the possible provincialism of separate departmental audits, and insures a broad review of interdepartmental responsibilities and controls.

Internal auditors in most companies and their external auditors recognized this principle in the late 1970s, when they started to perform system audits. These auditors recognized that unless a system was reviewed in its entirety, certain controls could be overlooked or omitted. What was the standard practice for the first operational auditors is gradually becoming the standard for all auditors.

The important factor in all audits is the constructive approach, with the ultimate objective of more effective and profitable operation.

PROFESSIONAL STANDARDS

In 1977, the IIA published the *Standards for the Professional Practice of Internal Auditing*. This document was produced after three years of diligent effort by their Professional Standards and Responsibilities Committee. The purpose of the *Standards* is to define the criteria by which the operations of an internal auditing department are to be evaluated and measured. They are intended to represent the practice of modern internal auditing and are intended to be a dynamic and living document to meet the changing needs of auditors worldwide. The *Standards* have been adopted by many major firms.

The *Standards* discuss the auditors' responsibility in Standard 300, Scope of Work, when it states, "the scope of the internal audit should encompass the examination and evaluation of the adequacy and effectiveness of the organization's system of internal control and the quality of performance in carrying out assigned responsibilities." Specific Standards include:

> *Standard 310—Reliability and Integrity of Information.* Internal auditors should review the reliability and integrity of financial and operating information and the means used to identify, measure, classify, and report such information.

Standard 320—Compliance with Policies, Plans, Procedures, Laws and Regulations. Internal auditors should review the systems established to ensure compliance with those policies, plans, procedures, laws, and regulations that could have a significant impact on operations and reports, and should determine whether the organization is in compliance.

Standard 330—Safeguarding of Assets. Internal auditors should review the means of safeguarding assets and, as appropriate, verify the existence of such assets.

Standard 340—Economical and Efficient Use of Resources. Internal auditors should appraise the economy and efficiency with which resources are employed.

Standard 350—Accomplishment of Established Objectives and Goals for Operations or Programs. Internal auditors should review operations or programs to ascertain whether results are consistent with established objectives and goals, and whether the operations or programs are being carried out as planned.

SPECIAL CONSIDERATIONS PERTAINING TO OPERATIONAL AUDITING

Management's Principal Interests

Since an objective of operational auditing is "to assist members of the organization in the effective discharge of their responsibilities" (*Statement of Responsibilities*), the auditor must imagine himself in the position of both general management and departmental management in order to render constructive service to the business. The essential objective of the management of any department or function is the attainment of the objectives outlined by general management. For example, in a manufacturing department, the objective is production of merchandise of acceptable quality at minimum cost; for a sales department, maximum sales of the most profitable items at minimum selling expense. The operational audit must begin with the auditor having a clear understanding of management's objectives for the organization or function under review.

To a good manager, the formal reports of operations will bring few surprises. The manager knows (based upon day-to-day work and contact) how this section of the business is doing; and the reports confirm in figures the facts of which the manager was already aware. For this reason, the auditor should give particular attention to any areas where the manager expresses concern.

Management of an operating unit will be particularly interested in the reports to higher management that show the degree to which planned objectives have been met. When reports include allocations of such expenses as advertising or home office expense, a manager will be concerned with the basis of distribution principally to be assured that the department is not being unfairly charged for these items. Occasionally there may be undue concern with these locally uncontrollable items, to the point that diminished attention is given to those controllable expenses that should have the constant attention of local management.

In brief, the manager of an operation will be interested in:

1. Suggestions to improve operations or to gain better control over them, or otherwise help achieve objectives.
2. The manner in which the results of operations are reported and interpreted to superiors.
3. The impact of home office policies, instructions, and allocations on operations.

Items in Which Operating Management May Not Be Greatly Interested

To work effectively with operating managers, the auditor must understand that they have comparatively little interest in matters that do not contribute directly to the attainment of their objectives. For example, while no manager would question the need for protective controls over cash, the manager will not be much interested in the details of the application of these controls unless something goes wrong. As long as all goes well, the manager will regard such controls as insurance—they are necessary, but they do not help to do a better job in the eyes of superiors.

A manager is interested in protective procedures and controls only insofar as they help operations run economically and effectively. Most managers regard procedures as the plumbing of the business, which should work quietly and effectively behind the scenes to accomplish the planned results. Like plumbing, procedures should come to attention only when there is some unpleasant situation—a leakage or stoppage in the normal flow.

Nothing can hurt an auditor more than nit-picking—or criticizing for the sake of criticism. Managers sometimes suspect that auditors are rewarded according to the number of audit findings reported. Internal auditors should make sure that only significant findings and recommendations are presented in the final report.

Appraisal of Performance

Although it is essential that the internal auditor think in management terms, it is also essential to constantly bear in mind that the auditor is not the manager or the manager's supervisor. Situations sometimes come to light indicating that management made an error in judgment. With the benefit of hindsight, it may be easy to see how a different course of action might have been better for the company. In such situations, the auditor should remember that perfect information may not have been available at the decision-making time. In addition, it is not always possible to determine the effectiveness of a particular management action on a particular business situation. An example of this is a promotional sales activity that was unsuccessful because it coincided with a similar activity by a competitor.

Because of previous background and experience, the auditor may be better qualified to be definite in appraisals and recommendations. If the internal auditor has had broad training and background in financial and accounting matters, he or she may be definite in criticism and positive in proposing corrective measures in these areas.

When auditing various operating departments, both the auditor's own experience and the nature of the departmental operations may preclude any black and white appraisal. This means the auditor must differentiate between opinion and expertise. A formal expression of an improper opinion may lead to inconclusive and confusing disagreement between the auditor and the head of an operating department. The recommendations may also be impractical and/or unworkable. Much care must be exercised by the auditor.

What Is Appraised?

The internal auditor's assignment begins with the examination and appraisal of the controls governing the operations under review. Some of these controls will originate with general management, some with the department.

One function of properly designed controls is to highlight unusual situations that should have further investigation. (A common example is a report that gives a comparison of actual performance with standards.) If the auditor, in observing actual operations or in working with operating controls, notes some condition that appears questionable, the auditor should first determine if that condition was revealed to operating management through the normal controls, such as records or reports. If not so revealed, then:

1. The controls may be deficient, and recommendation for improvement may be in order.
2. The condition may be one not easily susceptible to routine control measures. Further study by the auditor (or others) may be needed.
3. The auditor's preliminary opinion may be incorrect.

Although unable to specifically appraise the efficiency of operations, the auditor is constantly using broad experience in company operations, a natural aptitude for observation, and a background as a business analyst to be of help to operating managers "in the effective discharge of their responsibilities by furnishing them with objective analyses, appraisals, recommendations and pertinent comments concerning the activities reviewed" (*Statement of Responsibilities*).

In summary, the auditor (1) appraises controls in theory and in practice, (2) works with operating management to increase their efficiency and effectiveness, and (3) offers recommendations to improve the operations of the business—both in the field of control and in matters coming to attention in the normal course of the auditor's work.

Qualifications of the Internal Auditor

Since operational auditing is concerned with business analysis and judgment, the success of the audits in helping the business improve operations is largely dependent on the attitudes and talents of the auditor. As previously stated, the auditor should understand accounting and financial records and the principles and techniques of verification and analysis. If possible, this understanding should have been gained in practical fashion through prior experience in operations or auditing. In addition, and of at least equal importance, the auditor should have a broad background and approach to business problems. Scholastic training should have included courses in the humanities, management principles and practice, communications, information systems, accounting, quantitative techniques, and so on.

The specific Standards dealing with the professional proficiency of the individual auditor include Standards 240 through 280, which state that internal auditors should:

1. Comply with professional standards of conduct
2. Possess the knowledge, skills, and disciplines essential to the performance of internal audits
3. Possess the management skills to deal with people and to communicate effectively
4. Maintain their technical competence through continuing education
5. Exercise due professional care in performing internal audits

In addition to the Standards, internal auditors can pass a proficiency exam to become Certified Internal Auditors (CIA). Once certified, internal auditors are expected to maintain their certification by continuing professional development by attending seminars, college courses, or other educational offerings. In addition, the Certified Internal Auditor is expected to maintain a high standard of professional conduct in the performance of his or her profession. The CIA Code of Ethics (see Appendix B) is a prerequisite for maintaining the designation.

he following are some of the characteristics of a competent auditor:

1. *Curiosity.* Interested in and curious about all of the operations. Always asks such questions as: "What is being done? Why is it being done? How does this fit into the business? Is someone else duplicating this work? Is there an easier or better way? Do we need to do this at all? Does this seem to be an efficient operation?"

2. *Persistence.* Investigates until satisfied that the situation is fully understood. Tests, checks, or obtains satisfactory evidence that things are actually done as described.

3. *Constructive Approach.* Looks at those matters that seem wrong as clues, not as crimes. Is interested in seeing how repetition of mistakes may be avoided, not in recrimination as to who was responsible. A mistake is considered as a possible guide to areas of future improvement.

4. *Business Sense.* Reviews everything from the broad viewpoint of the effect on the profitable and efficient operation of the business. Is not governed by dogmatic ideas as to what is right or wrong. Appraises each situation on its own merits. When evaluating any particular area, keeps in mind the relationship of that operation with others and with the business as a whole. Brings to the analysis a global perspective rather than a narrow, green-eyeshade view.

5. *Cooperation.* Considers him- or herself as a partner, not a rival of the manager of the organization or function under review. The objective is not to criticize the department but to improve the operation of the business. The auditor is more interested in having the improvement made than in receiving credit for the accomplishment. Therefore, the auditor works, consults, and reviews recommendations with the auditee and higher management.

The internal auditor must be truly interested in people's problems from their standpoint, not from a narrow protective control angle. When internal auditors learn and understand the problems of operating personnel, they can bring their experience and talents to bear on constructive solutions that will help the operating department and the business as a whole. The auditor should strive to have empathy for the problems of the auditees.

Organizational Status and the Internal Auditor

The *Statement of Responsibilities of the Internal Auditor* describes the organizational position of the auditor as: "Organizational status should be sufficient to assure a broad range of audit coverage, and adequate consideration of and effective action on audit findings and recommendations."

The *Standards for the Professional Practice of Internal Auditing* states that "the organizational status of the internal auditing department should be sufficient to permit the accomplishment of its audit responsibilities."

In spite of recent improvements in organizational status since the implementation of the Foreign Corrupt Practices Act, the majority of businesses still have the audit function assigned organizationally to the financial group, usually under the direct supervision of the vice president of finance. Many audit directors also have access to the audit committee of the board of directors. This status is very acceptable. The *Standards* state that the department should report to a level sufficient to permit the accomplishment of its responsibilities. The most important item is still the backing and support given by the superior.

In summary, both relatively high organizational status and unquestioning support by top management are essential. To perform successful operational audits, the auditors must be in a position to deal as equals with operating managers, not as subordinates.

Relationship with Independent Accountants

The relationship between the internal auditor and the public accountant has received increased emphasis in recent years. In 1975, the American Institute of Certified Public Accountants issued its Statement of Auditing Standards (SAS) No. 9, *The Effect of an Internal Audit Function on the Scope of the Independent Auditor's Examination.* The SAS indicates that the external accountants should evaluate the various internal audit functions and that the results of those evaluations should have a bearing on the nature, timing, and extent of their audit procedures and the degree of reliance they place on the work of the internal auditors. Standard 550 states that the director of internal audit should coordinate internal and external audit efforts.

In fact, the auditors for many large companies have formal and/or informal programs in effect for cooperation with their public accounting firms. For example, one company has a formal plan coordinating overall coverage. Certain predesignated locations are reviewed by the internal auditors with an approved program, and the workpapers are reviewed by the CPA manager and partner. The smaller to midsized plants, divisions, and/or subsidiaries are included in the scope of the internal auditor's review. Coordination of the two groups can be part of the internal audit department's responsibilities. Areas of coverage and the current-year audit schedule should be communicated and discussed with the CPA manager or partner. Reviewing progress and even follow-up of action taken on items in the CPA's management reports can also be part of the internal audit department's responsibility.

Another company negotiated for their auditors to work for the public accountants and to perform an entire audit segment from the procedural documentation review through to detail testing (rather than just supplying an auditor to be stuck with the grunt work as assigned by the in-charge accountant). This work is usually rotated on a biannual basis. Internal auditors are also being used by CPA firms to assist in their audit of company pension and benefit plans.

Some companies include the difference between the CPA average billing rate and the internal audit average cost per hour in calculations to define departmental savings to the company. In this analysis, the CPA manager must also agree to the quantity of total hours saved, if any.

When a staff member works for the public accountants for two or more weeks, the internal audit director should request a performance appraisal of the staff person assigned. This will assist in communications between the two groups; and if any problems occur it brings the problem and the employee to the director's attention on a timely basis.

Essentially no conflict should occur between the functions performed by the independent public accountant and those of the internal auditor. One of top audit management's responsibilities should be to ensure that there is adequate description, cooperation, and complete understanding of the scope of the work of each. When properly done, the work of both will be complementary; confusion, duplication, and conflict will be minimized.

PERFORMING THE OPERATIONAL AUDIT

Objective

The general objective of the operational audit is described in the IIA's *Statement of Responsibilities:* "To assist members of the organization in the effective discharge of their responsibilities. To this end, internal auditing furnishes them with analyses, appraisals, recommendations, counsel, and information concerning the activities reviewed." The fulfillment of this general objective may be considered by the auditor engaged in an operational audit in such matters as:

1. The adequacy of the control structure for which the operating department is responsible
2. Departmental control over its operations relative to:
   a. General company and division policies
   b. Other company departments
   c. Requirements of departmental management
   d. Financial and accounting matters
   e. Government laws and regulations

f. Fulfilling its objectives (charter)
g. Evaluating missions and projects for achievement of goals

The internal auditor should perform operational audits from a businessperson's perspective and not approach audits from a narrow viewpoint, looking only at protective issues. The auditor must look at the impact of recommended actions on the total business.

Objectivity

In considering the steps of the operational audit, it is necessary to understand the nature of the objectivity that is a basic requirement for the auditor's work. Among *Webster's* definitions of "objective," the one that best covers the nature of objectivity is: "expressing or involving the use of facts without distortion by personal feelings or prejudices."

Ideally, objectivity requires that no opinion be developed until all facts have been ascertained and appraised. In practice, this rarely is done. Any individual will begin to develop theories and impressions about a problem from the moment the first facts are developed. Objectivity requires that the auditor be willing to adjust prior theories and assumptions—or to develop entirely new ones—as further factual findings are developed.

In the final appraisals and recommendations, therefore, the internal auditor must be unbiased in recommendations, basing them on the complete facts of each situation encountered during the audit.

Audit Scope and Plan

Operational audits may follow organizational or functional lines, as well as departmental audits, emphasized in the prior sections. The current trend is multifunctional, since such audits should result in a complete appraisal of the internal control and procedures of a total system. Since the Foreign Corrupt Practices Act was enacted, total system audits such as Material Requirements Planning have become more common. However, these audits, covering many departments, can be confusing and very time-consuming. Caution should be exercised. The audit scope can become very large when doing system audits.

The internal auditor must always have in mind the division of functional responsibilities between organizational units. In auditing an individual department, an auditor must be alert to possible duplication or gaps where a functional responsibility crosses departmental lines. An audit of a specific function through all affected departments, or in a number of semiautonomous operations, can be valuable in determining whether the pattern of control over the entire functional operation is economical and effective.

The audit of any department or function comprises four basic steps:

1. Familiarization
2. Verification
3. Evaluation and recommendation
4. Reporting

Familiarization

The first step is to learn with the help of operating management (1) what the objectives of the department are, (2) how it works to accomplish the objectives, and (3) how it determines the results.

In familiarization, the auditor should conform to the primary dictionary definition of an auditor—as a listener. The auditor encourages the operating department heads to tell of their plans and problems. Since the purpose of this discussion is to provide the auditor with background for later study of departmental controls, the emphasis should be on discussion and learning about what is being controlled, not the controls themselves.

For example, in a manufacturing operations audit, a walk through the plant with the manager is essential. The auditor can then visualize and inquire about problems of physical operation, such as handling of scrap, receipt of materials, orders for shipment, scheduling of production, and storage of finished goods.

Very few executives will be reluctant to talk with an auditor who shows a sincere interest in the nature of the actual operations and operating problems. These are the matters in which executives are truly interested. For example, a purchasing manager will be enthusiastic in telling of working with other departments in reducing material costs through a value analysis program. And if the manager believes the auditor is a sympathetic listener and not a troublemaker, he or she may also tell of difficulties with other departments and of how some deal directly with vendors even though procedures prohibit this.

The importance of familiarization with actual operations and problems cannot be over emphasized. Unless the auditor knows what is being done, how it is being done, and why it is being done in the attainment of departmental and company objectives, the auditor cannot perform a competent audit. Specifically the auditor cannot perform the required appraisal of the controls without a thorough knowledge of what is being controlled.

The second step in familiarization is to learn about the controls that establish and maintain the environment within which management operates—the controls that management uses to govern its operations and attain its objectives.

First comes organization structure. Here the auditor is interested in learning the assignments of authority, responsibility, and accountability; the related organizational checks and balances, and the relationships with other departments and between subordinate groups within the department. If an organization chart is not available, the auditor should prepare one to assist during the audit.

Next comes the review of the policies and procedures that govern the work of the department. Here the discussion may be with a departmental administrative supervisor, who will probably be more familiar with detailed procedures than will the operating head. Written policies and procedures are a necessity in practically all operations. Through them, individual employees know what they have to do and how they should do it—and those directly responsible and others are informed as to the scope of responsibility and methods of operation. Written procedures establish standards for work performance. When a violation occurs, it provides a definite signal for further investigation. Something may be unusual about a particular transaction, or the procedure or policy itself may be incomplete or incorrect.

If no written policies and procedures exist, the auditor should learn from operating management the standards that govern the activities that are being reviewed.

With knowledge of departmental operating objectives and procedures, the next step is to become familiar with the structure of accounts and the other records maintained by operating management—both those specified under company policy and those that operating management originates to meet its own requirements. Where the reason for a record is not understood, the auditor should ask.

In becoming familiar with the standards used to gauge departmental performance, the auditor may find numerous interesting sidelights. For example, the general office may have established a budget or other standards that are not entirely acceptable to the operating department. Consequently, the department will prepare and maintain what the general office prescribes, but may not make use of it. Instead, some special record that is considered a more effective means of control will be maintained.

Whatever the situation, the auditor should ask the operating department head what is used to appraise the department's work. How does the manager decide if individual employees in the department, or in the organization as a whole, have done an effective job or a poor one? How good is supervision? What is the most valuable tool or measure in controlling the department? Many managers maintain their own personal file in which they keep the reports and records that they consider to be of greatest value to them. A review of this file, if possible, can be highly valuable to the auditor as an indicator of management thinking— and as the basis for recommendations for improvements in the structure of reports.

The reports prepared to show operating performance will cover a variety of subjects, ranging from those that depict total departmental performance for general management down to detailed listings of such items as material issues or overtime premium pay. In reviewing reports, the auditor should inquire as to:

1. Who receives the report?
2. What does, or can, the recipient do with data contained?
3. Are arbitrary allocations used?
4. How well are reports coordinated?
5. Do reports duplicate other available information?
6. How valid and usable are the comparisons shown in the reports?
7. Do the reports meet management needs?
8. What would result if the report was discontinued?

Reports are usable in control only when they are prompt, fair, concise, and complete. The auditor should have these factors constantly in mind when reviewing the control structure provided.

The process of familiarization continues throughout the audit, as the auditor learns more and more about the details of the operation in the course of his or her examinations and appraisals. However, as has been mentioned, the initial familiarization is the essential first step in the operational audit. If an adequate working knowledge of the objectives and the controls of the operating department does not exist, the auditor cannot perform an intelligent audit.

Verification

Having become familiar with the objectives and responsibilities of the operating department and the manner in which departmental controls are designed to fulfill these objectives and responsibilities, the auditor should then proceed to verification. In this phase of work, the auditor's objective is to ascertain the degree to which actual operations and controls conform to the written and oral descriptions and understandings that departmental management has given to the auditor.

Verification requires that a selected sample of transactions or a selected area of work be examined in detail. The size of the original sample or area will depend on the auditor's judgment and will usually be comparatively small. If a number of deviations or discrepancies are found in the selected area, the auditor can extend sampling to the point where a conclusion can be reached as to the extent of conformity with, or deviation from, the control plans of departmental management and company policy. Where there is a very large volume of transactions or records, statistical sampling techniques provide a possible means for appraising the accuracy of work within predetermined limits of acceptable error.

In verification, the auditor is concerned with establishing facts, to learn whether or not in actual practice:

1. The organization structure and assignment of responsibility follow the control plans of departmental management.
2. Procedures prescribed by management are adequate, reasonable, and are being followed.
3. Prescribed internal checks are being performed.
4. Prescribed procedures and controls provide effective coordination with other departments.
5. Operating records and reports are complete, prompt, factual, and meaningful.
6. Standards of performance provide an effective basis for appraisal of operating results.

Evaluation and Recommendation

A rather definite dividing line separates the process of familiarization, where the auditor is dealing largely with management personnel, and that of verification, where the auditor is dealing with operating personnel and records. In contrast, the verification phase of the audit merges gradually into evaluation as the audit progresses.

When a deviation is found, the auditor must discover the reason and develop certain tentative corrective measures. As the work progresses, the auditor will continually adjust his thinking to conform with additional factual developments. Thus, one cannot conclude that the auditor works only on fact finding, and then proceeds to an entirely separate task of evaluation and recommendation. Instead, evaluation and recommendation are both constantly in the auditor's mind throughout the operational audit.

The auditor will be concerned with correlating the knowledge gained through the familiarization and the factual findings in verification, to determine the answers to such questions as:

1. Do departmental controls operate effectively? If not, what constructive measures can be recommended?
2. If there are numerous deviations from established policies and procedures, does the reason lie with the policies and procedures or with other factors?
3. Do departmental controls and practices conform with company policy? If not, what should be recommended?

4. Do controls help management attain operating objectives?
5. Does operating management understand and utilize controls to its best advantage?
6. Does the structure of accounts, records, and reports follow the pattern of operating responsibility, and does it conform to the way management looks at operations?
7. Is there adequate coordination and cooperation with related departments; are there duplications or gaps in control?

In evaluation and recommendation, the internal auditor must think first in terms of the welfare of the business—and then be sure that the recommendations include adequate protective safeguards. If the auditor begins with protective controls, these may be overemphasized at the expense of effective and economical operation. Beginning with protective controls would be like an architect giving first consideration to the fireproof characteristics of a building, and then fitting the major purpose for which the building was intended into these characteristics. Protection is important and must be provided for, but first emphasis must be given in recommendations to the attainment of operating objectives, followed by attention to any modifications necessary to meet protective standards. When the auditor thinks in these terms, the auditor is thinking as management thinks, and the recommendations will be better understood and appreciated.

The auditor will encounter many situations where no definite recommendation may be possible, either because the facts of a situation may not permit a specific recommendation or because the auditor does not feel qualified to give a definite opinion. Here evaluation is confined to determining whether the established controls revealed a questionable situation to management; if they did, and the problems were recognized by management, no specific action or recommendation may be feasible for the auditor.

Reporting

During the process of verification, evaluation, and recommendation, the auditor will probably have encountered a number of comparatively minor deviations and discrepancies. As soon as he or she is satisfied that these are not symptoms of some major or widespread deficiency, the auditor should proceed to discuss and settle these items at the lowest possible supervisory level. For example, a normal minor error found in verification should be brought to the attention of the supervisor who can authorize its correction; and no further action or reporting should be required aside from a notation in the auditor's working papers. Also, during the course of the audit, the auditor will have discussed on an informal basis with various supervisors the findings and possible recommendations on both major and minor matters.

The auditor should now have in the working papers those findings and recommendations that are to form the subject of the audit report to operating management. This report may also be distributed to senior management of the corporation and to the managers of all affected operating departments.

More capable audit work and constructive recommendations are wasted because of poor reporting than through any other single factor. Many auditors are capable of doing a constructive piece of investigative work, but lack the ability to communicate their ideas to those who must accept and adopt them. Many good books have been published and are available about report writing.

Summarized below are a number of items to be considered in report preparation:

1. Emphasize the items that will improve the operation of the business. Any operating manager will be interested in a procedure change that will reduce costs, and far less interested in one that only improves protective control.

2. Include favorable or betterment findings showing improvement since the last audit, or laudatory comments for a job well done as well as those involving serious deficiencies.

3. Omit minor items not warranting executive attention.

4. Keep the report as short as possible.

5. Do not expect the operating manager to think as an auditor; write the report in terms in which the manager is accustomed to thinking.

6. Make no criticism without a constructive recommendation and supporting factual information. In technical matters, where the auditor may not be qualified to make a specific recommendation, audit findings should be reported with a recommendation for further study by qualified experts where the situation appears to call for such action.

7. Discuss the draft report with all operating supervisors affected by its findings and recommendations.

8. As much as possible, secure agreement on recommendations from operating management and present them as joint recommendations.

9. Where agreement on recommendations cannot be reached, be sure that there is agreement on factual background material. This material is then presented in the report, with statements of the position of the operating department and of the auditor. Higher management then has the basis for making a decision.

10. Send copies (or excerpts) of the final report to every operating department head affected by the report and to senior executives responsible for the audited operation. (If excerpts are used, care should be taken to give an unbiased synopsis of the background and the reasons for recommendations.)

Some companies make the closing conference (the final discussion with local operating management) the occasion for meeting the senior executives of the divisions affected by the auditor's report. This is an excellent means to demonstrate to line operating personnel the support and interest of senior executives and will give the auditor the means of pointing out the constructive contributions that an audit can make to the better operation of the business.

Audit Programs

The remaining chapters describe the control structures and related operational audit activities in the various functions pertaining to the subject function.

A major portion of each chapter will give a description of actual operations and problems to assist your understanding of the related controls. Included in the text or appendices of each chapter are programs that describe the general nature of audit coverage.

All of this material is intended as a guide to the auditor in developing a program. Operational auditing is characterized by an attitude—a manner of approach, analysis, and thought. It is not a distinct and separate type of auditing characterized by special programs and techniques. Creativity is limited only by an individual, not by a company. Effective operational auditing depends on the auditors and the auditors' state of mind, not on the programs. The auditor must develop programs to meet the needs of any operating department being reviewed.

CHAPTER 2

Manufacturing Resource Planning (MRP II)

INTRODUCTION

In the 1960s, direct labor was the dominant cost in many manufacturing environments. Accordingly, much time and effort was expended for industrial engineers to establish work standards, process flows, and human factors engineering. As labor became more educated and more expensive, it decreased as a percent of total product cost; material has become the dominant cost in the 1980s.

We now expend much time and effort tracking material. Direct labor expense is still decreasing, while indirect labor expense to track material is increasing. While accountants consider inventory an asset, operations management considers all inventory above an absolute minimum as a liability. As a general rule, as the amount of inventory increases, the amount of problems increase. Inventory must be purchased, expedited, received, inspected, controlled, expedited to the factory floor, inventoried, further inspected, moved through the plant, packaged, and finally shipped. Scrap, spares, safety stock, and so on create residual inventory, which continues to be subjected to the same processes mentioned above.

In the mid- to late 1960s, Material Requirements Planning (MRP I) was initiated to assist the inventory control process. Most of these areas

TABLE 2–1
Material Requirements Planning Materiel Topics

Chapter	Topic
3	Purchasing
4	Receiving
5	Scrap, Salvage, and Surplus Material (including Inventory, Stores and Warehousing Topics)
6	Traffic Operation and Organization

can now be found in the materiel function (see Table 2–1). MRP I assisted inventory and production control, purchasing, and expediting. Combined with other techniques, companies could better control materiel, but not the manufacturing process. Something was missing.

Currently Manufacturing Resource Planning (MRP II) has come of age. While some people consider MRP II an application system, it is more than that. MRP II is:

A management process
A management philosophy
A management commitment
A fully integrated, formal, closed-loop system
A starting point, not a final destination
A different way of thinking

MRP II requires (and instills) discipline. It is a fully integrated corporate system used to plan and monitor all resources of sales and marketing, engineering, and finance, as well as manufacturing. It requires continuous feedback and modification. Planning time is reduced from months to weeks and sometimes requires daily reaction time.

Benefits to be derived from a fully functioning MRP II system usually include such items as:

Improved communications
Increased employee morale
Team building
Decreased inventory levels (at all levels of the process)
Reduced warehousing needs
Less expediting labor
Better plant utilization
Greater throughput

Better quality control (faster feedback on problem identification)
Increased disciplines throughout the organization
Better financial planning
Better matched supply to customers' demand

With all these benefits, management is still challenged to control the data base and ensure that the (ideal) on-line, real-time, closed-loop system has proper segregation of duties. The data base must be reviewed to see who has update capabilities in the data base, and to what fields. Security must be reviewed for access control—especially when employees change jobs or leave the company.

MRP II topics are discussed in general in this chapter (see Table 2–2). The materiel topics are discussed in detail in the referenced chapters.

A corporation, similar to an automobile, is an integrated entity that works best when all parts work and fit together. If all cylinders don't work in tandem, the car as a whole suffers; it bucks and eventually will fail. The same is true of an organization, especially with today's highly sophisticated systems. Maintaining this fine tuning is an ideal job and the challenge for the operational auditor.

Each auditor needs to become as knowledgeable as possible in the manufacturing process and the control systems in existence at a given location. Avoid departmentalization when auditing—look at the total process flow; ask for the concerns and frustrations of the controller, the president, as well as the manufacturing personnel interviewed.

ENGINEERING

The manufacturing process/cycle starts in engineering. Research and development (R&D) develops a prototype product based on marketing or on someone else's idea. Engineering provides the initial construction (prototype) to put an idea into reality. Manufacturing design takes R&D's prototype one step further toward a manufacturing reality. Engineering

TABLE 2–2
Additional MRP II Topics

Engineering Design and Manufacturing Engineering
Shop Floor Data Collection
Inventory Planning and Control
Production Planning and Control
Production Scheduling
Vehicle Administration

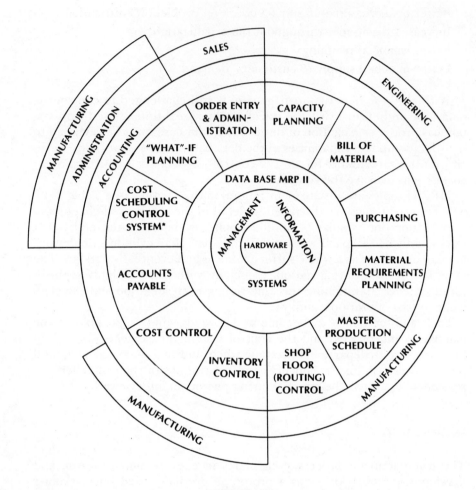

EXHIBIT 2–1

drawings describe specifications to the purchase agent and to potential vendors. The parts, as assembled, must fit together within certain tolerances. However, specifications should not be so tight that purchasing cannot do its job.

Engineering involvement may only be the product or could extend into designing equipment to produce the product, or into package development, and so on. Here we shall concentrate on the product itself. For example, if one company were to build a personal computer, the engineers would probably:

1. Identify major components:
   a. Monitor
   b. Keyboard

    c. Cabling

    d. Central processing unit (CPU)

2. Identify subassemblies such as:

    a. Disk drives

    b. Hard disks

    c. Major circuit boards

    d. Large scale integrated chips

    e. Cabinets

    f. Special purpose (color) boards

3. Identify specific parts and purchased components

4. Develop manufacturing standards and specifications for:

    a. Routing labor for component assemblies

    b. Housing production in sheet metal shop

    c. Wiring harness assembly

    d. Material tolerances: incoming parts inspection, in-process sub-assembly performance, final test, system integration, protection from voltage surges.

We now have computer aided engineering (CAE), design (CAD), and manufacturing (CAM) equipment, which eventually expedites the engineering and manufacturing drawing process. Accuracy is improved, and what-if modeling techniques can be explored faster and with less cost. This becomes increasingly true with large-scale products (buildings, planes) and modifications therein.

Controls over engineering blueprints and drawings should be logged in by drawing number and date. A master list showing the latest version should be catalogued. In addition, for warranty, recall, and maintenance records, the company may need to know what parts are contained in the product, or *what version* a final product's serial number consists of. With blueprints and drawings on disk, the auditor has to be additionally concerned with security, write access, and backup and recovery of data. If the product is defined or highly confidential, access to all drawings or blueprints should be limited.

Product life cycle is circular. Changes can occur in technology. The state of the art can create different, stronger, lighter, healthier, safer, or less costly materials/products. All or some can be beneficial to the producer and/or the consumer. Accordingly, inventory obsolescence via engineering change notices (ECNs) can be common. This may be quite evident if significant amounts of obsolete or slow-moving inventory are noted.

The auditor should review interdepartmental relationships among engineering, purchasing, manufacturing, marketing, cost accounting, and so on. Engineering should get feedback from marketing and sales on product performance and customer satisfaction. This can be very important input to new product development or current product enhancements.

MANUFACTURING

The auditor should find out what departments are within the manufacturing manager's responsibility. It may include only those departments directly involved in in-plant production of the product; or it may encompass production control, quality control, assembly, inspection, and so on.

The methods used by the company should be periodically reviewed to determine if they are the best available (within the allowed cost parameters).

Research should have been done on materials-handling techniques and equipment. Plant layout and product movement should be analyzed. The optimum number of forklifts, flatbed trucks, skids, and pallets should also be determined.

The amount of supervision on the day shift should not be disproportionate to that on the night shift. The safety of the workers may be diminished by a lack of adequate supervision. Review the productivity of the day shift versus the night shift. Review all shifts. Reduced interference and management interruptions can cause greater efficiency on the night shift. Otherwise, lack of attention can also reduce the motivation to produce.

Supervisors and foremen should have enough time to do their own jobs, and they should not constantly be pressed into service as machine operators due to manpower shortages or work backlogs.

The company should not be reluctant to promote its better machinists and other hourly employees into positions of authority because of fear that production will suffer. (This may not only be true in production but throughout the company. In some industries, companies pay some hourly employees so well they refuse promotions into management positions.)

The company should take adequate steps to protect both its products and its manufacturing processes against theft and/or imitation. Infiltration and corporate espionage can occur. Some companies design their own equipment and their own processes. Proprietary formulas should be properly protected.

Product recalls can be very harmful to a company's reputation and very costly to implement. Accordingly, a good quality control program should be in effect. Product recall programs should be tested periodically for all locations and for at least one slow-moving and one fast-moving product.

Production Control—A Diagram of Its Elements

Production control coordinates and controls the four basic elements of a plant: money, machinery, material, and manpower. The harmonious movement and integration of these elements is extremely complicated and calls for a great deal of operational control.

Production control is the central function of the total manufacturing process at most plants. It is responsible for the complete material flow from raw material through manufacturing and subassembly fabrication to final assembly and testing of the finished product.

Areas of special concern in the manufacturing process include:

Short- and long-range forecasting
Finished parts requirements planning
Economic order sizing and control
Machine floor loading and scheduling
Basic input to manpower and facilities load planning
Customer order scheduling and control
Interdepartmental communication
Inventory analysis and evaluation
Computer analysis and evaluation
Computer production application systems
Warehousing methods and materiel control

The company should compare its production schedule to actual output and attempt to find the reasons for discrepancies. Expectations should not be unrealistic. Production control should be evaluated by management to:

1. Determine whether the total system is functioning
2. Determine what degree of variation from plan exists

Large material usage and labor variances in cost may indicate inadequate control in establishing performance standards.

Substantial over- or under-absorbed overhead may reflect inefficient utilization of equipment. Excessive inventories of raw materials, work-in-process, or finished goods may indicate ineffective production control. Machine downtime from lack of work may indicate inadequate planning and scheduling of production.

Production Scheduling

Production schedules should be designed using sales forecasts as a starting point. The schedules should be followed. If they are modified too often, they probably serve little or no purpose. Seldom-enforced schedules are usually ignored.

Production problems may be traced to internal sources such as absenteeism or insufficient equipment or to outside vendors who consistently fail to meet delivery requirements.

Items that require the same extensive setup procedure should be scheduled so that the procedure is done only once. If a worker must perform the same setup operation two or three times a day for different production runs, the worker will think poorly of the company of his or her supervisor.

Economic lot sizes should be calculated and used.

Production Schedule Guidelines

The following guidelines are used by one company:

1. Both the planner and the supervisor will agree on scheduled commitments. If a conflict of interest occurs, the production manager and the project coordinator will settle it during the scheduling meeting.

2. Material shortages not anticipated by the planner will not count against the schedule attainment of the supervisor, but against the planner's scheduling efficiency.

3. Quality assurance is considered part of the work center for scheduling purposes, and its work must be complete as well.

4. Materials movers must ensure that completed work is moved forward to the next stage in the routing. Credit will not be given until the scheduled work is moved. This will require timely input to the data collecting system.

5. Activity on anything not on the schedule (outside of routine production maintenance and overhead activity) must be approved in advance by the appropriate planner.

6. Schedule-related problems that will affect commitments must be communicated to the appropriate planner in advance of any action.

7. Manufacturing usually refers to an assembly operation; however, similar concepts and approaches can be followed in process-flow and service operations.

8. The scheduling cycle data is analyzed by the planners and developed into achievable shop floor production schedules based on individual shop backlogs, capacity constraints, priority of project milestones, and material availability.

9. Schedules will be generated on a weekly basis at the weekly schedule meeting. At this meeting, performance to the prior week's commitments will be discussed and recorded, and the current schedule distributed, discussed, and committed to. Also, problems and other items concerning scheduling will be discussed. The focus of the meeting is for the supervisor and the planner to officially agree to the next week's schedule. The meetings will be individual-oriented, with one supervisor and one planner at a time.

10. Each month, all planners and supervisors, along with selected interested management personnel, will gather for a monthly schedule

performance meeting. Discussion will contain indices on schedule attainment, planning efficiency, and other schedule-related information.

The shop schedules are a listing by scheduling unit showing shop orders, part numbers, quantities required, when due, and so on. They are the primary device of all planning and scheduling activity. Adherence must be absolute. They will be maintained on a weekly basis by the planners using the data collection system. The overall success of the schedules is based upon systematic discipline. As such, guidelines must be followed and maintenance activities kept current.

Shop Floor Data Collection

One company's shop floor schedules are based upon block scheduling rules, using weeks as the primary scheduling unit. The shop floor work centers are arranged into schedulable units using the criteria of logical, associated, and similar functions; individual supervisory responsibility; and individual planner responsibility. This methodology promotes the concept of teamwork between planning and shop floor supervision. It also accomplishes individual accountability for planning and performance.

Overtime normally is authorized in advance and factored into the cost of the budgeted (forecast) product cost.

MACHINE UTILIZATION

Requested investment (money) in computerized machinery is always increasing. The demand for faster, more reliable and precise production tolerances gives rise to the need for and the utilization of computerized machines.

Equipment now can be programmed to:

Assemble components onto circuit boards
Etch electrical circuits
Calibrate to test subassemblies within a defined tolerance

Primary machine purchase justification rests with manufacturing management. Justification factors to be considered are both tangible and intangible, and must be weighed carefully.

The company may have too many or too few machines. Determine how they use mathematical (minimum-maximum) formulas or other methodology to determine the optimum number of machines. The research should entail something more advanced than a survey of actual machine hours used versus potential machine hours available to reveal how extensively the company uses its resources, but not if its resources are sufficient.

Manufacturing should do its own forecasting with regard to which machine will be required to do what job for how long.

Such significant capital investment in machines warrants an adequate basis on which machine utilization and performance evaluation can be made.

An adequate and meaningful method of determining machine utilization and productivity should exist. At the same time, management should agree with the evaluation measurements used, and should continually review these factors.

PARTS REQUIREMENTS—EXCESSES AND SHORTAGES

Space availability should be considered an important constraint and not be disregarded in production scheduling. With the introduction of computer integrated manufacturing (CIM) and the just-in-time (JIT) concept, space may not be allocated for inventory storage. Recent theories consider inventories a liability (operations viewpoint), not an asset (accounting viewpoint).

Plant inventories usually increase to levels far beyond projections, with the corresponding capital expenditures needed to maintain and control them. An adequate inventory analysis control therefore must be maintained if parts overages are to be kept to a minimum, as well as precluding a shortage of parts that could seriously affect production schedules.

Inventory Control

Material may be issued at standard, actual, or an adjusted standard cost. In defense contracting, cross transfers are not allowed unless approved. Other MRP II systems may transfer at average cost, which may or may not meet a company's needs.

Naming standards and conventions are used, but different part numbers may exist for the same part used on different jobs/contracts/spare parts.

Standards may be established for lot sizes of 100, when in fact the average run size may be 10. This can result in higher per-unit costs and overall startup costs. Shop floor practices can change, while the engineered standard may not have.

Bills of material should be reviewed for missing parts and subassemblies, and to determine if quantities listed are accurate. One common input should correct, update, and create file maintenance for all relevant systems.

Key reporting areas for controlling inventory include:

1. Production and labor reported by workstation should be complete, accurate, and timely.

2. Material received and issued via move tickets from one department to the next, with both department supervisors signing for the quantity transferred.

3. Move tickets should account for scrap, rework, and rejects.

Inventory overages may appear tolerable but can also be indicative of trouble. Offsets will eventually come. Also, more harm can come to the company if customers are being shortshipped.

Scales should be periodically checked to see if they are in proper working order. Tolerances should be within limits; overages (and, in CIM and JIT, shortages) cost money—quickly.

Fast-moving products should be segregated (and stored closest to the door) from slow-moving products in warehouses. Uniform product codes (UPC) should be reviewed. If the UPC is similar on two or more products, they should not be stored near each other. As a further safeguard, a check digit should be used to reduce improper product pulls. High-volume products stored close to the door will reduce movement for both incoming and outgoing merchandise. A manufacturing production line can be designed not to move products into a warehouse but directly onto a loading dock for shipment. Use others' vehicles to the fullest extent.

Inventory should be secured, and nothing issued without using a controlled prenumbered receipt and issue form. An integrated stock status/ inventory accounting system should be used. The inventory control clerks should periodically verify bay/bin locations and buy-before dates.

Manufacturing should have effective controls against the theft of tools and equipment. Tool cribs are normally used to safeguard tools.

Inventories

Inventories should be reviewed periodically for bad material, shortages, unsalable inventory, and adjustment to inventory accounts, and approved by individuals independent of those with physical custody over the inventories.

Periodic (annual) inventory or cycle counts should be done and reconciled to subsidiary records. Appropriate action should be taken on unreconciled differences. Physical inventory/cycle count should be identified and adjustments made to books of account and subsidiary ledger. Is a reworked product considered good? Maintain appropriate procedures to add/deduct from inventory records.

Physical Inventory

For physical inventory planning, a review of shipping and receiving documentation should be done. For a proper cut-off test, using two to three days minimum is better than using just one. This will capture most, if not all, in-transit, shipped-not-billed material, and inventory that is FOB shipping point.

Missing inventory and negative balances should be reviewed as a matter of course. Unprocessed/missing inventory tags, shipments relieved from paper stock prior to actual physical pull, and coding errors in identifying parts issued (use computer assigned check digits) all can be a probable cause. Consigned inventories (to customers/from vendors, stored in trailers, railroad cars, or tankers), rejected material, material on hold, and materials at vendor plants should be properly controlled and periodically confirmed and examined.

When pricing the inventory, the accounting department should double-check the units-of-measure (also review calculations on conversions) and review issues and stated values for equivalents, such as:

Pounds versus gallons (liquids)

Metric versus avoirdupois (dry weight)

Quantity to a box/carton

Boxes/cartons to a pallet

Determine if a common pallet pattern is used; if so, determine if the pallet pattern changed recently.

Was there a change in assumptions or labor input in work-in-process? What is the source of input data? Is it the same (a common) input used for different systems? Do they control via cutoff the amount of production for the various shifts? Review and determine if one shift's ending production count is the same as the next shift's beginning number.

Examples of possible exception reports for inventory include:

Parts by contract by part number, indicating rejected transactions or those suspected of being in error.

All stock in part number sequence regardless of contract number.

Potential shortages on kits. A before-the-fact report measures selected kits against the stock-status-on-hand column before the kits are sent to the stockroom to be filled. The report lists all part numbers that do not have sufficient quantity on hand to meet the kit requirements. For each part short, the report lists the kits the part is required on, the kit number, the item number on the kit, the quantity required per assembly, and the total quantity.

List of parts that have been scrapped during the course of the contract in part number sequence.

List of adjustments resulting from physical inventories recorded. List the quantity adjusted, plus or minus for each part number, and the total dollar value of the adjustment. The summary page gives the net total dollars adjusted as a result of the inventory.

All parts that have a minus quantity on hand in the available column. Also, another report could show (if allowed by the system) all part numbers with a negative inventory on hand.

Causes of shrinkage commonly can result from:

1. Items counted more than once or not at all: dual counts, recounts of probable errors, in-process, storage on railroad trailers, van storage, outside (overflow) warehouses, in-transit goods, and so on.
2. Counts taken from inaccurate perpetual records; the system may accept negative balances.
3. Wrong items counted, or items counted incorrectly. Items could be on consignment, defective/rejected parts on hold from manufacturing, not released by quality control. Items in incoming inspection or at outside vendor for testing, rework, and so on.
4. Incorrect part/product number. Units of measure or cost standard used is incorrect: feet versus pounds; cases versus units; units versus square feet; improper conversion factors: metric versus avoirdupois; volume versus weight. Mathematical errors, extension/footings.
5. Improper cutoffs—work-in-process, receiving, shipping. No-charge shipments not relieved from inventory, interplant company transfers.
6. Drop shipment not recorded.
7. Production material used for nonproduction purposes.
8. Substituted material usage, not properly recorded.

Fraud

Examples of potential fraud in the movement of inventory include such items as:

1. The selling of scrap using wrong weights (usually involves collusion); less stock is recorded on the bill of lading than is actually sent.
2. Issues to floor from stock can be made, with no actual movement to the floor; the goods are diverted and sold.
3. The ending balance one month, to the beginning balance the next, is changed.
4. Work-in-process is lost due to lack of move tickets, or no prenumbered move tickets.

Cycle Counts

Effective cycle counting should concentrate counting efforts on the items requiring the greatest attention. Major benefits can be accrued with minor investments in time and labor. The results will be cost savings, not an added expense.

Potential savings could include reducing the obsolete inventory and increasing manufacturing efficiency (without stock-outs). Expediting shortages will not be necessary, and they are, shrinkage should be spotted earlier and identify the source(s) of the shortage.

Cycle counts should be established with a desired frequency based on: the size of available staff, a slow time period (quarter, week, year, season, or plant shutdown). Cycle counts can be developed by an individual item or for a class of items. Characteristics could include high-dollar items, high-usage items, long lead-time items, multiple product usage items, and the probability of pilferage (item marketability).

Cycle counts should be conducted with enough time prior to major production runs to purchase additional items if required. Recount criteria in some companies incorporate automatic part inclusion when a part's inventory balance is at a low point, or shows a zero or negative balance.

Cost Accounting Systems

For changes in the cost accounting system, someone in accounting should be responsible for following up on input controls, parallel processing, and determining that the new system works as intended.

Paperwork flow, accounting entries, and input/output controls should be documented. Accounting should approve all adjustments to the inventory.

The system may default to zero cost if no standard is contained, rather than rejecting the item. What controls are contained in the system to identify changes in price, market, and/or product cost?

Inventory shrinkage and obsolescence can be affected by:

Major product design changes
Product recalls
Make or buy decisions
Change in equipment (startup, etc.)
Work-in-process
Changes in an operating system, cost accounting system or inventory system.

Other causes include inadequate physical security and unreported production and paperwork delays.

Engineering Changes

Considerable time and expense is usually involved in engineering changes. Such changes, however, are necessary to insure the safe and improved operating standards of parts and machines. Engineering changes should be geared to improvement of the product and not be made for the sake of change itself.

The auditor's purpose should be to determine that engineering changes are properly processed and recorded. Emphasis on the cost of the engineering change must be considered, and the proper levels of approvals for the change secured.

An overall evaluation should be made of each engineering change selected in the sample to determine its total impact on current inventories, current production schedules, and current purchases.

Joint participation in value analysis programs that are established to try to reduce overall company expenditures should be tried.

Audit Approach

Depending on the size of the plant, the auditor may either conduct an overall operational audit, including all areas specified in Table 2–2; or, if the plant is too large, the auditor can audit the areas individually.

Ideally, 100 percent machine utilization and productivity is desirable but, in practice, unattainable.

The machine manufacturer supplies percentage factors based on operations performed during factory tests. However, revisions of these guidelines are necessary based on conditions and operations unique to each plant.

For machine utilization, the auditor should determine:

1. What reports and analyses are available to management for machines that show utilization and efficiency figures
2. If management accepts such figures as being realistic and conclusive
3. Whether, if various jobs and operations have industrial time standards assigned, they are:
   a. Established by manufacturing-engineered methods
   b. Temporary standards
   c. Educated estimates
4. Whether manufacturing and industrial engineering departments are in agreement on estimated time standards being used. Does an active program exist to review and update jobs and operations with and without time standards?

5. What the economic justification was for the original purchase of computerized machines selected for review. Are any of the significant purchase justification factors being realized?

The auditor will find that direct labor time recording is usually the basic factor for determining machine utilization. However, the accuracy and reliability of these time recordings will have to be established.

If direct labor time recordings are made against various jobs and operations without established industrial time standards, then an effective and reliable comparison is lacking. Machine operators could be recording time against a machine-in-operation labor code when in reality the operator may be setting tools, and so on, and the machine is idle.

This situation may raise several questions:

1. Are there enough direct labor time codes to cover any given machine situation?
2. Are established industrial time standards being prepared for machine operations?
3. What is management doing to improve time recording accuracy and reliability?

Inaccurate labor time recording has the following adverse effects:

1. It directly affects machine utilization and performance ratings.
2. It forces production scheduling on a computerized basis with on-line adjustments.
3. It directly affects the unit cost of parts worked.
4. It reduces effective report use by management.

Machine efficiency (output) measurements used will have to be ascertained. Most plants have a weekly machine load report that is compiled via the same labor input. Recording deficiencies also directly affects computations in this report.

Inventories

In reviewing inventories, the auditor's concern is that an evaluation and analysis of the current inventory portion for selected production parts is being made to determine if production controllers are actively reviewing their parts and adjusting purchasing requirements in lieu of changing production conditions.

An audit sample selection should be made of those parts from inventory control records that appear to be excess to current production requirements. Likewise, those parts that are in short supply to production requirements as indicated on a short, or hot, list should be sufficiently sampled and reviewed. Parts selected in the two categories above should be scheduled by the responsible controller.

Following are several audit programs that one company uses to review its manufacturing operations.

INTERNAL AUDIT PROGRAMS—MANUFACTURING RESOURCE PLANNING

The following data is presented as one company's individual audit programs. The material includes questionnaires and audit programs for MRP II areas, including production planning, control, and scheduling; inventory control; and physical distribution. Physical distribution is further segmented into transportation/traffic, warehousing, shipping/receiving, packaging, and vehicle administration.

Once again, these programs are presented to give the reader ideas as to how companies structure their programs, and to present the reader with different program styles. The programs for traffic, inventory, and receiving are significantly more brief than the programs following the chapters devoted to those topics in this book. They are intended to be; they are from different companies and are to be used with different intents.

Production Planning, Control, and Scheduling Function

Introduction

This program is concerned with (1) material controls and the flow of material through the plant; and (2) scheduling and planning (relating production to sales, determining material and labor requirements, and comparing planned results with actual). In the event all functions are to be audited, the various programs should be reviewed to eliminate duplication of steps.

General

1. Prepare an organization chart of the departments showing job classifications and duties.
2. Review budget reports and obtain explanations for line-item variances from the year-to-date budget. Schedule and vouch the major actual charges to departmental expenses for a particular month.
3. Obtain copies of the reports issued by the departments and explain the purpose and how the data are compiled.

4. Obtain copies of the reports received by the department and inquire as to their usefulness.

5. Obtain copies of forms used in the department and prepare a brief write-up and a procedural flowchart showing the flow of all paperwork. Flowcharts should be prepared for each scheduling phase (from a sales order to a finished product) and the material control phase (the flow of documents supporting the flow of material).

Sales Forecast

1. Ascertain that sales forecasts are accurate and realistic to a degree that reliable production forecasts and requirements can be prepared.

2. Determine that production schedules are properly prepared on the basis of the forecasts and sales orders.

3. Ascertain that the production planning department is promptly notified of all sales-order changes and specification changes that may affect the flow of work and cause variations in previous plans.

Production Planning

1. Determine that production schedules are established and approved with an objective of economical operations; determine that standards are set up for the most economical group of orders.

2. Obtain reasons for any carryover of items from month to month in the production schedules; determine the effect of the backlog and if this is an indication of lack of cooperation or failure to attain projected production.

3. Determine that production schedules are being followed and met by examining daily department and machine reports, such as: shutdown reports, attainment-of-schedule reports, inspection releases, and reports of delivery to stock or shipping room.

4. Ascertain that equipment is efficiently utilized by examining equipment utilization reports; determine if low utilization is directly associable to the scheduling function.

Material Purchasing

(See Chapter 3, Purchasing, for a more detailed review of purchasing controls and a more detailed audit program.)

1. Evaluate the accuracy of the projected schedules for ordering raw material; determine that the production planning department is notified by the purchasing department of vendors' lead

times; determine that such lead times are considered in the projections.

2. Determine the specific causes of material returns (unrealistic inspection requirements, lack of quality consciousness on the part of the purchasing department, short lead cycles); ascertain that returns are not disproportionately high.

3. Ascertain that possible obsolescence, storage costs, delivery costs, price changes, and economical quantities are considered in placing requisitions.

Material Control

1. Trace selected production orders from the raw material stage through the operational phases to finished goods shipped; tie in consumption from one operational unit to the next; determine that the actual material put into production agrees with the standard material requirements; determine that engineering changes are properly coordinated with the planning; note any delays at any stage of the operation.

2. Determine if material controls are realistic and if the control records are adequate as perpetual inventory records; ascertain that accounting records are not duplicated; determine if mechanical equipment is being properly utilized.

3. Determine that major book and inventory differences are promptly and thoroughly investigated; ascertain if differences indicate possible flaws in the system; ascertain that differences are reconciled before further purchases are made.

4. Review the system of recording production and determine if production is recorded at the point where it is most feasible to collect information for use in cost determination, budgeting, and inventory control; review controls over scrap, defective material, and other losses; determine that losses are reported at the point incurred.

5. Review finished-goods inventories for overstocked and obsolete items; obtain explanations and determine if the situation was caused by improper assumptions in planning.

Additional

1. Review completed orders and compare promised, completed, and actual shipping dates; obtain reasons for significant variances.

2. Examine incomplete order files; ascertain whether the planning department is currently advising sales of the status of unscheduled orders and revised promised dates; obtain explanations for old orders for which work has not been started.

3. Evaluate the size, scope, personnel, and duties of the production planning department; ascertain that the department is given sufficient authority to perform its duties; evaluate the results of the department's operations.

Preaudit Questionnaire

When the arrangement letter is sent, the following questionnaire should be sent to the location's materials manager. The completed questionnaire should be available upon the auditors' arrival.

General

1. What is the function (charter or mission) of the production planning and control organization?
2. Prepare an organizational chart of the production planning and control department, including job titles, names, and grades:
   a. Number of people in production control
      Salaried _____
      Hourly _____
   b. By job description
      Number of managers
      Number of production planners
      Number of production schedulers
      Number of clerical
      Number of other
   c. Review job descriptions for each position.
3. What was the total production planning and control operating budget for last year? $ _____
4. Is there a regular sales forecast?
   a. Who prepares the forecast?
   b. How often is it issued?
   c. In what detail is it prepared?
5. How does planning adjust for peaks and valleys in sales to level factory loads?
6. How is plant capacity determined?
7. What role does production control play in
   a. Authorizing stock orders
   b. Changing lead times
   c. Changing direct labor manning

8. Are schedules made
   a. According to the production plan
   b. To obtain the highest possible labor efficiency
   c. To minimize set-up costs
   d. Based upon known manufacturing intervals
   e. With allowances for rush orders
   f. Considering other factors
9. How does the department coordinate the quantity requisitioned and the purchase price to the cost allowed in the proposal/quotation or other pricing of an item?
10. Does the department have access to production contracts between the company and the customers?
11. Does production control issue periodic delivery performance reports? What were the attainments for the last two years?

    Current year _____ %

    Prior year _____ %

    a. Is delivery performance measured against company promise or customer request?
12. Does production planning and control advise sales/contract administration or the customer, in advance, when delivery dates are going to be missed?
13. Is production planning and control, manufacturing, or both responsible for assuring movement of an order through the shop?
14. How are production levels determined and how often are they reviewed?
15. Who schedules priorities in the final quality function?
16. Who identifies the need for overtime?
    a. Who authorizes and approves the overtime?
17. What formal training has been afforded the production planning and control group in the past two years?
18. What Information Systems (IS) assistance is in use for production planning and control?
    a. What is planned?
    b. What is needed?
    c. What (if any) problems are being encountered?
19. List the various reports issued by the production planning and control department. Have one copy each available for the most current period.

20. List the various reports distributed to the production planning and control department. Have one copy of each available for the latest period.

Internal Audit Program

Preliminary

This audit segment is concerned with (1) sales forecasting, (2) production planning and control, and (3) production scheduling.

1. Review all division and/or local policies and procedures in these areas.
2. Follow up on the most recent audit report and ascertain if corrective management action has been taken. Obtain reasons for any deviations noted.
3. Review the preaudit questionnaires and discuss the content with the materials manager.
4. Tour the production plant to gain familiarization with the plant operations.
5. Update the permanent files.

Audit Steps

General

1. Explain the purpose and how data are compiled for the copies of reports requested in the preaudit questionnaire.
2. Evaluate the lines of communication between the production control department and the other departments (because of the wide and varied contacts within the organization, the planning and control activity becomes a coordinating function). No one group should dominate the others at the expense of the organization. The following are to be considered:
    a. **Sales department.** Exchange information regarding consumer needs; production control should notify the sales department of slow-moving items for appropriate action in the forms of special sales promotions.
    b. **Purchasing.** Exchange information on vendor's lead times, planned production, and economical purchase quantities.
    c. **Accounting.** Understand the others' roles in inventory control and exchange information on operating costs, effects of schedule changes, and other factors that may influence planning.
    d. **Engineering.** Advise of new developments that may affect the

demand for present products and aid in overcoming production problems.

3. Is the production control department unduly influenced by other departments?

Sales Forecast

1. Who participates in the preparation and approval of the sales forecast?
2. What procedures and techniques are used to develop sales forecasts?
3. Ascertain that the sources of data for forecasts are adequate.
4. Ascertain that the sales forecasts are accurate and realistic to a degree that reliable production plans can be prepared.

Production Planning

1. How does the sales forecast flow into the production plan?
2. Are sales forecasts and production plans issued far enough into the future to avoid peaks and valleys in production and manpower requirements?
3. Does the production plan include a review of
   a. Inventory availability
   b. Sales forecasts
   c. Historical sales data
   d. Maximum and minimum inventory levels
   e. Previous production results
   f. Special orders that would influence production plans
   g. Priorities and lead times required for
      (1) Engineering
      (2) Industrial engineering
      (3) Tooling
   h. Machine capacity
   i. Manpower requirements
4. Obtain a copy of the latest production plan, and perform an overall test of reasonableness of the data obtained by
   a. Comparing them to previous sales for this period
   b. Comparing them to previous production for this period
   c. Reviewing overall plant capacity
   d. Reviewing overall manpower requirements

   Access the reasonableness of the current production plan to historical performance, plant capacity, and marketing forecast. Any variances should be explained.

5. Select items (group/family, machine type) from the current production plan for detailed testing. Obtain a reason for the items' inclusion in the plan (i.e., to cover customer order, build inventory for peak periods, maintain a steady labor force, etc.).

   a. Obtain reports and records to support the reasonableness of this production plan.

   b. Verify the reasonableness of the production plan by reviewing the calculations and methods used to determine this plan.

   c. Review reasonableness of additions or deletions made to production plan for bringing production requirements into agreement with manning or machine capacity.

6. Test the accuracy of the production forecast by obtaining previous production plans and comparing them to actual results.

7. Verify and ascertain if changes to the plan are made to the production plan and distributed to other departments.

8. Determine if the accounting department uses the production plan in its financial projections.

9. Determine whether the production plan is approved at an appropriate level.

10. Evaluate the effectiveness of the system used in production planning and the overall conclusion on production planning.

Production Scheduling

1. Determine that production schedules are properly prepared on the basis of the production forecast.

   a. Are these schedules approved at an appropriate level?

2. Determine that production schedules are established with an objective of economical operations; determine that standards are established for the most economical group of orders.

3. Is work dispatched to the shop floor based on schedules?

4. Ascertain if the equipment is efficiently utilized by examining equipment utilization reports; determine if low utilization is directly associable to the scheduling function.

5. Determine if production schedules are being followed and met by examining daily department and machine reports, such as: shutdown reports, attainment-of-schedule reports, inspection releases, and reports of delivery to stock or shipping room.

6. Obtain reasons for any carryover of items from month to month in the production schedules; determine the effect of the backlog and if this is an indication of failure to attain projected production.

7. Is there feedback of information from production to scheduling?

8. Are the efficiencies or yields applied to production plan to cover shrinkage or loss reasonable?

9. For items selected in Production Planning, Step 4, perform a detailed test of the schedules prepared supporting this production plan. Explain any deviation from the production plan.

10. Evaluate the effectiveness of the procedures used in production scheduling and write an overall conclusion on the reasonableness of production scheduling.

Production Recording

1. Review the system of recording production and determine if production is recorded at the most feasible point to collect information for use in cost determination, budgeting, and inventory control.

2. Prepare or obtain a flowchart of all documents applicable to production control. Do documents provide sufficient information and provide proper controls?

3. Review the procedures and controls over scrap, defective material, and other losses. Determine that losses are recorded and reported at the point incurred.

4. For the period selected, perform a detailed test of production recording from final production figures to supporting documents. On a sample basis, verify current production on floor to reports to see if all information is properly processed, controlled, and recorded.

5. Evaluate the effectiveness of the production recording and scrap reporting system.

6. Write overall conclusion on tests performed.

Inventory Control

Preaudit Questionnaire

When the arrangement letter is sent, the following questionnaire should be sent to the location's materiels manager. This information should be available for the start of the audit.

1. What is the function (charter or mission) of the inventory control organization?

2. Prepare an organizational chart of the inventory control department including job titles, names, and grades:
   a. Number of people in Inventory Control
      Salaried _____
      Hourly   _____

   b. By Job Description
      Number of managers
      Number of material analysts
      Number of inventory control supervisors
      Number of inventory control clerks
      Number of other
   c. Review job descriptions for each position.

3. Do you have a division or local policy on inventory levels and controls?

4. What are your rules regulating inventory control?

5. Does an inventory plan exist? Is the plan being met?

6. Are inventory level goals determined by
   a. Executive opinion
   b. Overall financial considerations
   c. Employment level and seasonal fluctuations
   d. Production plan related to forecast
   e. Optimum inventory calculations (i.e., A-B-C)
   f. Reorder point—EOQ
   g. Inventory turnover
   h. MRP I (Material Requirements Planning)
   i. Other factors (describe)

7. Do clearly established and understood policies exist for
   a. Authorized maximums and minimums
   b. Service levels (percent)
   c. Safety stocks
   d. Surplus and obsolete classifications
   e. Use of inventory to level factory loads

8. Who has physical responsibility for
   a. Raw materials
   b. Work-in-process
   c. Finished goods

9. What is the dollar value of

	Current Month	Same Month Last Year
a. Raw material	_____	_____
b. Work-in-process	_____	_____
c. Finished goods	_____	_____

10. What are your planned inventory turns and how do actual results compare to plan?

11. What type of records are used to record and control
    a. Raw material
    b. Work-in-process
    c. Finished goods
    Is there any duplication of inventory records?
12. Who has responsibility for the analysis and action on
    a. Slow-moving inventory
    b. Obsolete inventory
    c. Defective and damaged material
    d. Scrap material
13. How often are physical inventories taken to verify the accuracy of perpetual records?
14. Are there formal instructions for the taking of physical inventories?
15. Is there a formal procedure of cycle counting to verify the accuracy of perpetual records?
16. What is the dollar status of slow-moving inventories?
    a. No movement in last 12 months $ _____
    b. No movement in 12–24 months $ _____
    c. No movement in more than two years $ _____
17. What is the current inventory reserve status?
    a. Is it adequate?
18. Are there inventories consigned?
    a. To us
    b. By us
    c. How are they controlled?
    d. Are they periodically confirmed?
19. What is the current dollar value of any goods in subcontractor locations? How frequently is it verified?
20. How is stockroom control established?
    a. Enclosed area
    b. Issues, move ticket, receipt system
    c. Stock clerk responsibility

Internal Audit Program

Preliminary

This program is concerned with: (1) material requirements; (2) flow of material through a plant; (3) controls over: raw materials, work-in-process, and finished goods; (4) control over damaged, defective, and scrapped materials; (5) physical inventories.

1. Review applicable policies and standard practice plus any division and/or local policies and procedures.
2. Follow up on the most recent audit report and ascertain if corrective action has been enacted. Obtain reasons for any deviations, if any.
3. Review the preaudit work steps as supplied by the location and discuss the content with the materials manager.
4. Update the permanent files.

General

1. Tour the plant and storeroom facilities to obtain a grasp of the physical operations.
2. Prepare or obtain a flowchart of all documents applicable to the inventory control system. Identify the controls and appraise the efficiency of this system.
3. Obtain copies of reports issued by inventory control departments.

Material Control

1. Evaluate the accuracy of the projected schedules for ordering raw material. Is the ordering of raw material based on the explosion of the production plan into raw material requirements?
2. Do the material requirements include a review of available inventory?
3. Is the material control department notified by the purchasing department of vendors' lead time, and are such lead times considered in the requirements?
4. Does purchasing transmit price breaks and other economical buying information to production control?
5. Do requirements include an estimated allowance to cover scrap, shrinkage, and other nonproductive usage?
6. Ascertain that possible obsolescence, storage costs, delivery costs, pricing charges, and engineering charges are considered in placing requisitions.
7. Evaluate the accuracy and reasonableness of material requirements schedule. Write overall conclusion.
8. Determine if material controls are realistic and if the control records are adequate as perpetual inventory records.
9. Is corrective action taken when a vendor:
   a. Ships early
   b. Ships late

    c. Overships

    d. Short ships?

10. Determine specific causes of material returns (unrealistic inspection requirements, lack of quality consciousness, and ascertain that the returns are not disproportionately high.

11. Are the following items stored and identified separately:

    a. Rejected material

    b. Returned goods

    c. Slow-moving items

    d. Obsolete items

    e. Stock?

12. Is storage space adequate?

13. Are storage areas well protected, orderly and clean?

14. Are there any inevitable major risk factors in carrying excess inventory quantities such as limited shelf life, style and engineering obsolescence?

15. Write overall memo on the effectiveness of the material control department.

Raw Materials

1. Review raw material procedures and update the permanent file (kardex, method of determining materials consumed, cycle counts, etc.).

2. Select a representative sample of raw material inventory items from the significant classifications of raw material.

    a. Physically count the selected items in the presence of plant personnel.

    b. Reconcile the kardex balances for receipts and issues to the date of the physical counts.

    c. Compare the physical counts to the adjusted kardex balances and compute the dollar amount of the differences.

3. Material consumed for the month to be tested is usually determined by material classification as follows:

Beginning inventory—priced out kardex	$200
Plus: Purchases—journal register	300
Less: Ending inventory—priced out kardex	(150)
Equals: Material consumed	$350

Material consumed may also be computed as follows:

Beginning inventory—G/L	$200

Plus:	Purchases—journal register		300
Less:	Materials consumed		(150)
	Beginning WIP	$ 50	
	Priced out issues	400	
	Material returns	(75)	
	Ending WIP	(25)	
			(350)
Equals:	Ending inventory		$150

(If material consumed is computed by the second method, perform Audit Step 3-A; otherwise, perform Audit Step 3.)

a. Obtain copies of location worksheets for the determination of material consumed.
b. Trace beginning and ending inventory balances to the General Ledger.
c. Obtain the priced out kardex summaries for both the beginning and ending inventory.
d. Tape the summaries by material classification.
e. Tape the detail of the significant material classification and tie into the tapes obtained in Step 3d. Select the large-dollar items on the tapes and enter the code, quantity, and standard unit cost on the tapes.
f. Trace the quantities of the codes selected in Step 3e to the kardex.
g. Trace the standard unit cost of the codes selected in Step 3e to the standard unit cost cards or tab run.
h. Verify extensions for the items selected in Step 3e.
i. List the detail (voucher register, suspense entry, journal entries, etc.) of amounts totaling to purchases for the classifications selected in Step 3e.
j. Cross-reference detail obtained in Step 3i to applicable workpapers and trace to support on a limited basis.
k. Trace materials consumed to cost report.

3A. a. Obtain copies of location worksheets for the determination of material consumed.
b. Trace beginning and ending inventory balances to the general ledger.
c. Tape the summaries by material classification.
d. Tape the detail of the significant materials classifications and tie into the tapes obtained in Step 3Ac. Select the large dollars

on the tape for detail testing. Enter the code, quantity, and standard unit cost on the tape.

e. Obtain the issue slips for the codes selected in Step 3Ad.

f. Trace the standard unit cost of the codes selected in Step 3Ad to the standard unit cost cards or tab run.

g. Verify extensions of the items selected in Step 3Ad.

h. List the detail (voucher register, suspense entry, journal entries, etc.) of amounts totaling to purchases for the classifications selected in Step 3Ad.

i. Cross-reference detail contained in Step 3Ad to applicable workpapers and trace to support on a limited basis.

j. Trace materials consumed to cost report.

4. On a limited basis trace issues on kardex to issue slips. Examine to see that quantities and codes agree.

5. Perform a clerical accuracy test of the kardex on a limited basis.

6. Perform a raw materials price test on the codes selected in Step 3d for the ending inventory.

a. List the code, quantity on hand, and standard unit cost on a schedule.

b. Obtain current invoices to cover the quantity. List the vendor, date of receipt, quantity, and cost per unit.

c. Compare the standard unit cost to the unit costs obtained in Step 6b and compute the dollar difference.

7. Perform a purchase price variance test on material classifications that have a significant purchase price variance.

a. Tape the detail making up the purchase price variance and cross-reference to the cost report.

b. On the significant items on the tape obtained in Step 7a, compute the purchase price variance by comparing the invoice cost to the standard cost (standard unit cost times quantity on the invoice).

8. Compute inventory turnover (material consumed average inventory) for a minimum period of six months and compare to same period in prior year.

9. Determine adequacy of current reserve balances by computing potential dollar amounts of obsolete and excess items.

10. Write conclusion on raw material tests.

Work-in-Process

1. Review procedures and update permanent file.

2. Trace quantities on a test basis from inventory count sheets to inventory summary for one month.

3. Verify standard prices on a test basis used for inventory valuation to material, labor, and overhead standards.
4. Verify extensions and footings on inventory summarizations on a test basis.
5. Review WIP reconciliation for any major adjustments and determine reasons for such adjustments.
6. Write conclusions.

Finished Goods

1. Review finished goods procedures (production recording, cycle counts, etc.) and update the permanent file.
2. Select a representative sample of finished goods.
   a. Physically count the selected items in the presence of plant personnel.
   b. Reconcile the kardex balances for production recorded and sales or shipment to the date of the physical count.
   c. Compare the physical counts to the adjusted kardex balances and compute the dollar amount of the difference.
3. Verify finished goods production recorded for one month.
   a. Obtain production summary for the month. Foot and extend on a test basis and trace total to journal entry.
   b. Obtain production report for two days.
   c. Trace daily production reports into monthly production summary.
   d. Examine move tickets (production copy and warehouse movers copy) for the two days selected to see that they agree as to code and quantity. Examine to see they are properly signed.
   e. Trace standard unit costs for the two days selected to the standard unit cost run.
4. Using the same sample, trace standard unit costs of finished goods at plant to division run of standard unit costs, and to cost of sales.
5. Obtain summary of finished goods inventory and trace to the General Ledger.
6. Test adequacy of current reserve balance by computing potential dollar amounts of obsolete and overstocked items.
7. Examine support of cycle counts and verify that the procedures are being followed.
8. Write conclusion.

Damaged, Defective, and Scrap Material

(Review control of damaged, defective, and scrap materials and obsolescence losses.)

1. Determine that company policy for reviewing slow-moving, obsolete, and dormant stock items is valid and in use.

   a. Determine that periodic reviews are made of all inventory categories based on age of items or date of last issuance. Are the time periods selected for review appropriate for each category of inventory under study? (Aging data may be obtained from the records, information on packages, etc.)

   b. Ascertain whether slow-moving, obsolete, or dormant goods are reported at specified intervals to the consuming department.

   c. Select a random sample of items from the dormant list and determine why each of the selected items is on the report.

      (1) Has the item been replaced by a later model or different item; that is, is the item obsolete?

      (2) Is there an excess of the item on hand? Should the excess be disposed of before the item becomes obsolete or deteriorates? Consider these facts in appraising procedures for determining order quantities.

      (3) Should dormant inventory be written off or be capitalized?

   d. Test the dormant list by tracing from such items listed in the course of physical inventory observations.

2. Review procedures for disposition of damaged, deteriorated, and overstocked goods.

   a. Determine whether damaged, deteriorated, or overstocked goods are reported at specific intervals to the consuming department.

   b. Determine who has been delegated responsibility for approving the adjusted value and disposition of such goods. Test that disposition documents and verify company policy is being followed.

   c. If appropriate, determine whether deteriorated, damaged, or excess goods are disposed through proper bidding procedures.

      (1) Ascertain that lists are kept of prospective purchasers and bidding forms are sent when appropriate.

      (2) Determine whether sealed bids are required.

      (3) Verify whether bids are opened in the presence of two or more authorized people.

      (4) Are the highest bids always accepted? If not, describe circumstances when other bids or no bids might be approved.

      (5) Select a few of the latest bids submitted and

         a. Determine whether the bids were dated and mailed by the deadline

         b. Ascertain whether the bids were signed by a responsible official of the bidding firm.

   c. Were the highest bids selected? If not, why not?
   d. Determine whether only a few groups always have the
       lowest bid. Investigate if considered necessary.

Physical Distribution

Introduction

A complete audit will include an examination of each of the following
responsibilities within physical distribution:

   Transportation/Traffic
      Truck
      Air
      Rail
      Sea
   Warehousing
   Shipping/Receiving
   Packaging
   Vehicle Administration
      Autos
      Trucks

   The intent is to evaluate each of these functions (1) as stand-alone
functions, and (2) as they interact and interrelate with the other functions within the company.
   If one individual does not have responsibility for all of the named activities, an effort should be made to contract all the responsible individuals to achieve a completely integrated review. In this way, the auditor can
be more effective in assisting locations to increase their effectiveness.
   To (1) allow us to prepare better for evaluating the activity, (2) allow
you to better prepare for the audit, and (3) provide a more complete,
meaningful, and expeditious evaluation, we request you provide us with
the following information in time for our arrival.
   Note: For more detailed narrative and audit programs, please refer
to specific chapters for Receiving, Traffic, and Inventory Scrap and
Salvage.

Preaudit Questionnaire

When the arrangement letter is sent, the following preaudit requirements should be sent to the location materiels manager. These data will
be required 10 days prior to commencement of the audit. Additionally,
following the preaudit questionnaire for physical distribution are five

modular sets of preaudit questions relating to the five subsections of physical distribution. (We intend for the supervisor of each subsection to complete the respective questionnaire.)

1. What is the function of the organization? Indicate the scope of control and/or the responsibility of the department.
2. Prepare an organization chart of the physical distribution organization as defined at the location level. The chart should include the name, grade, and job titles of all physical distribution exempt and nonexempt personnel.
3. Complete a physical distribution organization staffing level breakdown by job definition and salary grades.
4. What was the total physical distribution operating budget for last year? $_____
   a. Transportation _____%
   b. Warehousing _____%
   c. Shipping/Receiving _____%
   d. Packaging _____%
   e. Vehicle administration _____%
5. What was the total physical distribution cost last year? $_____
   a. Transportation _____%
   b. Warehousing _____%
   c. Shipping/Receiving _____%
   d. Packaging _____%
   e. Vehicle administration _____%
6. What were the actual savings (profit contribution for the last five years)? $_____
   Define the method of determining the savings:
   a. Favorable variance to budget _____
   b. Profit Improvement Program projects completed _____
   c. Other (explain) _____
7. How is quality of service defined and measured?

Transportation Traffic

Preaudit Questionnaire

1. What is the function of the transportation department? Indicate the control and/or responsibility of the department and its relationship within the organization.

2. Prepare an organization chart of personnel in the transportation department. The chart should include the names, grades, and job titles of all transportation personnel. Do not include drivers of leased vehicles.

3. On an attached sheet, estimate the total transportation cost for the last two years and what percent of the total physical distribution cost transportation costs represent.

4. What was the total tonnage shipped the last two years?
   Last year   _____
   Year before   _____

5. What was the total tonnage received in the last two years?
   Last year   _____
   Year before   _____

6. What were the average shipments per week leaving the plant(s)?   _____

7. What were the average shipments per week received by the plant(s) last year?   _____

8. What was the mean weight per shipment?
   a. Shipped   _____
   b. Received   _____

9. Are freight bills audited? If so, by whom?
   a. Transportation department   _____
   b. Outside audit firm   _____
   c. Other (specify)   _____

10. Estimate the percentage of outgoing shipments last year that were:
    a. Carload (truck and rail) lots   _____
    b. Less than carload (LTL)   _____
    c. Small shipments   _____
       (less than $100 in transportation cost each)

11. On an attached sheet, for the last two years list the names of the top 10 carriers (by dollar volume assigned), the total yearly cost, and the percentage of total outside transportation cost.

12. Check off those cost reduction programs presently in effect:
    a. Quantity discounts   _____
    b. Commodity rate investigation   _____
    c. Pool-car arrangements   _____
    d. Reclassification projects   _____
    e. Freight consolidation   _____
    f. Shippers Association   _____
    g. "Marriage cars"   _____
    h. Negotiated contracts   _____

     i. Company trucking   _____

     j. Other (specify)   _____

13. What policy controls are used to control the use of premium transportation and private carriers?

14. Be prepared to present to an auditor, upon arrival, copies of:

    a. Job descriptions for each employee in traffic/transportation

    b. Traffic/transportation department manual of divisional and/or local policies and procedures

    c. Reports, internal and external, used by traffic/transportation during the current fiscal year

    d. Computer-generated information reports used by the location

    e. Current copy of the operating budget for the department and the most recent monthly comparison and year-to-date report

15. Are freight bills audited:

    a. For correct rate

    b. For correct classification

    c. Against FOB point on purchase or sales order

16. Are routings specified

    a. To vendors for inbound shipments

    b. To the shipping room for outbound shipments

    c. With preferred or alternate carriers

17. Is there a program to schedule and combine shipments to obtain optimum transportation costs?

18. Are shipping containers provided by common carriers used to reduce packaging costs?

19. Are vehicles and equipment owned or leased? Why?

20. Are economical long-distance shipments made by coastal or inland water routes where time and location factors are found to be favorable?

21. Are shipments of certain items made by rail rather than truck?

22. What are the controls to prevent

    a. Duplicate payment of freight charges

    b. Demurrage

    c. Shipping via premium methods

    d. Unnecessary shipment by premium methods

    e. Minimum carload weights

Audit Program

Preliminary

1. Read applicable Policies and Standard Practices.

2. Follow up on the most recent audit report and ascertain whether

or not corrective management action has been enacted. Obtain reasons for any deviations.

3. Review the preaudit work steps as supplied by the location and discuss with the Traffic Department Supervisor.
4. Obtain copies of all forms used in the department and prepare procedural charts showing the flow of all paperwork.
5. Prepare organization chart of personnel in the traffic department showing job classification and duties.
6. Obtain copies of all reports issued by the traffic department and explain their purpose and how compiled.
7. Update the permanent files.

Audit Steps

1. If trucks are leased, determine if the company is in compliance with the lease agreement.
2. Determine if controls exist over fuel and service of vehicles; investigate the advantages of installing fuel or service facilities. Determine if an adequate inventory of spare parts and supplies is in line with requirements.
3. On a test basis, examine freight bills for proper product distribution, supporting papers (bills of lading), payment within time specified by ICC regulations, and determine if the invoices are audited by the traffic department or by a traffic audit bureau.
4. On a limited basis, examine selected freight bills. Obtain the assistance of the traffic department personnel in performing Steps a, b, and c, below.
   a. Verify freight rates, classes, and weights.
   b. Verify description of articles to insure they are classed to provide for the lowest rate.
   c. Ascertain whether correct routing is selected.
   d. Determine if method of packing does not add undue weight.
   e. Determine if receiving department checks and reports weights to the traffic department.
   f. Determine how weights on outbound shipments are verified.
5. Review claim and adjustment procedures; determine the value and age of claims filed but not settled; schedule claims for follow-up to final disposition; determine cause (packaging, receiving, or shipping); ascertain if there is any indication of carelessness on the carrier's part.
6. Determine methods the traffic department exerts to reduce transportation costs; that is, recommendations to division and warehouse personnel regarding the best method of shipping.

7. Evaluate the lines of communication between the traffic department and sales, production planning, purchasing, warehousing, and the controller's departments.

8. Review the open bill of lading file in the traffic department; determine if it is maintained on a current basis.

9. Verify the adequacy of insurance coverage; compare the cost of such insurance against the claim experience over a recent past period.

10. Review the cost and evaluate the performance of the trucking operations (both leased and owned) supervised by the traffic department.

   a. Determine whether trucks are being utilized to capacity.

   b. Determine if ICC regulations governing weight limits are not exceeded.

   c. Determine that inbound and outbound shipments are coordinated to attain maximum utilization and that interdivisional and divisional coordination occurs.

   d. Review procedures for accumulating costs and billing out of these charges; on a test basis, examine supporting vouchers.

   e. Compare costs of shipments to costs if shipped by common carrier; compute savings and compare to traffic department report.

   f. Review comparable costs of leasing or owning vehicles; investigate significant differences.

11. Review driver control records:

   a. Ascertain that ICC regulations governing hours and service are not exceeded.

   b. Determine if records are sufficiently analytical to distinguish between economical and uneconomical runs.

   c. Ascertain if measures are taken to correct the uneconomical runs.

12. Review procedures for ordering and approving transportation; determine if current rate survey charts are maintained; ascertain whether bulk shipments are utilized to the maximum degree.

13. On the basis of the results of audit Step #4 and the review of procedures, evaluate the freight invoice audit procedures.

   a. If audited by the company, determine

      (1) The amount recovered

      (2) If auditing is up to date

      (3) The degree of thoroughness

   b. If audited by an independent agency, determine

    (1) Fee and savings

    (2) Thoroughness of the agency

    (3) If it is worthwhile for the company to perform this function in-house

14. Review transportation charges to determine the extent of the premium mode of transportation.

    a. Determine the use, frequency, and reasons for using the premium method (air freight, air express courier).

    b. Ascertain if consideration is given car load versus LTL; investigate shipments other than full car loads to field warehouses and shipments of finished goods between field warehouses.

    c. Ascertain if vendors have definite shipping instructions and if they are billed back when they ship via premium mode without proper approval or instructions; determine if the production planning department has properly coordinated inbound shipment with the traffic department.

    d. Review demurrage records; determine cause (receiving, shipping, storage, or scheduling) and reasonableness; determine methods to limit such charges and to increase credits (if credits are allowed for the prompt release of cars and may be offset against charges).

15. Review claim and adjustment procedures; determine the value and age of claims filed but not settled; schedule claims for follow-up to final disposition; determine cause (packaging, receiving, or shipping); ascertain if there is an indication of carelessness on the part of the carrier.

16. Before leaving audit location, obtain explanations from responsible official of all questionable or open items and include in the working papers.

17. Prepare listing of items to be discussed with management at audit exit conference; if none, so state.

18. List here omitted, additional, or suggested future audit steps and reasons:

Steps Omitted

    Step #   Reason

Steps Added

    Step Description   Reason

Steps Suggested for Future
    Step Description   Reason

Warehousing

Preaudit Questionnaire

1. What is the function of the warehousing department? Indicate the scope of control and/or responsibility of the department and its relationship within the organization.
2. Prepare an organization chart of personnel in the warehousing department, indicating names, grades, and job titles of all warehousing personnel.
3. For the last two years, estimate the total carrying cost of inventory including warehousing costs:

   19X8 Production materials   _____
         Finished goods   _____
         Maintenance/Repair   _____
   19X7 Production materials   _____
         Finished goods   _____
         Maintenance/Repair   _____
4. What was the total usage (in square feet) of public warehousing space for the past two years? If square footage total usage is not available, provide the total yearly cost of a cost per carton basis.

   19X8 $_____   19X7 $_____
5. Estimate the total square footage of warehousing space (include both company owned and publicly leased space):

	Gross Sq. Ft.	Usable Sq. Ft.
a. Bulk	_____	_____
b. Rack	_____	_____
c. Shelving/bins	_____	_____
d. Assembly	_____	_____
e. Reconditioning	_____	_____
f. Dock	_____	_____
g. Offices	_____	_____
h. Other (specify)	_____	_____
Total	_____	_____

6. Estimate the percentage of net usable warehouse space used by:
   a. Security   _____
   b. Raw materials   _____

    c. Production material   _____

    d. Maintenance/repair   _____

    e. Distribution   _____

    f. In-plant finished goods   _____

    g. Other (specify)   _____

7. What percentage of the storage system is:

open   _____

closed   _____

8. Explain location system including any control or segregation of items (eg: slow moving).

9. Describe any automated systems presently installed.

10. Be prepared to present to an auditor, upon arrival, copies of:
    a. Job descriptions for each employee in warehousing
    b. Warehousing department manual of divisional and/or local policies and procedures
    c. Internal and external reports used by warehousing during the current fiscal year
    d. Computer-generated information reports used by the location
    e. Current copy of the operating budget for the department and the most recent monthly comparison and year-to-date report

Audit Program

1. Prepare an organization chart of personnel in the warehousing department showing job titles and people.
2. Review the adequacy of procedures and controls over the warehousing function and records.
3. Tour the warehouse and observe the condition of the raw material and finished goods inventory.
   a. Determine that the merchandise is neatly organized with like items together.
   b. Ascertain whether or not evidence of deterioration of stock exists due to improper storage or inadequate storage facilities.
   c. Determine if partial cases and individual items are segregated in a secured and controlled reconditioning area.
   d. Determine if shipments are made on a FIFO basis.
   e. Determine if any other companies' products that may be detrimental to the company products' condition (i.e., soap or ammonia products near food products) are not stored near them.
4. Determine if the physical security of the warehouse is adequate to assure the safeguarding of the inventory.
   a. Ascertain whether the security and control over expensive and/or highly marketable products is reasonable and adequate.

5. Determine whether the warehouse has adequate fire extinguishing equipment (sprinkler system) to satisfy corporate insurance requirements.

6. Determine if the sanitary conditions of the warehouse are adequate to satisfy corporate quality control requirements with periodic inspection of traps, proper logging of inspections, periodic safe spraying of chemicals, and appropriate maintenance of buildings and grounds, and so on.

7. Determine whether the handling and storage of inventory is done efficiently.

   a. Is the raw material inventory located by frequency of issue?

   b. To what extent does the location utilize stock-locator systems?

   c. Determine whether the degree of mechanization in stocking and shipping is adequate and effective.

8. Ascertain whether the location stores and separately identifies:

   a. Rejected materials

   b. Returned goods

   c. Slow-moving items

   d. Obsolete items

   e. Stock-outs

   f. Requests for nonstock items.

9. Determine the warehouse space utilization:

   a. Utilization of shelf and rack space   _____%

   b. Utilization of floor space   _____%

10. Ascertain the cost of warehousing and materials handling for last year. $_____

    a. Determine the cost per square foot to perform the warehousing functions. $_____

11. Determine whether the location is using outside warehousing.

    a. What is the amount of space (square footage)?

    b. What is the percent utilization?

    c. If leased, is the location in compliance with the lease agreement?

    d. Does the warehouse have adequate security?

Shipping/Receiving

Preaudit Questionnaire

1. What is the function of the shipping/receiving department? Indicate the control and/or responsibility of the department and its relationship within the organization.

2. Prepare an organization chart of personnel in the shipping/receiving department, indicating the names, grades, and job titles of all shipping/receiving personnel.

3. For the last two years, estimate the dollar amount of damage on incoming shipments.

    19X8 $_____

    19X7 $_____

4. For the last two years, estimate the number of claims processed against incoming shipments and the dollar amount of those claims:

    19X8 #_____ $_____

    19X7 #_____ $_____

5. What percentage of incoming shipments arrive via:

    a. Corporate trucks   _____
    b. Common carrier trucks   _____
    c. Rail   _____
    d. Air   _____
    e. Sea vessel   _____
    f. Air express   _____
    g. Parcel post   _____
    h. Other (define)   _____

6. How is incoming material identified?

7. List the distribution of the copies of the receiving report in each of the following situations:

    a. Regular completed shipment
    b. Partial shipment
    c. Damaged short or over shipment.

8. What is the total warehouse space used by the shipping and receiving department? _____ square feet.

9. Estimate the percentage breakdown of usable shipping and receiving warehouse space used by:

    a. Transit   _____
    b. Security   _____
    c. Floor storage   _____
    d. Shelf/bin storage   _____
    e. Outside storage   _____
    f. Trailers   _____
    g. Other (define)   _____

10. Be prepared to present to an auditor, upon arrival, copies of
    a. Job descriptions for each employee in shipping/receiving
    b. Shipping/receiving department manual of divisional and/or local policies and procedures
    c. Internal and external reports used by shipping/receiving during the current fiscal year
    d. Computer-generated information reports used by the location
    e. Current copy of the operating budget for the department and the most recent monthly comparison and year-to-date report

Audit Program

Preliminary

1. Prepare organization chart of personnel in the shipping/receiving department showing job classification and duties.
2. Obtain copies of all reports issued by the shipping/receiving department and explain their purpose and how compiled.
3. Obtain copies of all forms used in the department and prepare procedural charts showing flow of all paperwork.
4. Ascertain if access to the receiving and shipping areas is properly controlled.

Shipping

1. Determine whether all shipments are covered by an authorized shipping advice.
2. Ascertain whether shipping orders are prenumbered and sequentially accounted for.
3. Determine whether a copy of the shipping order is validated and forwarded directly to the billing department after shipment is made.
4. Ascertain if quantities shipped are summarized daily.
    a. Are the quantities shipped reconciled periodically with the customer billings?

Receiving

1. Review the open and closed receiving report files and determine if the records are in good order and properly controlled.
2. Ascertain whether or not all items clearing the Receiving Department are covered by a formal purchase order.
3. Ascertain if the receiving department functions include
    a. Inspection of all receipts as to quantity and quality
    b. Comparison of receipts to a copy of the authorized purchase order

    c. Preparation of receiving report for all receipts

    d. Prompt transmission of materials to stores, rather than to production floor or other uncontrolled areas

    e. Obtaining a signed receipt from the storekeeper for the merchandise transferred

4. Determine what control receiving has over deliveries made directly to the requisitioners.

5. Review the controls maintained over partial receiving reports.

6. Determine whether copies of the receiving report are forwarded directly to accounting and purchasing.

7. Review receiving report log or other means of controlling receiving reports and determine whether receivers are properly accounted for.

    a. Are receiving reports prepared for rejected material returned by customers?

8. Ascertain if overshipments in excess of allowed percentage are referred to purchasing for disposition.

9. Determine if procedures provide for check of open purchase orders in the receiving file against accounting and/or purchasing open orders.

    a. Are open purchase orders investigated by a responsible person?

Summarization

1. Before leaving audit location, obtain explanations from a responsible official of all questionable or open items and include in the working papers.

2. Prepare a listing of items to be discussed with management at audit exit conference; if none, so state.

3. List here omitted, additional, or suggested future audit steps and reasons:

Steps Omitted

    Step #   Reason

Steps Added

    Step Description   Reason

Steps Suggested for Future

    Step Description   Reason

Packaging

Preaudit Questionnaire

1. What is the function of the packaging department? Indicate the control and/or responsibility of the department and its relationship within the organization.
2. Prepare an organization chart of personnel in the packaging department indicating the names, grades, and job titles of all shipping/receiving personnel.
3. For the last two years, what was the cost of packaging materials?
   19X8 $_____
   19X7 $_____
4. For the last two years, what was the damage cost attributed to improper packaging?
   19X8 $_____
   19X7 $_____
5. Estimate the mean weight and mean size of outgoing packages:
   a. Mean weight   _____
   b. Mean size   _____
6. What percentage of outgoing shipments are packed in:
   a. Fiber cartons   _____
   b. Plastic containers _____
   c. Reusable cartons   _____
   d. Wooden crates   _____
   e. Other (specify)   _____
   f. Wooden skids   _____
   g. Cardboard slips   _____
7. Be prepared to present to an auditor, upon arrival, copies of:
   a. Job descriptions for each employee in packaging
   b. Packaging department manual of divisional and/or local policies and procedures
   c. Internal and external reports used by packaging during the current fiscal year
   d. Computer-generated information reports used by the location
   e. Current copy of the operating budget for the department and the most recent monthly comparison and year-to-date report

Audit Program

1. Prepare organizational chart of personnel in the packaging department showing job classification and duties.

2. Obtain copies of all reports issued by the packaging department and explain their purpose and how compiled.

3. Obtain copies of all forms used in the department and prepare procedural charts showing flow of all paperwork.

4. Review the adequacy of procedures and controls over the packaging function.

5. Ascertain whether packaging is coordinated with pallet sizes as well as truck size or other mode of transportation.

    a. Determine whether the packaging meets the requirements of the shipper.

6. Determine whether any correlation is made between damage incurred in transportation and the type of packaging used.

7. Investigate the use of packaging materials and the possible application of less-expensive alternative materials.

8. Determine whether complete destruction testing of packing materials is performed prior to being put into use.

9. Ascertain if specifications exist for all packaging materials and supplies to insure adequate product protection and proper handling by production machinery.

Vehicle Administration

Preaudit Questionnaire

1. What is the function of the vehicle administration department? Indicate the control and/or responsibility of the department and its relationship within the organization.

2. Prepare an organizational chart of personnel in the vehicle administration department indicating the names, grades, and job titles of all vehicle administration personnel.

3. For the last two years, estimate the annual repair costs:

    a. 19X8   Trucks $ _____

               Tractors   _____

               Trailers   _____

               Boxcars   _____

               Cars   _____

               Forklift trucks   _____

    b. 19X7   Trucks $ _____

               Tractors   _____

               Trailers   _____

               Boxcars   _____

               Cars   _____

               Forklift trucks   _____

4. What is the number of vehicles under your control?
   a. Trucks _____
   b. Tractors _____
   c. Trailers _____
   d. Boxcars _____
   e. Cars _____
   f. Forklift trucks _____

5. What is the total direct operating cost per mile for the last two years for:

	19X8	19X7
a. Trucks	$_____	$_____
b. Tractors	_____	_____
c. Trailers	_____	_____
d. Boxcars	_____	_____
e. Cars	_____	_____
f. Forklift trucks	_____	_____

6. What is the mileage or time criteria for vehicle replacement?

	Mileage	Time
a. Trucks	_____	_____
b. Tractors	_____	_____
c. Trailers	_____	_____
d. Boxcars	_____	_____
e. Cars	_____	_____
f. Forklift trucks	_____	_____

7. Estimate the percentage of idle time in a 40-hour week for:
   a. Trucks _____
   b. Tractors _____
   c. Trailers _____
   d. Boxcars _____
   e. Cars _____
   f. Forklift trucks _____

8. Be prepared to present to an auditor, upon arrival, copies of:
   a. Job descriptions for each employee in vehicle administration
   b. Vehicle administration department manual of divisional and/or local policies and procedures
   c. Internal and external reports used by vehicle administration during the current fiscal year
   d. Computer-generated information reports used by the location

    e. Current copy of the operating budget for the department and the most recent monthly comparison and year-to-date report

Audit Program

Usually, vehicle administration is assigned the responsibility of obtaining, operating, and maintaining the automobile, truck, and rail fleets, and other special types of equipment required by a manufacturing or utility company in its operations. It may also be responsible for rental equipment.

Close liaison should occur with the purchasing and operating departments to ensure that adequate, but not excessive, equipment is provided to effectively consummate the assigned mission of each department. To accomplish this, certain equipment is generally assigned to a department (such as sales), and other equipment is retained in a vehicle pool for general use.

Since recommendations given by vehicle administration may be given considerable weight in procuring new equipment, adequate records by individual piece of equipment should be kept to support their recommendations. The use of equipment should be logged by vehicle administration with particular emphasis placed upon gasoline and oil cost, idle vehicle time, and control of replaced parts, batteries, tires, and tubes. Likewise, this department expends a sizable amount of the annual operating budget in the operation and maintenance of equipment, and accordingly should have the necessary supporting records (by vehicle identification number) available for periodic review to effect the most economical results consistent with good operating practices.

Reports required by the accounting and other departments should be regularly scheduled to provide management with information essential to its needs.

Adequate insurance coverage and equipment inventory control is essential.

A safety program (zero defects) including investigation of vehicular accidents may also be the responsibility of the vehicle administration department.

Adequate controls should be maintained to prevent unauthorized use of equipment, supplies, and parts.

1. The audit program should be divided into four phases of review, as follows:
   a. Acquisition and disposition of equipment
   b. Utilization of equipment
   c. Operation and maintenance analysis
   d. Record-keeping and procedures review
       Three separate sections are introduced in Steps 1a–1c. For Step

1d, the auditor must review current rules, procedures, policies, and laws that apply to the first three areas. No individual audit steps are applicable for Step 1d; the principle applies throughout the audit program.

2. Prepare an organizational chart of personnel in the vehicle administration department, showing job titles and people.

Acquisition and Disposition of Equipment

1. Company policy with regard to the purchase and replacement of passenger cars, trucks, and other related equipment:
   a. Who makes the decision as to whether major repairs should be made on old equipment, or if new equipment should be purchased?
   b. Is an economic formula used for computing when a vehicle should be replaced rather than overhauled? Or is replacement based on the judgment of the supervisor of transportation, or on a fixed mileage basis?
2. Review the company policy for disposition of old equipment:
   a. Are cars traded-in or sold? Are they sold to employees at that company location?
   b. Compare Blue Book trade-in values with actual amounts received.
   c. Review bids obtained and the analysis sheets outlining these bids.
   d. Review other price data and approvals.

Utilization of Equipment

1. Determine company policy regarding assignment of vehicles:
   a. On what basis are vehicles assigned to individuals or departments?
   b. Are such vehicles used sufficiently to justify the assignments? Check mileage assigned to individuals or departments.
   c. Would it be practical for persons now being assigned vehicles to use pool vehicles?
   d. What is the basis for assigning vehicles on a drive home basis?
      (1) What control exists over this perquisite when an employee changes classification?
      (2) What control over personal mileage is used? How is it accounted for and summarized for tax purposes?
2. Review use of equipment for little-used, idle, or surplus equipment.
   a. Review time or mileage reports to see that the equipment is being used.

3. Review the policy and control over employees using personal cars on company business.

   a. Determine if usage justifies the need for the personal car.

   b. Determine whether proper authorizations have been obtained for each personal car used.

   c. Review rates established for payment of personal car use.

   d. Review control over payments to employees for use of personal car.

   e. On a test basis, determine whether all payments are proper.

Operation and Maintenance Analysis

1. Review overall cost of transportation.

   a. Are transportation costs budgeted?

      (1) What are budgeted costs?

      (2) How do actuals compare with budget?

      (3) Investigate reasons for large variations.

   b. Compare actual cost for the current period with prior periods on a per-mile or per-hour basis.

   c. Compare this company's/division's costs with other companies/divisions.

   d. Are adequate segregations made in classes of equipment for determining costs and for reporting mileage to be used in distributing costs from the clearing accounts?

   e. Are adequate cost centers (detailed expense accounts) established?

2. Review gasoline and oil cost and control.

   a. Review the company policy on purchasing gasoline and oil.

      (1) To what extent are credit cards used?

      (2) Are records maintained of employees to whom cards are assigned?

   b. Review the procedures and the adequacy of the procedures to detect vehicles using excessive amounts of gasoline and oil.

      (1) Current period compared with prior period.

      (2) Compare similar vehicles between different locations.

      (3) Compare license plate listed on the charge ticket to the car the employee is assigned.

3. Review the cost and controls over tires.

   a. Determine whether the activity of new-tire issues is comparable to the size of the automotive fleet.

   b. Compare the number of new tire issues against the number of used tires traded in or returned to salvage for general reasonableness.

    c. Review the procedure for handling tires removed from automotive equipment.

    d. Compare the cost-per-mile with that of prior periods.

4. Review the policy and procedures on servicing and maintenance inspections.

    a. How often are vehicles serviced? Is service based on mileage or on length of time?

      (1) If on a length-of-time basis, is any allowance made for the period of time when the equipment has been idle?

    b. Determine if routine preventive maintenance inspections are being followed.

5. Taxes and Licenses

    a. Check all transportation and construction equipment listed on Ad Valorem Tax statement to capital records.

    b. Test fees paid:

      (1) Compare the current fee with the previous one.

      (2) Compare the fees by general type of equipment; that is, the fees for like vehicles of the same year should be the same.

      (3) Test check any fees of a questionable amount to the rate book.

      (4) Verify whether all equipment (for which fees are paid) are recorded in the capital records.

      (5) Determine whether licenses are not obtained for vehicles that have been retired or that are to be sold.

      (6) Are licenses transferred from old equipment to new acquisitions when provided for in state laws?

6. Insurance coverage

    a. Insure whether all equipment is properly covered in policies.

    b. Insure whether notification of all equipment changes are promptly forwarded to the insurance department.

    c. Investigate liability policies to insure that proper coverage is maintained when use of personal cars is authorized.

7. Inventory of equipment

    a. Obtain a listing of all equipment from property accounting records as of a given date, and reconcile to licenses purchased.

    b. Verify inventory by visual check or other satisfactory means to insure that all equipment is accounted for.

8. Before leaving audit location, obtain explanations from responsible official of all questionable or open items, and include explanation in the working papers.

9. Prepare listing of items to be discussed with management at audit exit conference; if none, so state.

10. List here omitted, additional, or suggested future audit steps and reasons:

    Steps Omitted

    Step #   Reason

    Steps Added

    Step Description   Reason

    Steps Suggested for Future

    Step Description   Reason

CHAPTER 3

Purchasing

IMPORTANCE OF PURCHASING

Virtually every organization has a purchasing department. All manufacturing concerns and most other companies purchase materials, supplies, or services. The importance and difficulty of purchasing these items can vary from being minor, as in a small office where office supplies and printed material may be the principal items procured, to being a major concern in the cost of commodities, advertising, marketing supplies, ingredients, packaging supplies, automobiles, computers and computer services, and other products, as in a Forbes 100 business. In some manufacturing enterprises, the cost of materials, supplies, and outside services can be more than half the total sales price of the products produced.

The importance of the procurement function in the profitable operation of an organization is recognized through:

1. High organizational status of the purchasing department. In the majority of manufacturing companies, the head of purchasing reports to the president or a senior vice president.
2. Responsibility for purchasing is usually centralized within a company.
3. Participation of the purchasing department in such programs as value analysis with other departments such as engineering and

79

manufacturing. The three departments work cooperatively with vendors to lower costs through consideration of alternate materials, quality, quantity, work locations, and sources of supply.

PURCHASING DEPARTMENT (PROCUREMENT) ACTIVITIES

Procurement has been defined as the act of obtaining the right product at the right price, in the right quantity, at the right time, and at the right place. In this definition the word *right* is obviously relative, reflecting a basic standard for evaluating the activities related to obtaining products from others. Normally *right* is interpreted to mean what is best in the long-term interest of the business as a whole. However, *right* can also mean what is best to keep the manufacturing line from shutting down within the next hour.

Businesses do not necessarily organize or assign responsibilities for procurement in the same way. Important differences can be found among different industries, different companies in the same industry, and within the same company.

Some companies specifically delegate parts of the procurement activities to other departments. For example, one company may have a purchasing department whose principal responsibilities are to perform certain procurement activities that are limited as follows:

1. The purchasing department may have no responsibility for procuring nonmanufacturing services such as advertising, media, public accounting services, engineering consultants, transportation services, and so on. This may also extend into the manufacturing areas of emergency repairs, building maintenance, and the machine shop.

2. The purchasing department may share some of its responsibilities with other groups. The responsibility for judging the most suitable quality and quantity and the most suitable time and place of delivery is sometime assigned to others (such as engineering, or the customer—such as the government, when dealing with defense contracting).

These limitations are often modified to a considerable degree by the participation of a purchasing agent in cooperative endeavors with other departments in such activities as purchases of specialized equipment, and determination of purchasing and inventory policies in relation to market trends and value analysis programs. Such participation may be part of a formal program, or it may come as a result of the informal auditing done by purchasing upon requisitions they receive.

This section explores the internal control and audit of a moderately complex purchasing department that is responsible for purchasing materials, supplies, and commodities and for certain other activities that are often assigned to them.

In every organization, all departments end up doing some part of the procurement activity without involving the purchasing department. Within the auditing department, you may purchase books, travel services, seminar registrations, operating supplies, or software for your microcomputer without going through the purchasing department. In some of these cases, procurement may have occurred without going through the proper procedures.

ASSIGNED RESPONSIBILITY FOR PURCHASING

Assume the purchasing activity begins with participating in the initial contact between vendors' representatives and operating departments prior to the origination of the purchase requisition. The actual purchase operation begins with receipt of an authorization for the purchase of a specified quantity of a specified item, to be delivered to a specified place at a specified time. In this process, the principal functions performed by purchasing include:

1. Securing authorizations for purchase
2. Obtaining quotations and selecting vendor
3. Issuing a purchase order
4. Issuing routing instructions to the vendor
5. Following-up for delivery (expediting)
6. Negotiating any adjustment with the vendor

In brief, the procurement area begins with the negotiation and authorization for purchase and ends with the determination by purchasing and the ordering departments that the purchase transaction has been satisfactorily concluded.

Please note that the following is excluded from the discussion:

1. The determination of the appropriateness of the (right) quantity to be purchased. We will consider purchasing's responsibility for bringing more favorable purchasing arrangements to the attention of operating departments. As previously stated, purchasing will normally participate in decisions of general policy concerned with market trends, inventory levels, or special company requirements. However, do not assume that purchasing has sole or final jurisdiction over the quantity to be purchased.

2. The procurement of materials or services that are usually handled outside of purchasing. In general, these items are usually the subject of negotiation, rather than competitive bidders; for example, engineering consultants, insurance, and public accounting services. In addition, the primary responsibility for negotiation of construction contracts and purchase and installation of heavy manufacturing equipment can be delegated to the engineering department. (However, one company had their own capital expenditure purchasing department that worked closely with the engineering and plant services departments to effectively reduce costs.) If the purchasing department is not primarily responsible, it normally participates in conferences and negotiations on construction and equipment projects so that the company negotiators may take advantage of the knowledge of purchasing negotiation techniques.

3. The procurement of finished products for resale by a retail or wholesale business. These procurement activities are separate and distinct from most other purchasing activities.

OTHER RELATED DEPARTMENT RESPONSIBILITIES

Departments dealing with material often are assigned responsibilities that are indirectly concerned with the procurement of materials, supplies, and services. These may include:

1. Sale of scrap
2. Purchases for employees' personal use
3. Operation of material and supply storerooms
4. Expediting
5. Material estimating

After reviewing the normal purchasing operations that are concerned with the placing of orders, we will discuss these collateral responsibilities. The considerations will be limited to the problems in internal control and audit that arise because of the inclusion of these responsibilities under the same supervision. A complete review of receiving and scrap operations is provided in later sections of this book.

PROBLEMS OF DECENTRALIZATION

As in the case of other business functions, the trend in large organizations toward the establishment of autonomous divisions has introduced a problem in the control of purchasing operations. The vice president of a division usually wants to operate with as few restraints and controls as possible. He believes the unquestioned closer contact with the problems and operations of the division permit him to control the various operating functions more effectively than can be done from a remote home office. Thus, as the size and complexity of a business increase, the centralized purchasing department is presented with ever-greater problems of control, coordination, and cooperation with other operating units. As will be described later, the internal auditor, in appraisal and evaluation, may render valuable constructive service to both field and home office purchasing departments.

INTERNAL CONTROL AND AUDIT

The following sections of this chapter will consider the operations customarily handled in a typical purchasing department, and the problems of control in each operation. Later in this chapter we present a typical internal audit program.

The narrative and program endeavor to bring out the twofold responsibility of internal auditors in their appraisal activities for (1) the protection of the interests of their company against waste and loss, and (2) constructive recommendations that will lead to better operation and more profit for the company.

Examples of this responsibility are illustrated in the following segments from two audit reports:

EXAMPLE 1

The internal audit department of a large manufacturing corporation was asked to appraise buying activity and to report any suggestions for improvement. The examination covered a detailed study of 170 purchase orders placed during a five-week period. The selected orders totaled $2,750,000, representing all sizes of purchases, all buyers, and all general types of material. Each order was reviewed by using a questionnaire, on which the entire history from origination or requisition through securing of bids and determination of vendor was compiled. The information for the questionnaire was secured by talking with buyers and requisitioners, and from reviewing purchasing files.

From the data compiled, the handling of each order was then appraised by the auditor, and a conclusion reached on the transaction. A summary of all transactions formed the basis for the auditor's report, which included:

1. A statement that 98 percent of the orders had been well handled by purchasing.
2. A recommendation for earlier contacts between the purchasing and engineering departments, so that purchasing expertise could be better utilized.

3. A recommendation for increased coordination with the material planning department in determining quantities to be ordered.
4. A recommendation for the redesign of purchasing price record forms, to overcome deficiencies noted.
5. A recommendation of a simpler routine for small orders.

In this assignment, the basis for the work and the resulting recommendations lay in the internal auditor's discussions with departmental employees; the auditor's background and contact in the organization enabled the appraisal and recommendations to be of maximum value.

EXAMPLE 2

In another audit, separate orders were generated for identical material required in the manufacturing process. The reason was that five identical job orders were in process. Someone deemed it simpler to issue separate requisitions and thereby obtain separate invoices and receivers for each job. Combining the orders resulted in a savings of several thousand dollars. In this example, the fault lay with the accounting department, which sought to simplify its recordkeeping. Purchasing should have insisted upon the economies of consolidated purchases.

APPRAISAL OF PURCHASING DEPARTMENT OPERATION

Factors in Effective Purchasing

Superficially, the purchasing operation may appear to be simple. In most purchases, the sources of supply are usually known or may be readily ascertained. It appears to be relatively easy to get comparative quotations from several sources, then to place the order with the lowest bidder and thus fulfill the basic requirement of purchasing (to get the right item in the right place at the right time and at the right price).

In practice, this unimaginative procedure may be adequate for many purchases. Effective purchasing, however, must go beyond this and may take many factors into consideration, including:

1. Was the knowledge of materials and markets available in the purchasing department used to advantage by the requisitioner in the determination of the right item and the right quantity?
2. What incidentals, such as discount and delivery cost, affect the price quotation?
3. Is there some assurance of the reliability of the supplier through previous experience or investigation? Reliability includes such

factors as ability to meet delivery schedules, quality control, and financial responsibility.

4. Has the supplier given special services in the past, or in connection with the pending order, that might justify awarding it the business even though its price is somewhat higher?
5. Do considerations or corporate policies involve purchasing from local suppliers or from companies to whom the buyer's business sells its finished products?
6. What are market trends? Should a suggestion be made that only a minimum quantity be purchased in anticipation of a lower price, or an extra quantity in anticipation of a higher price (especially for purchasing commodities)?
7. Is material ordered available elsewhere in the company?
8. Could material be made at a lesser cost in the company, instead of being purchased from an outside source?
9. Are special factors, such as conditions applying to government contracts, taken into consideration?

Consciously or subconsciously, the effective buyer will have these and similar questions in mind for each order placed.

In summary, purchasing involves business judgment, weighing and combining a number of factors so each purchase order may be placed to the organization's best advantage.

Importance of Cooperation, Coordination, and Communication

With recognition of the importance of effective purchasing in the making of profits, higher organizational status has come to many purchasing executives. Their participation in coordinated programs aimed at increased profits through reduction of costs of purchased materials is evidence of this.

Value analysis programs are a typical example. Here, purchasing works with vendors and the affected company departments (such as engineering and production) in the analysis of specifications, consumption, and requirements. Through such analysis and cooperative effort, major savings are possible through redesign, a change in specification, purchasing more economical quantities, or in-house manufacturing of the product itself. Purchasing should be fully informed of production schedules and plans. With this knowledge, the department can make full utilization of its knowledge and contacts in making forward purchases to maximum advantage and in staggering deliveries to minimize carrying costs (investment).

Such cooperative efforts will result in savings and in greater acceptance of purchasing as an essential member of a profit-making team. Any appraisal of a purchasing operation must give consideration to the degree of mutual confidence and respect that appears to exist between purchasing and the other operating departments.

Evaluation of Purchasing Department Operations

Because the work of purchasing is dependent upon business judgment and cooperative effort with other departments, and because the prices paid are often governed by market trends, it is highly difficult to establish any direct means of reporting or determining how effectively the purchasing operation is performed.

There is no question that the purchasing department plays a vital role in the making of profit. The difficulty comes in attempting to determine the exact amount of the profit contribution for which purchasing is responsible. Since the materials and supplies that are purchased are usually consumed by other departments, the profits made through better purchasing will usually show up in the reports and accounts of the using departments. For example, if the unit cost of an item of sales promotion material is reduced through the efforts of the purchasing department, the result will show as a favorable variance in the sales promotion budget; therefore, the sales promotion department is more apt to receive this credit variance than the purchasing department.

Many attempts have been made to set up a mechanical means of measuring purchasing performance, but none have resulted in plans that have gained any degree of acceptance. The simplest measures are those covering such items as the number of orders placed, value of orders, departmental cost per order, and so on. While these measures are of value to a purchasing executive in gauging the work load and the operating cost of the department, they have no value as indicators of whether or not business judgment (the prime requisite in the making of purchases) has been exercised to the best advantage of the business.

This inability to summarize the effectiveness of a purchasing department operation in numerical report form means that other gauges must be utilized. These usually take the form of reports as follows:

1. Special memos covering individual projects such as savings made in contract renewals or through revisions of specifications.
2. Regular reports to management: monthly, quarterly, or annually. These reports usually include summaries of mechanical performance (orders placed, value, departmental expenses versus budget, etc.) on a comparative basis. In addition, and possibly of greater importance and interest to management, the reports will describe specific accomplishments in making purchasing arrangements that have resulted in savings, better service, or other benefits to the company. Categories of purchasing performance measurement may

encompass such topics as price effectiveness, efficiency, vendor quality and delivery, material flow control, and inventory levels.

One must recognize that memos and reports originating in purchasing will emphasize favorable elements; unfavorable happenings will be minimized or not reported.

Approach of the Internal Auditor

The lack of any definite form of numerical report or other standards of purchasing department accomplishment means that the approach of the internal auditor will differ as compared with an audit approach to departments where such reporting is possible.

For example, in a manufacturing plant audit, the internal auditor will review the operating reports. These reports have been designed to bring out just how effectively the plant has operated. By examining such items as current unit costs, labor expense, and plant overhead in comparison with standards or previous periods, the auditor is able to select certain items (such as those with unfavorable variances) as the subjects for particular attention.

In a purchasing department operation, it is desirable that the mechanical operations be handled with economy. However, as has been mentioned, economical operation is not a fair indication of how well judgment has been exercised, or how effectively the purchasing operation has been performed.

In the examination of the purchasing department, the internal auditor must give particular attention to some considerations that are difficult, or impossible, to reduce to figures. These include:

1. Cooperation and coordination with operating departments so full advantage may be gained from the purchasing department's knowledge of markets, materials, and processes. Mutual interdepartmental confidence and coordination is an indicator of a good purchasing operation.
2. Good relationship with vendors so the company can gain from the specialized knowledge and suggestions that can usually be had for the asking.
3. Routines in relation to results. Far too often, a rather involved and inflexible routine is followed when a simpler method would take care of a large proportion of the work.
4. Inventory writedowns at close of year—the reason may be traceable to purchasing, or may be due to conditions beyond the knowledge or control of the purchasing department.

CONTROL OF PURCHASING OPERATION

So far, we have been concerned with relationships between purchasing and other departments and with problems of appraisal. We now proceed to more detailed consideration of the operating controls with which purchasing is concerned.

Policy and Control

The determination of definite policies is a prerequisite to the development of control. In purchasing, policy must be established by management on such matters as:

1. The placement of the purchasing department in the organization structure.
2. Extent of purchasing responsibility; for example, the purchasing department may not be concerned with the purchase of manufacturing equipment.
3. A plan for delegation of authorizations of purchases.
4. Assignment of limited purchasing responsibility to decentralized operations or specialized departments.

The determination of definite policy sets the limits within which the control structure must be organized and administered. Inadequate definition or failure to support established policy will certainly result in weakness of control and ineffectual operation.

With policy established, operating control begins with the setting of an organization structure that is given definite assignments of authority and responsibility. Next comes the specification of procedures, which gives an explicit description of how operations are to be conducted—within the boundaries of prescribed policy. Remember, policies and practices should be established and used to *manage* the organization, and not be perceived as mechanisms used to punish people.

The general standard of organizational control in purchasing, as in any other operation, is that no one individual or organizational subunit should have entire and sole responsibility for a given transaction from origination to completion without being subject to accountability through review or approval of actions by another individual who is not subordinate. Applied to purchasing, this means a single buyer should not have authority to originate a requisition, determine the vendor, place the order, approve the quantity and quality of received material, and approve the vendor's invoice for payment.

Authorization for Purchase

The standard of protective control over the authorization for purchase is usually met by a formal requisition of some type that is approved for purchase by an authorized employee. A common plan is to delegate the authority for approval on the basis of organization position and the type of product purchased. Authority for approval of capital equipment purchases will usually be more restricted than for purchases of standard materials and supplies used in current operations.

Purchasing's first step in departmental control is the verification of authorization.

In the *preventive* phase of internal audit, the principal concern is that prescribed procedures are used and that purchase requisitions are approved in accordance with established policy. At the same time, the audit should also consider the source of the requisition and the extent to which the ordering department may have assumed purchasing authority. Once the internal auditor has determined that prescribed routines are being followed and that there is adequate protection against fraud and waste, the auditor should be concerned with:

1. The adequacy of policy
2. Any alternative methods that would improve operation or control, or would be more profitable to the company

Examples of matters covered in the constructive appraisal of purchase authorizations include:

1. Identifying situations where the determination of product and vendor was made outside of the purchasing department. These are divided into two groups:
   a. Situations where the value of the services of the purchasing department are limited. Examples include requisitions where the specifications are so restrictive that the order is limited to a single vendor. Similarly, requisitions marked "Confirming Order" sometimes indicate situations where the selection of material, the quantity to be ordered, and the vendor have been determined prior to the formal authorization for purchase.
   b. Situations where routines call for clearing the procurement transaction through regular purchasing routines, even though it is doubtful that purchasing is in a position to make any constructive contribution to the transaction, such as in orders for technical or consulting services or memberships.
2. Identifying situations where the need for immediate delivery may not give purchasing sufficient time for adequate coverage of

available sources. The usual indication will be requisitions marked "Rush," "As Soon As Possible," and so on.

3. Situations where the ordering department may not have given adequate consideration to quantity or usage in relation to ordering, shipping, or storage requirements.

In every company, there are times when rush or confirming orders are necessary, or when an operating department must take immediate steps to secure a wanted item. Occasional cases are normal and usually do not call for any comment or action. Often, however, a concentration of rush or confirming orders can be found in a few operating units, while other units carry a normal proportion of these transactions.

The constructive appraisal of these matters may require further study in other departments. The reasons may be logical, as in a maintenance department, where rush orders for repair parts are often unavoidable. For many other times, the reason may lie in the administration of the operating department, and recommendation for improvement or further study may result.

One of the most common deficiencies to be found lies in the failure of operating departments to bring in purchasing at the beginning stages of the procurement transaction. This lack of coordination and cooperation can be the source of considerable monetary loss; at best, there is sure to be irritation and confusion.

Selection of Vendor

The most definite policies and procedures in purchasing operation in many companies are those concerned with securing bids and in selecting the vendor. The following composite description may be considered typical:

1. Maintain a vendor file by purchased item to show from what vendor the item is purchased.
2. When a requisition is received, attach the vendor card.
3. Company policy requires three competitive bids on all purchases exceeding a limit of $10,000, for example. If under this amount, the buyer may place the order with a previous or new supplier without bidding. Usually this will be done if the price is the same as before or in line with changes in the general market since the previous order. More elaborate procedures and additional approvals should be in effect for items over $20,000.
4. Summarize competitive bids on a bid record with the buyer's recommendation. If the order is given to the lowest bidder and the total amount is under a limit such as $20,000, the buyer may process the purchase order. The bid record will be filed with the order.

5. If the buyer recommends the order be given to a vendor other than the low bidder, or if the total amount is over the established limit, the director of purchasing must review and approve the purchase order.

6. When the order is placed, enter the name of vendor, the price, and the quantity on the vendor card.

The above skeleton routine is indicative of procedures used in controlling the selection of a vendor. Naturally, each company will have special situations governed by special policies or procedures. Often these situations will be concerned with contracts for bulk commodities or for periodic purchases over a considerable term. For example, in printing a periodical, it would be poor practice to shop around for prices at frequent intervals. The work of breaking in a new printer on the handling of copy, proofs, and other details of production would nullify any but a substantial price advantage. A workable plan would be to have a continuing arrangement for one or several years, with competitive bids checked prior to renewing any arrangement.

The auditor's appraisal of the routines used in selecting vendors should be based on (1) verification that procedures are adequate and complied with, and (2) the business judgment exercised in awarding the purchase. Where bidding procedures are not followed, or where an order is awarded to a vendor who is not the low bidder, a readily determinable reason for what was done should be documented.

When reviewing competitive bids, be alert for unique situations where (1) a buyer's judgment may have been overridden by the supervisor, and (2) there is a reciprocal situation where the vendor is also a customer.

Some of the documentation you should expect to find available in purchasing should include, but not be limited to (1) a numerical file of purchase orders issued/voided, (2) a purchase history file by part/item, (3) a vendor file, including correspondence and quality evaluations, (4) a quotation bid file, (5) a contract file, and (6) general correspondence that should include the buyers' monthly activity reports. All of these items will assist the auditor in identifying how well the department is operating, and where to address the audit effort.

Favoritism—Gifts—Bribery—Collusion

The maintenance of a friendly relationship between the company buyer and the vendor's salesperson is a definite advantage in the satisfactory completion of the purchasing transaction. In this atmosphere, questions and adjustments that often arise may be resolved with minimum difficulty.

The vendor realizes it is beneficial to promote this. To this end, it is common practice (where the buyer is receptive) to give gifts at Christmas or at other times. These gifts may be of nominal value, or they may be of considerable value, or they may be outright presentations of money for favors received.

The entire situation involves a complexity of human relationships, rationalization, and business interests. The offering may come in a form that is difficult to refuse without appearing antisocial; the buyer may rationalize a gift with the explanation that the lowest bidder was used so that it is none of the company's concern if the vendor chooses to be nice to the buyer.

Many companies do not particularly question a small gift or limited entertainment—a bottle of liquor or a ticket to the theatre. The problem is to determine where friendly contact ends and bribery begins, and there are no standards for drawing the distinction. In considering the problem, all should agree that any extensive gift-taking or entertainment cannot be anything but a handicap to the professional, independent basis that should characterize the relationship between buyer and seller.

The possibility of undue influence thus exerted upon his buyers is in the back of every purchasing executive's mind. A number of plans have been used by purchasing executives toward control of the situation. Some of these are:

1. A company policy that acceptance of gifts of any description is sufficient cause for immediate dismissal of the buyer.
2. Publication for buyers and vendors of a statement of principles and standards similar to that promulgated by the National Association of Purchasing Management (see page 93).
3. Sending a letter to principal vendors at Christmas time thanking them for pleasant relations during the year and stating that no gifts are necessary and that employees are required to refuse them.
4. Rotation of the products handled among buyers on a regular basis (such as every 12 to 24 months). This plan controls the building of long-term personal connections between buyer and vendor and has the advantage of broadening the experience of the buyers. This also helps with departmental backup in case of illness or resignations. It has the disadvantage of losing some of the benefits gained by having buyers who are specialists in assigned areas of purchasing.

The problem of protective control in this situation is not one of verification, because in almost all cases the records will be in order and prescribed routines will have been followed. The internal auditor, therefore, must be alert to situations such as:

1. Continued purchases of competitive items available from several vendors from a single source of supply particularly when

   a. Competitive bid records show that the successful bidder is the last one to bid and is just slightly lower in price. (The buyer may be tipping off the favored vendor to competitive prices.)

   b. Continued purchases from a favored jobber at higher prices on the excuse of better service, without careful exploration of other and more direct sources of supply.

   c. Competitive bid records showing oral bids, which may (or may not) be confirmed by written bids of a later date.

2. Purchases from a single source of supply of such work as specialty printing of sales promotion material. The reason given will usu-

PRINCIPLES AND STANDARDS
OF PURCHASING PRACTICE

Loyalty to Your Company
Justice to Those with Whom You Deal
Faith in Your Profession

(From these principles are derived the N.A.P.M. standards of purchasing practice.)

1. To consider, first, the interests of your company in all transactions and to carry out and believe in its established policies.
2. To be receptive to competent counsel from your colleagues and to be guided by such counsel without impairing the dignity and responsibility of your office.
3. To buy without prejudice, seeking to obtain the maximum ultimate value for each dollar of expenditure.
4. To strive consistently for knowledge of the materials and processes of manufacture, and to establish practical methods for the conduct of your office.
5. To subscribe to and work for honesty and truth in buying and selling, and to denounce all forms and manifestations of commercial bribery.
6. To accord a prompt and courteous reception, so far as conditions will permit, to all who call on a legitimate business mission.
7. To respect your obligations and to require that obligations to you and to your concern be respected, consistent with good business practice.
8. To avoid sharp practice.
9. To counsel and assist fellow purchasing agents in the performance of their duties, whenever occasion permits.
10. To co-operate with all organizations and individuals engaged in activities designed to enhance the development and standing of purchasing.

WE SUBSCRIBE TO THESE STANDARDS

ally be the special creative talents of the vendor or his knowledge of company problems.

In a questionable situation, the indication cannot be concealed, since it will be the awarding of business in disproportionate volume to a single vendor. Yet the internal auditor must at the same time remember that normal and mutually profitable long-term relationships with individual vendors will often exist with no element of undue favoritism. There must never be hasty conclusions or condemnation.

Issuing the Purchase Order

Order placement is completed when a purchase order form is prepared, signed, or otherwise validated by an authorized company employee and forwarded to the vendor. Protective control over this phase of the purchasing operation should begin with the blank purchase order forms. The importance of controlling these forms may be better appreciated if a comparison is made with the importance of blank company disbursement checks.

There is considerable agreement that blank checks should be serially numbered and carefully accounted for. Yet if an unauthorized individual can secure a blank check, it has little value unless signed. The authorized signers are specified and the bank on which the check is drawn is responsible for checking the validity of the signature. Many losses resulting from stolen blank checks end up as the responsibility of the bank or a third party who cashed the check for the thief, and represent no out-of-pocket loss to the company.

By contrast, a vendor receiving a purchase order has no means of knowing whether a signature is genuine or who the authorized signers may be. An order may be prepared for delivery to another location, at a deferred billing date, or confirming delivery of material. In view of these and other hazards, the need for control of blank purchase orders and accounting for issued purchase orders is obvious.

Each individual or department affected by an order should be notified when the order has been issued. This is accomplished by preparing multiple copies of the order, with a copy going to such departments as (1) ordering, (2) receiving, (3) inspection, (4) storeroom, and (5) accounts payable.

The auditor's control evaluation (protective appraisal) of purchase order issuance will be concerned with the handling and storage of order forms and routines and approvals before the order is issued. The constructive appraisal will center around procedures and routines, particularly in the handling and need for extra copies of orders. As in the case of purchase requisitions, a rather involved procedure may be followed uniformly on all transactions, whereas a simpler procedure might apply to a substantial proportion. For example, where frequent small purchases of repair parts are made at catalog prices, a blanket order with handwritten releases and monthly invoicing might offer considerable economy with no weakening of control.

As another example, some companies require the vendor to sign and return one copy of the order showing acceptance and concurrence to specified prices and other conditions. In some cases this may have value; in most instances, this serves no purpose except to increase the costs of procurement.

Controlling Costs

For many years, most companies have looked for ways to increase the productivity of purchasing while minimizing the impact on internal controls. As a result, many methodologies have been developed to assist the buyers. Based on the 80/20 rule, 80 percent of the volume of purchase orders accounts for less than 20 percent of the dollar volume in purchasing. In some firms, this dollar volume can be as low as 5 to 10 percent. Accordingly the following methodologies are used to increase purchasing and organizational productivity:

1. *Traveling Requisitions.* Standard stock items are logged in and out in inventory control on individual stock cards. When the stock gets to a predefined level, the stock card is sent to purchasing and is used as the requisition; thereby reducing the time and paperwork necessary to initiate a purchase order.

2. *Petty Cash Purchases.* Individuals within the company are able to purchase items of minor value and to be reimbursed (with supervisory approval, etc.) through petty cash. Usually the amount of reimbursement must be less than $25 and must be properly supported.

3. *Blanket Orders.* Various companies issue blanket orders to office supply houses and firms able to supply maintenance items on a prompt basis. Prices are usually based on a discount to a published catalog price. Material is requisitioned directly with the vendor by authorized individuals. The vendor will then bill on a periodic basis (weekly or monthly) attaching copies of all requests and shipping documents with the invoice.

4. *Contracts.* These are usually referred to as national contracts where a company, utilizing its buying power with a national vendor, agrees to a minimum amount of annual business at reduced rates. Examples include the purchase of liquid gases, duplication

equipment rentals and service, computer paper, security, and maintenance and other service contracts.

5. *Combined Draft (Check) Purchase Order Form.* Sometimes this is also referred to as a Direct Purchase Order (DPO). Normally a supply of these prenumbered forms are given to a department that deals with a quantity of small purchases or with new vendors. Instead of C.O.D. or processing a check in advance, the DPO is used as the requisition, purchase order, and payment—all in one step.

   Obviously, much control must be exercised over these particular forms. The dollar amount is usually limited to an amount less than $1000, and the approval process must include two independent departments. This form can be compared to drafts sometimes given to salespersons.

6. *Automated Material Requirements Planning Systems.* This refers to several software packages on the market that fully integrate inventories, minimum reorder points, requisitions, purchase orders, receiving reports, shop floor systems, scheduling, production and inventory control, and part of the accounts payable system. Because of their diversity, they are mentioned for your awareness.

Routing

A usual responsibility of purchasing is to indicate the carrier and mode of shipment of the material purchased. A common weakness in the control of transportation costs is to consider them as uncontrollable and to concentrate only upon the price of the material. The true cost is the cost of material delivered to the specified place at the specified time. Therefore, the control of the delivery cost must not be disregarded.

This phase of ordering presents a number of ramifications that must be explored before an auditor can render an opinion or recommendation. Some questions to consider are:

1. Were delivery costs included in considering competitive bids?
2. Is the company transportation (traffic) department consulted as to the preferred and most economical means of delivery?
3. Where material is bought F.O.B. vendor's shipping point, is freight allowance verified before the invoice is paid?
4. What attention is given to possible savings in shipping expense through such means as pooled-shipments, backhauling, or most favorable tariff rates?
5. Where a requisition specifies shipment at premium rates (for services such as air express or express mail), how much effort is made to determine whether paying the premium rate was necessary?

Order Follow-Up

Another responsibility regularly assigned to the materiels department is that of expediting—following-up with the vendor to insure that shipment is made according to the terms of the order.

The internal auditor's examination and appraisal of this phase is again principally concerned with routines and policies.

1. Does standard procedure call for follow-up of all orders, where such following may in many cases be unnecessary?
2. Could order follow-up be reduced by prenegotiation and establishment of critical due dates?
3. Are purchasing and operating departments duplicating each other's efforts in expediting?
4. Is purchasing informed of follow-up by other departments?
5. Is follow-up activity documented?
6. Is there regular review of activity by supervision?
7. How do actual delivery dates compare with dates specified on orders?

Adjustments with Vendors

The final phase of completing the purchase transaction usually assigned to purchasing is the negotiation of adjustments with vendors for variations from the specifications of the purchase order in such items as quantity or quality of received material. These adjustments are often handled by accounts payable with assistance from individual buyers, without any definite requirement for approval of additional costs involved.

The problems may be best illustrated by several examples:

1. In one company, certain materials did not meet purchase specifications. Management decided to do the necessary corrective work, rather than return the material to the vendor. The total shop cost was determined and charged to the vendor. The vendor protested the amount and, in the final negotiations, the buyer charged only for the direct shop costs for labor and material with no allowance for normal overhead expenses.
2. Vendor shipments (plus or minus 10 percent) are common, and duplicate shipments do exist.
3. Additional cost is frequently incurred due to variations in the method of shipment from the specifications of the purchase order. For example, a carload order may be shipped in several less-than-carload lots, thus losing the advantage of the carload transportation rate.

4. Damage incurred on incoming shipments should be pursued to insure that recovery is made from the vendor or transportation company.

Although it is difficult to set any definite rules or procedures for the handling of such items, the principal control standards include:

1. Departments affected should be informed of and approve adjustments.
2. Adjustments should be followed to completion.
3. Final settlement should be approved by a level of management as appropriate.

Commodity Purchasing

If the purchasing department is buying the right product at the right price at the right time, the department is personified by the perfect competition offered by the Chicago Board of Trade! The Chicago Board of Trade was established in 1848 to reduce the drastic fluctuations in the price of commodities between buyer and producer. Current futures traded in this market include grains, oilseeds, precious metals, forest products, and interest rate futures.

People can buy or sell what they want when they want. A buyer or seller can hedge to protect themselves from future higher or lower prices. Contracts (set volumes of a contract) can be bought and sold. They may be bought if you believe prices are going up.

What affects price? Basic economics: supply, demand, imports, exports, product substitutes, periodic government reports, the weather, and psychology. Psychology is the *anticipation* of governmental reports and *forecasts* of bad weather and/or bad crops.

The daily price fluctuation by product is limited by the Board. Not included in the price are items such as storage and shipping costs. Further adjustments can also be made; in the purchase of grains, for example, adjustments are made for moisture content.

This topic may be better explained by example:

Example 1.   A grower will sell futures to lock in a firm price for the crop being raised.

Example 2.   A rancher will buy futures to firm up a price for cattle feed. This will protect his forecasted cost used to determine at what price cattle must be sold to make a profit.

Example 3.   A food processing company forecasts its profit based upon budgeted volumes. Certain assumptions are made about the cost of the grain used. Weekly reviews are held to determine the average cost-to-date and what posture to hold based upon manufacturing needs for the next 90 days.

CONTROL OF COLLATERAL RESPONSIBILITIES

As previously mentioned, many material departments have responsibility for operations other than the actual buying operation. Where these collateral responsibilities are assigned can create certain problems or possible weaknesses in control. The following sections consider some of these responsibilities and the related control factors.

Receipt and Inspection of Incoming Material and Supplies

The reporting of receipts should be assigned to a group reporting to the head of the materiel's organization.

In appraising the internal control risks, the auditor should consider:

1. Whether any future check on quantities received is done—for example, in an operating department or a storeroom.
2. Routing receiving reports—do these go directly to departments other than purchasing and accounts payable?
3. Handling differences between quantities reported as received and quantities billed or ordered. If these are referred back to the buyer, who then decides what is to be done; control is weak.
4. If the purchase includes a charge for services, who determines that the services have actually been rendered?
5. Is there a possibility for introducing a fraudulent receiving report into the vouchering system?

Frauds have been perpetrated through agreement between a dishonest vendor and a dishonest buyer; material of a low grade would be supplied, with billing rendered for material of a higher grade. Thus, in controlling situations where a buying department approves either the quantity or the quality of incoming material, the greater risk is probably in the case of quality.

A mitigating factor will arise if there is a further check of quality in the course of manufacturing operations; for example, if coal of an inferior grade is supplied, the production of steam in relation to coal consumption will be poor and the boiler room supervisor will be quick to notice and report it.

Authorization of Payments to Vendors

Disregarding all other considerations, the optimum standard of control is one where:

1. The purchasing department, having ordered material on the basis of a requisition from an outside department, sends a copy of the order to the accounts payable group.

2. A receiving department, not under the supervision of purchasing, sends a report of the quantity of received material directly to accounts payable.

3. An incoming inspection (or laboratory) not under the supervision of purchasing sends a report of the quality of received material to accounts payable.

4. Incoming invoices are delivered directly to accounts payable.

5. Accounts payable, having matched order, receiving, and inspection reports and invoices, prepares an accounts payable voucher to authorize payment to the vendor.

Where this standard cannot be met, the control requirement is to provide as much separation as possible between the responsibilities for (1) originating requisitions, (2) placing orders, (3) reporting receipt, and (4) approving invoices for payment. The less the separation of these functions, the more exhaustive the internal auditor must be in verification and appraisal.

Operation of Material and Supply Storerooms

In some organizations, the maintenance and operation of storerooms is under the materiel's department.

Effective control calls for as much separation as is feasible between storeroom operation and buying. This may be accomplished by the natural segregation of storerooms in a separate operating unit that reports to the head of materiel.

It is important in this situation to study the control over storeroom inventories through perpetual inventory records and through charges for materials received and issued. The degree of authority purchasing has over the specifications of materials carried in the storeroom should also be considered.

The following questions should be in the internal auditor's mind when making an evaluation:

1. Could substandard materials be purchased and issued without effective complaint from operating departments?

2. Could materials be charged-off or diverted without adequate disclosure?

3. What are the dangers of overstocking or understocking or of carrying obsolete materials because of lack of contact between purchasing and the operating departments?

The protective and constructive internal audit of storeroom operations is a subject in itself. Here the objective is to bring out only special factors arising when storerooms are under materiel's supervision.

Sale of Scrap

Responsibility for the sale of scrap is assigned to the purchasing department in some industries. The handling and disposal of scrap material
presents a number of control problems and hazards, ranging from failure
to realize adequate values, to losses through theft and collusion. In itself,
scrap (as a by-product of any business operation) may be neglected to the
point where there is almost an invitation to mishandling.

Purchasing department responsibility normally begins after a quantity
of scrap has been accumulated elsewhere in the organization and is ready
to be discarded. The usual practice is to secure bids from dealers and to
then award the material to the highest bidder. Protective and constructive internal audit examination over this function has many requirements,
which may lead the internal auditor into operating departments. Among
the questions to be asked are:

1. How effective is control over scrap material quantities? When are
   weights determined and when is accountability established?
2. Is scrap material segregated and classified for most-profitable disposition?
3. Is any material (for example, containers) being discarded as scrap
   when it might be returned for credit to the original supplier?
4. How are the weights of scrap sold determined? Scrap dealers
   alone should not be able to decide exactly what they will pay for.
5. Are prices offered by dealers checked with trade quotations,
   where available?
6. What is the possibility of material or equipment being disposed of
   as scrap by one department when another department is purchasing similar material?
7. Are shipping documents used for scrap sales prenumbered?
8. Are trucks picking up scraps weighed in and out of the facility?

The internal auditors will undoubtedly develop numerous other questions in their examination and appraisal of this hard-to-control section of
the business.

Purchases for Employees' Personal Use

Companies have policies ranging from complete prohibition of personal
purchases for employees to giving quite extensive service in the purchase
of most items other than food and clothing. In addition, company products may be sold to employees at substantial discounts with payments,
without interest, through payroll deductions.

The simplest plan from a control standpoint is where the company recommends the employee to a dealer, and from that point all transactions

are direct between dealer and employee. In this situation, there is comparatively little work for the company and no problem of billing and collection with the employee.

When the dealer is to bill the company, there are these evident control requirements:

1. Assurance that items billed to the company by dealers are rebilled to employees.
2. Assurance that collection is made from employees.
3. Assurance that billing for personal purchase may not be diverted so that purchases are charged out as company expense.

SPECIAL AUDIT PROBLEMS

Field Purchasing

As previously mentioned, the decentralization of a company's operating units will usually be accompanied by some decentralized purchasing responsibility. The control of these decentralized units brings a twofold problem of internal auditing:

1. The appraisal of the internal control of the decentralized units. Depending largely upon the size of the operations, this may or may not be done as one part of a complete audit of the unit.
2. The appraisal of the effectiveness of the home office policies, procedures, and instructions prescribing the limits of responsibility and authority and the methods of operation of the field purchasing offices.

The internal audit of a field purchasing office must be prefaced with a review of company policy on purchases by field offices. Policy limitations customarily include such provisions as:

1. A requirement that items of general company usage be ordered via national contracts negotiated by the home office.
2. A dollar value or quantity limit upon individual orders placed by the field office.
3. A requirement that the field office send copies of purchase orders or releases against master purchase orders to the home office purchasing department. This may cover all orders, or may be limited to orders over a certain dollar amount or quantity limit.

Whatever the control measures, it is necessary to review the field office situation to see (1) if corporate policies are being followed, and (2) whether any revision in policies should be considered. Compliance with established policies is verified in the field office audit, with an eye to such obvious evasions as placing multiple orders for the same item to circumvent an established dollar limit, or local purchase of material that is available elsewhere in the company.

A situation where a revision of home office policies may be desirable would be where audits of a number of field locations indicate similar evasions or deficiencies. For example, if a policy sets a low limit (such as $100) on the maximum order that could be placed without home-office approval, the field office would probably resort to placing several small, identical orders for needed materials. This situation would probably call for a functional study of field purchasing responsibilities to combine and compare the purchasing experience of all locations. This combination and comparison would give the basis for a constructive recommendation regarding policy revisions.

The general problem of control of decentralized purchasing operations is no different than is the control of other decentralized functions. A principal requirement is coordination of home office and field. The internal auditor, having direct contact with both home office and field, can be of major assistance in communication and coordination.

Purchasing should also promote communication and contact between purchasing agents in the different field offices and the home office. For example, one company has an annual meeting of its purchasing staff. In this company, authority is completely decentralized, and the head office exercises comparatively little control over purchasing arrangements except for negotiation of general contracts covering a few major materials and supplies. The annual meeting, which lasts for one week, gives purchasing agents an opportunity to present their accomplishments and problems. Through group discussion, each agent can benefit. As a group, they are able to offer constructive suggestions on items handled through general purchase contracts, and to each other with their local purchasing problems.

Petty Cash Purchases

There will always be some degree of purchasing by other departments. These purchases and their nature will be evident through the payments that are usually petty cash vouchers or employees' expense accounts.

Whatever the means of payment, the internal auditor should check the nature of these purchases in the course of the other audits to ensure there is no extensive procurement of items that might be more effectively handled through regular purchasing channels.

DESIGNING THE AUDIT PROGRAM

The foregoing sections described the operations and the related internal control elements and problems found in some purchasing departments. To present a description or program usable in any situation naturally is not possible without allowance for local conditions. Both the descriptive matter and the specimen program that follow are sufficiently comprehensive to enable the internal auditor (who has not reviewed a purchasing department) to develop an adequate program. Also, the internal auditor who is auditing a purchasing department may find this material of value as a standard against which the present program may be compared. Finally, the purchasing executive may find the material of value in the establishment and maintenance of an adequate internal control plan over the purchasing operation.

The operation of a purchasing department is governed by the requirements of the rest of the organization. The fulfillment of these requirements cannot be completed by set formula or routine. Effective purchasing requires knowledge of company requirements and the exercising of sound business judgment by the purchasing executive.

The internal auditor can be of valuable assistance in bringing broad knowledge of company operations to bear upon the internal control and operating problems of the purchasing department.

INTERNAL AUDIT PROGRAM*

The program that follows has been developed from programs secured from a number of companies. Because this program is a composite, it should be applied to any individual company only after allowing for the normal differences between industries and companies.

As is customary with audit programs, this program endeavors to show what is to be covered and how this is to be done, without going into detail. The steps may be considered as forming the foundation from which the audit and resulting recommendations and comments will develop. How this development will occur will depend on what is found, and on the imagination and initiative of the auditor, whose objectives are (1) protection of the interests of his company, and (2) improvement of operations and profits.

The program is divided into five principal sections, which correspond generally to the sequence of the audit. These are:

1. Company policy and organization
2. Purchasing department operation

*For defense contractors, an important phase of the purchasing audit is verification that federal procurement requirements are complied with.

3. Collateral operations
4. Records and reports
5. The audit report

Review of Other Audits

The audit should begin with a review of any previous purchasing department audit reports and with notation of purchasing matters coming to attention in other audits, such as those covering receiving, accounts payable, or branch offices.

Company Policy and Organization

I. Organizational Status of the Purchasing Department
   A. To whom does the head of purchasing report?
   B. What control over purchasing policy is exercised by
      1. Company executives outside of purchasing organizational lines?
      2. Administrative committees?
      3. Board of directors?
   C. Secure or prepare organizational chart of purchasing department, with outline of duties and responsibilities of employees, including division of purchasing responsibility among buyers.
II. Responsibility for Purchasing
   A. Is the responsibility of the purchasing department clearly defined and understood by members of
      1. Purchasing department?
      2. Other departments?
   B. Does purchasing have knowledge of conflicting purchasing responsibility assumed by other departments?
   C. Is the company policy on purchasing covered in a written manual?
   D. What are the principal procurement activities for which the purchasing department has
      1. No responsibility?
      2. Limited responsibility?
   E. What is the policy covering the relationships of other departments with vendors
      1. On contract or discussions with sales personnel?
      2. On correspondence?
   F. Is purchasing consulted by, or does it originate discussions with, operating departments on such purchasing matters as

1. Favorable purchasing opportunities?
2. Economical order quantities?
3. Revision of purchase specifications?

G. What is the policy on
   1. Making purchases locally where possible?
   2. Purchasing from users of company products?

H. Does the purchasing department maintain or participate in a value analysis program including
   1. Determination that price revisions covering changes in materials and methods are negotiated with vendors.
   2. Review of market trends, particularly on long-term contracts and contracts containing escalation clauses.

III. Authorization for Purchasing

A. What is the general policy for approval of purchases by departments requiring material?

B. Are approval limits covered in written instructions?

C. Are approval limits definite as to amount and classification of expenditure?

D. What are the policies regarding special approvals, such as:
   1. For capital expenditures?
   2. By budget department prior to commitment?

E. What is the approval policy where the final cost of an order exceeds the amount originally estimated on the requisition or purchase order?

F. What is the approval policy where changes are made in the quantity or specifications of the original purchase requisition?

G. Secure copies of each form used to authorize purchases.

IV. Physical Facilities. Study the layout and general facilities of the purchasing department with particular attention to:

A. Arrangements for reception and interviews with salespeople

B. Office layout for effective operation

V. Decentralized Purchasing. Determine what the company policy is for purchases made by decentralized operating units, through petty cash, and so on:

A. Limits of authority

B. Reporting responsibility

C. Review or control by home office purchasing department

NOTE: The purpose of this portion of the audit is to learn of the policies and general conditions under which the purchasing department operates. The sources of information will usually be the head of the purchasing department and company manuals.

Where policies are lacking or indefinite, there may be weakness in control, duplicating fields of responsibility or other deficiency that will be evidenced in the course of the audit. Also evidenced will be variations between policy and actual operations.

Purchasing Department Operations

I. Department Procedures
   A. Are purchasing department procedures oral or written?
   B. Prepare chart showing the handling of requisitions, placing of purchase orders, and the flow of requisition, purchase order, and other purchasing forms within the purchasing department and to and from other departments.
   C. Study procedures related to bidding by vendors.
      1. Policy as to amount of order on which bidding is required
      2. Procedure on requesting bids
      3. Form of bids (sealed, oral, etc.)
      4. Summarization of bids and selection of vendor
II. Department Forms. Secure a copy of each specialized form used by the purchasing department. These should be studied so the purpose and usage is thoroughly understood. Typical questions would be:
   A. Is the purchase order form wording clear and complete, so the vendor understands all terms and conditions?
   B. How are blank purchase order forms protected?
   C. What is routing of copies of forms?
   D. How necessary is each copy of a form?
   E. Is some form of traveling requisition provided for repetitive orders for storeroom purchases?
   F. Are forms designed for efficient and simple completion?

NOTE: It is common to find overelaborate routines relating to preparation of purchase order copies. The result is unnecessary and duplicating files in various departments.

III. Selection of an Audit Sample. Examine files covering all purchase orders placed over a period of three months. From these, select for detailed examination orders that will include some of each of the following:
   A. Purchases made by each buyer
   B. Requisitions by each major operating department
   C. A number of "Rush" and Confirming Delivery" orders

D. Single orders divided between several suppliers
E. Orders where purchase is not made from lowest bidder
F. Orders where final specifications or quantities are revised from the original requisition
G. Orders where freight is allowed
H. Orders for capital equipment
I. Orders where price is not specified or that include some variable pricing arrangement
J. Orders providing for trade-in allowances
K. Orders where substantial overshipment is made and accepted
L. Blanket or continuing orders where a number of deliveries are made over a period of time
M. Orders where specification of item, quantity, or price is not definite
N. Orders placed under long-term purchase contracts

NOTE: The selection of an adequate sample is of utmost importance. The objective is to set aside for detailed examination a group of purchase orders that will adequately represent both the normal and the abnormal. Enough normal items must exist for the auditor to verify general policies and to reveal situations that may call for more extensive examination.

IV. Examination of Purchase Orders Selected in the Sample. The examination of each purchase order selected in the sample should be done in enough detail, through examination of all supporting records, to enable the internal auditor to be confident of knowing how each of the operations, from origination and approval of requisition to the completion of the order, was handled. The auditor must be constantly concerned with what was done and why—to be satisfied that each order was placed and handled in the best interests of the company.

Through this examination, the auditor becomes aware of situations that require further study in purchasing or in other departments. The objectives are (1) through verification, to provide the basis for appraisal of current policies and procedures, and (2) to give a basis for constructive recommendation.

The following listing is intended only as a sample of questions that will occupy the auditor's attention and may be the subject for further inquiry:

A. Where an order is divided among several vendors, what was the reason?
B. On "Confirming Orders," did some operating department really assume the purchasing function?

C. If orders are placed for such items as memberships, just what is gained by clearing these through purchasing routines?

D. Are there any indications of favoritism to vendors?

E. Where changes are made from original specifications in requisition or order, are these adequately approved and brought to the attention of those who should be concerned?

F. How are allowances and adjustments handled and approved?

G. Are transportation allowances verified?

H. If price is omitted from the order, why?

I. If the order calls for services or materials on a cost plus or other basis that is indefinite as to exact amount, how are final charges verified?

J. Does the employee approving a requisition appear to have adequate information to enable intelligent approval?

K. How are trade-in arrangements determined and approved? (Sometimes more can be secured for replaced equipment than from a trade-in.)

L. How completely do possible sources of supply seem to be covered?

M. Are F.O.B. points and routings shown and followed?

N. Does it appear that effort is made to ship by most economical methods? Is the traffic department consulted regarding routes and methods?

O. How were long-term contracts negotiated?

P. What consideration is given to tax status of materials, sales and use taxes, excise taxes, and so on?

Collateral Operations

Determine and describe briefly all operations performed in the purchasing department that are not directly concerned with placing orders and follow-up for delivery. For example, the purchasing department may be assigned responsibility for such operations as:

1. Reporting on quantity and quality of received materials
2. Authorization of payments to vendors
3. Operation of material and supply storerooms
4. Sale of scrap
5. Purchases for employees

In the audit of the collateral operations of the purchasing department, the internal auditor will have a twofold concern: first will be the effect that the inclusion of these operations under the responsibility of the purchasing department will have as far as internal control is concerned; second will be the internal audit of the assigned collateral operations.

Because of the many variables, no definite program for the audit of specific collateral responsibilities of the purchasing department can be specified. The internal auditor must study to cover each situation, and it may develop that a supplementary interdepartmental survey of a particular field should be made. In general, the collateral responsibilities present a challenge and an opportunity for both protective and constructive recommendation.

As an example, when material and supply storerooms are the responsibility of the purchasing department, there is a protective hazard in having the origination of orders, placing of orders, approving for quantity and quality, and issuance of materials and supplies all combined under a single responsibility. Here the internal auditor will be concerned with the organizational separation and responsibility for these operations, and will shape the examination accordingly. Beyond this, the internal auditor should look into the liaison between purchasing and operating departments with consideration of such factors as overstocking, understocking, or obsolescence.

Records and Reports

The various records used in current operations will have been reviewed and appraised in the study of departmental procedures. This will include such records as those showing sources of supply and numerical listings of purchase orders placed.

Beyond these will be a variety of records and reports not required in the normal flow of work but maintained to provide information considered valuable for administrative reasons.

Examples of this type of record or report will be:

1. Records of orders placed with each vendor
2. Records of orders placed by each buyer, showing number of orders and total value
3. Reports of future commitments
4. Reports of departmental operation to management
5. Reports of commodity price trends to operating departments
6. Reports that have been rendered to management covering special savings or other accomplishments.

Examination and appraisal of records and reports has two objectives:

1. First should come verification of the accuracy of the records or statements that are maintained or reported. This should be done on a test basis. For example, if a saving was claimed, there should be a test to be sure that the claimed saving was actually realized.
2. After verification of the general accuracy, the second step is appraisal of the value to the department or executive using or receiving the record or report. In this appraisal, the internal auditor should ascertain the answers to such questions as:
   a. Is each record really used?
   b. Does each report serve a useful purpose?
   c. Does each report give a complete and accurate picture?
   d. Are reports incomplete so important factors are not brought to management's attention?

The answers to these and other questions that will arise will require discussion with those who prepare the records and reports and with those who receive and use them.

The Audit Report

The form and content of the audit report covering the purchasing department will be similar to reports covering any other section of the company. In the report, the auditor must be careful to separate his findings and recommendations in matters of internal control from his findings and suggestions in matters outside the field of control.

In matters concerned with the appraisal of control, the internal auditor has a duty to point out deficiencies and to make constructive recommendations. For example, the audit examination might disclose a situation where substantial revisions affecting the cost of a purchased item were made by direct contact between an operating department and a vendor. In this case, a recommendation for clearing all such transactions through the purchasing department would be in order.

A number of matters outside the field of control or outside the scope of authority of the purchasing department might come to the auditor's attention in the course of the audit. There is no standard treatment; however, the report should draw attention to situations that merit further consideration or action. For example, company policy may require that a particular item be purchased from a prescribed supplier for reasons of reciprocity without a stipulation that the price must be competitive. In the course of work, the auditor learns that the item may be secured at a lower price from another supplier. It is not the auditor's responsibility to recommend that the policy be changed, but the auditor can point out the excess cost of the policy. Having done this, it is management's responsibility to decide whether to pursue the matter further.

As soon as the draft copy of the report is prepared, it should be reviewed and discussed with the head of purchasing by the auditor in charge. A number of findings and recommendations could be agreed upon as a result of this discussion. This agreement may then be noted in the report, so attention may be focused on any areas of disagreement. In these areas, the discussion would result in agreement on the factual data in the audit findings, so that the final decision by management may rest on a sound factual basis.

The report is then prepared in its final form, with a copy routed to the head of purchasing.

CHAPTER 4

Receiving

IMPORTANCE OF RECEIVING OPERATIONS

Definition

Receiving operations are the middle stage in the cycle of procurement. The main objectives of the receiving operation are to assure that items are received in the quantity and quality specified in purchase orders, and that materials received are properly protected and efficiently handled from receipt to entry into the flow of operations.

Importance of Receiving

The internal audit of receiving operations is and must be concerned not only with paperwork, but also with the physical handling of materials. In manufacturing companies, a well organized receiving operation is essential to the orderly flow of materials and supplies into production. Delays or interruptions in the flow may lead to serious disruption of activities.

Effective control over receiving activities is an important safeguard against fraud and loss. The misreporting of quantity and grade of received materials has been an essential element in many large frauds. Poor facilities for storage and handling in the receiving department can lead to damage, loss, or pilferage.

This chapter deals with the following aspects of receiving operations:

1. The flow of materials from outside sources into the receiving activity
2. The determination that quantity and quality conform with purchase specifications
3. The delivery of materials to the point of use or to storage for future use
4. Related procedures, which should provide prompt and complete reporting to all affected departments, including the
   a. Ordering department
   b. Purchasing department
   c. Stores department or user
   d. Accounts payable department
   e. Traffic department

The following sections are arranged in a logical sequence to be followed in the internal audit of receiving operations. A discussion of the organizational relationships of the receiving function is followed by a description of the physical facilities for received materials and related controls. Next, determining quantity and quality of received materials are dealt with. After discussing the physical requirements and handling, procedural controls are described.

Verification of Services Received

Since this section deals with the operations of receiving materials and supplies, no specific attention is given to reporting the receipt of services—such as repairs or maintenance. Customarily, specifications and charges for these items are approved for receipt and payment by those who have direct responsibility for the facilities to which the services apply.

Reporting Responsibility

The most desirable relationship, from both control and operating standpoints, is where the receiving function is a part of the general organizational grouping responsible for material requirements planning.

The main objective of effective receiving is the accurate reporting of the quantity and quality of materials received to assure that the company receives what is ordered and what it will pay for. In appraising the organizational control over receiving, one should bear in mind that there are certain organizational structures that are basically weak, since the checks and balances that will assure objectivity are not fully provided.

1. Having the receiving operations under the supervision of the purchasing function is undesirable. If this situation exists, the purchasing function is in the position of first specifying what is to be ordered and then attesting that the requirements of the purchase contract have been met.

   In such cases, a minimum control requirement is to make the head of the receiving activity responsible to the head of the purchasing function and not to anyone who has line responsibility for day-to-day dealings with vendors. Even in this arrangement, control is not satisfactory.

2. The rather common assignment of receiving responsibility to the storeroom function does not present the risk of collusion with buyers or vendors inherent in the assignment to the purchasing function. However, if the storeroom and receiving records and operations are closely intermingled, there is the possibility that records may be manipulated to conceal losses or fraudulent diversion of materials. This may be minimized by definite separation of the responsibilities for the handling of materials and for the keeping of records in the receiving and stores activities.

Relationship to Other Departments

The receiving department generally operates as a service activity for the entire organization. This requires that close cooperation be maintained with operating departments and with such service departments as purchasing and traffic. An important part of this cooperation is the prompt reporting of received materials. For example:

1. The department responsible for ordering should be informed when material has been received and is available.
2. The purchasing department should be informed when:
   a. Variations occur from the specifications of purchase orders
   b. Materials are received that cannot be identified with purchase orders.
3. The traffic department should be informed when:
   a. Cars have been unloaded
   b. Difficulties arise because of the scheduling of incoming shipments
   c. Materials have not been received after some set period of time
   d. Damage and loss is found.
4. The accounts payable department should be notified promptly when material has been received and accepted so vendors' invoices may be processed on a timely basis.

PHYSICAL FACILITIES AND HANDLING

Entry and Exit of Carriers

Control over received materials should begin at the point of entry on company property. At most industrial plants, the first stage of a delivery by outside motor carrier is the securing of a vehicle pass from the company guard at the entry gate.

The truck driver is then instructed to go directly to the receiving area, where he either makes delivery or is in turn routed to another plant location. After delivery is made, the receiving clerk makes a notation on the driver's copy of the vehicle pass, indicating whether the outgoing truck will be empty (having unloaded completely) or will contain goods to be delivered elsewhere. This notation is checked by the guard when the pass is surrendered and the truck is inspected at the plant exit. Partially loaded trucks leaving company property are usually subject to a close inspection to ascertain that packages are not arranged so as to conceal pilfered materials.

Materials coming into the plant over railroad sidings are readily controlled since movement within the plant will be governed by the location of trackage. Most such deliveries will be full carloads or tankcars, since less-than-carload shipments will usually be delivered by truck. One necessary control is the assignment of definite responsibility for determining railroad cars are completely unloaded before leaving company property. In most cases, this is done by visual examination.

In addition to controls over movement of trucks and railroad cars, plant security procedures should provide for restricting the movement of truck drivers and train crews to specified plant areas and for their surveillance while on company premises.

Goods delivered by mail, express, or messenger may present a problem because some may be personal packages addressed to individual employees. Three methods of handling this situation are:

1. All packages are delivered to the receiving department, which then sorts out those that appear to contain company-ordered materials and delivers the others to the addressees.

2. The incoming mail department endeavors to make the separation, delivering personal packages to employees, and sending packages bearing order numbers and similar identifying data to the receiving department.

3. The receiving department opens and delivers all packages delivered to company premises (similar to the mailroom opening all mail so all invoices will go to the accounts payable department).

Any misrouting of incoming materials will subsequently be revealed when the vendor seeks payment for materials for which no receiving report has been rendered. A preventive measure to minimize such occurrences is to require adequate labeling by the vendor.

Track and Truck Scales

Where a considerable volume of bulk materials is delivered by truck or rail, it is desirable that scales be available to determine gross weights of incoming trucks and cars, and tare weights after unloading. For some materials (i.e., coal), these weights may serve as the basis for reporting the net quantity received. For other materials (i.e., liquids in tank cars) these weights will provide a cross-check on the volume determined by gauging at the point of delivery. (The use of scale weights will be discussed below in the section that covers the determination of quantities received.)

Docking and Unloading Delays

Any accumulation of trucks or rail cars awaiting unloading may be the symptom of:

1. Inadequate docking facilities
2. Inadequate receiving personnel to handle incoming volume
3. Inadequate mechanical facilities for moving received materials
4. Inadequate facilities for holding received materials
5. Poor scheduling of incoming shipments by the traffic, purchasing, or production control departments
6. Slow inspection by quality control activities
7. Poor checking procedures and practices
8. Trucking companies not coordinating deliveries

Inadequate Facilities

Facilities for handling, unloading, and storing the major materials used or consumed in the production activity should be adequate and well planned. Most manufacturing plants are designed with these facilities in mind; any major deficiency in this area will normally have continuing attention until corrected. (Some companies have an agreement with a common carrier to provide a quantity of trucks as additional storage during peak production.) It is more common to find deficiencies in the facilities for handling miscellaneous materials.

Delays Due to Personnel Limitations

It is not unusual to find that delays in handling incoming shipments occur because sufficient personnel are not available to handle the volume of materials received in peak periods. Where this condition is only occasional, it may be due to a temporary breakdown in the scheduling program or other unavoidable factors. Where this condition appears to be chronic, detailed study followed by appropriate corrective action is indicated.

Where there is a temporary shortage of personnel, it may be less expensive to pay demurrage on rail cars than to pay overtime for unloading, assuming that the incoming materials are not required immediately.

Delays Due to Inadequate Mechanical Facilities

Such mechanical aids as forklift trucks are essential in a modern receiving operation handling any sizable volume. In general, any manual handling of incoming materials in large volume is usually uneconomical, and normally only found in countries with very low labor wages.

Forklift handling can be maximized by arranging with vendors to ship in a way that facilitates handling in the receiving operation. Examples are packing incoming items in containers of standard sizes or packing in standard units on pallets or slips so materials can be readily checked for quantity and handled by forklift trucks in the receiving and/or stores departments.

Delays Due to Inadequate Storage Facilities

Adequate space must be provided in receiving facilities to hold materials until they are cleared to production or stores. The determination of what is adequate is difficult, since the requirements may be markedly changed by changes in the routing of materials. For example, arrangements may be made to deliver certain materials directly to production departments instead of through the receiving department, thus helping avoid an overcrowded condition. Or, arrangements for more rapid deliveries to production and storerooms could reduce space requirements. Short-cut measures should not be permitted to weaken the essential receiving responsibility for examination and correct reporting of quality and quantity.

Where storage facilities prove temporarily inadequate, the situation can occasionally be handled by not unloading incoming cars (or by agreement to use the trailers as temporary storage), provided demurrage charges are less than the cost of other arrangements for storage and handling.

Delays Due to Scheduling

Scheduling deliveries from vendors with the objective of obtaining an even flow of materials is an essential of inventory management—but is usually feasible only where large volumes of materials are received on a regular basis. Examples of this include automotive parts shipped to an assembly plant; basic materials and supplies delivered to an oil refinery; and commodities, raw materials, containers, and supplies to a food processing plant. In these circumstances, the scheduling is an integral part of the broad production control and inventory management plans.

If the flow of incoming materials is uneven, the receiving operation can usually be improved by scheduling incoming shipments to reduce bottlenecks. One company was faced with a situation where various small deliveries were made by 20 different trucking companies. This resulted in congestion at the receiving docks, with truckers required to wait long periods to make small deliveries. The condition was corrected by having the purchasing and traffic departments issue specific routing instructions to vendors. Under these instructions, only five truckers made deliveries, thus reducing the incoming trucks to a manageable level.

Delays Due to Inspection for Quality

Certain materials are retained in the receiving department or in temporary storage pending approval by quality control laboratories. Often the required testing is incidental to what the laboratory technicians may consider more important work. The result can be delays in inspection and reporting that may materially affect:

1. Requirements for storage space
2. Demurrage payments
3. Accounts payable operations

The internal auditor's factual determination and reporting of the effect of such delays upon company operating units can be helpful in bringing such conditions to management attention.

Delays Due to Procedures

Unduly complicated or poorly executed procedures can cause delays in all stages of the receiving operation. Correction will usually require, and should include, thorough study and analysis of physical aspects of receiving activities and of related paperwork.

Delays Due to Trucking Companies

If the freight forwarder is unaware of a particular need for a product or if the company is not a regular customer, the shipment may not be handled in an expedient manner. To assist in the scheduling of deliveries, some companies have working arrangements with one or more freight companies. Accordingly, purchasing agents will request vendors to use these freight companies when shipping product.

Correction of Inadequacies

As mentioned, any delays in the receiving process are symptoms of possible inadequacies. In many instances, any of the several measures outlined in the preceding paragraphs may be sufficient to correct the condition.

The determination of optimum corrective measures is often a job for experts in materials handling and production control. In this circumstance, the internal auditor's job is to determine the symptoms—usually delay or confusion in receiving operations—and to direct attention to these symptoms in his report. If the auditor is not in a position to make specific recommendations for corrective action, the report can then recommend study by experts.

Inspection of Facilities

Since the receiving activity is concerned with handling, counting, inspecting, and safeguarding physical materials, the inspection of facilities and operations by the auditor is an essential and first step of the audit. Actual physical inspection of facilities is one of the principal means by which the auditor can appraise the controls over the completed transactions that are reflected in the majority of the receiving reports.

DETERMINATION OF QUANTITY AND QUALITY

Primary Verification

In attesting to the receipt of satisfactory materials, receiving department employees may rely extensively on the good faith of their vendors and on secondary checking in stores or operating departments. Sometimes the assumption is that vendors will ship materials that conform in quantity and quality to purchase specifications. Thus the verification activity of the receiving department may be limited because of mutual confidence between the company and its vendors. If discrepancies are revealed in secondary checks, experience shows that adjustments may be made with reputable vendors without undue difficulty.

For many received items, a brand name or other standard designation made will show this designation and the quantity in each container. In this situation, the common practice in most companies is to accept container markings and packing slipsheets as evidence of quantity and material identification.

However, reliance on vendors should not be carried to the point where recoveries for legitimate losses or claims are prejudiced because of an undue lapse of time between the original receipt of materials and the filing of claims arising from secondary checking. In this situation, or in cases where an unusually large number of discrepancies becomes apparent in shipments from certain vendors, more critical examination is required at the time of receipt.

Secondary Verification by Stores and Operating Departments

The verification activity of the receiving department tends to be limited by the extent to which quantity and quality may be checked in the routine operations of the departments that will use or store the materials.

Quantity

As an example, in one company automotive parts are delivered from outside vendors in cartons packed according to quantity and arrangement standards developed by company engineers. On receipt, the number of cartons is checked and reported, but no count of individual parts is made. The using department is instructed to report any omissions of parts from cartons—and the physical packing arrangements make any such omission evident. The only verification by the receiving department is an occasional test-check of a few cartons.

Another example is the receipt of paper that is delivered to a stationery storeroom. Such paper is often wrapped in ream packages (500 sheets) and packed in cases on which the total number of sheets and packages is marked. Here the receiving department counts the number of cases, and reports the number of packages received as verified by the stationery storeroom when the cases are opened and unpacked.

Quality

The final determination that the quality of received materials is satisfactory and in conformity with what was originally ordered remains with the department eventually using the materials. Thus any inspection in the course of receiving will be concerned with:

1. Making sufficient tests to insure that the identity of the material is the same as what was ordered, and that it is satisfactory to put the material into production or bulk storage.
2. Sufficient testing to provide assurance that it is in order to pay for the material.

Verification of Packaged Materials

Quantity

Where materials are received in packages, bundles, or separate units, quantity verification is customarily based on the packing slip accompanying the shipment. The first step consists of a count of the number of packages received; the receiving clerk then signs the carrier's form for receipt of material.

Where materials are in units of standard weight and quantity, very little checking of contents is done by most companies. Some test-checks are made, particularly where items are received in nonstandard packages. For example, a counting scale (one that works on a fixed ratio, such as 50-to-1) may be used to test-check quantities of rivets received in kegs.

In general, minimum verification of individual items received in packages or other units is permissible when:

1. Contents of packages are indicated on labels
2. Received quantities will be later verified by storing or operating departments
3. Prior experience has established vendor reliability

More detailed verification is required where contents and quantity are not clearly specified on packages or other containers.

Verification of Purchased Parts

Quality

Where fabricated parts are purchased from outside vendors for an assembly operation, some testing is desirable to insure that specifications are met. One company that makes equipment requiring accurately machined parts follows a statistical sampling procedure in testing identical purchased parts. In this process, a chart is developed showing lot size, sample size, and acceptance/rejection limits for various acceptable quality levels.

A testing procedure for such parts is important in the production activity since:

1. Assurance is necessary that parts conform with purchase specifications before being placed in production.
2. Production departments may be tempted to use substandard parts to meet production quotas.

3. Production shutdown may be forced if unacceptable parts are not detected before they reach production lines.

Verification of Bulk Materials

Comprehensive checking is necessary at the time of receipt when bulk materials such as grain, coal, and liquids are delivered in car or truck-load lots. In many cases, individual shipments will lose their identity in bulk storage. For this reason, both quantity and quality must be verified before final delivery of bulk materials into storage or production.

Quantity

The most satisfactory control exists when all incoming cars or trucks with bulk deliveries are weighed on company premises before and after unloading—particularly when scales are equipped with automatic printing devices that minimize the possibility of errors in recording. However, many companies do not have sufficient bulk deliveries to justify the cost of installing scales, and must rely on weights certified to by licensed weighmasters. For example, in some companies, deliveries of coal are reported on the basis of weights determined by railroad weighmasters.

There are certain disadvantages and risks in relying on outside weighing:

1. Loss or pilferage between the time of weighing and the time of unloading may occur. For example, small losses before final unloading, such as pilferage of coal from an open car or leakage from a hopper car, may not come to attention. (If noticeable loss occurs, unloading may be delayed pending another weighing.)
2. Outside weighing will usually cover only gross weight. The stenciled tare weight of the car or truck will usually be used in determining the quantity delivered.

Stenciled tare weights on railroad cars—which are determined and marked when a new or overhauled car is put into service—may be quite inaccurate. Due to accumulation of dirt, minor repairs, and other factors, actual car weight may be as much as 1000 pounds over the stenciled weight. In such a case this increases the costs of material not received and the related freight charges.

When the tare weight is taken after unloading, any appreciable variance from the stenciled weight may indicate that the car or truck has not been completely unloaded. The opportunity to use this check in verifying material receipts is lost when—due to cost and the difficulty of routing cars and trucks to outside weighmasters—tare weights are not checked.

In general, bulk commodities will not be physically handled through the receiving department. Instead, they will be unloaded at the location where they will be stored or put into production. Such an arrangement may result in the responsibility for reporting quantity received being assigned outside the receiving function. Where this is the case, the internal auditor should ascertain the exact delegation of responsibility as part of his appraisal of the control over receiving operations.

As mentioned previously, many bulk materials lose identity as individual shipments as soon as they are unloaded. For example, a carload of grain goes into an elevator silo with other grain; a tanktruck of oil is pumped into general oils storage. In such situations, the determination of quantity can readily be made only once; after that, an accurate recheck is difficult or impossible. In some cases, a cross-check may be possible by taking inventory of bulk storage before and after delivery. For example, the quantity of oil delivered may be verified or cross-checked by:

1. Converting the weight delivered into volume by the use of conversion tables
2. Measurement of oil delivered into storage by the use of meters
3. Measurement of oil in storage tank before and after delivery

While such cross-checks are feasible, they need not be regularly employed—but they may be applied to advantage in a program of periodic test-checking.

One company that uses large quantities of steel follows a plan of accepting incoming loads from steel mills at the reported mill weight—verifying these by 10 percent test weighings. Since weights from steel warehouses have been found to be less dependable, all incoming shipments from such warehouses are weighed on receipt.

Differences in Received Quantities

Differences often occur between the quantity of a bulk commodity reported as shipped and the quantity determined as received. Such differences are normal in bulk shipments in open cars, where sun and rain may affect the quantity of moisture in the cargo. Measured volumes of liquids will show variations with changes in temperature. Grain will lose moisture when shipped some distance in hot, dry weather.

Normal differences are usually provided for by trade practice or arrangements with vendors under which variances within specified limits are disregarded. The differences are not as important as comparing the received weights and quantities with reported shipments, so claims may be filed where specified tolerances are exceeded.

Quality

Assurance that basic components and supplies will be of acceptable quality and in conformity with purchase specifications is necessary in all productive processes. Such assurance is particularly essential with many bulk materials, since it is common to find incoming quantities merged with existing supplies in storage or production. To illustrate:

1. In receiving bulk deliveries of petroleum products, a sample of each delivered load is checked before unloading. This assures (a) the products meet purchase specifications, and (b) they are identical with those already in storage tanks into which unloading will be made.
2. In a chemical manufacturing company, a sample of each incoming shipment of bulk chemicals is analyzed by the factory control laboratory to ensure that it meets the rigid requirements of the plant processes.
3. Purchases of bulk grain are made in various grades and in specified moisture contents. (As the moisture is only contained water, a high moisture content adds to the weight—but not to the value—of the grain.) Since bushels delivered are based on standard weights per bushel for each kind of grain, a test of moisture content is necessary both to check the quantity received and to assure that the moisture content is not such as to affect the grading on which the per-bushel price is based.

Commodity Exchange Practices

Dealings in many major bulk commodities are governed by rules and practices established by commodity exchanges in such matters as:

1. Specifications of grades
2. Handling of disputes over grading and similar differences
3. Standards regarding deliveries, terms, and so on

These rules and practices apply in the settlement of any claimed differences in grade or quantity.

Other Inspection Methods

Independent inspection services may be called in regularly or in special cases to attest to the quality received or to the extent of damage to a received shipment as basis for a claim against a carrier.

In some circumstances, quality inspection may be performed at the source by a representative of the buyer. This is appropriate when

1. A large volume of purchases of an item is made from one supplier.
2. The nature of the inspection operation is such that it can best be done during the course of manufacture or assembly—rather than after completion.

Verification of Intercompany Shipments

The testing of quantity and quality of bulk materials or parts from other company operations is usually kept to a minimum sufficient to assure that there has been no loss in transit and that necessary specifications have been met. Recurring discrepancies should be corrected by investigation and action at the shipping point—rather than be the cause for extended checking in detail at the receiving location.

Substitute Materials

In certain circumstances, substitute materials that do not conform exactly with purchase specifications may be acceptable for productive operations. Unless a approved listing of specific acceptable substitutes is published, the receiving department should not be responsible for decisions as to the acceptance or rejection of such materials; such decisions should be by agreement between the purchasing and the consuming departments. Procedures should assure notification of the acceptance of substitute materials; any revised pricing is furnished to all affected departments, including accounts payable and cost accounting.

Control Hazards

When the receiving responsibility is widely delegated to using or storing departments, the auditor must recognize that there are definite control weaknesses. The following illustrates this:

1. A department requiring materials originates a requisition specifying the quantity and quality of items needed. The specifications may often be so restrictive as to limit procurement to a single or to very few suppliers.
2. The purchasing department orders the requisitioned materials from the best source.
3. The received materials are generally checked as to quantity by the receiving department, although not always in detail.
4. The ordering department finally determines whether it received what it ordered.

The obvious danger in this situation is that a company employee in the using department may enter into collusion with an unscrupulous vendor—and attest to the receipt of materials different in grade or in quantity from those actually supplied.

The following control measures are necessary to provide minimum safeguards:

1. Require that received materials clear through the receiving department to the maximum practical extent. (One company requires that receiving reports for material not cleared through the receiving department be approved by a supervisor of a higher organizational level than the employee receiving the actual material.)
2. Deal with reliable vendors. Such vendors will usually maintain controls making the issuance of the documents necessary to collusive fraud difficult.
3. Be sure the purchasing department performs more than an order-placing function. Whenever possible, materials should be described by standard specifications that give the purchasing department freedom in the selection of vendors (see Chapter 3).

Internal Audit Approach

When inspecting the means by which the quantity and quality of received items are determined, the internal auditor should give due consideration to the factors set forth—and consequently should not expect every incoming shipment to be carefully inspected and measured when received. As previously mentioned, procedures should provide reasonable assurance that an adequate determination of quantity and quality is made by some independent means before the shipment loses its identity in production or storage.

The cost of controls should have economic justification. For example, the cost of routing empty freight cars to an outside weighmaster for checking tare weights should be matched against the possible losses due to incorrect stenciled weights. If the ratio of cost to possible benefits is high, one solution may be a program of test checking to determine that differences are maintained within acceptable tolerances.

CONTROL PROCEDURES

Need for Definite Procedures

The volume of transactions handled by most receiving departments, the importance of prompt and accurate notice to operating departments, and the exposure to loss or possible fraud bring the conclusion that receiving operations should be governed by specific written procedures. If the receiving department does not have specific procedures for its own department, they may be covered under those for the purchasing or accounts payable departments.

Notification of Expected Incoming Materials

The customary methods of notifying the receiving department of anticipated materials receipts are through distribution of a copy of:

1. The purchase order.
2. A shipping schedule covering a series of deliveries to be made under a blanket order of a purchase contract. This applies usually to major production materials and supplies.

Purchase order copies and shipping schedules are held in a pending file until the materials are received.

Notification of anticipated arrival dates of large-volume incoming shipments—such as carload or truckload deliveries—will be forwarded by the traffic department to the receiving department (or the department that will be responsible for unloading) so plans may be made for spotting incoming cars or trucks and for personnel to handle the unloading.

When an occasional large-volume shipment arrives without prior notice and requires facilities and personnel beyond the normal capacity of the receiving department, receiving should immediately consult with the traffic, stores, and production departments to decide how the shipment will be handled.

Receipt of Materials

When a packing slip or bill-of-lading copy accompanies the incoming shipment—as is usually the case—the first check will be the number of containers delivered against these documents. Any signs of damage will be noted and the receiving clerk will sign the carrier's receipt, after which the incoming vehicle will be released.

Carload or truckload deliveries are separately recorded in a register or journal including the type of material, gross, tare, and net weights received.

After unloading, the next procedural step is to check the delivery against what was ordered and to notify the interested departments of the material received.

When there is no particular urgency about using the material, the routine where single deliveries are made against a purchase order is to check the quantity received with quantity on the purchase order (or enter quantity in the space provided on the order), sign copies of the order to show that the materials have been received (or prepare a receiving report), and forward copies to the

1. Purchasing department
2. Requisitioning department
3. Accounts payable department

The receiving department copy may be signed by the department using the material to evidence receipt. This basic control procedure will be modified to meet company requirements or situations where there are deviations from the specifications of the order.

In one company, most of the deliveries are made on a scheduled basis, and many of the items are parts used in assembly line operation. In this company, the vendor's packing slip is assigned a serial number and is used as a receiving report. Notice of receipt is sent to the production, inspection, and purchasing departments via input to a shared data base.

In another company, the purchase order package sent to the receiving department is reproduced after notation of receipt, with copies going to the departments affected.

Minimum Controls

The detailed procedures in effect should provide for:

1. Notification to the purchasing, ordering, and storing or using departments of the material receipt
2. Separate notification to the accounts payable department of material received, so a payment voucher may be processed
3. Safeguards against the introduction of fraudulent notice of receipt into the accounts payable operation, such as:
   a. Separation of receiving and procurement responsibilities
   b. The use of registers of serial numbers by the receiving and accounts payable departments covering such forms as purchase orders and receiving reports to give assurance that unauthorized forms are not introduced into the vouchering routine
   c. Follow-up action to locate serially numbered forms that are not accounted for
   d. Restricting authority for signing receiving reports to supervisors whose signatures are on file in the accounts payable department
4. Follow-up by the accounts payable department of receiving reports that do not match with purchase orders.

5. An adequate record of material receipts that are not subject to the usual purchase and accounts payable routines, such as:
   a. Materials returned by customers
   b. Materials belonging to suppliers, such as items sent in for testing

Reporting Quantity Received

As pointed out earlier, no detailed quantity determination is made on many of the shipments that are cleared through the receiving function. The actual count taken will be largely confined to a count of cases or packages containing identical items, and the number of units reported as received will be based on contents stenciled on cases or labels or quantities shown on the packing slip accompanying the shipment. Detailed checking of units will be principally of a sampling nature.

There is some difference in opinion and practice as to whether or not the quantity ordered should be shown on the receiving copy of the purchase order. Those favoring showing the quantity take the position that questioning and rechecking will be minimized if the receiving clerk knows the quantity expected. Those favoring omission of quantity on receiving's copy believe the quantity checking will be done more objectively if the receiving clerk has to make a blind count.

Observation in several companies in which there were examples of each practice indicates there is little advantage either way as far as quantity determination is concerned. The reasons include:

1. Reliance is placed on the vendor's packing slip.
2. Unit counts of many deliveries are not made in the receiving department.
3. Reliance is placed on an eventual unit count by the department to which material is delivered.

One advantage of showing the quantity on receiving's copy of the purchase order is that quantities will be reported in units that may be checked in the accounts payable department with quantities specified in the purchase order. Another advantage is that the receiving department knows immediately upon receipt of materials whether there is an undershipment, an overshipment, or whether the order is completed. Another important benefit is the showing of quantity provides notice of what is expected, so the receiving department can plan for storage space and handling labor.

Overshipments; Partial and Early Deliveries

The customary practice is to accept a certain percentage of overshipment without question—the usual is a 10 percent allowance. Deliveries in excess of this allowed percentage are reported to the purchasing department, and the quantity overshipped is set aside pending instructions from the purchasing department as to disposition.

When partial delivery is made, a usual plan is to note the quantity received on the purchase order copy, which is retained in receiving pending completion. The initial and subsequent partial deliveries are reported on serially numbered receiving reports.

In the past, companies have been content to receive deliveries slightly in advance of the anticipated delivery date. However, as companies progress toward just-in-time manufacturing systems and plants are built for efficient manufacturing processes, less space is allocated for inventory storage. Therefore, if a product is received too far in advance, physical storage problems can result. Additional handling or storage costs can result. In such cases, early shipments should be documented and monitored. Vendors should be notified if they continually cannot ship in accordance with the schedule.

Materials in Damaged Condition

When materials are received in evidently damaged condition, the receiving department may refuse to accept the shipment if the damage appears to be extensive, or it may accept the materials after noting the damage on the receipt given to the carrier. The decision whether or not to accept the delivery will usually be made after consultation with the purchasing and traffic departments.

If accepted, the shipment is then segregated in the receiving department until inspection of the damage has been made by traffic department and carrier representatives and a decision is reached as to filing an appropriate claim.

Similarly, when damage is not evident at the time of delivery but is revealed during unpacking or checking, the materials are segregated until possible claim action is decided.

Rejected Materials

When materials are rejected because they do not meet specifications of the purchase order:

1. The materials must be segregated pending action as to disposition.
2. If materials are to be returned to the vendor, procedures must insure charge back is made for materials and any related costs, such as transportation charges.

Decision as to handling will usually be made after consultation with the purchasing and requisitioning departments. Pending this decision, the materials are usually held in the receiving area.

Unidentified Receipts

While not a serious problem in most companies, every receiving department will receive materials that cannot be identified with any pending orders on file. The usual practice in these cases is to report such deliveries to the purchasing department—asking for identification. A considerable portion of such deliveries will be represented by items for which informal orders have been placed—for example, by telephone—and delivery has been made before the confirming order was issued. Whatever the reason, unidentified deliveries should be segregated in the receiving department until they can be identified and reported.

Emergency Direct Receipts

In emergencies or for more efficient handling, normal receiving routines may be bypassed and mail delivered directly to the location where needed. For example, a machine breakdown may call for the purchase of repair parts for immediate installation by maintenance personnel. Some time later, the necessary receiving procedures will be followed on an after-the-fact basis.

There is a definite control hazard in such transactions. Bypassing the receiving function means receipt is attested to by an interested party. This simplifies the perpetration of fraud through misappropriation of materials or collusion with vendors. Such emergency handling of material receipts can become a habit—a bad one. Frequent occurrences should be sufficient cause for review by purchasing and receiving personnel to be sure they are justified.

After-Hours Receiving Practices

Most deliveries from carriers are made during daytime hours, even when a plant is operating on a 24-hour basis. Consequently, most receiving is done only in daytime hours. A skeleton staff, if any, is on duty at other times. However, some sort of receiving capability should be provided when receiving personnel are off duty.

After-hours receiving is usually handled by plant security personnel, who will have access to receiving areas. They will check the carriers' delivery form (such as a bill of lading) with the materials received, and sign for receipt. When materials held in receiving are required, plant security personnel should satisfy themselves that the requisition is in order and issue the materials. These after-hours transactions are then reported to the receiving department and are included in the following day's reports.

Safeguarding of Materials

Materials in the receiving department should be physically safeguarded in at least the same degree and manner as apply to corresponding materials in storerooms. If anything, safeguards in the receiving department should be somewhat more stringent since a greater variety of personnel—such as material handlers and truck drivers—may have comparatively free access to the premises, even though they may not be permitted to enter the receiving department.

Receiving areas and delivery personnel should be under the surveillance of plant security personnel. Naturally, particular protection is necessary for valuable and desirable items, such as precious metals and small tools. These items should have separate storage facilities with limited and specified receiving personnel having access.

Facilities in many companies include a locked enclosure in which the smaller and more valuable materials are held pending delivery to production or stores departments. Bulky—and comparatively undesirable—materials are less carefully protected, since the risk of pilferage is low.

Off-Premises Receipts

Materials may be delivered for the account of a company directly to outside locations, such as warehouses or processors. In most businesses, such transactions are few in number and represent large-volume deliveries. For off-premises receipts, the procedural requirements are:

1. Notice of receipt from the receiving locations to affected departments—including the accounts payable department—as a prerequisite to paying the vendor
2. Entry of quantity and value on cost, inventory, and other control records to insure materials are properly accounted for
3. Verification that the recipient maintains adequate controls over the received materials.

AUDIT OF RECEIVING OPERATIONS

Objectives of the Audit

The internal audit of receiving operations has as objectives:

1. To examine and appraise the controls over the flow of materials through the receiving function

2. To examine and appraise the controls that govern the verification and reporting of the quantity and quality of received materials

3. To review performance to determine the effectiveness of controls.

The work of a receiving department is primarily concerned with handling materials. As far as records are concerned, the receiving department should process or originate only the minimum necessary to report its operations.

A testing or verification of the records covering completed transactions reported by a receiving department is but one phase of the internal audit of receiving operations. To some extent, these records should be covered in the internal audit of accounts payable, where evidence of satisfactory quantity and quality receipt is an important requirement for processing payments to vendors.

The audit of receiving operations is principally concerned with actual operations and operating procedures. The auditor must be in attendance to observe how materials are handled. The auditor must be alert to conditions that may be clues to situations that should have attention in the receiving operations themselves or in those areas with which the receiving activity does business. One should remember that responsibility for the correction of unsatisfactory conditions often lies outside the confines or direct responsibility of the receiving activity. This has been stated previously, but is mentioned again because it is particularly important in the internal auditor's approach.

INTERNAL AUDIT PROGRAM

Organization Chart

After discussing operations with the head of the receiving activity, the auditor should obtain or prepare an organization chart that indicates the

1. Direct line of organizational responsibility
2. Relationship (including indirect responsibility) to
   a. Purchasing department
   b. Storerooms
   c. Production department
   d. Quality control or inspection
   e. Traffic department
   f. Accounts payable

Inspection of Facilities

The next step is an inspection of all locations participating in the handling, inspecting, and reporting of received materials. These include truck docks, rail unloading facilities, scale-houses, and testing laboratories, as well as the headquarters of receiving operations. Throughout this inspection, the auditor should observe the manner in which

1. The quantity and quality of received materials are determined and reported.
2. Received materials flow through the receiving operations. The auditors should question indications of delay and investigate items that appear held for an unduly long time.

Like an efficient storeroom operation, a good receiving operation requires good housekeeping and orderly handling. The auditor can gain an impression as to these factors almost immediately and can confirm this impression by subsequent inspection and questioning.

In observing the flow of materials, the auditor should note the mechanical devices used to facilitate storage and movement, and should appraise the coordination between the storeroom, production, and purchasing departments, so materials are delivered in a manner assuring effective and economical physical handling.

In the inspection stage, the auditor should give particular attention to the facilities and methods for handling out-of-the-ordinary transactions. The auditor should observe and question receiving personnel as to how they handle such situations as

1. Received materials that cannot be identified with purchase orders
   a. Who is notified?
   b. How are materials segregated?
   c. What is the follow-up procedure?
2. Materials received in damaged condition
   a. Who is notified?
   b. How are materials segregated?
   c. How are they disposed of?
3. Overshipments
   a. Who is notified?
   b. How are materials segregated?
   c. How are they disposed of?
4. Early/late shipments
   a. Who is notified?

     b. How are materials and paperwork handled?

     c. Are any associated costs segregated?

5. Receipts of substitute materials

     a. Who is notified?

     b. Who authorizes acceptance or rejection?

     c. How is the accounts payable department notified?

6. Rejected materials

     a. Who authorizes rejection?

     b. Who is notified?

     c. How are materials segregated?

     d. How is disposition handled, and who is responsible?

7. Valuable or specially attractive items (i.e., precious metals, small tools, and gifts or novelties for advertising purposes)

     a. How are these protected while in receiving?

     b. How are these safeguarded until delivery to operating department?

8. After-hours deliveries

     a. How are these controlled?

     b. How are they reported?

9. Deliveries made directly to requisitioner (i.e., repair parts picked up by maintenance personnel)

10. Deliveries—such as bulk materials—made directly to storage or productive facilities. What is the receiving department's responsibility for

     a. Quantity determination

     b. Quality determination

     c. Unloading

     d. Reporting

Examination of Receiving Procedures

The internal audit of procedures will usually comprise a review and appraisal of actual operations in comparison with established procedures. In this review and appraisal, preparing a flowchart showing the routing of forms may be helpful and informative.

To find forms created that duplicate other records or that are retained in files far beyond the time of any normal reference is not unusual. For example, the internal auditor in one company noted that copies of receiving reports were retained in the receiving department for an indefinite period. Such retention served no purpose after a few months, since practically no reference is made to the copies. In those few instances where reference may be necessary, receiving report copies in purchasing and accounts payable files were readily available. The obvious recommendation was to establish a specific retention period of one year after completion of orders.

Written procedures governing receiving routines are desirable. Where procedures are in written form, the auditor should compare actual operations with the standards prescribed in the procedures and illustrated on the flow charts.

Various types of transactions should be tested. For example:

1. Purchase orders covering materials not received for some time beyond the specified delivery date should be selected from the pending file and examined on an individual basis. Inquiry should be made as to

   a. Reasons for delay

   b. Failures of other departments to notify receiving of materials delivered

2. Purchase orders covering materials returned because of overshipment, rejection, or other reasons should be selected. Items to be checked are

   a. Reasons for return

   b. Authorization for return

   c. Delays in handling

   d. Charge back to vendor (including applicable transportation expense)

3. A selection of regular receiving reports should be made from accounts payable files, including some cases where there were delays in payments to vendors. Points to be investigated should include reasons for any delays in reporting receipt of materials to the accounts payable department.

4. Cases should be selected where payment was made for demurrage. Items to be checked would include:

   a. Reasons for demurrage payment

   b. Demurrage cost versus overtime payroll cost for unloading.

5. From materials being held in the receiving department, a selection should be made to include, where possible:

   a. Materials that cannot be identified with purchase orders

   b. Materials to be returned to vendors

   c. Damaged materials

   d. Materials being held for any other reason

   e. Materials held for an undue length of time

   f. A test count of the material

The internal auditor should determine whether reporting, follow-up, and other procedures are being followed.

6. Tests should be made of transactions involving products returned by customers that come into the receiving department. In determining how such transactions are handled, items of the following nature should be checked:

   a. How is return authorized?
   b. What notice of expected return is given to receiving?
   c. What acknowledgment goes to the customer?
   d. What disposition is made of returned materials?
   e. Who decides and authorizes such disposition?
   f. How is the customer given credit?

Completion of the Audit

The internal auditor may identify matters to report definite findings and make definite recommendations. This is readily possible in factual situations where indications of operating deficiencies caused by either inadequate procedures or deviations from approved procedures are definite.

In other situations, the internal auditor's examination may indicate where a practice or a routine is questionable. While the auditor may be able to suggest some corrective measures, the final determination as to what is best may be a matter for further study and decision by experts. For example, the auditor notes congestion and resulting confusion in handling received shipments. The causes may lie in areas within the receiving department, or the department may be handicapped by deficiencies in the facilities or activities of other departments.

The corrective measures may require study and changes in other departments. Here the internal auditor should expand the audit scope to describe the condition and recommend the measures that appear applicable—for example, a detailed study by materials-handling engineers.

In submitting the report and recommendations, the auditor should always consider the general effect upon the business. For example, if freight car tare weights are not being determined, is there a sufficient risk of loss to justify

1. The installation and cost of operating a track scale on company premises, or
2. Checking weights on outside scales, with resulting switching and weighing expenses, or
3. The cost of occasional test checks on outside scales?

Based on a general familiarity with operations, the internal auditor should examine and question those phases of receiving activity that appear to be duplicated in operating departments. For example, if counting and inspection of certain materials is promptly performed in both receiving and operating departments, can such verification be modified to avoid duplication? Some factors to be considered before recommending any modification include:

1. Has past experience with vendors shown they are reliable, and that differences between their reported shipments and actual receipts are negligible?
2. What has been the experience in settling discrepancies with vendors?
3. What verification—either of quantity or quality—does the operating department perform that might be curtailed to reduce duplication with the receiving department—or vice versa?

On the other hand, inquiries by the internal auditor in the receiving, using, and storing departments may well disclose that inadequate verification procedures are due to such factors as:

1. Reliance on vendors to the exclusion of normal verification or testing.
2. Incorrect assumptions by one department that another department is performing certain verification activities

The objectives of the receiving operation are to assure items received are in the quantity and quality specified in purchase orders and that received materials are properly protected and efficiently handled from receipt to entry into the flow of operations. The objective of the internal audit is to determine whether such assurances are being provided effectively.

INTERNAL CONTROL QUESTIONNAIRE: RECEIVING AND INCOMING INSPECTION

The following questionnaire is used by one company. It is presented in addition to the preaudit program as another tool for the auditor.

1. Are receiving department operations segregated from other operations?
   a. What is the relation to shipping activities?
2. Are specific receiving points established?
3. Is all incoming material required to clear receiving?
4. Is the receiving area physically protected for control of goods?

5. Is the receiving department advised of purchases as commitments are made?

6. Are receiving reports serially numbered?

   a. If not numbered, what control exists over their issuance?

7. Are all documents accounted for?

8. Are receiving reports prepared for all materials received?

9. Are receiving reports signed by the person receiving the shipment?

10. Are copies of receiving reports sent directly to accounts payable, purchasing, and other interested departments?

11. Are receipts from suppliers independently counted, weighed, or otherwise measured and identified without reference to packing slip?

12. Are scales or other measuring devices checked periodically?

    a. Are trucks and rail cars weighed "light" and "heavy"? If all are not, what are the exceptions?

13. Are shortages, rejections, and so on reported immediately to the purchasing, accounts payable, and traffic departments?

14. Are over and under shipments within allowable company or commercial limits?

15. Is quality inspection adequate to protect the company's interest?

16. Is quality inspection evidenced by inspection reports or notations on receiving reports?

17. Are procedures set up for the handling of materials received but not ordered?

18. Are possible claims against carriers for materials lost or damaged in transit reported to the traffic department?

19. Are rejected materials returned to vendors through the shipping department?

20. Do the procedures followed assure the minimum of delay in the handling of paperwork?

21. If material is received at other than authorized receiving points, is verification of quality and quantity made by both the receiving and inspection department employees?

22. Is a specific receiving department employee responsible for noting shortages, overages, or deviation from specifications?

23. Is another employee responsible for rechecking differences?

24. In case of services that are not subject to physical inspection, what procedure is followed by the receiving and inspection departments?

CHAPTER 5

Scrap, Salvage, and Surplus Materials

NATURE OF THE PROBLEM

Scrap—A Universal Problem

Every business is confronted with the problem of the disposition of the waste and surplus materials that are a normal product of the business operation. These wastes take many forms. For example, every office has the problem of disposing of an imposing volume of waste paper—a normal byproduct of office operation; every organization has the problem of what to do with surplus or replaced equipment. In a service institution, such as a bank or an insurance company, waste paper and surplus equipment may comprise the major part of the scrap problem, and the controls may be similar and relatively simple.

In firms where material is processed in the manufacture of finished goods—or where extensive properties must be maintained—the value of scrap may become a major item; that is, a metal manufacturing operation or in a public utility.

In a metal manufacturing operation, large volumes of such raw materials as metal sheets, bars, and rods will be bored, turned, or stamped to produce the parts that are assembled into an end product. Large quantities of scrap material will be generated in this process. For example, in one company the production of large electric motors requires the stamping of laminations from high-grade, and relatively expensive, electric-steel sheets. The quantity of metal in the finished lamination may in some cases be less than the quantity punched out; in other words, the weight of scrap may exceed the weight of usable parts produced. A similar situation may arise in screw machine operations, where borings and turnings generated as scrap may exceed the weight of the completed finished parts.

A utility is faced with continual change in its facilities to meet the requirements of the public in its service area. Facilities must be maintained and expanded when required; extensions of service must be made to meet demands of business and private consumers. The normal situation is one of continual work on facilities, with resultant replacements, additions, and removals—all of which generate scrap, obsolete, or surplus material. One utility maintains 74 service trucks, each using new material and turning in scrap material every day. Another (and larger) utility accounts for six million pounds of scrap underground cable in the course of a year.

Such companies must maintain effective control of the considerable quantities and values of scrap materials. They must be alert to whether stocks of materials on hand are in excess of current requirements or are in danger of becoming obsolete because of operating improvements. Constant study is done to determine the best possible methods for utilizing scrap—for example, by reconditioning some of the scrap material for further use. In the electric motor operation previously mentioned, it is sometimes possible to use the punchings from larger motor laminations to make laminations for smaller motors.

On the other hand, one can devote too much attention, control, and expenditure to scrap of little value. For example, the cost of mutilating, baling, and disposing of waste paper may not be justified by the financial amounts to be realized. Yet, even here, it is hazardous to generalize. While the paper from wastebaskets may not be worth much effort, endless outdated printouts will usually be well worth selling to an outside dealer. But don't forget that scrap paper (reports, etc.) accumulated may not have value, but may have to be destroyed by burning or other means due to the confidential nature of the data.

The problem of scrap, salvage, and surplus materials is not simple since it varies from company to company. The handling and control—and the development of a related internal auditing program—call for a combination of curiosity, ingenuity, and business acumen so that optimum value may be realized while effective control is maintained.

Definitions

1. *Scrap*—is considered as material created in the course of manufacturing, maintenance, or other operations that is not usable material at the time of its creation, although subsequent inspection, reprocessing, or other

operation may result in the creation of a usable material. For example, in an electric utility a considerable portion of the used cable turned in by a maintenance crew might, upon inspection, be found suitable for reuse. Since the decision as to reuse is made as a subsequent operation, the cable is considered scrap until the possibility of reuse is determined.

Scrap, as defined here, does not include normal byproducts of a manufacturing operation that in themselves have identity and value as usable products or materials. For example, such byproducts as seconds in a textile mill—or wet or dried grains remaining after a distilling operation—are not to be considered as scrap. The control of such items is a part of manufacturing and production control, which is outside the scope of this section. Scrap will usually be disposed of in essentially the same state in which it was created, with only such simple operations as sorting or baling performed prior to disposition.

2. *Salvage*—occurs when special treating, rebuilding, or similar operations are performed upon scrap or other materials to derive further usage or greater value from them. Salvage may or may not change the condition or form of the scrap material. For example, one company manufactures an abrasive cloth and generates an appreciable quantity of trimmings and defective product that is turned over to the company salvage department. Although the scrap abrasive cloth has no junk value, it is possible to perform a simple laundering operation that removes the abrasive. The cloth then has an appreciable value that is realized through this salvage operation.

3. *Surplus Materials*—relates to overstocks and obsolete items, such as factory supplies, manufacturing and maintenance materials, and similar items that enter into the day-to-day operation of a business.

The examples in this section describe major control problems, and the control measures described may be considered as representing the most effective—and often the most elaborate—required. In business where the importance and value of scrap and salvage are minor—for example, a bank—much less stringent control measures may be necessary and desirable. As in other functions of business, it is not feasible or reasonable to attempt to apply any set of axiomatic principles of control to each situation. Each business will be different in such important factors of control as assignment of organizational responsibility, policies, procedures, layout of physical facilities, and records. All of these must be given consideration in working out the control and audit plan to fit an individual business.

CONTROL OF SCRAP

Importance of Establishing Control

Most scrap is created as a byproduct of some productive operation. In some cases the quantity of scrap that is generated may be closely related to the materials consumed. In this situation, an original control point is established by computing the theoretical production of scrap based on specifications or standards. Actual production is then compared to this calculation. In other cases, very few standards may exist by which to gauge whether the volume of scrap is what it should be. In either situation, physical control over actual scrap should be established as soon as possible after the scrap has been produced—to provide a base for effective control of subsequent transactions.

The nature of the controls will vary according to the physical requirements, which are very different in different industries. The following examples illustrate how control is applied in several kinds of organizations.

Machinery Manufacturing

A large volume of scrap is created in manufacturing in the form of borings, turnings, and stampings. In one company, the weight of scrap generated is determined when collected from the machines area. This weight then serves to establish an inventory that is subsequently accounted for.

In another company, which produces a large volume of scrap, scrap from various presses and other machines is accumulated in trailer bins, with a separate trailer for each type and grade of scrap. When filled, these trailers are weighed on a public scale; this weight establishes the quantity that is to be accounted for.

In still another company, where a large part of the scrap is stampings, scrap is loaded by grade into containers. When filled, these containers are taken by a scrap dealer, and the company accepts the weights given by the dealer as the basis for its accounting. (As is later pointed out, acceptance of dealer's weights is inadequate control.)

One concern of particular interest to the internal auditor is the relation of the volume of scrap actually produced to what should have been produced under ideal conditions (the standard). Excessive production of scrap may be an indication of something wrong in the manufacturing process or with the quality of the materials used. In many companies, the primary control over the usage of materials is effected through standard costs. If something is wrong with the materials or the manufacturing operations, the result will be an unfavorable variance from the material standards. Such a variance—assuming it is not due to price—will be confirmed by the unusually large volume of scrap produced.

Public Utilities

Public utilities find it possible to maintain much closer control over the generation of scrap than do manufacturing companies. This occurs because the principal sources of scrap in public utilities are (1) replacement of facilities and (2) construction of additional facilities.

One company controls the scrap from general service work by operating its service trucks with an imprest stock of standard items. Each morning a truck starts with a standard load of new materials. When the truck returns at night, used and scrap material is checked into stock as scrap and replaced by equivalent new material for the next day. Thus, accountability for scrap material can be established on a definite basis.

On new construction of outside facilities, the original layout prepared for the line crew establishes quite accurately the requirements of each installation. Incidental scrap is returned to stock and picked up on control records at the completion of the job.

General Manufacturing

In one general manufacturing business, the treatment of scrap varies according to product. Each phase of this company's operations has its own problems; for example, in one plant not only does the scrap have no value, but the cost of disposal represents an actual expense. Constant study is required of the problems resulting from creation and disposition of scrap in the various company units. How this company handles this problem is described in the section of this chapter on Salvage.

Control at Point of Disposition

Control of certain scrap or other byproducts may not be feasible until the point of disposition is reached. Examples of such scrap are cinders and fly ash from a power house, which may be sold at varying prices or may not be sold at all; waste paper from offices where there is no good method of establishing control over quantity or value; and liquid slop from a distilling operation, some of which may be salable as cattle feed; if not sold, the slop must be destroyed.

In any of these situations, the primary control will be to insure that the portion of scrap that is sold is accounted for at the time of sale and that the proceeds of the sales reach the company cash accounts.

Examination of Control over Generation

The internal auditor's examination and appraisal of controls over the generation of scrap will be concerned with such factors as the following:

1. What means exist to determine whether the quantity of scrap generated is normal or excessive? For example:
   a. Material standards
   b. Weighing of scrap at point of production
   c. Comparison of production with related scrap

     d. Reports of scrap and spoilage

     e. Application of scrap and spoilage losses to incentive plans

     f. Reports and approvals of supervisors

     g. Comparison of scrap with replacing materials

2. Is material being scrapped that should be reconditioned or reused? (For example, one company found expensive subassemblies were being junked when they could have been easily adapted for use.)

3. How soon after generation of scrap is accountability for quantity established?

4. What are the physical facilities or safeguards that insure that scrap created is channeled to a location where accountability is established?

Control over Storage and Handling

After scrap has been created and has reached the location and the condition where it can be treated as a separate item, the controls have the objectives of:

1. Protecting the scrap just as other materials

2. Handling to derive the maximum benefit from disposition.

Scrap must be protected so excessive deterioration and loss are guarded against. At the same time, the value of the scrap may not be great, and the possibility of pilferage may be remote. Accordingly, elaborate storage facilities may cost more than they are worth. No standards can be set for this; the requirements of each situation must be separately determined. Good judgment is required.

More important is the necessity for handling scrap in a manner that brings the maximum benefit to the company from the final use or disposition of the scrap. For example, some scrap can be reworked or reconditioned and put into the process for reuse. Where a transmission line is replaced by one of larger capacity, the wire from the replaced line may be returned to stock for reuse. The burned-out windings of a burned-out transformer may be replaced, making the transformer returnable to service.

In a factory, scrap parts may be reworked so that they can be used. In one company, large pieces of scrap are usable in the making of smaller parts. In another company, steel borings and turnings are made into briquettes, which are then usable as manufacturing scrap in the company's foundry. This eliminates the outside purchase of a corresponding quantity of scrap for the foundry operation.

Where scrap is to be sold, separation by type of material and grade of scrap is essential; for example, heavy melting scrap, clips, borings and turnings, copper, and bronze. If not done, the payment received for a composite lot of scrap is much less than would be realized if the same scrap were graded. To facilitate this grading, one company publishes a schedule showing the classification of scrap that results from each machine operation.

Examination of Control over Storage and Handling

In examining the storage and handling of scrap, the internal auditor is concerned with:

1. Physical facilities for the storage and handling of scrap
2. Procedures for the examination of scrap and the separation of items that may be reworked, reconditioned, or reused
3. Procedures for the separation of scrap by types and grades
4. Facilities for putting scrap into best condition for use or disposition, such as the use of baling machines and treating to remove oil, grease, and dirt
5. Cost of sorting, conditioning, or other handling in relation to price advantages

Control over Disposal

The essential problem in the disposal of scrap is that of obtaining the maximum benefit to the company in terms of either usage or a sale that maximizes revenue.

Internal Usage —Accounting Control

Scrap that can be reworked or reused in the normal production cycle usually brings a greater return than if it is sold, since there is no element of dealer's profit to increase the cost.

Where scrap is returnable to parts or material storerooms after repairing, reworking, or other reconditioning, the practice is to charge any costs to current manufacturing or other expense accounts, and to take the materials into storeroom accounts at a cost that reflects usable value.

Outside Sale —Control of Prices

When scrap is available for outside disposition, the usual practice is to ask for quotations from scrap dealers, either for a specific lot or for all scrap produced over a period of time. For example, dealers are asked to quote on scrap generated for a three-month period.

Scrap quotations are published in metal trade publications. The usual practice is to check bids from dealers with these quotations, but sometimes a certain dealer may have a demand for a specific type of scrap and may therefore offer more than the published quotations. One company has given all of its scrap business to a single dealer over many years; control over the prices paid is exercised by checking the prices given by the dealer with metal trade publications. Most companies follow the plan of securing periodic competitive bids from dealers.

The bids offered highlight the importance of having scrap graded prior to disposition. When not done, the price offered for ungraded scrap will be much less than when the same scrap is separated into grades and types. Experience shows it is usually profitable for the business to do the grading.

Outside Sale—Control of Weight

The importance of establishing a control weight as soon as feasible after scrap is generated has been mentioned previously. This weight will provide a control figure against which the weight of what is sold may be checked.

Whether or not this is done, an independent verification of quantities and grades of scrap is required at the time it is sold. Failure to exercise control at this point opens a vital gap that may be the source of fraud or loss. For example, if a dealer's weights are accepted, any collusion between an employee and the dealer—or even no collusion—will leave the business in the position of relying entirely on the integrity of the dealer.

In checking weights, it is equally important to check loaded weights and the tare weights of vehicles or other containers. Empty vehicles and containers should be examined when the tare weight is determined. At one company, trucks were being driven into the plant with several inches of water in the body of the truck. This water was included in the tare weight—and was then drained out when the truck was being loaded with scrap. In another company, drivers stayed in their cabs when the tare was being determined, but got out to chat with the scale operator when being weighed out. Another driver left company premises with two bills of lading—one with the proper weight of the scrap, and another with less weight, to be used if the driver is not stopped and checked.

The standards for weight control should provide for:

1. Weighing out over company scales, with weights then checked by the dealer over his own scales, or weighing on licensed public scales, with dealer and company agreeing to accept the result
2. Examination of vehicles and containers and adequate control over determination of tare weights

3. Observation of weighing by a company employee, where weighing is handled on public scales
4. Safeguards over transmission of weighing data to the billing department

Outside Sale—Control of Disposition

Responsibility for securing quotations and arranging for the sale of scrap is usually assigned to either (1) the purchasing department or (2) the stores department. From a control standpoint, either assignment should be satisfactory. If the responsibility is given to the stores department, the responsibility for selling should be completely separate from that for sorting, grading, and weighing.

The optimum control over disposition should provide that:

1. Prices be determined by competitive bids obtained from a group of representative dealers. (Some companies obtain bids from as many as six dealers.)
2. Bidding be rigidly controlled. Definite closing times should be set and all bids opened immediately after the closing time and not before. Bids should be opened and tabulated in the presence of one or more employees other than those responsible for negotiating the sale.
3. Weights be determined either by company personnel or licensed public weighers.
4. Billing be rendered and recorded in accounting records at determined weights and agreed prices and grades.
5. Any subsequent adjustments, usually arising from claims by dealers for such items as misgrading or excessive dirt, be separately recorded and handled by credit memo. Such memos should be approved by a high authority.

Examination of Control over Disposition

In the disposition of scrap, the internal auditor's program should include:

1. Physical inspection of storage, protection, and weighing facilities
2. Review of procedures and assignment of responsibility for sale
3. Verification of prices obtained with published quotations
4. Appraisal of control of weighing procedures in relation to billing rendered
5. Examination of adjustments claimed by purchasers of scrap for authorization and reasonableness

6. Examination of controls over weighing, handling, and collection of proceeds from sales of such uncontrolled items as cinders and waste paper
7. Appraisal of physical control through plant protection facilities
8. Test checking by confirmation of sales to selected scrap dealers
9. Observation of the weighing process

The plant accounting department of one public utility prepares an overall annual reconciliation of cable scrapped and salvaged and metals reclaimed to determine the percentage loss in the overall operation. The materials control department of one metal manufacturing company prepares an occasional quantity reconciliation of metal used with the total weight of usable parts produced plus the weight of scrap. Almost every company that makes extensive use of materials has the possibility of relating the scrap produced to the materials used. Such reconciliations, where feasible, provide a good medium of control over the quantity of scrap produced and a good point of departure for the verification work of the internal auditor.

CONTROL OF SALVAGE

Distinction Between Salvage and Scrap

As previously described, salvage is distinguished from scrap because there is an inspection, reconditioning, or other special operation performed on the scrap or other materials to derive further usage or greater value. This means that some of what is originally classified as scrap may be transferred to salvage while the remainder may be processed and disposed of as scrap. In addition, an item replaced in service or surplus may be repaired, reconditioned, or otherwise adapted for further use in company service. This is also considered as salvage.

Operation of a Salvage Department

A manufacturer of a diversified line of products with several decentralized plants finds it profitable to maintain a salvage department. The manager of the salvage department visits each plant to study the scrap and waste accumulated in the normal process, and to develop means for the best handling. For example, certain scrap from one location could be used profitably in another plant. In yet another plant, better methods of scrap disposal were developed at a considerable savings in expense.

Items that have little or no value for the plants and that may be treated to produce greater value are turned over to this salvage department for handling and disposition. Methods were developed for better utilization and reclamation of the large number of metal drums used by plants.

This salvage department operates in an available old building with few employees. Enough is realized from direct sales to more than cover the cost of payroll and premises.

Economics of Salvage Operations

As is the case with any scrap operation, the appearance of profit in the operation does not constitute proof that the operation is economically justified. Effective control requires that periodic study be made of present operations and costs in relation to possible alternatives. For example, a higher price obtained as a result of salvage operations might be more than offset by the cost of salvage.

A profit and loss statement on salvage operations includes as costs:

1. Materials delivered for salvage at their scrap value
2. Direct costs applicable to salvage—labor, materials, and direct expenses
3. Directly applicable overhead expenses

Comparing these total costs with the amounts realized from use or disposition will give some indication of the worth of the salvage operation. For example, assume that a utility company replaces a length of underground cable, and that the replaced cable is inspected, found satisfactory for further use, and returned to stock. The cost of sorting returned material between scrap, salvage, and good material is part of the cost of the job. Salvage costs begin when additional work or expense is incurred by the scrap material.

By contrast, the formula could be justifiably applied in the case of a burned-out transformer, where the cost of replacing the burned-out windings is added to the scrap value of the useless transformer, against which could be matched the useful value that the repaired transformer has as an operating unit.

One company studied its diamond drilling operation, resulting in the reclamation of diamond dust valued at $2000 per month from the wiping rags used in the machining departments.

Another company with a large number of factories issues to all plants a material utilization bulletin describing cost-saving and salvage ideas. By learning of these ideas, other plants are often able to make similar economies in their own operations.

Examination of Control of Salvage

In examining controls over salvage operations, the internal auditor is concerned with:

1. Controls over quantities and values of salvaged materials
2. Controls over storage and handling
3. Controls over salvage labor and material costs
4. Methods by which best utilization or disposition is made of salvaged materials
5. Controls over disposition—in general, these will be similar to the previously described controls over the disposition of scrap
6. Profitability of salvage operations.

CONTROL OF SURPLUS MATERIALS

Nature of Surplus Materials

Surplus materials comprise materials and supplies that are in essentially the form as acquired, but for which no immediate usage is anticipated, such as:

1. Stocks of maintenance or manufacturing materials and supplies in excess of normal operating needs
2. Supplies and repair of service parts that may become obsolete
3. Materials left over from construction projects
4. Replaced or idle facilities

This section does not give specific consideration to controls over the acquisition of major manufacturing commodities and original assembly parts, since these belong in the area of internal audit of production controls rather than surplus materials. However, the disposition of such surpluses is generally subject to the same controls that apply to other surpluses.

Control Against Acquisition of Surplus Materials

The best control over surplus materials averts the original acquisition of materials that may later become surplus. This is not possible in every instance, but should be borne in mind at all times. For example, normal controls over maintenance and manufacturing supplies will center around relating usage and total cost to an economical ordering quantity. Likewise, the use of maximum ordering quantities and minimum reorder points is an almost universal means of control. One company provides the following mechanism for determining the order quantity:

1. When an item is to be reordered, calculation is made of total quantity and value of usage for the preceding calendar year, and also for the preceding 12 months.
2. The formula for ordering is as follows:

   Two month's supply, if the total order exceeds $10,000

   Four month's supply, if the total order is between $5000–$10,000

   Six month's supply, if the total order is between $1000–$5000

   12 month's supply, if the total order is below $1000
3. Variations to meet economic order quantities or special conditions are permissible, but must be explained.

In construction projects, the determination of what is surplus is the responsibility of the company engineer, architect, or field representative. A most important control is the physical and accounting control over material at the job site to insure that material received and charged to the job is either used on the job or, if not used, is (1) turned in for credit, or (2) transferred to records of surplus material. Both opportunity and temptation to consider all materials charged to a construction job as being disposed of on the job is always present. Surplus materials may then be treated as having no value and disposed of at low prices or given away.

Whatever the recovery is, the construction job should bear the resulting loss in value. This is usually done by charging the original cost to the job, then crediting the job with values realized through the disposal or transfer to stores of the surplus material.

Controls against acquisition of surplus materials belong primarily in the control structure of the functions for which the materials are to be used. An element of these controls should provide against materials becoming surplus or unusable because of such poor procedures as:

1. Improper handling or storing of materials
2. Failure to follow first-in, first-out practices in storeroom handling

The internal audit program should provide for examination of ordering, handling, and stores procedures under such functions as construction and storeroom operations. Specific attention should be given to safeguards against overbuying.

Determination of What Is Surplus

A principal problem is setting up and maintaining controls that bring attention to those materials that are or may be considered surplus. This determination will be comparatively simple in the case of materials remaining from construction projects. If the materials are not used on the project, they are surplus as far as that project is concerned and are available for other disposition.

Where items are carried as stores or supply inventory, most companies provide for a periodic review of inventory records or bin cards to determine slow-moving items. Several companies issue annual reports of items in which no or few transactions have occurred during the preceding 12 months. Departments responsible for using or stocking these items are then required to recommend the disposition.

The advent of personal computers and the coordinated MRP II systems add a new dimension to tracking inventories. Major manufacturing plants will now have computerized inventory systems. Some of these systems go so far as attaching universal product codes (UPC) to materials as they go through receiving. From that point on, the materials will be tracked by the computer.

A more difficult situation arises where it is necessary to keep special repair parts or units on hand in case of emergency breakdown. Often, when such items are not carried, an entire operation might have to be closed if a breakdown should occur. Materials of this nature might be carried in stock for many years, and never used. Here, the determination of what is surplus will of necessity rest with the engineering or other department that is responsible for the operations for which the part or units are designed. The special materials should not be disposed of until the equipment is retired from service.

The problem of maintenance of adequate stocks of repair parts by machinery manufacturers is important enough to be the subject of a separate audit in the companies to which it applies. The first control requirement is the establishment by management of a specific policy covering the length of time that such parts will be available to customers. The next requirement is the determination by the service or engineering department of the quantity to be carried. As the term of years for which parts are to be carried draws on, a periodic review of quantities on hand in relation to past usage and estimated future requirements should be performed. Where surpluses develop, a decision must be made as to retention or disposition. In general, the tendency is to retain any moderate oversupply, since the scrap value is not great. If an unexpected shortage should later develop after a surplus has been disposed of, the expense of setting up for a short production run is usually very costly to the company. The point of no return on parts is reached when a decision is made on the scrapping of dies or special tools used to produce the parts. In one machinery company, this decision is assigned to a committee composed of representatives of the production, sales, and engineering departments.

Similar committees are found in other companies, with representatives of the purchasing, maintenance, and engineering departments making decisions as to retention or disposition of all surplus or slow-moving materials. This appears to be essential where such materials are concerned with the maintenance of facilities.

Replaced or Idle Facilities

The appraisal of control over replaced or idle facilities belongs logically as a part of the internal audit of facilities. In some instances, the storage and handling of such facilities is assigned to the department that handles the storage and disposition of scrap and salvage. (A description of controls applicable to surplus facilities is given in Chapter 7, Fixed Assets.) In general, provisions should exist (1) for centralized recording and control of available facilities, (2) for clearing orders for new facilities against records of current idle facilities, and (3) for disposing of facilities in poor condition or those for which no use is anticipated.

Disposition of Surplus Materials

When possible, the best method to dispose of surplus materials that are in the form in which they were purchased is to return them to the original supplier for credit. This is often possible in the case of such materials as storeroom and maintenance supplies and materials left over from construction projects. Sometimes the supplier may impose a restocking charge but the recovery value will usually be greater than can be secured through other channels, and greater than the cost of maintaining the material until another use can be found for it.

Disposal of surplus materials as scrap should be a last resort, used only after all other channels of sale or usage within the company have been explored.

Examination of Control over Surplus Materials

In examining controls over surplus materials, the internal auditor is concerned with:

1. Policies and procedures to guard against overbuying or other acquisition of materials that might become surplus
2. The effectiveness of procedures for bringing surplus materials to attention
3. Policies and procedures to insure that surplus materials are followed up for disposition
4. The effectiveness of procedures to insure that optimum usage or value is derived from surplus materials; that is:
   a. Reconditioning and usage within the company

  b. Return to supplier
  c. Outside sale
5. Physical facilities for handling surplus materials to protect against deterioration and misappropriation.

SUMMARY OF CONTROL PROBLEMS

Lack of Interest

One of the greatest handicaps to effective control of scrap, salvage, and surplus materials can be a lack of interest on the part of employees in the maintenance of control. The employee at a production machine is interested in producing completed parts; the scrap produced is a nuisance, and the employee wants as little to do with it as possible. The engineer supervising a construction project is interested in getting the job completed, not in the incidental leftovers that are only in the way. The storekeeper with a stock of obsolete or surplus materials may wish to clear them out of his storeroom, but the employee originally responsible for purchasing these materials may not wish to have his errors in judgment brought into focus, as they will be when disposition finally occurs.

This lack of interest or incentive on the part of many employees requires that responsibility for control over salvage and scrap operations be assigned to an employee or department that will take a positive interest in the establishment and maintenance of effective control. For example, the supervisor of the company salvage department took a real pride in seeing just how much could be recovered for the company from materials deemed worthless to other departments. The results amounted to a recovery of $72,000.

Handling

Where companies are comparatively large and generate and handle a considerable volume of scrap material, controls and facilities for physical handling of scrap will usually be well developed. However, this is not the case in many businesses, and poor facilities for handling, storing, and grading result in definite monetary loss to the company.

Disposition

The most profitable use of scrap material is almost certain to result when the salvage or scrap can be used in company operations. Even here, the cost of handling and the potential value of such salvaged scrap must be weighed against what might be realized from some other form of disposition.

When scrap is sold to dealers, the company must be constantly alert to ensure it gets a good price. Dealers in waste products handle large volumes of materials at a small margin of profit. These dealers realize much of the material is not important to those selling it—and naturally will pay no more than necessary to secure it. In addition, high bid prices may be offset by claims of misgrading, misweighing, or foreign materials when final settlement is made.

Summary

Effective control over the handling and disposition of scrap, salvage, and surplus materials presents a rather unique problem. As described, most of those who are directly responsible are not greatly interested and would probably rather be assigned some other duty. When this factor of disinterest within the company is coupled with the give-and-take bargaining that must be undertaken with highly interested outside dealers, one can see a situation that readily can lead to waste, loss, or outright fraud.

INTERNAL AUDIT PROGRAM

Development of the Program

The program for internal audit of scrap, salvage, and surplus materials should be tailored to meet the requirements of the organization. The whole control structure and the related audit program will be markedly influenced by factors including:

1. Nature of materials generated
2. Manner in which material is generated
    a. Production
    b. Maintenance
    c. Construction
3. Physical facilities for storage and handling
4. Manner of disposition
    a. Reclaiming for further use
    b. Use within company
    c. Return to supplier
    d. Sale to dealer

Because a program must be developed for each company, it seems preferable to list the check points covered in the development of any program, rather than to present a detailed program that could have no more than limited applicability. A number of such check points have been given in preceding chapters wherein control requirements for scrap, salvage, and surplus materials were considered.

Application of Program

We assume the internal auditor applying the program is familiar with the elementary auditing techniques of sampling and other testing as a foundation for his subsequent evaluation and reporting. Consequently, the check points indicate only what should be considered; they do not show the details of size or the nature of samples or other verification.

The auditor should understand that a question as to the nature of a control implies an appraisal by the internal auditor of the effectiveness of that control. In other words, if a question states "What is the control over . . . ?" the complete program of the internal auditor on that particular point should cover (1) familiarization, (2) verification, (3) evaluation, and (4) reporting.

As with any audit, the first step is a careful and complete review of all written policies and procedures applying to the subject of the audit. From this starting point, the internal auditor then proceeds to the normal steps of audit procedure.

AUDIT CHECK POINTS

The audit check points that follow are in question form, and are arranged in approximately the sequence of the descriptive material in this chapter.

Scrap

The internal auditor should make a physical inspection of the locations in which scrap originates, and examine the facilities for accumulation, storage, and handling.

Generation of Scrap

1. How is scrap generated?
2. What control exists that relates quantity of scrap actually produced to what should have been produced?
   a. Total production
   b. Material standards
   c. Relation to preceding periods, and so on
3. When is control over scrap established?
   a. Should this be done earlier in the production cycle?

b. What are the facilities or safeguards to insure that scrap cannot be diverted or disposed of without an accounting?

Storage and Handling

1. What is done to best utilize or realize the value of generated scrap?
   a. Use as reconditioned material
   b. Sorting by grade
   c. Baling
   d. Use in other operations of the company
   e. Cleaning, and so on
2. What control exists to insure that best realization is received in relation to cost and handling expense?
   a. Reports of sales or other usage versus cost of handling
   b. Periodic study and reporting (who is responsible for such studies?)
3. Do there appear to be any situations where value realized from scrap is not enough to cover costs of accumulation, handling, and disposition?
4. What organizational responsibility exists to insure that adequate control is maintained over storage, handling, and utilization?
5. How adequate are the records covering quantity and values of scrap on hand awaiting disposition?

Disposition

1. Who is responsible for disposing (controlling shipment) of scrap to outsiders?
2. How are selling prices of scrap determined?
   a. Competitive bids
   b. Contract
   c. Whatever dealer will pay, and so on
3. What control exists over weights or quantities delivered to purchasers?
4. How are prices received from purchasers checked as to reasonableness?
5. What control is exercised over adjustments or other differences between company records and billing and amounts received?
   a. Claims for differences in weight
   b. Claims for excessive dirt
   c. Claims for misgrading

6. Do adjustments claimed by dealers appear reasonable?
7. Where such materials as cinders, fly ash, and other scrap are sold, what are controls over
   a. Weight or quantity delivered
   b. Charge to purchaser
   c. Cash received (if a purchaser pays cash, how effective is control in insuring that cash is actually received by company?)
8. What is the possibility that an item of value (such as returnable containers) might be mishandled as scrap?

Salvage

1. How is responsibility for salvage operations assigned?
2. Is adequate control maintained over quantities and values of materials transferred to salvage?
3. Is cost of salvage related to benefits gained, so that unprofitable salvage operations will be highlighted?
4. How effective are controls over disposition of salvaged materials?
   a. Quantity
   b. Price
5. How effective are procedures designed to insure optimum realization from salvaged materials?
6. Are salvage operations profitable or unprofitable?

Surplus Materials

1. How effective are procedures to insure that surplus materials are brought to light?
   a. Obsolete materials
   b. Materials of declining usage
   (The internal audit of such functions as storeroom operations and production control should examine controls against overbuying.)
2. On construction projects, what controls exist to insure that materials not used on the project are turned in as surplus? (Internal audit of construction should examine controls over materials used in projects.)
3. What appear to be the principal reasons materials have become surplus?
4. What controls are applied to minimize the possibility of materials becoming obsolete?

    a. First in, first out materials handling

    b. Adequate storage facilities

    c. Adequate stores location records

5. What controls are applied to such items as emergency repair parts?

6. What are arrangements for segregation and storage of surplus materials?

7. What is the assignment of responsibility for disposition of surplus materials?

8. What are the means by which optimum value is realized from surplus materials?

    a. Return to supplier

    b. Use in some section of company

    c. Sale as surplus

    d. Sale as scrap

INTERNAL AUDIT PROGRAM

Handling, Disposal, and Sale of Production Scrap

A. Review the categories of production scrap as established, and determine the comprehensiveness of the classes of segregation.

1. Evaluate the sales for the past three years to identify the different types of scrap sold. This evaluation shall be updated in each audit.

    a. Also ascertain the various major types of material procured and note whether there is corresponding scrap generated.

2. Obtain studies made by the various departments responsible for conservation of assets. In addition, discuss with the methods engineering department conservation problems noted by them. (The auditor should recognize the comments from the viewpoint of their contribution to an economical conservation program.)

3. Obtain market reports and trade papers printed by the scrap industry and review the various sales reported, noting the market status, prices obtained, and whether the trend of the company's recent prices is consistent with the market.

4. From the information obtained in Steps 1, 2, and 3, evaluate the effectiveness of the company's segregation of production scrap.

5. Ascertain if the purchasing manager maintains a list of approved scrap dealers.

    a. Is a periodic review made of the scrap industry for the purpose of inviting new sources to bid for scrap?

  b. Determine how the latest scrap dealers were located and subsequently considered for sales of production scrap.

  c. What qualifications must a scrap dealer have to be invited to bid on production scrap?

   (1) Determine if the dealers who have been invited within the past 12 months to bid have fulfilled these qualifications.

   (2) Are any qualifications waived? If so, (a) what qualifications were waived, (b) what were the reasons for so doing, and (c) what approvals were obtained for the waivers?

  d. In performing Step A5c1, verify the information noted to the list of approved scrap dealers and note what approval was obtained for the list.

6. Determine that the purchasing representative observes the requirements for obtaining bids and for the sale of production scrap in accordance with regulations.

  a. Determine what regulations are applicable

  b. Evaluate the timeliness of soliciting bids and ensure that invitations are sent out in such a manner as to insure against discrimination against any bidder.

   (1) By a review of price trends of the scrap market for an extended period, evidence may suggest the company should reconsider the length of time that a commitment is made to sell certain scrap to one source or that bids should be invited in a month other than that presently selected.

  c. What controls exist to ensure invitations to bid are sent to the maximum possible number of approved scrap dealers?

   (1) Note whether any approved scrap dealers are consistently ignored in soliciting bids. If so, determine why and ascertain that management is aware of this information.

   (2) If certain dealers repeatedly fail to bid for scrap, determine what action is taken (a) to remove the dealer from the bidders list, and/or (b) to contact other dealers to determine their interest in bidding for production scrap.

7. How does the purchasing representative estimate the categories of scrap and the amount of each category available for sale in any given period?

  a. Recognizing that this information is of prime concern to any bidder, evaluate the estimate made within the last 12 months and compare to the amounts of scrap actually received by the dealers. If a wide variance exists between estimates and actual quantities, determine why the company can't obtain bids based on variable quantities.

   b. Determine to what extent coordination is effected with production departments in estimating the amount to be sold.

     (1) What consideration is given to production schedules established for the forthcoming period?

     (2) Are inquiries made questioning the major types of material to be used in the next period?

     (3) Are any ratios or formulas used (based upon historical records establishing production scrap generation to production output) in estimating quantities of scrap?

8. Examine scrap bid control records in the billing department for the period under review.

   a. Was the form signed by all members of the Scrap Bid Committee?

   b. Was there evidence to indicate that bids were received in sealed bid return envelopes before the date of opening?

     (1) If any evidence to the contrary is noted, investigate fully and determine that sealed bid envelopes were sent to bidders.

     (2) Inquire whether bids received after the date of opening are considered and, if so, note approvals obtained of this action.

     (3) Determine that the sealed bid envelopes were directed to the purchasing agent. If for any reason this is not the case, the auditor shall determine that the theory of the use of sealed bid envelopes has not been violated.

   c. Were the bids opened on the established day? If not, why not?

   d. Were the prevailing market prices entered?

     (1) From what sources was this information obtained?

     (2) Were the high bids comparable to prevailing market prices?

     (3) If there appears to be no significant relationship noted in (2) above, determine if further action is taken.

   e. Determine for the period under review that each bid contains (1) (for sales where the government has an interest) a signed scrap warranty by period for each successful bidder, (2) a signed quotation of bids, and (3) a signed condition of sale document.

     (1) If any of the above are missing, note the action taken to obtain the required signed documentation before authorizing removal of scrap by successful bidder.

9. Internal audit has obtained the cooperation of the purchasing department by being notified when the opening of bids is to occur. As a part of this audit, the auditor should attend the opening and observe the operations.

10. Determine whether the director of security and the manager of stores are notified in writing of the names of successful bidders for scrap for the period under review.

    a. Ascertain that this information is relayed to the personnel who have frequent contacts with scrap dealers.

    b. Further determine that supervisory personnel having contact with scrap dealers are aware of the conditions imposed on scrap dealers and that scrap dealers comply with these conditions.

       (1) Further determine what action is taken in obtaining the compliance of the scrap dealer and that the action is directed by proper supervision.

11. Tour the facility and note if appropriate containers appear to be adequately identified.

    a. Areas to be covered include cribs, fabrication departments, and manufacturing departments that draw substantial amounts of raw materials from stores.

    b. Ask the stores foremen assigned to the scrap docks what outlying buildings deliver scrap to the dock and whether he encounters segregation problems relative to these buildings.

       (1) Dependent upon an estimate of scrap delivered from outlying buildings if the quantity of scrap is significant, the auditor shall include those buildings in the review.

12. Determine what action is taken and by whom for the purpose of returning poorly segregated scrap to originating department.

13. Review the list of guards scheduled for scrap weighing detail and note if they are irregularly rotated. How far in advance do they know of this assignment? Are any guards consistently assigned when one particular dealer is a successful bidder for certain major categories?

    a. Ascertain that active and unused scale ticket books are kept under lock and key and that the supply of books in the guard's possession does not exceed three.

    b. Determine that the cashier does not issue a new book unless a completely used book is turned in.

    c. Determine the number of books in the cashier's possession, noting the accountability, and whether these books are secured.

14. During the course of the audit, the auditor should make several visits to the scrap dock and note:

    a. Is a guard assigned to the area?

    b. Are assigned areas for accumulation of different types of scrap properly placarded?

    c. Note whether the contents of trailers and trucks seen at the assigned area agree with the placard description and whether the contents are contaminated.

    d. List the trailers in the yard by license, together with description of scrap. Follow up to see that the same type of scrap was billed and that only successful bidders have trailer trucks at our docks. In addition, trace the license numbers to the incomplete book of scale tickets, noting that trailers are represented for each open ticket and that the in date of trailer on premises is shown.

15. Accompany at least one truck to the scales to observe that weighing procedure is being followed for both empty and loaded trailers.

   a. Determine if the guard accompanies the trailer and observes the trailer at all times and witnesses the weighing. To be as effective as possible, the guard should not be aware of the auditor's presence.

   b. Determine if the guard examines the placing of the trailer on the scale to insure that the trailer is properly weighed.

   c. Determine that during the weighing of the trailer (1) the driver is not weighed in, (2) the trailer is detached from the tractor, and (3) empty trailers do not contain loose equipment that could be removed after weighing in and subsequently not weighed in when trailers are loaded.

   d. Determine that every precaution possible is exercised to insure that neither company nor dealer personnel operate the public scale.

16. Note if the guard observes the proper placarding of the trailer or the placing of the trailer at the placarded area. In what manner does the guard insure that no scrap is loaded until the trailer is placarded?

17. Determine that the receiving and shipping inspection departments initiate a scrap condition report for each trailer.

   a. Are daily inspections made of the condition of scrap in each trailer?

      (1) Determine the approximate time of day these inspections are made. Are there any inspections of second-shift operations?

   b. Determine how the inspector decides the condition of a load to be unsatisfactory.

      (1) Does the inspector have instructions defining the various types of scrap?

   c. Obtain scrap condition reports used within the last full quarter and note if any loads were described as unsatisfactory.

      (1) Was the supervisor notified promptly of the condition?

      (2) What action did the supervisor take in determining the cause of improper segregation?

      (3) Review the various causes noted and determine the corrective action taken.

      (4) Determine what manufacturing supervisory personnel have

recently been contacted by the supervisor and evaluate the corrective action taken by them to prevent recurrence.

18. To what extent does the foreman insure that scrap is loaded into trailers in conformity with descriptions indicated on placards?

19. Determine whether the guard verifies the type of load inserted on the scrap ticket by the foreman.

20. Ascertain that the foremen signs the scale ticket and that the supervisor determines that the trailer is properly loaded and authorizes removal. Is this removal authorization by telephone?

21. Are the copies of the scale ticket distributed in accordance with subject procedure?

    a. Are **all** copies legible?

22. Determine what personnel are authorized to have access to the scrap condition report.

23. Are scrap bid control records, scale tickets, and scrap condition reports prepared in ink or indelible pencil, and are these documents complete in all information required?

B. The following audit steps should be performed at irregular intervals during the audit:

    1. Update from prior audit working papers the scheduling numeric accountability of scale tickets. Update the schedule, "Analysis by Classification by Month," and prepare a schedule listing all scrap trailers currently being loaded at scrap dock. The purpose of this schedule is to insure that all trailers have scale tickets.

    2. Obtain from the billing department all scale tickets received by them since the time of the last audit activity. Note any alterations to scale tickets and investigate the cause and necessary corrective action.

        a. Were the alterations approved by supervision?
        b. Did the scale ticket contain sufficient information explaining the reason for the alteration?
        c. Was the signature of the person making the alteration indicated?
        d. Compare the altered ticket to the copy retained in the book.

    3. Examine the scale tickets to determine whether they contain:

        a. License and number of the trailer
        b. Signature of authorized guard at weigh-in
        c. Signature of authorized guard at weigh-out
        d. Signature of dealer representative
        e. Signature of scale operator
        f. Signature of stores foreman
        g. Dates of weigh-in and weigh-out
        h. Load description

    i. Steps b,c,e, and f should be test checked to facsimile signatures on file.

4. Investigate any credits allowed dealers and, if credit is for poorly segregated scrap or incorrect scrap, review the scrap condition report for the particular trailer.

    a. Evaluate the extent of investigation of dealers' claim for credit and the approvals obtained to issue credit.

        (1) Were the approvals obtained in Step (a) proper?

            (a) Are approvals by personnel removed from routine policy, and do sufficient internal control features exist?

        (2) What precautions have been taken to prevent recurrence?

5. Perform the following audit tests of scale tickets (percent tested can change depending on volume):

    a. Test 33 percent of the net weight of scrap tickets to the weight billed.

    b. Test the unit price billed to the scrap bid control record of the highest bidder and, in addition, check the category of scrap billed.

    c. Test an alternate 33 percent of the scale tickets' mathematical computations to billing records.

    d. Test the remaining 33 percent of scale tickets descriptions with billing descriptions.

    e. Verify the mathematics of 50 percent of the scale tickets for net weight computations.

6. Reconcile total scrap billings by month to account #_____ Scrap Sales.

    a. Prepare an aging schedule of dealer receivables for the period audited and evaluate the efforts to collect monies due.

C. Account #_____, Scrap Sales

  1. Analyze this account for two representative months.

  2. Review the reconciliation performed in Step B6, and note any debits offset in the sales figure of this account.

    a. Substantiate the reasons for the debit offset noted above.

  3. Determine what departments charge labor to this account.

    a. Is the department engaged in the type of work that would normally be charged to this account? If not, determine the validity of the charge.

  4. Investigate other charges to this account, evaluating the documentation and approvals thereon. Any discrepancies are to be fully investigated.

  5. The months analyzed should be footed and charges, from journal vouchers and cash voucher reports will be traced to this account.

CHAPTER 6

Traffic Operation and Organization

INTRODUCTION

Importance of Traffic Operations

The traffic operation is one of constant change, influenced by factors from inside and outside the company. Changes in products, packing, selling, modes of shipment, and the rate structure of carriers all affect the traffic operation—and costs must be the constant concern of the traffic department.

The importance of control of traffic operations is readily appreciated when one looks at the amounts that are spent in moving materials and finished goods from one place to another. In different industries the traffic bill for finished goods varies from 1.5 percent to about 8 percent of sales revenue, and in other industries this can be much higher. Consider that a dollar saved in transportation expense increases net profits one dollar; and that one dollar of profit translates into several dollars of additional sales. The effective control of traffic operations, particularly in manufacturing and processing companies, is a must.

An upgrading of the traffic function in companies' organization structures has occurred in recent years. In most companies, the traffic manager reports to a senior executive, or enjoys vice presidential status.

Definition and Scope

As a starting point, the objective of traffic operations is to provide adequate service covering the movement of materials and finished goods from the point of origin through the manufacturing processes to ultimate destination at minimum cost. In this definition, much depends on what is considered adequate. Adequate service must meet timing requirements, based on such factors as the needs of customers, manufacturing schedules, and the perishability of the commodities to be shipped.

This chapter's consideration is limited to common carrier domestic transportation, as described below, including the movement of nonspecialized commodities where published tariffs are usually available for competing types of carriers. In general, this grouping includes railroads, parcel post, united parcel service, air freight, common carrier trucks, and contract carriers (where contract rates are available).

CONTROL OF TRAFFIC

The simplest approach to understanding the problems of traffic control is to begin with an ideal situation, where a manufacturing plant has been so located that the cost of transporting materials and manufacturing supplies bears the most favorable relationship to the cost of moving finished products to customers. (The traffic department should have been represented in the group responsible for recommending the plant location.) Both incoming and outgoing shipments move in carload or truckload lots into the plant and out to a relatively small number of distribution centers or customers. Manufacturing schedules and customers' requirements are completely coordinated, so no special handling or rush shipments are necessary.

A few companies, principally those dealing in bulk commodities, are able to approach this ideal, and for them the problem of traffic control is relatively simple. Far more companies cannot meet and many cannot even hope to approach this situation. In such companies, effective control by the traffic department requires constant study and coordination of company policies and problems in relation to the continually changing picture of common-carrier transportation.

Control cannot be really effective unless records and reports show results in a form that is understandable and usable by operating management. In the control of traffic costs, shipping costs should be segregated and reported so that total and per-unit transportation costs are shown and can be related to some standard of performance—for example, prior years or standard cost factors.

Misconceptions Regarding Traffic Operations

Often those who have only a general knowledge of transportation tend to oversimplify their problems. They are apt to believe that each mode of transportation has its own special characteristics that are not shared with other modes. Thus, some hold the belief that rail and truck offer the least expensive and slowest method of shipment, with savings possible through shipping in carload or truckload quantities. If quicker shipment is desired, or if shipment must be made in quantities below the economical minimum acceptable to railroads or trucks, then a more expensive mode of transport is used. In an approximate cost sequence, the next cheapest would be United Parcel Service, parcel post, and, finally, expensive but fast air freight.

Such illusions can be misleading and expensive. For example, in one company, the sales promotion department wished to secure quick delivery of an exhibit to a city 400 miles away. Without consulting the company traffic department, the sales promotion executives assumed that a premium-cost method of shipment would provide expedited handling, and shipment was made accordingly. Delivery took three days. If the traffic department had been consulted, the shipment would have gone via a regular overnight truck to the destination. Delivery would have been made the next morning, and the cost of shipment would have been $150 less.

Consideration of the problems of transportation was begun with this wrong approach so the reader may eliminate any thought that the problems of control of traffic are essentially simple. They are not. The control of traffic costs involves complex operations and interrelationships, some of which are controllable in one way or another. Others are relatively uncontrollable.

Comparison with Purchasing

The factors that the traffic department uses in controlling its judgments are in some respects very similar to those required in control of purchasing. In fact, the simplest approach is to consider the work of the traffic department as a specialized form of purchasing. The job of the traffic department is to make an optimum decision between competing vendors (the carriers) who, for a price, offer different degrees of service. The decisions, as already pointed out, are not easy—nor can they be permanent, since conditions, carriers, and rates are always changing.

The parallel with purchasing applies principally to the procurement of transportation services. Beyond this, the traffic department has to provide for much more elaborate verification of charges, and for the control of more expenses and similar items, than does purchasing.

Traffic Department Functions

The organization of a traffic department must provide for two distinct groups of functions. The first is concerned with procurement of traffic services, with analysis, and with constant study of routes, rates, and carriers in relation to the operating requirements of the company. Rate and route studies may include involvement in proceedings of regulatory bodies. Traffic personnel will participate with the production and sales departments in projects to expedite and improve receipt and shipment of materials and finished goods through improvements in materials handling, better packaging, safer methods of packing and shipping, and similar activities. Many of the clues to situations that may be profitable subjects for further study will come through analysis of charges made by carriers and losses that occur in the course of shipment. Consequently, the procurement section of the traffic department will have responsibility for checking bills rendered by carriers, and handling or reviewing claims for loss, damage, and overcharge.

The second group of functions is concerned with administration of the day-to-day operations of receipt and shipment, relations with carriers, and general control, similar to those prescribed for the first group of functions.

This logical separation into two groups of functions works to advantage in the situation where a number of field offices are operated on a semiautonomous basis under the staff control of the head office. In the head office are the specialized experts who have the ability and the time to make the continual studies that are a necessity for effective traffic control. On the basis of these studies, instructions will be issued to field offices covering such matters as standard and alternate routings, packing, car handling, and relations with carriers.

Assignment of Responsibility

The following outline, which is adapted from one large company, may be considered reasonably typical of the plan of assignment of traffic responsibility.

Home Office

General Traffic Manager—in charge

1. Traffic research
    a. Studies traffic costs for possible plant and warehouse locations

    b. Studies how general traffic policies of routing, carriers, and service are working out

    c. Studies division of business between carriers, reciprocity, and similar matters

    d. Studies rates and classifications, with view to reduction of cost

    e. Recommends general traffic policies

2. Commerce

    a. Maintains relationship with regulatory bodies

    b. Prepares rate petitions

    c. Represents the company in rate proceedings

3. Materials handling and packaging

    a. Works in cooperation with sales and manufacturing departments

    b. Studies methods of packing or shipment that will provide the most effective handling and minimum losses

    c. Studies damage claims

4. Rate audit and claim

    a. Checks freight bills for rate and classification

    b. Prepares claims and follows for collection

    c. Reviews claims prepared in plant traffic offices

    d. Handles relationship with outside freight audit agency or arranges for in-house

5. Traffic service

    a. Prescribes routings for incoming materials and outgoing shipments to be used by plants and sales offices

    b. Works with sales departments on special routing problems to meet customer requirements

    c. Handles moving arrangements for transferred employees

Field

Plant traffic manager

1. Has line responsibility to plant manager
2. Has functional responsibility to home office traffic department
3. Handles administration of local traffic operations according to policies prescribed by home office traffic department
4. Watches controllable costs and extra cost items (penalties), such as demurrage and switching
5. Prepares claims (principally loss and damage) and forwards to home office for review before filing

In this organization, functional control over the actual traffic operations in the field is exercised by

1. Review of freight bills and claims in the home office traffic department (after the fact in some cases)
2. Review of operating performance from reports submitted on such items as demurrage, detention, transportation charges paid, routings, excess transportation charges, and transit times
3. Annual visits by home office traffic personnel to field offices

Payment of bills is now offered as a service by some banks. Instructions are given on bills of lading to forward the bills to the company agent for payment.

The above listed functions are commonly the responsibility of the traffic department. These operations must be controlled by that department; the job of the internal auditor is to examine and appraise how control over these functions is established and maintained.

FACTORS PERTAINING TO TRAFFIC OPERATIONS

Common Carriers

Common carriers offer services to the general public covering the transportation of property and passengers for compensation. By doing this, a common carrier becomes subject to detailed regulation of the routes over which it may operate and the prices it charges for its services. This regulation is handled by the Interstate Commerce Commission and Civil Aeronautics Board for interstate carriers and by applicable state regulatory commissions for intrastate carriers.

Railroads offer a range of equipment, routes, and services that can cover virtually any shipping problem.

Motor trucks are the most widely used carriers. They provide fast intercity services at rates that may be higher than rail. Offsetting the higher rates for some shipments is the lower capacity of trucks compared with freight cars. The result is truckload rates that are based on lower minimums. An important factor in the consideration of motor truck tariffs is the door-to-door service that is provided.

Contract carriers are motor trucks that operate on specific contracts to haul specified commodities between definite locations. Tariff charges must be published and are at favorable rates. Contracts are usually negotiated by the traffic department. Contract provisions must be simple and complete, and charges for accessorial services, such as icing, spotting and storage, and wait time must be specified.

Inland water carriers are principally barge lines, which are used for bulk cargo where fast service is not required. This service is often rendered in conjunction with rail service under a combination rate that is lower than all-rail or all-truck service.

Air freight service is provided by both air passenger and exclusively air freight carriers. This highly expedited service is at premium rates.

United Parcel Service (UPS) is similar to parcel post and motor trucks. Unlike parcel post, UPS has routes and will pick up packages daily; unlike motor trucks, UPS does not have a minimum weight or charge for picking up small deliveries. UPS has been very successful in establishing and maintaining its market niche.

Forwarders collect small shipments from individual shippers and combine them into large quantity shipments that are carried at lower rates to a single destination. At that point, the forwarder delivers the individual shipments to consignees. Forwarders operate via rail, truck, and air.

Parcel post is the small package service provided by the federal government. Shipments are restricted as to weight and size.

Classification and Rates

Classification. A publication, such as the Uniform Freight Classification, that lists thousands of articles and commodities, and the classes to which they are assigned for the purpose of applying class rates.

Classification Rating. The categories into which related articles are grouped for the purpose of applying class rates.

Class Rate. Class rates are established on an overall mileage zone basis and apply in conjunction with ratings established in a freight classification, such as the Uniform Freight Classification.

Commodity Rate. A commodity rate differs from a class rate in that it is a specific rate on a specific article from, to, or between specifically named points. Generally, commodity rates are created because of regular heavy movements between the same two points, and usually are lower than the applicable class rates.

All-Commodity Rate. The all-commodity rate permits the transportation of articles of various classifications by carload at a common rate. Application of this rate usually requires a mixture of six or more items in the carload, and restricts the proportion of any single item to 50 percent of the total shipment. This rate is particularly applicable to freight forwarders and shippers' associations that combine material of various classifications into carload lots.

Classification and rates is the most difficult field for the layman in traffic to understand. Each carrier publishes its price list in the form of tariffs that give the cost of transporting from one specified location to another. In the case of railroads and trucks, the cost will usually be shown for quantities shipped by carload (CL) or truckload (TL), with a higher cost for less-than-carload (LCL) or less-than-truckload (LTL) shipment. In addition to variation due to quantity, the rate will vary according to the nature of the commodity. In general, commodities of greater value, commodities more susceptible to damage or loss in transit, and commodities of greater bulk will carry higher rates. These commodity differences are described in general classifications.

Tariffs will also specify minimum quantities that will be acceptable as carload and truckload shipments. Where small shipments are made, an important factor is the minimum charge usually imposed by the carrier. For example, a tariff may specify a rate of $3 per cwt. with a minimum charge of $60. This means that any shipment of less than 200 pounds would in effect be at premium rates.

Tariff schedules are published by all common carriers, so that the cost of shipment by alternative methods is always determinable in advance.

Because of the complications due to classifications, rates, rate changes, and routings via alternative methods, looking up a rate is no simple matter. With all factors known (classification, point of origin, and destination), an experienced rate clerk may require 15 minutes or more to determine from published tariffs the exact rate applying to a specific shipment.

In the United States, the rate structure is under the national jurisdiction of the Interstate Commerce Commission, and on a more localized basis by regulatory bodies and associations of carriers. In effect, the picture is one of a constant cold war between the carriers, who want to derive as much revenue as possible, and shippers, who wish to secure maximum service at minimum cost. A cross-current in this cold war lies in the efforts of the various types of carriers to establish rates that will put them into a favorable competitive position with other types of carriers. For example, a higher rate may mean loss, instead of gain, to a carrier if the effect is the transfer of business by shippers to a competing carrier that offers better service or a lower rate.

Every traffic manager is particularly conscious of his responsibility to his company in securing optimum service at minimum cost. One common activity is the effort to secure commodity rates where they may be applied to advantage. At the same time (as with purchasing in relation to vendors), the traffic manager has a collateral responsibility toward the carriers to see that they are given equitable treatment; often factors other than cost must be considered in selecting the mode of shipment.

In brief, the classification and rate functions in a traffic department call for skilled personnel, continual study, and effective action.

Economical Shipment

More economical and faster movement of materials comes with a large quantity shipment, such as carload or truckload. The simplest form of such movement is a minimum carload (or truckload) shipment inbound to the plant or outbound to a single customer. Where such shipment is not feasible, some of the advantages of quantity shipment and rates may be gained through:

Pool Car. A car in which shipments to a number of customers in a single locality are combined and consigned to a distribution center for delivery to the individual customers. In the case of incoming materials, vendors may be instructed to deliver to an assembly location, where a carload will be accumulated for delivery to the plant.

Stopoff Car. A car on which the movement is stopped at originating, intermediate, and terminating points to partially load or to complete loading, to partially unload or to complete unloading, or to exercise other privileges in relation to the contents of the car as provided in a specific tariff. In general, the carload rate applies to the contents of the fully loaded car from point of origin to final destination, plus a stopoff charge for intermediate locations.

Consolidations. A means of reducing shipping costs through use of the most economical shipping units. This requires that the traffic department be informed sufficiently in advance of shipment to work out the optimum arrangement that will take advantage of carload and other low-cost incentive rates for volume shipment.

Freight Forwarders. Separate companies (some controlled by railroads) that assemble material from various sources into carload and less-than-carload lots. Freight forwarders often maintain definite schedules between larger cities and can offer quicker delivery on less-than-carload shipments.

Shippers' Associations. Cooperative groups that handle material in the same manner as freight forwarders—except that their operations are restricted to the members of the group. Here the rate charged to members will be the carload rate, plus a service charge to cover expenses. (Note: Public Distribution Centers also use this concept to combine shipments for their tenants shipping materials to the same customers; i.e., grocery manufacturers to grocery stores.)

Transit Freight Privilege

Essentially a transit freight privilege gives the shipper the privilege of forwarding a shipment from one location to another, where it is stored and processed, and finally reshipping it (or the product after processing) to a third location. The advantage lies in the charge by the carrier, which is based on a through rate direct from originating point to final destination, plus a designated charge for transit privileges.

Weight Agreements

A weight agreement permits a shipper to determine the average weight of specified items that are shipped on a regular basis. This weight is then marked on each case or other container, which is packed as specified. Average pallet weights are also marked on pallets. This universally used plan saves both carrier and shipper the cost and time that would be necessary if each shipment had to be weighed separately.

Warehousing

Since the ultimate objective of traffic is movement of material from source to point of final delivery, warehousing must be included in consideration of traffic operations. As far as control of cost is concerned, the problem is one of comparing the cost of inbound movement from source to warehouse, plus warehouse charges, plus outbound delivery charges, with the cost of direct shipment. This essentially simple problem may be complicated by consideration of such factors as inadequate storage facilities in factories or branches and sales department requirements for service to customers.

Free on Board (F.O.B.) Location

The determination of the f.o.b. location in the contract of sale is important, since this usually defines:

1. The point at which title to commodities changes hands
2. In the event of loss or damage, who is responsible for the claim against the carrier

Many companies purchase materials f.o.b. the vendor's point of shipment, since this gives them control over routing and the opportunity to work out the most favorable classification, rate, and in-transit arrangements with the carrier.

Suppliers of large-volume, low-value commodities often endeavor to ship freight-collect (f.o.b. point of shipment) to avoid tying up company funds in freight charges that must be billed to customers.

Credit Terms

The terms of payment to carriers are specified by regulatory bodies. In general, charges must be paid at time of delivery unless prior credit arrangements have been made. Railroads are allowed to extend credit for 48 hours on carload and 96 hours on LCL shipments, and somewhat longer under special arrangements. Trucks and certain others allow credit up to seven days. Failure to pay within time limits is punishable by fine.

Freight Payment Services

Some companies utilize freight payment services to process freight invoices and supply cost and traffic analysis. Freight invoices are sent directly to the service company, which screens and enters the data. The carriers are paid per ICC regulations, and the service company is reimbursed via weekly transfer of funds.

Claims

Acceptance of a shipment by a carrier includes the acceptance of responsibility for the safe delivery to the consignee. When loss or damage occurs, the carrier is usually responsible, and the value of the loss or damage may be recovered by making claim against the carrier.

A different type of claim exists when the carrier bills for services at an incorrect rate, or when arithmetical errors are made in billing. Losses due to such errors are recoverable through claim for overcharge.

Under ICC regulations, action at law by carriers for recovery of charges and complaints to the Commission by shippers for recovery of damages not based upon overcharges must begin within two years from date of delivery. In the case of overcharges, action at law or complaint to the Commission must be made within two years from date of delivery, except when an overcharge claim has been filed in writing within the two-year period of limitation. In this case, the period is extended six months from the disallowance of the claim by the carrier. If the carrier begins action for recovery of charges within the two-year period, the period of limitation for the shipper to file a complaint or initiate action at law is extended for 90 days from the time such action is begun.

Other Responsibilities of Traffic Department

Since the movement of household goods of transferred employees requires knowledge of routes and carriers, these functions are usually assigned to the traffic department and are discussed in this section.

Further Consideration

The purpose of this brief description of some of the factors of traffic operation is to provide background for more detailed consideration of the controls maintained by a typical traffic department and the related work of the internal auditor.

Traffic cost should always be watched and controlled, whether or not such cost is paid by the company. When material is purchased from a vendor on a delivered basis, a lower delivery cost will give the possibility of securing a lower price from the vendor. Likewise, lower outbound costs to customers who are billed f.o.b. factory give these customers the possibility of quoting lower prices or making more profit and, more importantly, give the company an opportunity to gain increased sales because of lower delivered costs.

Approach to a Traffic Department Audit

When it comes to the audit of a traffic department, some auditors are hesitant because they assume that a knowledge of tariffs is a prerequisite to a traffic audit. This belief may come from the fact that records (tariffs) may be checked with other records (freight bills). Tariffs are complicated and not easy to understand—hence the hesitancy.

In fact, the ability to understand tariffs is no more necessary for the auditor to make an effective audit of the traffic department than being an experienced purchasing agent is necessary to make an effective internal audit of the purchasing department. The auditing of rates on freight bills belongs to those who are expert in traffic matters—rate clerks and outside rate audit agencies. In that phase of the audit program, the internal auditor is concerned with the control over the checking and payment, not with the actual freight bill auditing. The requirement in auditing traffic payments is the same as in auditing payments to vendors: verification that what was paid was in accordance with the amount authorized by the expert in that function (traffic person or purchasing agent).

The following sections describe the controls and the related internal audit procedures applying to a traffic department. Through familiarization, verification, and evaluation, the internal auditor will develop a picture of the control over traffic. One must be particularly alert to interdepartmental, interoffice, and interplant communications. Unless these communications are well maintained, the traffic department cannot use its specialized talents with maximum effectiveness.

In the development of the traffic audit program, a predominant factor is the natural difference in operations of one company from another. The effect of such differences is to preclude any universal internal audit program that may be applied to any traffic department. *Each internal auditor will have to develop his or her own program—based on the auditor's knowledge of the company and the estimation of the areas in which control must be exercised.*

To illustrate, in one company, the principal inbound movement to one factory is over 100 cars per day of three basic bulk materials, which come from three established sources of supply. In this situation, inbound routings and rates are standardized. Outbound shipments go to a large number of customers in lots of varying sizes, with use of pool and stopoff cars as a customary means of handling. In this company the major work of the traffic department is on outbound shipments.

The control and audit requirements are very different in another company, where the various manufacturing materials and parts are shipped from a large number of widespread suppliers to a small number of assembly locations, from which the finished product is shipped to dealers. In this company, inbound shipments are the principal problem, since outbound shipments follow comparatively standardized channels.

In developing an audit program, however, the internal auditor should be alert that lapses and deficiencies in control are prone to occur in areas regarded by operating personnel as relatively unimportant. In the first company mentioned, lapses might occur because the incoming bulk materials were so large in volume as to neglect the comparatively small volume of other incoming supplies and materials not moving in large quantity. Therefore the internal auditor must plan a program for complete coverage.

ROUTING OF SHIPMENTS

Importance of Routing

The crux of the control of traffic operations lies in the routing assigned to a shipment. This is the purchase operation—once the routing has been fixed, the remainder of the job is concerned with seeing that the prescribed path has been followed, that commodities have been received in good order, and that the price paid is correct.

One cannot stress enough the importance of carrier selection—and the expert knowledge of both carriers and company problems necessary for the job to be well done. For example, if a truck shipment is assigned to a motor carrier that does not connect directly with a carrier serving the city of destination, the rate is often higher than if the shipment were given to an originating carrier that scheduled direct connection. In addition to the higher cost when direct connection is not made, the time in transit would probably be longer.

Inbound Routing

Control over routing begins with the procurement of commodities. The universal practice is to have close coordination between traffic and purchasing departments so that adequate consideration will be given to the cost of inbound shipment as an element of the delivered cost—and to routing as a factor in plant operation.

The necessary coordination may be effected as follows:

1. Traffic prepares routing and rate information for major suppliers of principal purchased commodities. This information is maintained for buyers on a current basis.
2. Purchasing obtains routing instructions from the traffic department prior to placing purchase orders.
3. Purchasing sends a copy of each purchase order to the traffic department so it can verify the routing specified on the order.

The necessity for control over inbound routing may be better realized by example. In one company, materials are purchased from a number of mills adjacent to each other and at a considerable distance from the manufacturing plant. Here the traffic department arranges for inbound stopoff cars that assemble complete carloads from various mills, thus gaining the carload rate on the long haul to the plant.

In another case, docking facilities at the plant permit the handling of no more than six trucks at one time. Here the inbound routings are scheduled so that the facilities will not be overloaded.

Outbound Routing

In most manufacturing companies, constant study and control are maintained over the movement of inbound merchandise. In a processing business, for example, the sources of supply may be few, and routing and rate problems comparatively simple. By contrast, the finished products sent out may go to a large number of customers in many different locations.

Outbound routing is commonly concerned with such problems as:

1. Economy in shipping cost by assembly of pool or stopoff cars
2. Comparative merits and costs of shipping and redistribution through warehouses
3. Requests by customers for special routings (that may be more expensive)
4. Deviations caused by requirements for rush shipment
5. Development of sales plans without consolidation with the traffic department

For example, some years ago in one company an entire sales and direct shipment campaign was planned on the assumption that minimum LCL freight rates applied to 100-pound shipments. After the campaign had begun, the sales department discovered that the minimum charges imposed by carriers resulted in actual per-pound charges considerably more than anticipated. (A 100-pound shipment at a tariff rate of $25 cwt might be subject to a $50 minimum charge—100 percent more per pound than anticipated.)

Routing and Rate Guides

Where repetitive shipments are made between stated locations, the general practice is for the traffic department to issue and maintain routing and rate guide sheets covering the movement of inbound and outbound commodities. These sheets will be developed in the routing and rate section of the traffic department after study of company requirements in relation to the various alternative modes of shipment. Such sheets will usually specify the standard recommended modes of shipment and may specify alternative modes where faster service is required. In a company that normally ships to a widespread area, these sheets will provide definite information for the majority of shipments and will often serve to indicate the routing for locations adjacent to those specified on the sheets.

By having these sheets in such departments as shipping, billing, and purchasing, the traffic department may maintain definite control over the purchasing of transportation—provided instructions are enforced that all shipments that do not follow recommended routings are referred to the traffic department for its specification of routing.

In companies that have quite a range in size of shipment, mode of transportation, and requirements for speed of service, the traffic department may wish to maintain a comparatively complete record of all modes of transportation, rates, and applicable information for certain locations to which frequent shipments are made.

A common difficulty in the control of routing arises when a routing is determined—or more or less forced—outside the traffic department. For example, a customer may require a particular routing as a favor to a particular carrier or because the carrier specified may offer advantages in handling, storage, or delivery, or the production department may instruct a vendor to ship by premium cost methods to meet an emergency. The control requirements in such situations are:

1. Inform the traffic department of the nonstandard routing.
2. Ensure that responsible management understood and approved the cost of shipment by premium methods.
3. Verify that the service purchased by premium methods was necessary and actually gained the advantage expected.

Division of Business among Carriers

Many companies maintain summary records to show the division of company business among carriers in terms of tonnage or dollar volume. In some instances, considerations of reciprocity exist; for example, a company may manufacture commodities used by trucking companies. Other companies feel a certain obligation to assign enough business among various carriers to insure the continuation of service. Most believe that the maintenance of such information, in total by carrier for the entire company, is essential in dealing with carriers.

These records are usually accumulated in the headquarters office on the basis of figures submitted by traffic representatives at shipping and receiving locations. The necessary information may be developed from records of payments to carriers. Another advantage of securing this information is as an indication to the headquarters office of any situations in which a local office appears to be giving unusual preference to a particular carrier.

INTERNAL AUDIT PROGRAM: ROUTING OF SHIPMENTS

Policies and Procedures

The internal audit of routing begins with the examination of policies and procedures. Points to be covered include:

1. How is determination of routing made?
2. Are there periodic supervisory reviews of routing decisions?
3. How is routing published to other departments and to the traffic organization?
4. What check is made by traffic that prescribed routings are followed?
5. Where prescribed routings are not followed, what action is taken?
6. Where prescribed routing covers shipment at premium cost, or where special shipment is made at premium cost:
   a. What approval is required?
   b. What record of excess cost is maintained?
   c. Where is excess cost charged?
   d. What action is taken to minimize premium cost shipments?
7. What plan is followed so that routings are reviewed regularly with a view to possible revision?
8. Does the traffic department conduct tests to learn if shipments are received as scheduled by customers?
9. What is done to insure that adequate shipping information for incoming materials is given to vendors?
10. What is done in coordinating traffic with sales and production, to minimize transportation charges? (Arrangements for pool cars inbound from vendors or outbound to customers are examples.)

11. Where material moves through warehouses for reshipment to customers:
    a. Who determines routing of shipments to customers?
    b. What effort is made to minimize warehouse charges through direct shipments to large-volume customers?
    c. Who determines warehouse locations?
    d. How and by whom are warehouse stocks controlled?
12. What records are maintained to show division of business among carriers? How is information accumulated and summarized? (For example, some traffic people use "ton-mile revenue" as a measure.)

Verification

Here the auditor examines in detail a sample of transactions to ascertain the extent to which actual operations conform with the established plans. In the outlines below and in following chapters, the size of sample specified is completely arbitrary and is intended to indicate the general approach. In actual work, each internal auditor will have to decide what and how much will constitute an adequate coverage.

Typical items to be covered include:

1. *Inbound Shipments.* From deliveries into stores and production, select _____ items. Examine purchase orders, freight bills (and routing and rate guides, if available).
    a. Was routing specified by traffic and followed in shipment?
    b. How were rates verified?
    c. Was sufficient time allowed by ordering and purchasing departments between shipping date and required date?
    d. Note any inbound shipments at premium rates, such as:
        Items normally received in large quantities delivered LCL or LTL
        Items delivered by premium cost carriers (air express, etc.)
    e. Was freight allowance from vendors verified?
    f. If purchase order was based on carload shipment and part of the shipment was made LCL, was allowance for increased transportation cost made by vendor?
2. *Outbound Shipments.* From shipping department records (or from billing by carriers) select _____ items. Include _____ items that are not regular shipments of company products (for example, returns to suppliers and advertising material).
    a. Was routing specified by traffic and followed in shipment?
    b. How were rates verified?
    c. Were routing and rate guides used up-to-date?

d. Where customer's routing is followed:

Is it more expensive?

Is any additional cost charged to the customer? If not, who approves?

e. Note any shipments at premium rates, such as:

Rush shipments to customers/third parties

LCL or LTL interim shipments to normal carload locations, such as warehouses

3. *Premium Rate Shipments.* From voucher files, withdraw vouchers covering payments during a 10-day period to such premium-rate carriers as air express and overnight carrier. For these, and for premium shipments noted in the verification of inbound and outbound shipments, determine:

a. Reason for premium shipment

b. Authorization for shipment

c. Approval for additional cost

d. Accounting distribution of additional cost (substantial premium costs are commonly found buried in a large transportation or material cost account)

e. Whether results anticipated through premium shipment was gained

f. What provision exists to recover excess cost from customers who request premium routings or special equipment

Similar verification should be performed for inbound, outbound, and premium rate shipments applying to company-operated or outside warehouse locations. (Detachment from the traffic department and a belief that local personnel has better knowledge of local requirements often operate to weaken general control over such shipments.)

4. *Warehousing.* The economic and other factors affecting the establishment and maintenance of a warehouse in a particular location are often the subject of a special study by traffic, sales, and other operating departments. Where such study is made and definite costs and savings are anticipated prior to establishing a warehouse, the internal auditor may give constructive service by comparing the actual operating results with those that were anticipated. For example, the internal auditor may find that unanticipated LCL inbound shipments may increase costs that were planned on the basis of carload shipments.

TRANSIT SHIPMENTS

As was previously stated, considerable savings in shipping cost is possible where transit arrangements can be applied. In effect, these arrangements permit the shipment of materials from an originating point to an intermediate location for storage or processing and reshipment to a final destination. The rate charged will be based on a through rate from originating point to destination plus a transit charge.

Transit shipping arrangements may apply to various general types of transaction. Three of the principal classifications are:

Milling in Transit, in which grain will be received from outside sources in a processing plant, milled or otherwise processed at the plant, and reshipped to distribution locations or customers.

Fabrication in Transit, in which a semifinished product, such as steel, will be shipped from a steel plant to a processing location, where it will be fabricated to meet customer specifications and reshipped to customers.

Storage in Transit, in which a finished product, such as frozen food, will be shipped from packing plants to a central storage location and later reshipped to distributing locations or customers.

The problems in the control of transit shipping arrangements will vary almost directly with the number of points of origin and destination. For example, storage in transit will usually present simple problems, since points of origin and destination will be comparatively few in number and routings will follow a repetitive pattern.

At the other extreme will be milling in transit, where originating points and final destinations may be all over the map. Moreover, differences in weights will occur due to processing, and also because of local receipts and local deliveries to which transit will not apply. In this situation, some problems that are of constant concern will be:

1. Selecting inbound transit billings for most favorable application to outbound shipments.
2. Balancing inbound and outbound shipments so that sufficient transit billing is available for application to outbound shipments.
3. Comparing cost of grain purchased locally (without transit privileges) with carload grain cost (including transit billings). Determining, where products are sold on a delivered basis, average freight cost factor that is to be added to the base price to recover shipping cost to customers (allowing for benefits from transit rates).

The application of transit privileges is subject to regulations established by carriers. Of particular interest in the general control of transit are usual requirements that:

1. Bills on inbound freight that are expected to be applied to outgoing shipment must be registered with a local transit freight bureau.

2. Inbound bills that have been registered must be applied to outbound shipments within a specified period; otherwise, the transit privilege lapses.

INTERNAL AUDIT PROGRAM: TRANSIT SHIPMENTS

Policies and Procedures

The internal audit program for transit shipment will naturally vary with the importance and complication of the transit operation. Some of the factors to be covered in a milling business are outlined below, in the section that describes the relationship between buying, production, sales, and accounting departments necessary for adequate control of transit freight.

In general, the internal auditor should examine the records and discuss the related procedures with the personnel responsible for control of transit arrangements. In this, the auditor will be principally interested in factors affecting company policy and interdepartmental relationships.

In situations where a freight cost factor applies, the internal auditor should review the plan followed in determining this factor—and the manner of analyzing variations between freight paid and freight recovered by inclusion in selling prices.

Verification

Verification will require the selection of a representative sample of inbound and outbound shipments to which transit privileges apply or should be applied.

1. *Inbound.* Select from receiving records _____ cars of commodities to which transit would normally apply. Include _____ cars from records more than 12 months prior to audit.

    a. Verify that transit privileges were used prior to expiration date.

    b. If transit privileges expired without application, inquire as to reason.

2. *Outbound.* Select from shipping records _____ cars of commodities to which transit would normally apply.

    a. Verify that transit was applied.

    b. If transit was not applied, inquire as to reason. (For example, insufficient available incoming transit billing.)

3. *Selection of Transit Billing.* The selection of transit billing that will be most favorable for outbound shipments is a job that calls for specialized knowledge of routings and tariffs. Verification of the effectiveness of this work will normally be outside the scope of the internal auditor's assignment.

ORDERING AND HANDLING TRANSPORTATION— INBOUND SHIPMENTS

With inbound routing established under the control of the traffic department, the next phase of the traffic operation is concerned with coordinating the movement of incoming commodities with factory and other operations.*

Scheduling

Cars or trucks must be delivered (spotted) at proper locations; the traffic department is responsible for seeing that necessary orders are issued to accomplish this. Coordinated with this, receiving personnel should be available to handle the unloading. Scheduling incoming shipments calls for study of physical facilities and available labor and for close coordination between traffic and production.

Weighing

Where track scales are available, all inbound and outbound cars should be weighed to show loaded and tare weights. Weighing is a necessity in the case of such bulk commodities as coal and scrap. If track scales are not available, cars may be weighed by licensed weighmasters on railroad scales.

Failure to secure weights and to check them with transportation charges and vendor's billing may result in overlooking weight discrepancies. For example, tare weights stenciled on cars are the result of weighing when cars are new or reconditioned. After being put in service, cars pick up dirt and other material that will increase the tare weight. One company reported that actual tare weights on a considerable number of cars averaged 1900 pounds in excess of the weights stenciled on the cars. This may also be true of ice and snow accumulations in winter.

Demurrage

Demurrage is a penalty charge assessed by a railroad (or by a trucking firm) for retention of cars (or trailers) by a company beyond a specified free time of two working days. The rate rises very rapidly after three or four days to a level that makes the car an expensive form of warehousing.

Demurrage charges are definitely a controllable cost—anything other than occasional charges is a symptom that calls for attention. Very often the fault will be in lack of coordination between the traffic and plant operating departments, resulting in poor scheduling of cars in relation to

*Further discussion of inbound handling is presented in Chapter 4, Receiving.

plant labor and facilities. Because demurrage charges are a penalty and an indication of possible inefficiency, they should be separately recorded and brought to management's attention.

Where carload volume is large, demurrage charges may be minimized through making an average demurrage agreement with the carrier serving the plant. Under such an agreement, the company is given credit for cars that are released to the carrier within 24 hours of receipt. Within restricted limits, these credits may be applied to offset demurrage on cars that are held beyond the free-time limit.

Truckers may assess a charge for excess waiting when equipment is held for some time pending loading or unloading. Such a charge, like demurrage, is a penalty for which the company usually receives no return, and may be an indicator of some deficiency in receiving or shipping personnel and routines.

In occasional instances, payment of demurrage may be worthwhile. For example, an outgoing car might be retained for a short additional period to complete a carload shipment. Here the savings in rate on carload shipment might more than offset demurrage charges. As another example, paying demurrage is often less expensive than paying overtime to shipping or receiving personnel to load or unload a car within the allotted free period.

Railroad Switching

Where traffic arrangements include trackage and other facilities on company-owned property, a switching and sidetrack agreement will be made with the carrier. This agreement will specify the details of the facilities and the basis on which charges are made. Switching charges are commonly assessed at a flat rate per car, regardless of size, and do not usually apply to line-haul movement. If the company uses enough railroad cars, it may own or lease them.

One company noted that a great many movements of a bulk commodity were made between adjacent plants in cars of varying capacity. By ordering cars of maximum capacity, the number of cars was reduced— and there was a substantial saving in switching charges.

ORDERING AND HANDLING TRANSPORTATION— OUTBOUND SHIPMENTS

Outbound shipments present many of the same problems of coordination of facilities, scheduling, weighing, demurrage, and switching that apply to inbound shipments. Transportation equipment must be ordered and available at the time and place that will coordinate with production and shipping schedules.

Established procedures should cover orders for transportation service to secure them on an optimum basis. In the case of cars and trucks, orders would specify the size and type that will keep charges at a minimum. Where frequent shipments of specialized items are made, specialized equipment may be available. For example, special auto frame cars are used for shipments from auto frame manufacturers to assembly plants.

Where shipments are made to specified locations at reasonably frequent intervals, routines should be set up to provide for notification of all interested departments, so shipments may be combined into full-car or truck loads. In one company, this work of building up shipments into full carload lots is the full-time responsibility of one traffic department employee.

Procedures for ordering from carriers should include definite routines and forms for ordering, switching, and weighing. Orders should be specific, giving car numbers, tracks to be used, locations, and service desired.

INTERNAL AUDIT PROGRAM: ORDERING AND HANDLING

Policies and Procedures

The internal audit of ordering and handling begins with examination of the routines for controlling this function and the related penalties.

The program covers such items as:

1. What are routines for handling and spotting incoming and outgoing cars and trucks?
2. What records are kept to report on incoming and outgoing cars and trucks?
3. How is demurrage recorded?
4. What is done to minimize charges for demurrage, waiting time, and detention?
5. What are routines for tracing incoming and outgoing shipments?
6. How much tracing appears necessary?
7. What are routines for ordering, switching, and weighing?
8. Are weighing records reported and used to verify both freight charges and vendors' invoices?
9. What is policy on weighing shipments between company locations? (Weighing costs may be saved by accepting the weight at the shipping location.)
10. What routines are followed (or studies made) to increase the volume of shipments made in full carloads or truckloads?

Verification

1. *Inbound and Outbound.* Examine traffic department records of inbound and outbound cars for a period of 10 days. Select (1) all cars on which demurrage applied, and (2) _____ cars that contained bulk commodities.

    a. Determine, as far as possible, the reasons for demurrage.

    b. Determine what follow-up action was taken by traffic to control demurrage.

    c. Compare gross and tare weights recorded for cars containing bulk commodities with:

        Receiving and shipping records

        Traffic department car records

        Billing from vendors or to customers

        Billing from carriers

2. *Receiving and Shipping.* Examine receiving and shipping records for a period of 10 days (other than the period for which traffic records were examined). Select a total of _____ cars:

    a. Check for entry on traffic records of cars.

    b. Compare net and gross weights.

In examination of shipping and receiving records, note instances where repeated shipments from the same vendors or to the same customers occur in less-than-carload (or truckload) quantities.

    a. Inquire as to the possibility of shipment in large quantity.

Attention and complete investigation should be given to items where poor interdepartmental coordination is indicated. Further items of a penalty nature may be revealed in the audit of charges for transportation.

CHARGES FOR TRANSPORTATION

Effectiveness of Controls

As has been explained, principal elements in the effective control of transportation costs are: (1) establishment of regular routings for normal movement of commodities; (2) contact and coordination of the traffic department with other departments; (3) establishment of procedures covering such items as weighing, car-ordering, and switching; and (4) checking freight bills. The test of the effectiveness of these controls in actual operation comes in the examination of the charges made. Weaknesses and failures in control will show up in the form of excess charges for premium services, or penalty charges, such as demurrage. Very often, the penalty incurred is not directly attributable to any failure on the part of the traffic operation. It is rather a symptom that indicates some failure in such operating responsibilities as receiving, production scheduling, or inventory control.

Before considering these implications, we will describe a normal operating procedure for the verification, payment, and audit of transportation charges.

Verification and Payment

The invoice for normal transportation charges (outside of switching and demurrage charges) will be concerned with four factors: description, weight, rate, and total charge. In the verification of charges for services, you must remember that each invoice is prepared as a separate item by itself. Duplicates are common. In addition, any error made in an invoice will not be more or less automatically found and corrected by the carrier preparing the invoice. When using a verification routine, determine if the bills of lading are keyed-in on a left- or right-justified basis (right is more important). Bills of lading can have 12 to 15 numbers. Field sizes may be smaller; so when a duplicate payment run is made, you will want to sort on right-justified numbers.

Charges for services and penalties, such as demurrage, switching, and weighing, will be on a unit basis—per car or per transaction. Such invoices require verification of the number of units charged for and the rate at which the charge is made.

Freight bills are payable within time limits specified by regulatory bodies. Failure to pay within these limits is punishable by fine (has anyone seen them applied?).

To facilitate payment of freight bills in locations where accounting facilities are limited, some companies use an envelope-type draft. Bills from each carrier are listed on the face of the draft (which is drawn on a headquarters bank) and enclosed in the envelope given to the carrier. The carrier then receipts the bills and replaces them in the envelope before deposit.

1. *Weight.* Weights of bulk commodities shown on invoices should be regularly checked either with shipping weights shown on the bills of lading or with weights shown on receiving reports or vendors' invoices for inbound materials, and shipping department records or copies of customers' invoices for outbound materials. Without question, the preferable practice is checking with vendors' or customers' invoices, since these will represent the actual quantities for which accountability is established.

On incoming packaged commodities, a test check is normally sufficient. This test check should always be made on initial shipments of new commodities or from new vendors.

When bulk commodities are handled in carload lots, an independent check of gross and tare weights of incoming and outgoing cars should be made; this verification should carry through both to charges for transportation and for the materials themselves. As was previously stated, tare weights are stenciled on cars at the time when they are new or overhauled and have no great accumulation of dirt and other material. Once in operation, the car will soon exceed the stenciled tare weight; therefore, any use of this figure can result in an overstatement of the actual contained weight by an appreciable quantity.

2. *Description, Rate, and Extension.* In the case of shipments that move in normal channels, the verification of the rate will usually require reference to established routing guides or lists. Where shipments move regularly in volume, rate clerks will know the principal rates without reference to any other media. Where established rate and routing information is not available, published tariffs may be referred to.

Descriptions and rates should be checked, since the rate structure is complicated. The carrier can easily make a mistake in class or commodity rate. Within the company, the best verification of rate is possible in the traffic department, where rate clerks are familiar with classifications and rates of the company's materials and products.

As with other invoices, a check of arithmetical correctness prior to payment is desirable. In companies making numerous small shipments, this final proof is sometimes waived for smaller charges, such as those under $50. The use of a limit such as this is a question that can be determined only by testing and considering the possibilities of over- and underpayment.

3. *Treatment of Errors.* One of the difficulties in establishing routines for checking transportation charges is the comparatively short time allowed for payment. This applies particularly to railroads, where regulations usually provide that charges must be paid within 48 hours, unless special arrangements for a longer period are made. For this reason, the checking of rate and extension is sometimes postponed until payment has been made. One may argue in support of this practice that any errors developed in postaudit may be recovered by making claim against the carrier. The preparation and filing of a claim require considerable routine—so much so that usually no claim is made for amounts under $20.

As a matter of practice, prepayment verification of carriers' invoices is definitely preferred. During this verification process, errors may be corrected and the filing of claims correspondingly reduced. One company states that such preaudit resulted in correction of errors totalling $100,000 in one year. Corrections in preaudit are confined to actual error in weight, rate, and extension; a change to a classification that has not been agreed upon with the carrier is not permissible. Disputes with carriers as to classification are handled as claims.

4. *Approval for Payment.* The responsibility for checking description, weight, and rate is commonly assigned to the traffic department. In the process, a notation will be made on invoice copies or bills of lading with which transportation charges are checked that the charge has been received and passed for payment. The control plan must provide for this notation in some form as a safeguard against duplicate payment of transportation invoices. With shipment, rate, and weight verified, the approved invoice then goes to the voucher department for payment.

5. *Special Shipping Arrangements.* A usual complication (which presents some difficulty in control) arises when special terms or shipping arrangements require the maintenance of follow-up records to insure charges paid to carriers are properly handled.

For example, purchase terms may provide that incoming shipment will be collect, with allowance for freight to be given by the vendor. In this situation, current routines must provide for verification that allowance for freight is to be given by the vendor. In this situation, current routines must provide for verification that (1) allowance for freight is actually made by vendor, and (2) that amount allowed is either the same as was paid or in accordance with other provisions of purchase.

On outgoing shipments, sales terms may provide that freight is to be prepaid and added to the sales invoice. Here again, routines must insure that charges paid are billed to the customer.

One company reports that it frequently finds that a shipment handled by several motor carriers starts out as being prepaid and then ends up on a collect basis at destination. The reason is that the billing clerk for one of the connecting carriers neglects to note that the shipment is prepaid on that carrier's freight bill.

The large number of individual payments, which is the usual situation in traffic operations, makes the control of such special arrangements a matter that requires careful handling and detailed checking. An overlooked item will be buried in the large volume of transactions, and appreciable monetary loss to the company may never be revealed.

As an example of the complication of special shipping arrangements, one company has parts depots to supply parts for its machines to dealers. To encourage larger orders, dealers are asked to send in monthly orders on a set date for parts that are regularly required. As an inducement, the company pays for shipping charges on these orders. In-between orders from dealers are shipped prepaid with charges billed to the dealer. An immediate problem comes when parts depots are out of stock on a part ordered on the regular monthly order. This situation requires that, in fairness to the dealer, the back-ordered parts be prepaid when they are available. As can be readily seen, the problem of charging (or not charging) for transportation on the numerous small shipments is one that requires careful follow-up.

Postaudit of Charges

1. *Checking by Rate Clerks.* To this point, we have been concerned with the normal operating routines. The complication of rate structures and the possibility of error are so great that virtually every company finds it profitable to provide for a recheck of invoices from carriers. Rechecking is done on a postpayment basis under which the paid freight bills are reviewed by experienced rate clerks. The errors developed in this review will usually apply to rate and classification, since weight and arithmetical errors should have been found and corrected in the original voucher preaudit.

This second check of freight bills is often modified to apply only to bills for larger amounts—for example, in excess of $100. In one company that operates a number of outside plants, the home office traffic department checks freight bills sent in by plants on a selective basis. In addition to checking only the larger amounts, the checking is limited to a test check of one month in several where experience has shown that previous checking of bills from that location is not particularly rewarding in the form of recoveries.

2. *Outside Rate Audit Agencies.* The variations and possibilities for error inherent in carrier billing are well exemplified by the operation of freight audit agencies. These agencies will undertake the rechecking of freight bills on a contingent basis; a usual arrangement is a 50–50 division of amounts recovered between the freight audit agency and the company. A number of companies use these agencies and believe that the outside audit provides a good check on the effectiveness of their own rate and classification work. In one company, recoveries were so small that the audit agency withdrew from the account—and the traffic department therefore felt that its own rate checking was quite effective.

Usual practice provides that copies of claims developed as a result of audit agency examination be given to the company—or that original claims be filed by the company, which then pays the agreed share to the audit agency when collection is made.

Outside freight audit agencies can unquestionably fulfill a real purpose in the technical maze of tariffs and classifications. The amount of recoveries will give some indication of how good a rate job is being done by the traffic department. Moreover, the claims that are filed through these agencies may give the company a clue to some change that might provide economy in shipment and eliminate similar future claims.

INTERNAL AUDIT PROGRAM: CHARGES FOR TRANSPORTATION

The internal audit of charges for transportation is concerned with examination and appraisal of policies and procedures, with particular attention to the exceptions revealed in the course of the audit. The program must provide for no more than a very minor test check of rates with tariffs—or for none at all. Most companies perform no internal audit verification with tariffs, since they believe that adequate verification of rate and routing by qualified rate experts is gained through the recheck of freight bills by the traffic department rate section and outside audit agencies.

Policies and Procedures

The internal audit program begins with an examination of policies and procedures covering the verification and payment of transportation charges. It will include such points as:

1. How are weights checked?
2. If agreed weights (for example, per case of product) are used on bills of lading, how often and how are these periodically verified? (A change in container or packing case may not be allowed.)
3. In what manner is rate and routing information published to line personnel who are responsible for rate checking?
4. What control is maintained to ensure that correct description is shown on shipping documents?
5. How are rates checked before payment of charges?
6. Where errors are discovered in freight billing, how are these handled?
7. What routines are maintained to ensure that such items as prepaid freight to be billed to customers and incoming collect charges to be allowed by vendors are properly handled?
8. What are the controls against:
   a. Duplicate payment of freight charges?
   b. Shipping material that is not billed? (In one company, a carload returned for further processing was credited when returned, but not rebilled when final shipment was made. The oversight was revealed when the customer asked for billing.)
9. Are there secondary checks of freight bills by an outside agency? What were the results?

Variations from Normal Pattern

In most companies, the routines pertaining to normal shipment and receipt will be well controlled. The movement of commodities will be under constant study by the traffic department to ensure that adequate service is rendered at minimum cost. Yet, in every company, situations will arise where the normal pattern is not followed. The variations from this pattern will show up as exceptions of one kind or another—and these exceptions will normally involve payment of premium or penalty charges.

The premium or penalty charges usually will not be segregated in the accounting records. (Some traffic managers favor having this done, in the same manner that overtime payroll premium pay is often separated in payroll accounts.)

Some of the exceptions commonly found are:

1. Demurrage. Excessive demurrage may indicate poor coordination with plant receiving or shipping departments. One company reduced demurrage charges 75 percent by improving this coordination. In many instances, the cause may be entirely beyond the control of the traffic department—for example, in production scheduling.

2. Shipping via premium methods of transportation. Some of this will always happen in any company. Regular use of such facilities is open to question and may be the clue to faulty ordering procedures. More attention will be paid to intracompany shipments at premium rates if the receiving location is charged with the cost.

3. Unnecessary shipment by premium methods. For example, in one company, 100 units of material were required for immediate production operations. The vendor was instructed to ship an entire order of 1200 by air freight—even though the 1100 units not immediately required could have been sent via regular routing.

4. Shipping via premium methods without consultation with the traffic department.

5. Minimum carload weights. In this case, applicable charges result in what is in effect a premium rate. This condition applies not only to small shipments, but also to carload and truckload shipments. For example, a shipment of 21,000 pounds may be billed at a carload minimum charge for 24,000 pounds because it is less expensive to pay for 24,000 pounds at a carload rate than 21,000 pounds at the LCL rate. Thus, 3000 pounds of additional freight could have been carried for the same charge. (This example assumes loading by the shipper or bill of lading instructions to the carrier to load and assess charges.)

In this case, several questions are of interest:

1. Could a larger shipment have been made to utilize the full minimum carload weight?

2. When a shipment is known to be below carload minimum, was the smallest possible car ordered?

3. What are routines to relate orders for various sizes of cars with cubic footage of carload shipments?

In examining the exceptions found in the course of verification, a good approach is to start with the assumption that with perfect operation these additional charges would not have been incurred. Since they have been, and since some will always occur, the concern of the internal auditor should be:

1. What is the policy on premium shipments?
2. Who is responsible for approval of premium shipment or penalty charges?
3. What records are kept of the additional expense?
4. Are exceptions from policy brought to the attention of those who can do something about them?
5. What is being done in the line of preventive measures to minimize penalty charges and to reduce the number of exceptions from normal routines?
6. Where premium costs are incurred because of requests from customers for special routing or handling, what is the policy as to charging customers for the additional cost?

Internal Audit Verification

The verification procedures covering charges for transportation should be coordinated (or may be combined) with those described above in Ordering and Handling of Transportation, since possible deficiencies in ordering and handling will often be revealed in the audit of charges.

1. Select _____ invoices covering incoming material on which shipping charges were collect, including at least _____ that provide for freight allowance by vendor. Check description, weight, rate, and routing with freight billing. Check freight allowed by vendor with amount paid. Check terms of purchase orders. (For example, not cases where partial shipments of carload orders were made, and check to see that difference in rate was allowed.)
2. Select _____ invoices covering outgoing shipments. Check description, weight, rate, and routing with routing guide sheets. Verify with traffic department if routing guide sheets are not available.
3. For a two-week period, examine freight bills from railroads and trucking lines. Note such items as:
   a. Demurrage or waiting-time charges

    b. Switching charges

    c. Underloaded carload or truckload shipments

    d. Timeliness of payment.

4. For a one-month period, examine bills paid to premium-rate carriers such as Federal Express, Courier, or DHL. Check authorization for shipment, benefits received, and other pertinent items.

This phase of the internal auditing program of the traffic department should be coordinated with the accounts payable internal audit program to minimize duplication. Many of the routines will be similar to those involved in handling other payments, and it should be necessary to cover only those elements peculiar to traffic operations.

CLAIMS

Claims against carriers fall into two classes:

1. Loss and damage, in which a claim arises because of loss or damage to commodities while in the custody of the carrier.
2. Overcharge, in which claim arises because of an error made in billing by the carrier. Errors may be arithmetical, but are more often due to wrong rates or classifications.

Regulations specify definite time limits within which claims may be filed and beyond which any claim is refused.

Loss and Damage

Common carrier liability is limited to actual loss or damage while shipment is in the custody of the carrier. This custodial responsibility is modified to preclude liability in certain conditions outside the carrier's control, such as floods and strikes. An understanding of the conditions under which carriers are liable is a necessary prerequisite to filing valid claims and may also affect the decision to carry insurance against excluded hazards.

In loss and damage claims, notice must be given to the carrier within a specified period of time, and an agent of the carrier must have an opportunity to survey the damage that forms the basis for claim.

With incoming shipments, the first notice of a possible claim will be the report of receipt of material in damaged condition or in quantities less than specified on the bill of lading, packing slip, or delivery copy of the freight bill. A concealed damage claim arises when a package in apparently good condition is opened and the contents are found to be damaged.

As a service to customers, many companies will file claims for damage or loss occurring to finished products while in transit to the customer. In such claims, the necessary loss and damage report forms are completed by the customer and forwarded to the company. The amount of the claimed loss will then be credited to the customer and charged to a pending claims account.

Overcharge Claims

Overcharge claims arise in the course of checking descriptions, rates, weight, and total charges during the audit of freight bills. The simple overcharge claims will be concerned with such errors as the use of an incorrect rate or an error in extension. Beyond this, claims can become increasingly complicated. For example, one can claim an erroneous classification has been applied and that the material shipped should have been subject to a lower classification and rate. These more complicated claims will usually arise from questions raised when rate clerks in the traffic department or in outside audit agencies do expert checking of freight bills.

Control of Claims

Filing a claim provides no assurance that it will be paid in the amount claimed. The claim may be denied completely, compromised, or paid in full. Because of the uncertainty as to the exact settlement amount, some companies defer the formal recording of claims in the accounting records until actual collection is received. Control will be exercised through a memorandum account or a claims register.

However claims are recorded, a continuing and complete record of all claims should be kept. The record should not be closed until final disposition of each claim is determined.

1. *Claim Procedure.* Because claims come in from many locations as exceptions rather than as matters of routine, all receiving units should be supplied with written procedures describing the handling of loss and damage claims. The instructions should cover such matters as the necessity for making claims where the loss or damage occurs, the method of notice to carriers, completion of claim documents, notations on documents, and time limits within which claims must be filed.

2. *Minimum Amounts.* Preparation and collection of a claim requires a considerable amount of original and follow-up work. For this reason, the practice is to set limits below which claims are not filed. In some companies, these limits range from $15 to $25.

3. *Place of Filing.* In some companies, all claims are filed through the home office traffic department. In others, the local traffic units that handled the original shipment file the loss and damage claims.

Those who file claims locally feel that filing by local units expedites handling the claims, since the local traffic representative has direct contact with carriers and a more direct knowledge of the details governing the claims. Where claims are filed through the home office, correspondence from there to the field and back again is necessary to resolve any questions.

The preferable practice, where reasonably qualified traffic clerks are in the field, would appear to be having the field offices handle loss and damage claims directly—bringing the home office into the picture when claims became involved or difficult. To some degree, field handling of claims may weaken the control by the home office. Any weakening may be allowed for by providing for home office review of completed claims or by review of claims and procedures at field offices by home office traffic representatives or internal auditors.

4. *Prices on Claims.* In filing claims for loss or damage, the shipper is entitled to recover the amount of the loss to him. In case of shipments to customers, this is construed to mean that claims may be filed at the trade selling price. One company uses a form that is attached to loss and damage claims and includes the following statement: "The prices shown are the same as would have been used had the material been shipped direct to our customer. In each instance, we have given you the benefit of the lowest (wholesale) prices."

Claim Prevention

Total amounts recovered through claims are usually recorded and form an item in periodic reports, summarizing traffic department operation. When such reports are made, separating loss and damage recoveries from overcharges is essential. Loss and damage amounts represent normal transactions that went wrong. Often the fault may lie in part with poor practices or inadequate materials used in packing and shipping. Thus, large recoveries from loss and damage claims may indicate a situation to be investigated. In general, traffic departments work with other departments responsible for production and shipping to improve handling and minimize losses.

Certain overcharge claims may represent basic changes in the carrier's rate structure. When any claim of this type is allowed, the company's shipping locations should be notified (e.g., by issuing revised rate and routing guide sheets) to take advantage of the revised rates and to eliminate future similar claims.

INTERNAL AUDIT PROGRAM: CLAIMS

The internal audit of claims is concerned with the cycle from the point of determination that the basis for a claim exists to the final settlement.

Policy and Procedure

1. How are claims originated?
2. Are receiving locations provided with written procedures for handling claims?
3. What assurance exists that all differences are reported so that loss and damage claims may be filed? What are the possibilities that valid losses may not be claimed?
4. How are claims followed up to assure disposition?
5. What basis of pricing is used for claims?
6. What control exists to ensure that all claims filed are recorded in the accounting or other control records?
7. What is the minimum amount for which claims are filed?
8. What control exists over claims filed by outside audit agency?
9. What is control over handling of remittances of claims from carriers? These should clear through normal cash routines.
10. When a claim is compromised or disallowed, who approves for the traffic department?
11. What is done to analyze and correct causes of loss and damage claims?

Verification

1. Select _____ pending claims from the traffic department records. Include loss, damage, and overcharge, and several claims not settled after six months.
   a. Check for entry on accounting or other control records.
   b. Examine traffic department follow-up records.
2. Select _____ closed claims from accounting records.
   a. Check for entry on traffic department records.
   b. Check details of claims on such items as product price, inclusion of paid freight, compromise adjustments, and so on.
   c. Check to see if interest was allowed on overcharge claims over 30 days old.
   d. Check approval for compromise or settlement.

      e. Check manner in which payments were cleared into cash records.
3. Examine receiving records for a two-week period.
      a. Check to see that report was made of any loss and damage and that claims were filed according to policy.

RELATIONSHIPS WITH OTHER DEPARTMENTS

Necessity of Cooperation

Since the basic objective of the traffic department is to provide transportation service for the benefit of other departments of the company, rendering service on an optimum basis requires close coordination and cooperation with these departments.

Management policy stressing cooperation should be implemented by written procedures that describe the mechanics by which this is done. An additional and usual means of assuring departmental interest is to have the accounting distribution of transportation expense shown as a distinct cost against the operations of the department that has responsibility for the commodities that are received or shipped.

The manner of coordination will vary in each company depending on the general policies of the business and on the responsibilities assigned to each department. Some indication of details of coordination has been given in previous sections of this chapter. To bring this into focus, certain specific ways in which the traffic department works with other departments are outlined below. These are indicative and cannot be complete, since each company will present a different situation.

Purchasing and Production

In most companies, a generally satisfactory degree of coordination exists between the traffic, purchasing, and production departments. This is expressed as:

1. Providing routing information on purchase orders
2. Quoting rates applying to competitive vendors
3. Providing information on quantities necessary to secure the lowest shipping charge
4. Arranging for assembly of incoming pool car shipments from several adjacent vendors
5. Advising on best way to secure expedited delivery at minimum premium cost

6. Tracing and expediting shipments
7. Scheduling incoming shipments to meet such requirements as:
   a. Physical facilities
   b. Labor available
   c. Production scheduling

Sales and Distribution

Sometimes less satisfactory coordination exists between traffic and sales and distribution responsibilities. A common reason is the desire of the sales department to service customers in the form that customers wish. Such service is often necessary to retain business (for example, the desirability of controlling the routing of incoming commodities). The situation often cannot be handled by any set rule; certain considerations of business judgment and bargaining are principal factors in any decision. Whatever that decision may be, the traffic department should be consulted—and should point out any possible disadvantage that may be anticipated.

More specific ways in which the traffic department may cooperate with sales and distribution activities include:

1. Arranging for pool and stopoff carload shipments
2. Providing rate and routing guide sheets for shipping locations
3. Arranging for tracing and expedited shipment
4. Participating in decisions on location of branches and warehouses
5. Developing transportation cost factors to be used in pricing and budgeting
6. Scheduling outbound cars and trucks to meet:
   a. Sales requirements
   b. Production and shipping facilities

Packing and Shipping

In one company, the traffic department participated in the development of a shipping container for one of the company's products. The product was being shipped in a large, heavy, returnable wooden case. The case had to be made in varying widths to accommodate different models. The problem of developing a new container was undertaken by a packaging committee, with representatives from traffic, manufacturing, purchasing, sales, and product engineering.

The result was a savings of 100 pounds per machine by using two corrugated containers. Also, less damage occurred in transit, and cost savings were incurred, since the case no longer had to be returned.

Similar cooperative efforts can result in cost savings to the company in areas such as:

1. Better loading of inbound and outbound shipments
2. Claim prevention by improvements in shipping and packaging
3. Shipment by alternative methods

General Coordination

In many instances, proposals or activities cover several company departments. Here the essential factor is that the traffic department be a participant in discussions and decisions.

Internal Audit: Relationships with Other Departments

Since conditions relating to departmental coordination vary in each company, it is not possible to set up a program to cover coordination as a distinct section of the audit. The auditor should be alert to this matter throughout the work in the traffic department. Indications of any failure in coordination will develop in discussions with personnel and in the testing of transactions. Lack of consideration of traffic problems or failure to coordinate and utilize the special abilities of traffic personnel can be the source of unsatisfactory service and a large out-of-pocket loss to the company.

CHAPTER 7

Fixed Assets—Facilities

FACILITIES AND THEIR CONTROL

Importance of Facilities

The importance of facilities and the control over their acquisition, maintenance, disposal, and replacement continue throughout the life of a business enterprise. In any manufacturing company, the consideration and the effort devoted to the authorization, acquisition, recording, and disposal of capital assets is undoubtedly greater in terms of the values involved than in any other phase of the business operation. Extensive executive consideration and approval is a prerequisite to acquisition and generally to disposal. Carefully detailed records should be maintained over installed facilities and over the cost of their maintenance.

One reason for such care is the large values; in most companies, the fixed asset accounts are of major significance on the balance sheet. A more important reason is the vital influence that facilities and their use have on a company's operations and its profits. This factor is recognized in the common yardstick of the investment field, where one means of judging the astuteness of management is the ratio of profits to invested capital.

Decisions affecting the acquisition and utilization of facilities are long term, since the effect of a decision will last over the useful life of the facility. Any error in judgment may have a continuously adverse effect, and the ultimate loss may exceed by many times the cost of an original piece of equipment. Even when the loss is great, the tendency is often to live with the mistakes and to try to make the best of bad situations—though the results may be unsatisfactory from a profit-making standpoint.

The point in making these observations is to help the reader realize the importance of facilities to any company. Sometimes this is not understood because the amounts involved in current transactions in facilities may not be large in relation to the amounts applying to such items as sales and inventories. Hence, an erroneous conclusion may be reached that proportionately much less internal audit time needs to be spent on the relatively static fixed asset accounts than on the fast-moving sales, cost, and expense transactions. Here, as in all internal audit work, no rule-of-thumb is available by which the justifiable audit time may be allocated; each internal audit group must analyze its own situation.

Definition of Facilities

The term *facilities* in this book is a simple and broad term used to include:

Land
Building
Equipment
Machinery
Leased equipment and machinery
Loaned equipment and machinery
Furniture
Tools

For purposes of definition, facilities comprise any tangible property that is not directly consumed in the course of the normal business operation. They have four major characteristics: They (1) are actively used in operations, (2) are not held as an investment or for resale, (3) have a relative long life, and (4) have physical substance. In all businesses, the decision on the accounting treatment is based mainly on the useful life and the values involved. Borderline situations exist in every company where a decision will have to be made as to whether the cost and the useful life of an item or a class of items are sufficient to justify the effort of recording and charging off such cost over the useful life.

Coverage and Exclusions

This section is compiled from reviews of facilities controls in various large companies. These large companies have a relatively large investment in fixed assets; hence, these companies would have more completely developed plans of control over their facilities than companies where such investment was relatively minor.

Thus, the control descriptions and techniques that will be described should represent an optimum situation. In companies where facilities represent less of a control problem, such as financial institutions, the plans described may be readily modified to meet less rigorous requirements.

Some companies had virtually all of their facilities in a single location; others had factories and distribution facilities scattered over a large number of decentralized operating locations.

Limited consideration is given to land as a distinct facility. In many businesses, the purchase of land is the usual preliminary to the erection of other facilities, and the authorization over original acquisition of land is highly centralized—usually with a company's board of directors.

The controls over the purchase of land are concerned with verification that a clear title has been secured. This is handled by a company's legal department or outside counsel, and is not usually the concern of the internal auditor. (The auditor should be concerned that clear title has been obtained, but is not normally expected to inquire into the legal technicalities of that title.) Land acquisition and control present an entirely different problem in natural resource industries such as lumber, mining, and petroleum, and in public utilities and common carriers. Here the acquisition of property or rights to extract resources or otherwise use the property may be a major phase of operations that is handled by a specialized department. For example, a public utility will acquire numerous rights-of-way, easements, and options in the normal course of its operations. In such companies, an internal audit program for land operations includes such factors as control of dealings with land agents, cash advances for options, payments for easements, and similar transactions. Because the problems of acquisition and control in these companies are largely unique to the nature of their businesses, they are not covered in this chapter.

After consideration of some general factors applying to the control of facilities, succeeding sections of this chapter treat individual phases under the following general headings:

1. Authorization and Acquisition
2. Auditing the Acquisition and Construction of Facilities
3. Control over Acquired Facilities
4. Depreciation and Valuation
5. Maintenance and Repairs
6. Control of Idle and Fully Depreciated Facilities
7. Control of Facilities not Capitalized
8. Disposition of Facilities

Assignment of Responsibility

Usually, the request for the acquisition of a facility includes some statement of the saving or other benefit that is anticipated as a result of the new item. The control plan usually involves an evaluation of the claimed benefits some time after the new facilities have been acquired and placed in use. In one company, this evaluation was made by the home office engineering department; in another, by a special property analysis group; in another, a report was rendered by the department using the facility; and in a fourth, an appraisal and evaluation of the cost/benefit—present value was reviewed by the internal auditor and a recommendation was rendered to the board of directors.

Similarly, in some companies the physical inventory of facilities is the responsibility of the corporate fixed asset accounting group; in others, a local accounting unit may have such inventory as its assigned responsibility. Internal auditors should not have physical asset responsibility, since they can best evaluate the pattern of control when they can be objective in regard to each phase of the operation.

Responsibility of the Internal Auditor

The auditor's first task is to study the existing controls: what they are designed to control and the manner in which control is supposed to be exercised. Then the auditor proceeds to examine and test to determine whether the controls are operating according to plan. Finally, the auditor appraises the effectiveness of the controls and reports this appraisal to management.

The internal auditor should be particularly concerned with apparent weaknesses, failures, or omissions in the control pattern. For example, does the control over acquisition provide for audit of cost-plus and other construction projects? Is an appraisal of savings resulting from new equipment made by someone other than those who originally advocated the purchase of that equipment?

The Internal Audit Program

The assignment of responsibility and related control procedures vary among different businesses; therefore, internal audit procedures should necessarily be established on an individual company basis to reflect these differences. The control procedures described in later sections of this chapter indicate the work to be covered, which can be performed either by a fixed asset accountant or by the internal auditor. When control details are covered by other means (which is usually preferable), the internal auditor has the job of appraising how well the work is done and how effectively it fits into the pattern of control.

AUTHORIZATION AND ACQUISITION

Original Authorization

In the case of major projects, the original proposal for construction usually originates at the executive levels of a company. Plans for acquisition, construction, and purchase require long-range forecasts and planning by many staff and operating departments. Lesser projects usually originate at operating levels, and may be developed by departmental organizations.

The first step is the preparation of a request for authorization of a specific project. This request describes the proposal to acquire facilities and the purpose of the acquisition; shows the estimated cost of the proposed project; shows the anticipated influence on operating costs and profits; and gives data relating to such factors as replacements, demolition, moving cost, and employee training. The request then serves as the medium for securing the approvals required under company policy.

After proposed projects have received executive consideration and approval, a summary showing a general description, the estimated cost, and the economic justification is prepared for submission to the board of directors. The summary usually shows an estimate of proposed expenditures on major projects over a five-year period. (In one company, a major project is one where the total estimated cost exceeds $1 million.) The summary and the analysis, according to the year in which expenditures are estimated, should give a good picture of what is immediately in prospect and what is proposed for years ahead as the basis for consideration and action by the board of directors.

Considerable care should be used by internal auditors reviewing these multiyear proposals. The financial impact of approving multiyear capital expenditures can now be so significant that a corporation's financial standing and viability can be threatened (e.g., General Public Utilities, the Three Mile Island problem, and Washington state's bond crisis).

Scheduling

In companies such as public utilities, it is possible and necessary to forecast requirements and make general plans for fixed asset acquisition for a multiyear time period (i.e., nuclear power stations, oil and gas refineries). As the tentative date for beginning actual construction draws near, forecasts and plans are reviewed and updated to conform with the current situation. The forecast becomes a scheduling reality when work and expenditures are finally authorized and a specific project is assigned.

Limits and Approvals

Every company establishes certain rules covering what is to be considered a distinct project and the approvals that are required. Typical limits found include:

1. Projects under a stipulated amount ($1 million) do not have to be included in the request for board authorization and can be approved by division (a semiautonomous section of the corporation) management or a corporate vice president.

2. Specific limits are established by which actual expenses can exceed appropriated amounts before supplemental appropriation is required. A typical restriction is to require further executive authorization if the actual expense is 20 percent or $50,000 (whichever is less) in excess of the original appropriation. Such authorization is approved by the same authority as that required for the original appropriation.

3. Approved projects must be completed and closed into final capital accounts within a specified time limit. After the limit, the approval lapses; it is then necessary to secure a new appropriation if the project is to be continued.

4. In cases where division management wishes to make a major substitution or revision after a project has been authorized, such revision may be approved by general management provided that the total cost of the revised project does not exceed the original appropriation.

Economic Justification

Depending on the nature of the business and the wishes of management, there are many ways to develop the economic justification for acquisition of new facilities. Some factors that enter into the determination of the justification are:

1. Effect on direct labor and material costs
2. Effect on indirect costs
3. Effect on inventories and receivables
4. Nonrecurring installation costs
5. Employee training costs
6. Salvage value of replaced facilities
7. Effect on depreciation charges
8. Return on investment
9. Investment tax credit
10. Inflation rate assumptions

Although the usual impression is that operating management will be constantly pressing for new facilities, this is not always the case. A restrictive attitude on the part of management may result in the failure to request facilities that are really needed and that could make profits for the company. In one company, which operated an incentive plan based on decentralized profit centers, the managers sometimes would not request replacement of fully depreciated facilities that should really have been replaced. The reason was that new facilities would increase the asset base and depreciation charges and thus decrease the return on assets (investment) and profits on which incentive payments were based.

Acquisition

After projects are authorized, the next step is procurement. On a construction project, the first consideration is the preparation of drawings, specifications, plans, and schedules by or in consultation with architects and engineers. (Normally, engineering studies and architectual design on major projects are accomplished in a Phase I, which authorizes funding prior to full economic justification.)

It is customary to assign a number to each approved project and to relate all subsequent orders to the project number. Where a project is simple (for example, purchase of a new item with no installation expense), all that may be required is a single purchase order. From this simple situation, acquisition may extend to large, involved projects that entail outside purchases, company work orders, contracts for construction, and/or contracting for a turnkey plant.

The department responsible for control over acquisitions—usually purchasing or engineering—should maintain control records to insure that proper approvals have been secured before orders are placed or expenses are incurred. Detailed purchase orders and work orders should show the project authorization number.

As charges are incurred, the usual accounting practice is to clear all facilities expenditures through an account for construction in progress. To keep management informed of progress on the various projects, a periodic report is usually issued listing all open projects and showing the amount authorized, expenditures and commitments to date, the estimated cost-at-completion projections, the percentage of completion, and the amounts by which the cost of completed projects varies from the original authorization. The processes of authorization and acquisition described are straightforward and generally involve no unusual control problems.

Construction Contracts

A number of different types of contracts may be entered into on major construction projects. Those commonly found are:

1. Fixed Price (Lump Sum) Contracts, in which the contractor agrees to provide specified facilities at a stipulated cost.

2. Fixed Price Incentive (Time Cost) Contracts, in which the contractor operates on a cost-plus basis with a guaranteed maximum cost for the completed job.
3. Cost-Plus Fixed Fee, in which the contractor charges for costs and a definite amount specified as fee.
4. Cost-Plus Percentage Fee, in which the contractor's fee is set as a percentage of the costs charged to the contract.
5. Time and Material, in which the contractor charges for hours worked and materials consumed on the job. Charges negotiated in advance include overhead and fees.
6. "Target" contracts, in which the contractor charges cost plus a fixed or percentage fee. The total payments are subject to a target estimate agreed between the company and the contractor. Savings under the target cost are shared. Costs in excess of the target are usually absorbed with a penalty imposed—such as a reduction in fee.

Where new construction is to be handled by an outside contractor on a cost-plus basis, the contract should be very specific as to what is and what is not reimbursable and as to the items to which the fee is applicable, when the fee is based on a percentage of cost. In addition, the contract should specify in detail those items that are chargeable by the contractor under the terms of the contract, items for which no charge is permissible, and the details of the access by company personnel to contractor's records.

In cost-plus contracts, the internal auditor should have an opportunity to review the specifications of the contract regarding allowable charges and terms of payment before the contracts are finally executed. When this is done, internal audit work can be planned to give effective protection to the company. The auditor can then also have some constructive input to the wording of the contract. Quoted sections at the end of this chapter cover reimbursable and nonreimbursable costs that form a part of the specifications for cost-plus construction contract used by one company, typical items to be considered in negotiating and auditing a cost-plus contract.

Control of Commitments and Revisions on Major Projects

After actual work has begun on a larger project, there is the problem of maintaining control over the purchase orders and construction work orders to insure that the cost of the completed project will be within the limit authorized. A major factor affecting expenditures are the revisions that arise in the course of any project. Since such revisions are usually not provided for in the original contract, any extensive changes may have a decided effect in causing the cost of the completed job to exceed the original estimates and appropriations.

An effective method of anticipating the difficulty from this source is the maintenance of a purchase commitment record on each authorized major project. The estimated cost of each contract, work order, purchase order, or other prospective charge against the project is posted to this record. When contracts and work orders are completed, the actual cost is substituted for the commitment amount. The pending and completed items of the commitment record, plus the estimated cost of items not committed (as secured from the details of the original appropriation or the latest cost-to-complete) may be combined to provide a forecast of the completed cost. Such a forecast will provide advance warning if anticipated costs are going to exceed the original authorization, so management may take appropriate consideration and action.

One of the principal reasons construction projects exceed original estimates is that revisions and other changes are made in specifications or construction during the course of the project. Such changes can be very costly, and the costs will usually not have been anticipated in the estimates that served as the basis for the original appropriation. (Most cost-to-completes have a management contingency included for such unidentified costs. In lump-sum contracts, such extras will be charged for as additions to the contract. In cost-plus contracts, the cost of extras may not stand out specifically, since they will be merged with charges for labor, material, and other costs.

Revisions (change orders) are very difficult to control, since they are virtually inevitable in every major contract. The internal auditor should see that:

1. A definite policy exists and is followed on authorization and approval of revisions.
2. An estimate of the cost of the revision is prepared before the revision is authorized and is applied to adjust the completed cost of the project.
3. When it becomes evident that the completed project cost will exceed the original appropriation beyond allowable limits, a revised appropriation request is prepared by those responsible and submitted for approval.

AUDITING THE ACQUISITION AND CONSTRUCTION OF FACILITIES

The Audit Approach

In auditing the acquisition and construction of facilities, the internal auditor's activities should vary according to the nature of each project. The approach and the program will depend on (1) the scope and complexity of the project, and (2) the degree of control that the company exercises over the labor, materials, and equipment used or installed in the course of construction.

To bring out the differences in audit approach, we will consider separately the requirements for:

1. Purchased acquisitions
2. Construction and installation by company personnel
3. Fixed Price (lump-sum) construction contracts
4. Cost-Plus construction contracts
5. Postcompletion audit of claimed savings
6. Internal audit of cost-to-completion reports
7. Leasehold improvements

In the case of large acquisitions—such as the erection of new buildings or major manufacturing equipment—and as far as practical on other acquisitions, the internal auditor should make physical inspections periodically during the construction of the facility. The auditor's viewing of the actual facility will be essential in appraising the manner in which such items as costs and retirements are handled on the accounting records. Some corporations maintain an auditor on-site throughout the construction phase.

Purchased Acquisitions

The audit of purchases of equipment or *minor* construction does not normally present a major problem for the internal auditor. Here the entire acquisition may be covered by one or two purchase orders and a related work order to cover installation or demolition expense. A principal job of the internal auditor is to (1) determine that appropriate purchasing controls have been followed, (2) relate the purchase and work orders to the approved appropriation, and (3) be satisfied that the accounting distribution of the total cost is properly made between capital and expense accounts. At the same time, the auditor verifies that company policies relating to original approvals, approval of costs in excess of appropriations, and disposition and write-off of replaced facilities have been followed.

Construction and Installation by Company Personnel

In larger and more complex construction tasks, the auditor is faced with larger issues. All labor and material costs directly identified with such construction should be capitalized as a cost of the new assets. Determining the amount of overhead cost that should be allocated to the construction is more difficult to determine. Also, the capitalization of interest cost to the job may be necessary.

Greater internal audit effort is needed when company personnel handle the construction or installation of facilities. In such situations, the internal auditor should be alert to the possibility that costs applicable to a project may be concealed by being charged to maintenance or repair accounts. On the other hand, a generous original appropriation may be misapplied to cover repair and maintenance costs that should be included in normal operating expenses. In such projects, the auditor should review the original authorizations in relation to operating and construction budgets. Company policies should be specific as to whether such expenses as overhead and overtime premium are to be included in capitalizing the final cost of the project.

In a large operation, it is comparatively easy to introduce distorting factors. The occurrence of any misapplication may be very difficult to determine since the distorting items will be concealed in a large volume of routine work orders. Moreover, the question of just what should and what should not be applied to a facility appropriation is often debatable. Here, the internal auditor's inspection of the acquired facilities is of considerable value. In many projects, this inspection will give the auditor some basis for an opinion as to whether the related purchase and work orders appear to cover the complete costs of the new facility.

Inspections should, wherever possible, be made within the company with an engineer or construction supervisor who is familiar with the technical requirements of the work. Interviews at this time will help the auditor formulate an opinion as to the appropriate accounting treatment of the finished job. Tactful discussion may also bring out information on such important items as added work, unanticipated costs, and troubles in keeping a project within the estimated cost.

On larger jobs, the internal auditor should be satisfied that effective control is maintained over the job as it progresses. This may be accomplished by:

1. An on-the-job test check of the work being done by a number of employees, with subsequent check of the labor distribution charges for these employees on the construction accounting records.

2. A review of the current checking and controls maintained by the accountant responsible for the job cost records. Here the on-the-job inspection of the internal auditor will be valuable in appraising the controls over such costs as labor and material in relation to the physical requirements of the job.

3. Examination and analysis of any major maintenance jobs conducted in the same general areas as the construction job. Construction crews are often transferred to other work in the same areas, and

materials intended for construction are sometimes used in maintenance. Examination of the time distribution for specific employees
between construction and maintenance jobs may give an indication
of situations to be questioned. In general, the objective of the internal auditor is to be satisfied that time and material charges to
both construction and maintenance jobs appear to be justified and
reasonable.

Particular attention should be given to the final close-out of jobs from
the construction in progress account. Unusual charges or transfers to or
from maintenance or other expense accounts should be given close examination; they may represent an effort to distort the actual situation so
final reports of finished jobs may compare favorably with original estimates and authorizations.

Internal Audit Program

This internal audit program is based upon various large companies' (with
decentralized operations) programs. Each local unit has an accounting department with responsibility for verifying that home office accounting
policies and procedures are followed.

Construction Audit Program

General

Company policy with respect to the uses of and requirements for appropriations and related orders is detailed in the accounting manual. The
auditor should review accounting instructions pertaining to appropriations, orders, acquisition, transfer, and disposition of facilities prior to
the start of the fieldwork.

The scope of the audit is based on minimum requirements that provide
effective appraisal of the degree to which company policy and accounting
instructions are being followed. Coverage shall be extended, however,
when unsatisfactory conditions are disclosed and for reasons such as
change in personnel assigned to handling property accounts or initial
audits at new locations.

Closed Property Expenditure Orders

Examine all closed property orders cleared from construction-in-progress
for two months. Coverage is planned to provide a representative cross section of the annual activity; selection of consecutive months should be
avoided.

1. For months selected, secure details of closed orders and trace to construction-in-progress ledger. Examine details to determine whether charges and credits properly apply to orders and items to which posting is made. Make a physical check of equipment or facility on the floor to determine propriety of questionable charges. Where equipment has been obtained from other company units, ascertain the charge is in accordance with company policy on intracompany transfers.

2. Review property orders for approval and ascertain that all expenditures were properly identified and chargeable to approved appropriations. Note any cases where work was started or facilities were acquired prior to approval of appropriations or orders.

3. Scrutinize approved account distributions on orders and investigate any that appear doubtful. Compare with accounts charged on subsidiary progress ledger and accounts finally charged when construction-in-progress was cleared.

4. Verify that any substitutions on appropriations or property orders are approved in accordance with procedures.

5. Verify that policy and procedures are followed regarding revision of order estimates in cases of over- or underexpenditures. Note deviations in work papers and comment specifically on larger items.

6. Test check labor charge tickets for costing and approval.

7. Examine monthly report of open property orders. Investigate orders on which estimated dates of closing or estimated costs compared with cumulative expenditures may indicate delay in closing.

Open Property Orders

1. In December 19X8, review all orders open in construction-in-progress at November 30 and ascertain they are properly held open. Considerations shall include date of last charge, expiration date of appropriation, and whether the facilities are in use.

2. Examine details of all open orders for propriety of inclusion in construction-in-progress and applicability to specific orders. Extend coverage to include orders opened in December, and December postings to other orders up to time of audit. Make notation in working papers of questionable items and follow before year-end closing for appropriate action.

3. Ascertain that open items in construction-in-progress are only those that will ultimately be cleared to capital accounts.

4. Verify subsidiary ledger balance of open orders with general ledger control for construction-in-progress by independent listing

or by test checking and footing month-end reconciliation prepared by accounting department.

Fixed Price (Lump-Sum) Construction Contracts

The acquisition of facilities on fixed price construction contracts presents comparatively few audit problems where the specifications of the original contract are followed through to completion without change. The internal auditor's program should provide for such items as:

1. Examination of the provisions of the contract
2. Inquiry into how the contract was negotiated to verify that company policies in such matters as competition were followed
3. Testing payments made under the contract against contract provisions
4. Checking to see that the company is adequately protected by contractor's insurance coverage
5. Certification from company engineering department or architects that the work was completed in accordance with contract specifications
6. Checking the allocation of the total cost to fixed asset and expense accounts
7. Confirmation that the equipment is actually received, installed, and in operation.

On large projects, the contract will seldom be completed and charged for in the lump sum specified by the contract. The contract itself may have provision for variation. A common example of this is an escalation clause, which provides that the contract value be increased by the additional cost of any increase in labor or other specified items that take place while construction is in progress. In virtually every large project, changes or additions in specification or construction will be made during the course of the job.

The usual fixed price contract provides that any changes from the original contract specification be charged on a cost basis. Thus, revisions are in many respects similar to cost-plus additions and must be carefully audited. Typical items in the audit program includes checking that:

1. Extras and revisions were properly authorized and approved.
2. Charges for extras and revisions did not include charges for items included as part of the original contract.
3. The basis for additional charges was in agreement with contract provisions. Particular attention should be given to any overhead items included as additional charges.

Cost-Plus Construction Contracts

The acquisition of facilities through a contract under which the company pays the actual cost plus a fixed or percentage fee to the contractor presents the internal auditor with a real challenge—and a real opportunity. In considering the internal audit program, the auditor finds that the following important factors distinguish the auditor's approach and work on a cost-plus construction project.

1. The job usually entails major construction and high cost. Typical cost-plus jobs are the erection of a large building, refinery, or power generating station.
2. A large proportion of the items entering into cost cannot be separately identified after the project is completed (e.g., labor, equipment rental, lumber for forms, small tools used on the job).
3. Since the contractor is to be reimbursed for everything chargeable to the job—in a percentage fee contract the compensation is based upon these charges—the natural tendency is for the contractor to charge the job with as much as possible.

Consideration of these factors brings the conclusion that control over a cost-plus contract of any magnitude must be more exacting than that over a fixed price contract. A more complicated and interesting task is presented the internal auditor. Since many of the items lose identity as the job progresses, an audit of a cost-plus contract after the project is completed will have much less value compared to an audit that is performed as the work progresses.

The customary, and recommended, practice is that a company accounting representative be assigned to work on the job with the company engineer assigned to the project. The engineer will have the necessary knowledge of construction requirements, and the accounting representative can relate these to the provisions and the billings on the contract. The accounting representative may be a specially employed or assigned construction accountant working under the control of the property accounting unit. Other jobs can require a full-time accounting staff. Sometimes an internal auditor is assigned full time to construction jobs. In general, the accountant should have direct responsibility to a line accounting department, with the internal auditor making periodic audits as the project progresses toward completion.

Internal Audit Program—Cost-Plus Construction

Since each project has its own characteristics and its own contract, no uniform program exist for a cost-plus construction audit. The internal auditor reviews the contract provisions to see that they have been followed in the best interest of the company. In practice, the application is far from simple. Major construction projects are usually complicated with a wide variety of situations and problems. No matter how carefully the contract is drawn, there are sure to be borderline items and unanticipated occurrences that demand the use of judgment and influence by both the accountant on the job and the internal auditor. These difficulties may be minimized by having the internal auditor attend meetings during negotiation and review and, prior to signing the contract, concur with the contract terms relating to such matters as payment, allowable and unallowable items, and access to contractor's records.

Typical Findings

The internal auditor's responsibilities on a cost-plus construction assignment are best illustrated by typical examples of audit findings:

1. Material transferred from other jobs and charged to project as new material
2. Material used on job transferred to another job for reuse without credit
3. Office or supervisory payrolls charged directly to job. Under contract provisions, these are usually nonreimbursable overhead expenses.
4. Equipment rented and not used
5. Equipment rented and used on some other job
6. Charges for repairs to rented equipment that should have been charged to owner
7. Payroll taxes charged in excess of actual amounts payable (e.g., payroll taxes in excess of a prescribed individual dollar limit)
8. No allowance given for credits or refunds to contractor for such items as refunds for good experience on compensation and unemployment
9. Charges for sick leave, holidays, vacations, and other time not worked that are absorbed by the contractor through overhead
10. Payroll charges applicable to individuals who did not work on the job
11. Duplicate billing for material
12. Billing for material or equipment not delivered to the job
13. Incorrect pricing of labor, material, and equipment
14. Incorrect calculation of additional cost on escalation provisions
15. Cash discounts taken and not credited to the job

16. Percentage charges for such costs as overhead, profit, and insurance applied to an incorrect base

17. Rental charges for equipment exceeding the original cost of the equipment. (Most contracts provide that ownership of the equipment is transferred to the company, or else billings cease, when this situation occurs.)

The foregoing items illustrate the necessity for broad coverage and consideration of every factor entering into the cost of the contract. An outline of the duties assigned to the accounting representative on the job site is given at the end of this chapter.

Postcompletion Audit of Claimed Savings

As previously stated, a usual feature of requests for authorization of projects are representations outlining the general advantages to the company if the proposed acquisition is approved. These representations specify such items as:

1. Savings as compared with present facilities
2. Estimated time in which savings or additional revenue will recover the cost of proposed facilities
3. Estimated percentage rate of return or present value that savings or additional profits will earn on the cost of proposed facilities.

Since these claimed advantages are often one of the principal factors in deciding on an authorization, effective control requires a postaudit to compare the claims that have been made with the actual results after the facilities have been installed and are in normal operation. Operating personnel sometimes become overenthusiastic and oversold on the advantages, and are intrigued by the glamour of new equipment—and thus overestimate its profitability.

Most companies have a provision for making an examination and appraisal of claims versus actual results. Usually, these appraisals are made by the property or engineering departments in which central control of property is vested.

In one company, an audit of an installation of material handling facilities that was estimated to save $350,000 per year showed actual savings of $40,000 in the first two years of operation. Such appraisal and evaluation should be made initially by the engineering department. The internal audit department should review the engineering reports and statements as a part of the audit work on facilities.

Appraisal and evaluation of facilities representations often calls for specialized knowledge of construction, equipment, and production beyond the usual skills of the internal auditor. For this reason, the preferred practice in most cases is for the internal auditor to:

1. Verify that the postaudit of claimed advantages is being made by qualified personnel.
2. Endeavor to assure that postaudits are objective. An ever-present hazard is that the proponent of a proposed facility will consciously or unconsciously distort the report or the results in favor of original claims.
3. Verify statements in the reports made in such matters as costs, labor savings, and maintenance.

In larger projects, it may be desirable that several postaudits of claimed advantages be made. New equipment and the personnel who operate it usually go through a breaking-in period, and some time may elapse before the anticipated efficient operation is achieved. The purpose of the program should be to present a balanced, objective analysis of results in comparison with expectations. To this end, comparative results over uniform periods may be developed and reported. For example, a comparative report might be rendered showing annual savings during each year of the first three years after the completion of construction.

Internal Audit of Construction Cost-to-Completion Reports

Ideally, the internal audit of construction progress reports should be a part of the audit of field locations. By auditing these reports, the auditor can verify that they are being correctly prepared for management and that expenditures applicable to projects have been included and correctly applied. As part of this audit, open purchase orders and other commitments against appropriations should be examined to determine whether revised appropriation requests are being promptly originated where anticipated costs will exceed prescribed tolerances.

Leasehold Improvements

Leasehold improvements represent the acquisition of property whose unusual characteristic is that it will have little or no remaining value at the end of the lease period. In the internal audit of leasehold improvements, the internal auditor must make a careful review of the provisions of the lease. By doing this, the auditor can often learn of situations where expenses are assumed by the company that, under the lease, would be chargeable to the landlord. In addition, the company's plan for amortization of the cost of leasehold facility should be considered in relation to the terms of the lease.

CONTROL OVER ACQUIRED FACILITIES

Property Records

When facilities of larger unit value are acquired and placed in service, they are recorded in a property ledger. These records are usually maintained on an item basis, to provide flexibility for the inevitable transfers and changes that will occur to facilities during their useful life.

The usual property records provide space for a reasonably detailed description of the item, the serial number of any tag affixed to the asset for identification, the details of acquisition (such as appropriation number, date put into service, machine cost, installation cost, and similar items), the location, the estimated life, the basis of depreciation, and the periodic depreciation charge. Records may also provide for minor additions or replacements and for recording the date the property is disposed of, the depreciation accrued to date, and the final profit or loss as a result of disposition.

To maintain effective control, property records should be in units corresponding to the changes that might occur before the property is disposed of. For example, a machine equipped with an electric motor may normally be expected to have a motor replaced or transferred as a separate transaction during the life of the machine. If this is apt to occur, keeping separate records for the motor and for the machine itself may be advisable.

Policy on Capitalization

The following discussion is for cash-acquired assets. For acquisition cost for assets acquired through the exchange of stock, and so on, FASB No. 34 defines what should be included in the acquisition cost of facilities.

Most companies have definite policies on the minimum cost of items that would be capitalized. These amounts vary with the nature of the facilities; for example, the minimum might be $500 on office furniture, $5000 for microcomputers, $10,000 on machines, and $50,000 on buildings. Items below specified amounts are expensed when acquired. In some instances, unit records are maintained for physical control of larger noncapitalized items.

Many companies now adapt a realistic accounting policy where expenditures under a specified limit are expensed as incurred regardless of the future benefit, and expenditures above the established limit are capitalized only if the asset acquired has a measurable benefit extending the life of the asset or facility. In a large company, any item of less than $5000 unit cost (which is to be capitalized) is considered semidurable and is not recorded on an individual property record. Control is maintained over these items through other records. The total value of such items acquired each year is distributed to appropriate ledger accounts (machinery, office furniture, microcomputers, etc.), and depreciation of each year's acquisition is handled on an account balance basis until the items are completely charged off. No changes are made in the ledger accounts for any physical transactions of these items.

Identification

Most companies identify property (except real property) via asset tags with an assigned number. This number is usually on a metal or plastic tag permanently affixed to the property item. Property such as microcomputers that bear a manufacturer's serial number(s) is sometimes used instead of, or in addition to, an assigned number. Numbers should be readily visible and accessible for reporting purposes.

Location of Property Records

In companies with multiplant locations, property and related depreciation records are usually maintained in the home office under the supervision of a property control or records accountant. This practice has several claimed advantages:

1. Availability of records for use and reference by staff engineering and property personnel
2. Availability of records to handle problems on depreciation, taxes, and similar matters
3. Availability of records for use in controlling transfers and utilizing idle equipment
4. Use of home office software programs for maintaining, summarizing, and reporting values of facilities and depreciation accruals and reserves on an individual-item or summary basis
5. Summarization of facilities and depreciation for book versus tax basis, including investment tax credits

In some companies where operations were decentralized to autonomous divisions, property records are kept in the field locations. Where accounting units are adequately equipped with personnel and machines to handle property accounting, decentralization has the advantage of keeping the records closer to the physical location—with consequently reduced reporting to the home office.

In companies where formal property records are centralized, field locations usually have memorandum records of all facilities for which they are responsible. These may be continuing individual records or periodic listings prepared on home office equipment from home office records and forwarded to field locations.

Inventory

As in the case of any asset, periodic physical inventories of facilities are necessary to insure that accounting records are in agreement with actual conditions.

Considerable variation exists in practice as to the intervals between inventories in various companies. Part of this difference can be ascribed to the degree of permanency of the facilities. For example, it is not usually considered necessary to inventory large, permanently installed pieces of equipment such as boilers, turbines, and generators. It is, however, very necessary to provide for regular and comparatively frequent inventory of such items as office furniture and machines, semiportable production equipment, mobile equipment (trucks, autos, lift trucks, etc.), store equipment, and all other facilities that are readily portable and might be transferred within the company or stolen for outside use or sale.

Each company should develop its own schedule of physical inventory dependent on the characteristics of its facilities and its business environment. For example, once a year may be adequate for most businesses, unless many items are leased. On the other hand, construction companies may take inventories more frequently because of the various job sites and mobile equipment.

Responsibility for Inventory

The principal responsibility for inventories of facilities is usually found to be assigned to local operating personnel, with internal auditors test-checking data in the same manner as for inventories of materials and supplies. Where records are centralized, the field operating department secures a listing from the home office property records department as the basis for verification.

Typical assignment of responsibility for inventory taking is to the plant accountant for a manufacturing plant, or to a store supervisor or store auditor for a retail store operation.

The Process of Inventory Taking

The process of taking an inventory of fixed assets, where the number of items is small, may be no more than to check off observed items with a prepared list, noting discrepancies for further investigation.

Where there are many items, it may be desirable to set up inventory teams that use prenumbered double tags to record each piece of equipment. One copy of the tag is attached to the equipment; the other copy, showing the serial number of the equipment and a very brief description, is checked with listings and used to follow questionable items to a final disposition. This plan has the advantage of saving time in searching for items. The inventory, since it follows the physical layout, can be taken quickly and completely.

Inventory Differences

Some of the differences revealed in the physical inventory will be caused by unreported transfer or disposition; others may be caused by actual misappropriation. Whatever the reason, all significant differences should be carefully investigated and followed to a conclusion.

For some items of comparatively small value and short life, such as small tools, there may be no unit record or identification and no check on the accuracy of the inventory. In this situation, attention should be focused on the rate of consumption and the control over storage, issuance, and return to stock of the items.

Transfer of Facilities

Transfer of facilities between company units is common. The usual accounting record of transfer will provide for identification and description of the transferred item, the original cost, and the depreciation accrued to the time of transfer.

Some transfers may be a part of a project in which the transferred items are to be reinstalled or rebuilt after considerable modification. The accounting treatment used, where extensive changes are involved, is to transfer the cost and depreciation of the original item from fixed asset and reserve accounts to the new job. The asset is then set up as an item on the new job and depreciation is taken directly on that job.

Internal Audit Responsibility

The internal auditor's responsibility in connection with acquisition is discussed above. In the inventory of facilities, the principal concern is to verify that the facilities that are in use are properly recorded as to value and location on the property records, and that the items on the property records are in use by the company. In any large operation it will be impractical for the internal auditor to take the actual physical inventory of facilities. Consequently, the auditor's responsibility is to:

1. Be satisfied that the amounts in the detailed property records total to independently controlled total balances
2. Verify that inventories are taken according to company policy
3. Examine adjustments of material differences revealed by physical inventories
4. Appraise the effectiveness of the review given to vouchers for proper distribution to property accounts

444444444

5. Appraise the effectiveness of company policies pertaining to the acquisition and control of facilities

This examination, verification, and appraisal will be on a test basis, with the internal auditor determining the extent of testing. Tests should be performed from the asset to the records and from the records to the asset. In the testing and examination, the internal auditor should be alert to such factors as idle equipment that has not been so recorded, and the apparent effectiveness of the company's repair and maintenance program. In other words, the auditor should be observant to see the condition of the machinery and the state of repair of usable assets in the production stream. Idle assets or a machine shop in disarray should be questioned.

DEPRECIATION AND VALUATION

Problems of Depreciation

Depreciation is defined as the accounting process of allocating the periodic expiration of the cost of tangible property, plant, and equipment against periodic revenue. Depletion is the similar process for *natural resources;* and amortization is the term used to allocate the cost of *intangible assets.* The problem with depreciation is spreading the total cost of an asset having a life extending into subsequent accounting periods over the useful life of the facility. A number of factors make this apparently simple problem a complicated one in actual practice.

Income tax considerations are paramount in establishing any plan of depreciation. Since tax laws, rulings, and regulations are entirely different in each country, it is not feasible to give separate examples or treatment for each country. In the United States, rates and bases for depreciation are established on a general basis in internal revenue laws and specifically by negotiations between company and internal revenue agents. Tax considerations are so important as to be a governing factor in the establishment of rates—even at the expense of consistency. In practice, companies use one depreciation basis for company costing operations, and another for tax purposes to maximize both tax benefits and reportable profits to stockholders. For example, a company might use a straight-line depreciation basis for operating reports and an accelerated basis allowed by the IRS for tax purposes.

In one company, an allowed rate is developed on production machines for each hour of normal machine operation. This rate is based on normal capacity hours divided into the depreciation allowable for tax purposes. In costing, this rate is applied to the actual hours each machine is used, with the difference between the developed charge and the allowable depreciation shown as a depreciation variance in cost accounts. The entire question of what an adequate provision for depreciation may be is a matter of opinion, discussion, and dissension. Our intention is only to indicate a few of the problems in the system.

Approach of the Internal Auditor

The internal auditor's review of depreciation has to consider the dominating influence of tax considerations. The auditor must have in mind (1) the objective of seeing tax policies defined by those charged with tax responsibility (i.e., the controller) are followed to assure maximum tax benefits through depreciation allowances; and (2) the necessity of having the figures shown in operating statements presents a reasonable approximation of actual depreciation experience. These two objectives are sometimes adverse and almost irreconcilable.

In reviewing depreciation of facilities, the internal auditor should apply his knowledge of the company to discover situations where obvious distortions are introduced through established depreciation policies, and should recommend possible solutions—even though the possibility of corrective action may often not be very great because of tax implications.

Internal Audit Program

The internal auditor begins the audit with the customary testing and verification and then proceeds to appraisal and recommendation. Typical items on a program are:

1. Determine the company policies governing depreciation and check to see if they are uniformly applied.
2. Check the basis on which salvage value is established as a factor in determining depreciation.
3. Examine entries for depreciation, test checking to original control, and detail records on which calculations are made.
4. Test distribution of depreciation to cost centers and examine for reasonableness.
5. Where depreciation is taken on account balances, test-check calculations.
6. Examine debits to depreciation reserve accounts covering disposal of facilities, and note profit or loss on disposition in relation to depreciation accumulated to date of disposition. (This will bring out the variance between actual experience and estimated depreciation, and may serve as the basis for challenging the useful life assigned for depreciation purposes.)
7. Determine and check the reason for any significant debits to depreciation reserve accounts other than those covering disposals (which were previously checked).

8. Examine depreciation reserves where special rates are used. Compare method of charging depreciation in this situation with that used for similar facilities not covered by special rates.

9. Where depreciation is based on production, compare developed depreciation with depreciation allowable for tax purposes, and examine method used to account for any difference.

10. Appraise the effect of any policy followed in assessing extra depreciation charges when property is subject to abnormally high usage.

11. Appraise the effect of the policy followed in establishing the starting date for depreciation charges from an operating standpoint.

12. Verify the basis used for amortization of leasehold improvements with leases or other determining factors.

Valuation

Because any basis of depreciation is at best approximation, and because recorded depreciation is largely influenced by income tax factors, it is erroneous to make any assumption that the book value of a facility minus accumulated depreciation represents anything other than a record of value according to the books. An amount thus arrived at may have no relation whatever to the going value of this asset to the company. The book value will give no consideration to the higher costs brought about by inflation or to the possibly great difference between the estimated life on which depreciation is based and the actual experience.

Valuation of properties on a current basis is possible only if an appraisal is made by qualified experts. Such appraisals are often made in connection with new financing or to determine insurable values. Particularly where facilities have been in use to a point where they are largely depreciated, any relationship between book value and current values may be rather remote.

The proper place for consideration of this factor is in the internal audit of insurance (see Chapter 10). It is mentioned here so that the internal auditor may be aware of it in the review of facilities to see if the review of reserves indicates the use of book figures for some purpose to which they are not applicable.

MAINTENANCE AND REPAIRS

Routine Maintenance and Repairs

From the time facilities are placed in service, maintenance of one sort or another is necessary to keep them in good operating condition so the maximum useful life may be attained. In our consideration of maintenance, a distinction is made between routine maintenance and repairs and special maintenance jobs that may involve overhaul or rebuilding a specific piece of equipment.

The distinctive factor of routine maintenance is that it should be on a continuing basis. Usually routine maintenance and minor repair work will be covered by blanket orders or by the full-time assignment of employees to a specific type of work. Typical examples of routine maintenance include:

1. Minor electrical maintenance, such as replacement of light bulbs and minor electrical repairs
2. Assignment of a full-time mechanic to a specified group of production machines
3. Work under a definite schedule of repainting

It is common to find that facilities in more or less continual use are covered by a preventative maintenance program. With such a program, the facilities (such as manufacturing machines and automotive equipment) will be given periodic inspection and possible overhaul on a regularly scheduled basis. The purpose of preventive maintenance is to insure that equipment is kept in good running order and that possible major trouble is anticipated through replacement of worn parts before they cause difficulty. Preventive maintenance work is customarily controlled by schedules showing date and work to be done.

Customarily, departments responsible for the physical control of facilities (such as plant engineering) maintain individual memorandum records of each major piece of equipment. These records show such information as the type and model, vehicle identification numbers, motor specifications, and location. Charges for major repairs and overhauls will be posted to these records so the expense of maintenance may be available as a factor when replacement is considered.

Control of Routine Maintenance

The principal control problem in routine maintenance lies in the fact that the charges to blanket orders are numerous and diversified and often difficult to identify as applied to individual assets. The cost of such work is a direct operating expense and, as such, is best gauged by such means as relation to budgets or standards, or comparisons between periods.

Because so many transactions are handled as routine maintenance, maintenance orders can be misused in such ways as;

1. Balancing out time tickets for the day by writing up one as a charge to a routine maintenance order.

2. Evading policy on capitalization by charging work on larger projects, such as power wiring in connection with a machine installation, to maintenance orders.

3. Losing control of the cost of major repairs or reconstruction by charging the cost to routine maintenance. It is important that such costs be segregated so they may be given consideration for possible replacement or else be discarded.

The internal auditor's principal problem in the examination of routine maintenance orders is to be satisfied that the charges conform with company policy and that the orders are not used to conceal some items that belong elsewhere. To accomplish this is difficult and calls for knowledge of the physical facilities and for ingenuity in recognizing possibly erroneous items. The preparation of comparative statements showing such expenses for several periods should be helpful as a starting point for the internal auditor.

In this work, a sense of proportion and values is essential. For example, on a closed-out construction project for $20,000, a $200 charge for rearrangement of wiring found to be necessary is hardly important enough to justify reopening the closed-out project records. However, such a job should have been covered by a separate work order so the amount will be identifiable as additional installation cost.

Where a preventive maintenance program is in effect, the internal auditor should examine the scheduled controls over the maintenance work and test the scheduled plan against the actual work performed.

For example, check lists, customarily used for preventive maintenance, should be examined to see that they are developed by competent employees (i.e., engineering department) and properly applied by mechanical employees. Similarly, the auditor should examine any individual machine records maintained by operating departments and test how such items as repair and overhaul charges are determined for notation on the machine records. It is important that costs of labor and materials used on such records be those that are used on the accounting records.

Special Maintenance

Special maintenance includes the larger jobs that will be covered by specific orders, such as:

1. Relocation of an assembly line
2. Major overhaul of a production machine
3. Alterations to office space

These projects give rise to such questions as: What is maintenance, what are repairs, and what are capital additions? Company policy should be definite in covering the accounting treatment for these types of expenses. For example, company policy might prescribe that office alterations be charged at all times to expense, since such moves are frequent and the benefit derived from the alterations is not apt to be long.

As another example, a grinding machine may have blades that require replacement after two years, although the machine itself has a life of 10 years. Here the entire machine might be treated as having a 10-year life, with blade replacements expensed.

Control of Special Maintenance

The internal auditor's examination of special maintenance expense is concerned with such factors as:

1. The verification of authorization and testing of charges to work orders
2. Confirmation that company policy has been followed on capitalization and on charges to maintenance and repair accounts
3. Observation that costs of repairs are recorded on individual machine records so excessive costs of keeping particular machines in operation are revealed to operating management
4. Inspection to verify that equipment appears to be kept in good repair. This may be done when physical inventory is taken

Emergency Repair Parts

Where specially erected machines or facilities are in use, special emergency repair parts will often be carried in storerooms. Since the failure of an essential part in the operating machine might bring about a serious interruption in operations, such parts are kept on hand to provide insurance against interruption, although they may never be used.

The principal question on emergency parts relates to their valuation. Sometimes parts may be carried at full value on storeroom inventories— even though the machine for which they are specially designed has been worn out in service. In such cases, when the machine is discarded, the parts may have no more than scrap value. One way to handle this situation is to consider the emergency parts as a part of the machine or other facilities to which they apply, and to depreciate them on the same basis as the machine. If the parts are relatively inexpensive, they might be charged to expense upon acquisition, with an inventory record maintained for storeroom control. In general, however, if emergency parts are specifically built, there is good reason for depreciating or expensing them at the time of purchase.

Records of Used and Rebuilt Facilities

Records of facilities should conform with the actual physical items. Sometimes the cost of a major repair job will be entered as an additional charge on the existing records. The result can be a combination of charges incurred at various dates, and depreciation reserves that may be difficult or impossible to reconcile with the assets themselves.

The purchase and installation of used machinery or other facilities present somewhat similar problems. The remaining useful life of the facility may be difficult to establish, and the complete installation may comprise a combination of new and used items.

As previously mentioned, a common practice where major alterations are made in a facility is to charge the gross book value of the original facility (cost and depreciation) into the construction-in-progress job records. Upon completion of the work, a new record is created for the rebuilt facility; thus there are no confusing combinations of records showing different dates, values, and reserves for what is really a single item.

The internal auditor should examine the final recording of used and rebuilt facilities in the property accounts to verify:

1. Individual property records conform to the actual physical facility as it is being used.
2. Values recorded represent a conservative valuation of used or rebuilt facilities as compared with the cost of a comparable new unit.

CONTROL OF IDLE AND FULLY DEPRECIATED FACILITIES

Idle Facilities

Over the course of time, changes will take place in manufacturing or distribution, in factory or in office, that will result in the replacement or the lack of use of certain facilities. Where replacement of older facilities occurs, the customary practice is to dispose of the old facilities when the new are acquired. As far as control is concerned, such replacement presents no particular problems. (The control over disposition of facilities is covered below.)

A different situation arises when facilities are rendered idle by some change, such as the closing of a branch office. In this situation, some furniture and equipment may be in good condition and available for use elsewhere in the organization. Company policy usually provides that it will be retained, rather than sold to used furniture and equipment dealers paying low prices.

In most companies, the usual practice is to provide for clearing all records of available facilities into a central unit, such as property control or purchasing. All orders for new facilities are then channeled through the central unit to see whether the requirements can be met from the stock of idle equipment.

This simple method of control has certain problems that may affect the handling just described. Probably the most important of these relates to the condition of the idle equipment. As is only natural, any facilities that are released by an operating unit will be the poorest or oldest.

The first point of control is examination of surplus facilities to see that the used equipment is of good appearance and in good working order.

Another point to consider in the control of idle facilities is the probability of future use. It is very easy to incur storage and depreciation charges on something that may never be used and might better be scrapped immediately. Particularly in the case of much manufacturing equipment, high obsolescence because of constant development makes any prolonged retention on an idle basis a questionable practice.

Human beings seem to fall naturally into two classes: those who are overly inclined to save items that may have little possibility of future use, and those who will discard items at the first reasonable opportunity. Both types are found in every company, and one of the problems is to see that the first group does not hold on to items that are better discarded and that the second group does not discard items too soon. This is naturally difficult to allow for in an internal audit program, but it is a factor that cannot be disregarded.

Accounting for Idle Facilities

Customarily, the costs and depreciation charges on idle facilities are separated from the accounts used for facilities in active operation. The reason is that inclusion of these nonproductive facilities results in distorted costs and expenses for the productive operations.

Internal Audit Program

The internal auditor's program for idle and fully depreciated facilities should include examination and appraisal of:

1. Control over idle facilities
2. Physical condition of idle facilities
3. Cost of maintenance of idle facilities
4. Accounting treatment of fully depreciated facilities

If idle property is leased to outsiders, the internal audit program should provide for reviewing to ascertain if:

1. Income from leasees is properly controlled and accounted for.
2. Terms of leases are followed in such matters as charges for repairs, taxes, insurance, and similar items.

CONTROL OF FACILITIES NOT CAPITALIZED

Expensed Assets

In every business, there are assets that have a comparatively long-term life, yet that are not included in capital asset accounts. These include:

1. Assets with a normal life or a minimum value below the standards for capitalization set by company policy, such as small tools, jigs, dies, plates, and furniture and equipment
2. Those acquired for a specific job—such as a research project—that are later transferred to active service

Assets below Minimum Standards

As mentioned above, assets below minimum standards for capitalization will be found in every company. Because such items as small tools may not be capitalized, certain weaknesses in control exist as compared with capitalized items where detailed individual records are usually kept to record asset and depreciation values. A further factor is the attraction that many small tool items offer to employees and contractors—either for use in home workshops or for outside sale.

Consequently, inventory records must be maintained. In general, the following control measures are used:

1. Carrying small tools as storeroom inventory items. When a tool is withdrawn for use, the employee withdrawing it must sign for the item.
2. Where such small tools as micrometers and surface gauges are used regularly in production, a memo record is maintained of the small tools for which each employee is responsible.

Less consistency in practice will be found in controlling such items as office furniture and equipment having value below the minimum set for capitalization. A principal variant arises in the limits themselves. In some companies, the limits are set so low that everything is capitalized. In others, a higher limit eliminates capitalization of all items, including $10,000 microcomputers. In general, the belief is that the control of detail items costs more than the items themselves.

Expensed Assets Transferred to Active Service

A common example of the transfer of expensed assets to active service occurs in connection with research projects, which call for the purchase of certain equipment. Since the outcome and the value of the project may not be predictable, the conservative and usual practice is to charge anything purchased for the project to research expense. When the project is completed, some of the equipment purchased or created in the project may have value for use in normal operations.

In this situation, assuming the equipment value and life expectancy are in conformity with company policy on capitalization, the preferred practice is to establish a sound value for the equipment. This value is then credited to the cost of the research project and charged to the fixed asset account.

Internal Audit of Expensed Assets

The internal audit of expensed assets should cover such items as:

1. Examination of the record-keeping system of expensed items
2. Comparison of total charges for expensed facilities with standards, budgets, or previous periods
3. Examination and appraisal of methods used by operating personnel in controlling purchase, issuance, and follow-up of small tools
4. Examination of procedures assuring the return of small tools and other company property at the time of an employee's transfer or termination of service
5. Test check of detailed charges to expense accounts for items that should be capitalized under company policy
6. Examination of methods by which special research projects are closed out and of how resulting residual equipment is handled

Facilities Not Owned

Commonly, not all of the facilities used in a business are owned. For example, automobiles and trucks are often leased. Buildings are often not owned, particularly in the case of retail stores or branch sales offices. In manufacturing businesses, dies or similar specialized production equipment may be owned by customers. Also, some states and local authorities will build and lease buildings to companies (at minimal cost) to bolster their economy and to increase jobs for their area.

In the United States, entire defense plants and production machinery may be owned by the federal government and operated by a defense contractor (Government Owned Contractor Operated (GOCO). In this particular instance, contractors are required to maintain control records in accordance with government requirements.

Internal Audit of Facilities Not Owned

In the internal audit of facilities that are leased or used by the company, the first requirement is a careful review of the terms under which the facilities are leased or used. Particular attention should be given to the responsibility for such items as cost of repairs, replacement, alterations, and payment of taxes. Expense and other records should then be examined to verify that the provisions of the rental or other arrangements have been followed.

One of the most frequent violations of rental agreements is repairs. When something needs repair, particularly in an emergency, instinctively the item is fixed—and the cost absorbed.

Another factor to be verified is that the interests of the company have been protected. This will require examination to see that the company is insured against destruction or damage to facilities and for public liability.

DISPOSITION OF FACILITIES

Physical Disposal

The life cycle comes to a close when facilities are finally disposed of. The usual means of disposition are sale, trade in, scrap, or demolition. The first concern of control is the approval for disposal and the physical handling incident to disposition.

The internal audit of disposals should cover such points as:

1. Was disposal authorized and approved in accord with company policy?
2. If disposal was made for any reason other than wearing out, were the surplus items cleared for possible use elsewhere in the company?
3. Were items disposed of cleared through prescribed procedures for scrapping or other disposal?
4. Does the salvage value obtained appear reasonable?
5. Were any cash proceeds from disposal properly received and controlled?

Clearance from Accounting Records

Where facilities are individually identified by tag number and individually recorded on accounting records, the accounting record of disposal presents no particular problem. The elimination of the assets and the related reserve is all that is required.

A different situation exists when items below the limit set for individual record are recorded in total by year of acquisition or other group identity until the original cost has been completely written off. Since individual items will not be identifiable in the property accounting records, the usual control will be to verify that total depreciation is accumulated to the amount of the total original cost, and that cost and related reserves are then written off the books.

In cases where the facilities are individually recorded, the internal auditor's program should provide for test checks of such points as:

1. Credits to asset accounts and charges to depreciation accounts to eliminate disposed-of items.
2. Taking profit or loss on facilities disposed of to provide optimum tax advantage. For example, where facilities are traded in, it sometimes is preferable from a tax standpoint to sell the replaced facilities rather than to use the trade-in value to reduce the purchase price.
3. Clearance from asset and reserve accounts of all related costs, such as installation costs and special power wiring, when an installed piece of equipment is disposed of.

The outlines that follow should be helpful in showing some of the factors to be taken into account in the negotiation and administration of a cost-plus construction contract.

These outlines differ since they come from different companies. Use these as guides and tailor them to your individual needs.

COMPANY A REIMBURSABLE AND NONREIMBURSABLE COSTS UNDER A COST-PLUS CONSTRUCTION CONTRACT

Contractor's Costs To Be Reimbursed with Fee

Owner agrees to reimburse contractor in current funds for all costs described, which are approved by owner as necessarily incurred for the proper execution of the work, and which are paid directly by contractor. The fee shall apply to:

1. Wages paid to labor employed directly by contractor in the performance of the work at this site;

2. Salaries of contractor's employees stationed at the site of the work in whatever capacity employed. Contractor shall furnish to owner a list showing salary rates of such employees;

3. Remuneration, the terms of which are previously approved in writing by owner, for the time actually spent at the site by contractor, a member of firm, or an officer of contractor, in the capacity of job supervisor;

4. The net cost to contractor of all material supplied including miscellaneous supplies, fuel, and lubricants;

5. The cost to contractor of all subcontracts; fees paid to subcontractors doing work on a cost-plus basis are excluded (see contractor's costs to be reimbursed without fee, below);

6. Permit fees; royalties; workmen's compensation; public liability and property damage insurance premiums; damage for infringement of patents; and costs of defending suits that may arise as a result of the use of equipment or processes furnished or specified by owner; and for deposits paid out and loss by causes other than contractor's negligence;

7. The cost of telegraph and telephone service, express, shipping, and freight, postage and similar costs incurred in the performance of, and for the benefit of, said work;

8. The cost of trucking by contractor's truck, for the benefit of the work, at ICC, negotiated, or other approved rates.

9. Rental charges at rates approved in writing by owner for construction equipment furnished by contractor, whether owned or rented from others;

10. Cost of construction equipment and tools purchased or leased by contractor, with the approval of owner, and used exclusively on the work;

11. Expense of loading, unloading, erecting, dismantling, and hauling contractor's equipment and tools from contractor's office, storeroom, or yard to the site of the work and back;

12. Expense incurred in making repairs to construction equipment and tools necessitated by ordinary wear and tear.

Contractor's Costs To Be Reimbursed Without Fee

Owner agrees to reimburse contractor for all the costs described hereunder that are approved by owner as necessarily incurred in connection with the proper execution of the work and paid directly by contractor, but the fee shall not apply to:

1. Losses and expenses, not compensated by insurance or otherwise, sustained by contractor in connection with the work, provided further that they have resulted from causes other than the fault or neglect of contractor, and that written notice of claim for such losses if filed with owner within 30 days from the time they are incurred. Such losses may include settlements made with the written consent and approval of owner.
2. All applicable federal and state taxes or charges levied on contractor and based on wages or salaries of labor employed on said work that contractor is by law required to pay; provided that (a) if at any time during a tax year, the total payments made by contractor to any employee attain the amount fixed by law, on which such taxes or charges are levied, whether such payments are on account of work done for owner or for others; the contractor shall make no further charge to owner for this purpose on account of such employee, and provided (b) unemployment taxes shall be computed at the statutory rate or at contractor's merit rate, whichever is lower. Contractor shall notify owner immediately of any change in his rate and the date it becomes effective.
3. Fees paid to subcontractors doing work on cost-plus basis.
4. Sales, transportation, and all other direct taxes.
5. The proportion of the labor payroll required by any employee welfare or comparable fund.

Contractor's Costs Not To Be Reimbursed

Owner will not reimburse contractor for, or pay a fee on, any of the following:

1. Salary of contractor if an individual; or salary of any member of contractor; if a firm, or salary of any officer of contractor, if a corporation; except as covered by "Contractor's Costs to Be Reimbursed with Fee," Section 1, above.
2. Salary and expenses of any person while employed in contractor's main office.
3. Overhead, or general items of any kind, except those that may be properly included under "Contractor's Costs to Be Reimbursed with Fee," Section 1 above, or "Contractor's Costs to Be Reimbursed Without Fee," Section 2 above.
4. Interest on capital employed either in plant or for expenditures on the work.

5. Cost of major repairs to rental construction equipment, used on the work either owned or rented by contractor.

6. Losses and expenses incurred through fault or neglect or both of contractor, his employees, agents, and subcontractors for any of them. This includes theft of tools or equipment and repair or labor cost, making good of defective workmanship and repair of damage of owner's property occasioned by such fault or neglect.

7. Damage for infringement of patents and cost of defending suits that may arise as a result of processes used or material furnished by contractor but not specified by owner.

8. Any item of equipment or tools loaned by owner for use on this work.

9. Small tools that may be necessary to accomplish the work, such as:
   Hammers, mallets, bull points, pinch bars
   Levels and blocks
   Shovels and spades
   Ladders: step, straight, extension (not over 20 feet).

Costs Paid Direct by Owner

The costs of the following items will be paid directly by owner, and no fee shall be paid contractor thereon:

1. Contracts for equipment and such other material that owner may elect to purchase direct;

2. Contracts placed by owner with others for labor or for materials or both;

3. Premiums on fire insurance.

Contractor's Records

Contractor shall check all labor supplied and entering into the work, and shall keep such full and detailed accounts of all costs as may be necessary for proper financial management, and the system shall be such as is satisfactory to the owner. Contractor shall keep daily time sheets for employees and other personnel engaged on the work, which shall show the name and classification of each person; also the number of hours worked and a description of work done by each person. These sheets shall be approved each day by the owner. Owner shall be afforded access to the work and to all contractor's books, records, correspondence, instructions, drawings, receipts, vouchers, memoranda, and so on relative to this work, and contractor shall preserve all such records for a period of two years after final payment, during which time the owner shall complete any audit that may be desired. Should discrepancy or question arise, the records shall be preserved until an agreement is reached.

COMPANY B EXAMPLES OF ITEMS TO BE CONSIDERED IN NEGOTIATING OR AUDITING A COST-PLUS CONSTRUCTION CONTRACT

Labor

1. Wage rates should be agreed upon in the contract or verified by reference to prevailing labor rates.
2. Overtime or night shift work should be approved by a company representative in advance.
3. Wages paid to which the contractor's fee would apply should exclude the premium portion of overtime, travel expense, and time not worked (vacation, sick leave, etc.). Time not worked should also be excluded from costs to be reimbursed to the contractor.
4. Payroll taxes are normally included in the base for computing contractor's overhead and profit. The amount of payroll taxes reimbursed should be limited, however, to actual cost, unless negotiated at a fixed rate.

Materials

1. The company should receive credit for deposits made on containers and drums that are subsequently returned.
2. Prices for used material furnished by the contractor should be agreed upon in advance.

Equipment

1. Equipment rentals for contractor-owned equipment often include an element of overhead, which should be excluded from the base for overhead and profit. Equipment rented for the job by the contractor from outside sources is included in the base.
2. Normal wear and tear to equipment should be absorbed by the contractor as it is covered by the rental fee. Unusual damage to equipment directly attributable to the job is usually reimbursable.

Miscellaneous

1. The company should approve subcontracts before they are placed.
2. The subcontractor's total charges, including his fee, should be included in the base for the prime contractor's overhead and profit.
3. Contractor's overhead and profit is usually payable on taxes such as transportation, gasoline tax, and all other direct taxes.

COMPANY C ON-THE-JOB ACCOUNTING AND CONTROL PROCEDURE FOR COST-PLUS CONSTRUCTION CONTRACTS

A. Check incoming materials, supplies, and equipment purchases.
   1. Verify count to receiving copy of purchase order if shipment is complete and purchase order is on file.
   2. Verify count and record portion received on receiving copy of purchase order. If shipment is partial and purchase order is on file, make up separate receiving report for each portion received.
   3. Record receipt on receiving report if no purchase order is on file.
   4. File common carrier claim when necessary.
   5. File supplier claim when necessary.
B. Maintain alphabetical file of receiving copies of purchase orders (and receiving reports).
C. Approve supplier's invoices for payment, attaching the following supporting evidence:
   1. Receiving copy of purchase order or receiving report, including attachments, if any
   2. Approval for payment (sticker)
   3. Partial shipment (stamp) if necessary
   4. Accounts payable copy of purchase order
D. Maintain freight paid and allowed register.
E. Maintain rental equipment register.
F. Approve equipment rental invoices for payment.
   1. Adjust for idle time charged after approval of engineer-in-charge.
   2. Adjust for repair costs, if not our responsibility.
   3. Adjust for overcharges based on contract rate.
   4. Adjust for rental fees on equipment not on job.
G. Maintain daily labor report.
H. Approve payrolls for disbursement.
   1. Verify to daily labor report for period covered.
      a. Hours worked
         (1) Straight time
         (2) Overtime
      b. Number of workmen, by classification
   2. Check extensions and addition.
   3. Verify rates paid to contract or union schedule.
   4. Eliminate vacation or sick time charged, if not provided for in contract.

     5. Verify deductions.

        a. FICA, not to exceed actual deductions in calendar year

        b. State and local payroll taxes, if any

        c. Federal income tax

I. Maintain earnings records.

J. Approve workmen's compensation insurance invoices for payment.

     1. Verify to earnings records for period covered.

        a. Gross payroll, excluding overtime premium

        b. Breakdown by work performed, for example, carpentry, masonry, and so on

     2. Verify premium rate charged to insurance department schedule.

K. Maintain returned goods file.

L. Maintain returnable containers register.

M. Maintain nonexpendable tool register.

     1. Verify inventory at least weekly.

        a. Report disappearance to engineer-in-charge.

        b. Follow contractor for credit for missing tools, if approved by engineer-in-charge.

N. Approve travel and living expense reimbursements for payment.

     1. Verify to contract terms.

        a. Individuals covered

        b. Allowances charged

O. Maintain gasoline purchases register.

     1. Arrange for contractor to obtain refund for tax paid on gasoline used off-highway. Request refund periodically.

P. File refund request for excess state unemployment taxes at the end of calendar year.

     1. Request the State Unemployment Compensation Committee to furnish rate paid by contractor.

        a. A favorable experience over a three-year period usually reduces the rate.

     2. Determine tax reimbursement that should have been paid to contractor by multiplying contractor's rate by total of wages paid for any individual.

     3. Subtract reimbursement that should have been paid from actual payments made to arrive at amount of refund expected.

     4. Follow up with contractor for credit.

Q. Approve contractor's statements for payment.

     1. Total supplier's invoices (which have already been audited and attached to receiving reports, approvals for payments, etc.).

2. Check extensions and additions of supplier's invoices.
3. Verify that cash and trade discounts taken by contractor have been passed on.
   a. Discuss missed discounts with engineer-in-charge and contractor, if substantial.
4. Verify fee charges to contract terms. Obtain approval of engineer-in-charge if based on percentage-of-completion basis.
5. Verify miscellaneous charges to contract.
   a. Fixed percentages of various bases
      (1) Percentage of gross payroll for FICA and state taxes for any individual
   b. Overhead charges of various kinds
6. Eliminate charges not in accord with contract terms.
   a. Small tool costs when included in fee
   b. Rental tool repair costs when included in rental fee
   c. On-the-job bookkeeper's salary when included in overhead and fee

CHAPTER 8

Personnel

INTRODUCTION

The cost of labor is the largest dollar expense for many companies. In addition to wages, salaries, commissions, and bonuses, also to be considered are the company's cost of unemployment insurance, social security (FICA), medical and other insurances, pension and savings plan costs, and other employee benefits (clubs, tuition reimbursements, cafeterias, seminars, conferences, and employee-assistance programs (alcohol and drug rehabilitation, and sometimes financial and emotional assistance)). In spite of this major investment in their personnel, the company shows no asset on their balance sheet! The only mention on the financial statements appears as period costs. In recent years, however, companies have begun to emphasize the importance of these costs by showing and commenting on the total labor cost of employees in their annual reports.

For purposes of this chapter, personnel is split into two main operational areas:

1. The operations of the personnel department as an integral part of the payroll function (its traditional role), that is, hiring, promotions, and other activities, and terminations, and
2. The services provided by the employee relations department, for

example, continuity programs, employee benefits, training, and employee relations.

The traditional role of the personnel department is hiring individuals, initiating and processing payroll additions, status changes, and termination transactions, employee counseling, and termination interviews.

In many organizations, personnel services have grown and become more important as a result of the various federal and state laws, as increasing employee benefits are added, and as the cost of the various medical, savings, and retirement plans increases. These areas may not receive the amount of audit attention and analysis they deserve if auditors continue reviewing the traditional role of the personnel function.

Compliance with the increasing number of federal and state statutory and regulatory agency requirements may result in potential exposure to an organization. Included among these programs are the Affirmative Action Program (AAP), Equal Employment Opportunity (EEO), the Equal Pay Act of 1963, and the Age Discrimination in Employment Act. Among the agencies involved are the Equal Employment Opportunity Commission, the Department of Labor (federal and state), state unemployment commissions, the Social Security Administration, the Internal Revenue Service, and the Commission against Discrimination.

The primary objectives of the personnel function could be to:

1. Provide personnel to meet corporate and department needs.
2. Meet staffing requirements through recruitment orientation and training.
3. Insure that each employee is properly classified and appropriately compensated in accordance with that classification.
4. Provide an employee relations program to maintain and motivate employees.
5. Provide employee benefit programs to protect employees and their families in case of serious medical problems or death.
6. Handle union negotiations, if any.

Usually more policies are related to personnel than to any other function. These policies should (1) reflect management's current employee and community relations philosophies, and (2) adhere to established federal, state, and local regulations.

Analysis of Current Activities

Care must be exercised to properly identify where certain activities take place. The larger the company, the greater the possibility that activities are split between headquarters and the field locations. In such cases, determine what activities are plant activities and responsibilities.

EXHIBIT 8–1
Comparison of Staffing
Company Versus Industry Averages

Function	Industry Average	Company
Staffing	20%	15%
Training	5	15
Personnel evaluations	5	10
Union labor relations	20	10
Employee relations	15	20
Medical, health, and safety	15	10
Wage and salary administration	20	20
Total Personnel Staffing	100%	100%

As with most operational audits, the analysis of trends and activities is important to understand how a department functions. These statistics can permit quantification and provide a basis for comparisons with other similar locations as well as with prior and subsequent audits of the same facility. Comparison of this or similar data may already exist at group or corporate headquarters, or at the local plant, and may include:

1. An analysis of arbitration decisions
2. Turnover ratios for various classes of personnel
3. Recruitment and employment costs
4. Staffing ratios as related to total employment and sales
5. Ratios of supervisors to workers by department
6. Accident frequency and severity measures
7. Workman's compensation costs
8. Unemployment compensation costs
9. Area wage and salary surveys
10. Analysis of wage and salary practices and merit review programs
11. Benefit plan participation ratios
12. Human resource planning
13. Comparison of company personnel staffing versus industry averages in a manner illustrated in Exhibit 8–1

The following documentation should be in the personnel department:

1. Union agreements, including highlights such as dates of agreements and the current expiration date of the contract, rates and their effective dates.

2. Governmental (state, local, and federal) regulations applicable to the function
3. Policies and procedures pertaining to the function

THE TRADITIONAL ROLE

The Payroll and Personnel Cycle Assignment of Responsibilities

Personnel departments are responsible for maintaining an independent and complete identification record for each employee and for initiating additions, deletions, transfers, and rate changes to payroll records. All changes to payroll records must be supported by management approval according to the level of approval required by the division/company/unit. Normally, records pertaining to exempt employees will be maintained by the headquarters/division personnel offices. Individual plant personnel departments are usually limited to records pertaining to nonexempt employees only.

Exempt personnel are not paid overtime due to the nature of their job duties and classifications. These employees may be set up on payroll records to be paid automatically, and adjustments are only made by exception. Exceptions are then recorded in the subsequent pay period. Nonexempt personnel are composed of the hourly workforce, and those salaried employees whose duties and responsibilities are such that if overtime is required they are paid for the additional time.

One of the primary responsibilities of the personnel function is hiring personnel. The usual process includes:

1. The review of an existing (or the approval and grading of a) job description,
2. The processing of an approved personnel requisition,
3. An internal search for qualified individuals and, if unsuccessful,
4. A search of resumes on file;
5. Outside advertising for the position,
6. Screening resumes to bring in qualified candidates,
7. Setting up appointments and interviewing qualified candidates,
8. Evaluating candidates, and
9. Making a decision to hire an individual.

Job descriptions are necessary and are used to evaluate one job against other jobs in other disciplines in the company and to measure duties and tasks within a department. Accordingly, much thought and effort should be placed in making the document as accurate as possible. Due to changes in laws and regulations, it is desirable that job descriptions be reviewed at least every two or three years.

Personnel requisitions should be based on actual workload, preferably on a zero-base budget. Requisitions should be processed by the departmental manager, and require at least one-over-one approvals if the position is budgeted. Additional approvals should be required if not budgeted. Personnel approvals should also be required to verify that the job is properly evaluated and graded.

Major companies usually have an internal search and/or job posting to inform current employees of job promotions. Companies wish to keep employees with promise as the employee learns the company and its environment. New employees have to adapt to their new environment.

While some companies encourage the hiring of relatives, others have definite policies discouraging nepotism. Knowing one relative is already employed in the company will motivate related employees to do well, so as not to embarrass the other. On the other hand, it is improper for one relative to supervise and give special, favorable treatment to a relative. (This information is presented for the auditor's awareness and consideration.)

Companies look at job advertisements in one of two ways. First, they may believe the company's name is very desirable and, therefore, will advertise with the company's name; or, second, they may not wish to identify themselves so that they will not have to answer all candidates who sent letters in response to the advertisement. Many firms also utilize placement agencies.

Other companies utilize employee referrals. The company pays money ($500) for any individuals hired who were referred by an employee. The logic is that the company saves money by not having to pay for advertising. Also, the applicant is usually told about the company by a satisfied employee. This generates desire and motivation by the applicant to work for the company. The current employee usually will not recommend an applicant who will reflect poorly on the current employee.

When candidates are brought in to interview, or for walk-ins, documentation is created and retained for each candidate interview. This includes the required employment application and other statistical data for EEO and AAP requirements.

Interviewing and screening candidates may be done first by personnel, with recommendations made to a line manager; or the interviewing and screening of candidates may be done by personnel immediately followed by a second interview by the line manager. The screening process is intended to ensure the candidate has the required skills, education (or equivalence), and interest to effectively fill a specific position.

Initial offers may be verbal to insure the candidate's interest in the position. However, written offers indicating the starting salary (stated as a monthly or similar dollar term), the position title, the supervisor, and any other specific items requested should be forthcoming. Offer letters are sometimes sent under the signature of the new employee's manager, while others are always sent by the personnel department. The offer should be made in accordance with the dictates of the company's policy and procedures and subject to the passing of a company physical and successful reference checks.

Among the multitude of forms for new hires to fill out should be medical, life insurance, payroll data, retirement, and savings plan data, bonding data, assignment of invention/patent, and other data regarding the new hire's family if benefits apply to them.

Payroll is responsible for maintaining similar but independent employee records and for receiving and processing additions, deletions, transfers, and rate changes as directed by the applicable personnel department.

Obtaining References

Although downplayed by some companies, we cannot overstate the case for thorough checks of employee references. Because (1) checking the current employer is usually difficult if not undesirable, (2) employers normally restrict the amount of information they are willing to give out on prior employees, and (3) most references given are usually friends, or people giving favorable feedback. Thorough collaborative checks should be made of prior supervisors.

Payroll Input

As previously stated, personnel will be supplying payroll with new-hire data to initiate a new person on the payroll. Good segregation-of-duties controls state that personnel is the only department to initiate these transactions. No matter who processes the input data, both personnel and payroll records must be in balance before and after updates. On-line system controls should allow for separate access to read and separate access to write or update payroll-related data.

No other accounting system impacts every employee in the company. No other system is so subject to criticism. Most corporate officers will condone minor errors in any system other than payroll. With such high visibility and concern, every precaution should be taken to ensure the payroll data are accurate.

Personnel should also define or dictate and/or recommend the final day to process changes in the payroll cycle in coordination with the payroll department's processing cycle. Departmental managers will have to abide by these schedules or increases for their employees will be delayed. Retroactive increases are to be discouraged, if not totally disallowed.

As a check and balance to the payroll function, personnel must receive and verify all activity it submitted for processing. Edit and activity reports must be reviewed and all exceptions cleared. This activity includes all payroll information for new hires and status changes impacting financial, tax, and personnel data.

Salary Change Activity

Major corporations usually have set criteria to guide managers as to how much of a merit increase to give employees based upon their performance and position within a given salary/wage range. Union contracts or other bargaining entities guide increases for line workers. Promotions and other changes in job classification usually do not apply to this established criteria.

Most corporations have payroll performance grids to help guide supervisors in the size of a salary merit increase. Based upon a person's (1) position within a salary grade, and (2) job performance during the prior period, a percentage increase range is dictated.

The personnel department's responsibilities should include the verification of proper percentage increases based upon performance in accordance with the published grid. All salary activity (not defined by contract) should be approved by someone in salary administration. The person's signature will verify the accuracy of the percentage increase in accord with published guidelines.

Transfers

Transfers involve the movement of an employee or group of employees from one location to another (normally another city is implied) because of promotion, staff reduction, or corporate need.

Documentation and procedures should be similar in all cases, including the physical transfer of files, payroll charges, and benefit and insurance coverage. The organization should have policies and procedures for such matters as (1) moving costs, temporary relocation costs, housing closing costs (on the sale and purchase of houses), and so on, (2) the selection of a carrier for the moving of household goods, and (3) the proper prior authorization for the approval of the move and expenses.

Corporate procedures should be in place to ease the relocation burdens for the employee. A personnel representative and a relocation service is possibly hired to introduce the employee and family into the new location. Relocation and housing closing costs are sometimes absorbed by the company. Coordination is necessary with the payroll and tax departments to assist the employee with laws and regulations usually not addressed on an annual basis.

Separate expense reports are required to identify the move and house-hunting trips so that accounts payable and the tax department can accumulate these moving costs and determine the allowable and unallowable costs and the subsequent tax payments for salary equalization for the employee.

Employee Records

Personnel is also charged with maintaining the accuracy of the employee data base for both active, retired, and other terminated employees. These historical records are subject to access (potentially) for 30 years and must be planned accordingly.

Terminations, Transfers, and Resignations

Termination is the voluntary or involuntary release of an employee or group of employees. One of the highest levels of potential exposures to the corporation can be involuntary termination of employees. Therefore, a standard procedure should be defined, followed, and documented to ensure that all activities have been completed and are correct.

Payroll is notified as soon as practical of terminations. This is very important in that some state laws require that an employee be paid within 24 hours of separation. Payroll can be notified either directly by the supervisor or through the personnel department.

Since corporations usually invest substantially in their employees, much concern should be given whenever individuals leave the company's employ. The real reasons why an employee left may help establish a pattern by which a poor manager may be identified, an error in the hiring practice may be identified, and so on. Personnel may also learn that the services for a particular skill are being bid very high in the marketplace, and salary adjustments may be in order.

Personnel should monitor managers' performance appraisal techniques. Favorable performance should be properly documented and rewarded. Poor performance should also be properly documented. The documentation is extremely important if the quality of performance is not corrected and termination for cause is necessary. Personnel should be the independent monitoring device to determine if proper procedures, documentation, and corrective action have occurred prior to proceeding with any termination action.

In addition, more serious conditions may also be found. Harassment, discrimination, or improper discharge may be alleged. With the potential for later legal action, all employees leaving the company should be exit-interviewed by someone from the personnel department.

A review of benefits for terminated employees should be completed by a personnel manager and explained in the exit conference. The employee should sign a statement indicating that the benefits were explained. This is to ensure that the employee receives the allowed benefits and is aware of any and all supplemental benefits that are available, especially if he is involuntarily terminated.

The exit interview also obtains any company credit cards, security passes, company identification badges, travel advances due, and notifies the employee of his/her final pay including, if appropriate, any unused vacation and personal time, severance pay, or pay in lieu of notice. Most personnel departments have developed an exit checklist addressing issues that are to be resolved prior to the exit interview.

Finally, the exit interview should outline when any monies due the employee can be expected (including payouts from savings plans and so on that can take an extended period of time), what group medical and life insurance benefits can be continued and at what costs, and, for retirees, who and where their continuing contact with the company and insurance representatives will be.

Outplacement services are sometimes provided to employees when major layoffs occur. In addition, when a management employee or executive is terminated, outplacement services can be provided, as well as an office and telephone.

Layoffs and Plant Closeouts

In years past, companies were able to control their own destiny in regard to the closing of plants and moving operations to other cities and states. This is no longer the case. Recent federal and state laws make the closeout of plants more expensive. Pensions must be properly funded and employees well treated to minimize the impact on the state's unemployment fund and the local economy as a whole.

Layoffs are also an undesired part of doing business; however, national economies and industries go through cycles that necessitate such actions. Most corporations have policies addressing such issues based on years of service with the company and/or based on salary grades.

The potential for significant layoff or closing may be challenged by either a labor force, a local community, or the state government. Operating management should investigate, anticipate, and plan for any potential exposures.

Demotions

A demotion is the reassignment of an employee to a position of lower rating or salary structure due to poor performance, reduction in work force, reassignment of grades, or bumping as part of a contractual agreement. Normally no immediate adjustment is made in the employee's pay or benefits. Future raises or promotions may be limited or nonexistent. Future performance may result in the employee's resumption as an employee in good standing.

Pensions

In the late 1970s, Congress passed a law protecting employees with many years of service from corporations that were laying off employees before full vesting of their pension benefits. Other companies would go bankrupt with pension funds inadequately funded. The pension reform law was passed in an attempt to protect employees faced with any of these situations.

Since the passage of this law, the Financial Accounting Standards Board continues to issue additional Financial Accounting Standards to describe the proper accounting methods to fund plans and to list the appropriate assets and liability accounts the company must list on its financial statements. The auditor should reference the latest accounting methods and review these data prior to the start of the audit.

The Payroll and Personnel Department Structure

The payroll and personnel department structures are normally segmented to allow for a logical division (allocation) of workload. This is accomplished either by division, geographic location, payroll account number, or alphabetic split. To avoid too much familiarization, to minimize collusion, and to maintain good internal control, job rotation should occur approximately every two years. This time frame allows for one to two payroll (increase) cycles to occur and is not overly burdensome to the administration of the department. Staff turnover can substitute for job rotation.

Special Considerations

Additional controls may be considered over personnel in the payroll, personnel, and data processing departments. Special controls should be in effect for all personnel and for payroll transactions for these individuals to ensure that no unauthorized transactions occur. These controls may be manual.

EMPLOYEE RELATIONS

Personnel also lends itself to an organized, systematic review. It is easier to understand the systems and to structure the audit according to how the personnel organization is structured.

Policies and Procedures

All departmental managers should know where their job responsibilities end and personnel's begins. Personnel policies should not fluctuate from unit to unit or between departments. This is especially true in the hiring and firing process. Clear-cut policy statements should be issued stating when and who should be consulted before initiating such actions.

Employee Benefits

The corporation's benefits should be comparable to those offered by other firms in the same industry and/or the same geographic area in order to be competitive and to attract the best possible workers. Surveys are periodically conducted by associations in which your company probably participates. Variations will occur. Larger companies will have set vacation policies and smaller companies can be more personal in their relationships.

The benefits program should be concerned with several areas, including:

1. Eligibility for benefits
2. Benefits presently being accrued (but not disbursed) for current and former employees
3. Benefits being paid to active employees
4. Benefits being paid to former employees
5. Previous employees' participation in any supplemental programs
6. Beneficiaries of former employees

Employee benefits include medical and life insurance plans, major medical plans, employee contributory and noncontributory pension plans, paid vacations, sick time, holidays, company cafeterias, company stores (offering company products at reduced prices), company-sponsored holiday parties, picnics, and company-subsidized athletic activities (softball, bowling, golf, racquetball teams, and health club memberships). Personal days may be allowed. More elaborate perquisites include profit sharing, stock options, and other items at the executive levels.

Others include self-help centers, drug counseling and dry-out centers, dental and eye plans, cafeteria plans, dependent life, savings, and retirement plans, stock purchase plans—employee and ESOPs, tuition assistance, long-term disability, 401-Ks, and encouragement of employee-affiliated credit unions.

Some of these benefits may be administered by a separate department or an outside organization. The employee's initial contact may be through the company's personnel function. Separate arrangements may also be made on an individual or group basis for funding to be provided by a third party for payouts at a later date.

Recent court rulings emphasize the importance of identifying and communicating all personnel practices in a distributed personnel handbook or manual. Included in such a manual are the usual business hours and procedures for reporting lateness, absenteeism, dress code, and time allowed for lunch and coffee breaks. Procedures for filing complaints against supervisors, entering self-help centers, and so on should also be identified.

As a result of the complexities of laws and regulations, many companies have arranged with outside insurance actuarial firms and management consulting organizations to assist in the design, development, and maintenance of these programs. Provisions must be made when negotiating contracts that allow for an audit review of these activities performed outside the company.

The determination and payment of these eligible benefits may be a complex matter with a corresponding potential of high exposure to the organization. The auditor may wish to obtain a professional opinion as well as the analysis of the results of the most recent review.

Human Resources and Human Resource Planning

Sales and production should periodically forecast their needs and adjust the number of employees so proper staffing levels can be maintained, and to avoid crash hiring and/or layoffs. The auditor should review to determine that appropriate structure, disciplines, and controls exist to maintain consistency among departments.

Procedures should also be in effect to define and limit the use of part-time (temporary) workers. A position statement should define how long a part-time worker should fulfill a job without the position being considered full-time. The purpose of this review is to avoid the use of temporary help to circumvent man-loading limitations, and to eliminate the possibility of circumventing corporate policies (possibly of employing relatives).

Employee Education and Training

At a minimum, the company should train supervisors in interviewing. What questions to ask and which questions *not* to ask are very important. Since hiring involves a major commitment on both sides, the company (through the interview) should be fair and honest with the prospective employee. Also, certain companies prefer subtle low-key interviews, while others may prefer team interviewing. Such techniques should be described and taught to prospective interviewers. If high-pressure interview techniques are not to be used, that policy should be stated to all applicable personnel.

Additional training should be offered through employee benefits (tuition reimbursement, training programs) and through budgeted seminars and conferences. Employee supervisory and technical skills should be maintained and enhanced. Human Resources should disseminate information to all management employees and track its usage.

Career Planning

Advancement is a major concern for employees and companies alike. At a minimum, job postings are made for positions at varying levels in the company. Other systems become elaborate and may include a listing of prior job assignments, skills, education, and job and location preferences. Internal job searches can be performed based on data contained in this employee data base.

In most corporations, all open positions above or below a certain grade level are announced or posted where all employees can be informed of the openings. If it is not the company policy to post open positions, the auditor may ask how qualified and interested employees are made aware of openings.

An internal posting program is good employee relations for the company and provides a vehicle for promoting from within. It shows a company is willing to invest in its own employees. The company also gains by having employees who are aware of how the company operates, who to see, and how best to get tasks accomplished. The employee broadens his or her perspective in the company. Start-up costs are minimized. Overall and individual employee morale is improved and/or maintained.

Performance Appraisals

A performance appraisal is a periodic evaluation of the employee or function against a predefined criteria, job description, or other standard. Objectively applied, this may be one of the primary instruments within a personnel function. However, care must be taken in its design, implementation, execution, timeliness, and so on. If possible, the system should be tailored to the department or group (accounting, sales, auditing, manufacturing, and engineering could have different criteria and standards applied).

The retention policy should reflect the need of the company and the confidentiality of the personnel records, and should have a defined period for maintaining records. The policy should ensure that records are kept for no longer than is required. This policy, when properly disseminated, can assist in the turn-around of some employees.

A definite, uniform program of employee appraisals should be administered within the organization. This process may never be defined as fair. The application of standards will differ by organizational discipline, manager, location, and personal bias. However, the company should strive for equity and equality in application. This can be attempted by training and education of managers and supervisors in how to conduct appraisal interviews.

When a performance appraisal review is finally over, both parties are usually relieved. Neither the supervisor nor the employee believe in the system or the words spoken. This is very unfortunate since such a review can be very beneficial to both individuals and to the corporation.

In some instances, the appraisal process is structured so that only below- or above-average performance must be explained (documented). In one company, some supervisors submit appraisals without employee signatures (implying that the employee has not been reviewed or has not even seen the appraisal). This practice should be discouraged.

Human Resources should be monitoring supervisors to determine whether appraisals are being done on a timely basis. Appraisals that have not been performed should be identified and brought to the attention of higher management.

Human resource planning should also engage in what-if situations—summarizing performance appraisals, identifying top performers, and outlining who replaces whom in case of promotions, resignations, and so on. Such a review will also address progression, job enhancement, replacements, employee interests, amount of personnel backup for critical positions, and, conversely, a lack of replacements and a lack of depth at or for a specific position. This can lead further to temporary expansion of personnel in a department to minimize the weakness.

Salary Administration

The individual grades and ranges and consistency in application and distribution should be in accord with the organizations' predefined written standards. Increases are usually outlined based on performance and location within the grade. Exceptions include contractual agreements with unions and with individual employees, officers, and directors.

Bonus (Incentive) Plans

If reviewed, the auditor should define what bonus plans are in effect. Performance may be based on the current-year budget. If so, the budget preparers may underestimate performance so the budget may be easily exceeded.

If performance is based on the prior year's sales/production, that basis may not be fair or equitable either. For example, in a mature market/mature product environment, it may not be fair to base performance on the prior year's data. If the product/industry is declining, the bonus may never be attainable. Performance may slip because of an unattainable standard. A good performance may not be rewarded if no sales increase is recorded. Other salespeople may not have to work at all if their territory is a high-growth area with booming sales. If the prior year reflected record sales, salespeople may want record low sales this year in order to get a high bonus every other year.

Within a manufacturing environment, similar situations can occur. If the assembly line is machine or worker limited, no one may be able to produce a given quota if the assembly line can work only as fast as its limiting station.

Discontinuing incentive plans can be difficult since, like other employee benefits, they are often viewed by employees as a permanent integral part of their job as soon as they are introduced. Therefore, the auditor can be of assistance in determining their continued viability.

Labor Relations

Labor relations is defined as the formal defined position and policy of the organization with their employees on an individual and organized basis. An objective is to define and maintain a consistent basis with all employees.

Procedures should be in place for the preparation and presentation of all regulatory agency and participation reports.

Compliance with contractual obligations with labor organizations and private employees should be scheduled and followed.

Community Relations, Donations (Matching Gifts)

Most companies have instituted a matching gifts program whereby employees can donate money to an institution or college foundation, and the company will then match the gift. Some companies match dollar for dollar, other companies match on a two-for-one or a three-for-one basis. This should motivate the employees to give freely to the organization of their choice, and it allows the company, through its employees' donations, to give to those organizations that the employees support.

Most companies also have recognized that they are part of a community and should support it. Employees are sometimes encouraged to participate in politics and to assist local universities, local school districts, and the local hospitals. Such activities create goodwill for the small amount of time invested. Such activities should be reviewed in lieu of the policy as established.

Summary

The 1970s and 1980s have seen an increase in employee benefits. Changes in regulatory requirements and standards have placed an increased emphasis on the personnel function. Therefore, the cost of these programs warrant significant attention by senior management and the audit department.

Prior to the start of fieldwork, a meeting should be held with the corporation's legal counsel and the administrative heads of industrial relations, labor relations, and employee benefits to discuss the current regulatory requirements and to identify the more significant exposures that may impact the company. To develop and complete an effective review of these functions, all input should be tailored into the audit program.

The auditor should determine that an appropriate management control system is in effect to ensure that specified requirements are observed.

Although this book reflects on the operational aspects of auditing, the need for the auditor to also review the financial aspects of the operation cannot be minimized. Reviewing the department's financial accounts can be equally revealing.

An audit should include the review of cumulative figures for savings and retirement programs, 401-Ks, and other voluntary deductions to ensure that amounts were properly calculated and deducted. A review should also be conducted to see if benefits were properly paid to the correct organization and credited to the employee or designated beneficiary account.

Audit Approach

Ample time should be allowed to review the general and specific regulatory agency requirements that pertain to the organization and to the personnel function with the legal department, the director of personnel, and senior management.

A review of the key activities will identify the primary areas and the associated control system that has been designed and put into place by management. The auditor selects an appropriate sample and tests to ensure the controls are functioning as designed and that the function is working properly.

An auditor should consider a verification of the primary activities associated with the following:

Personnel

The personnel audit should cross-check the grade and position classification for:

Correct assignment to the pay grade,

An appropriate distribution of employees within the grade structure, within the salary range, and within the pay grades. (i.e., all employees are not at the bottom of the grade, etc.),

Evidence that the equal opportunity laws are being complied with, and

An analysis of the time period since the last performance appraisal and salary review to ensure compliance with internal procedures.

Employee Benefits

Benefit and transfer accounts to be reviewed include:

The determination of employee eligibility for the benefits programs provided by the organization

Proper term life insurance amounts and deductions, and current beneficiary cards

Correct medical and dental insurance coverage and deductions (the number of and the coverage for eligible dependents)

Authorization cards for all other deductions (such as 401-K, pension, savings bonds, etc.)

These items are all worth reviewing periodically. If incorrect deductions were being taken from an employee's paycheck, or if an incorrect coverage is provided for insurance, or the wrong beneficiary was named, the embarrassment and cost to the corporation may not be desired.

Employees are responsible (which is a key control) for informing the personnel function of changes in their personal records and/or of errors in the deductions for coverages provided. However, the company should have a control system to assist the employees in periodically reviewing these data. This is usually accomplished by periodic or annual statements indicating coverages and benefits to all employees.

Other Employee Relation Areas

The auditor should identify the training capabilities available in-house, including the consultants brought in. The auditor should document what training is available and determine if it is effectively communicated to all departments and employees eligible to attend. Specifically, training is normally available on such topics as performance appraisals, salary administration, career planning, and other managerial topics.

Memberships

Memberships and departmental participation in local and national civic and professional associations:

Review the cost and participation by employees in various corporate memberships to major associations. What is the cost of membership; is value received in comparison to cost; who are the corporate representatives to the association? Are they fully utilized? Would someone else be appropriately involved?

General Approach

An analysis should be made of the related accounts, budgeted and variance amounts, and their associated control systems. The number of departments and/or individuals who have access to funds represented in these accounts is of concern, as are the review, approval, allocation, and distribution of expenses from the centralized accounts to the different operating and administrative departments within the organization.

AUDIT PROGRAM INTERNAL CONTROL QUESTIONNAIRE

Employment and Rate Authorizations

1. Who authorizes employment?
2. When a new employee is hired, is adequate investigation made as to the person's background and former employers?
3. Are unfavorable replies from recommendation requests carefully followed up?
4. Who authorizes initial rates of pay?
5. Who authorizes subsequent changes in rates of pay?
6. Are written notices of the employment of new persons, terminations, rate changes, and so on prepared?
7. Are employment or rate cards showing the authorized rates of pay maintained?

Other

1. Are special salary items (advances, casual and seasonal labor, etc.) subject to the same critical review as regular payments?
2. Do rules exist to determine the length of time a job can be defined as temporary (rather than being defined as a full-time position)?
3. What control is exercised over unclaimed wages?
4. Are comparisons made between payroll periods by department, job, or other classifications with explanations required for any significant variances?
5. What information is furnished to the employees as to their earnings, deductions, and so on?
6. Are historical records stored in dead-storage locations secured against unauthorized access and use and against deterioration or damage from fire, heat, humidity, exposure to chemicals, and so on?

Preliminary Survey

1. Obtain an understanding of the formal organizational structure and where personnel reports within the organization.

2. Identify the responsibility, authority, and accountability formally assigned to the function.
3. Review the activities that have been assumed by the function.
4. Identify the primary activities performed within the function.
5. Identify the primary financial accounts the department controls or is responsible for.
6. Review the organizational structure and staffing assignments within the function.

AUDIT PROGRAM HUMAN RESOURCES ORGANIZATION

Personnel

1. Analyze a block of personnel records to verify their accuracy and completeness. Establish that:
   a. An appropriate, accurate, and properly approved personnel form is on file for all personnel actions taken for the employees in the test sample.
   b. Personnel change notices are properly signed by authorized personnel of the concerned departments and prepared on a timely basis for prompt, timely processing by payroll.
   c. An accurate attendance record, in which all time off for sickness, jury duty, and other personnel reasons is maintained.
   d. The records accurately reflect actual rates, with effective dates for any changes.
   e. The records (payroll or personnel) contain disclosure agreements, signed conflict-of-interest statements, assignment of invention agreements, and personnel evaluations for the past two years (or whatever the records retention period is) as applicable.
2. Examine the position descriptions of randomly selected positions or a randomly selected department. Establish that these are consistent with policy-defined grades, categories and other job classifications by analyzing the responsibilities and activities listed, for example, direct/indirect, salaried/hourly, exempt/nonexempt, and so on.

New Hires

1. Establish that the personnel department has a formally organized recruiting process for the effective and timely recruitment of qualified, new employees. The process should incorporate:
   a. Routine use of standard application forms

b. Complete, consistent policies, procedures, and practices in:
   (1) Giving internal candidates first consideration for filling open positions
   (2) Choosing the method of recruitment in each case, for example, newspaper advertisement, employment agency, and so on
   (3) Screening, interviewing, evaluating, and testing candidates
   (4) Conducting experience and reference checks
   (5) Communicating offers or rejections to all screened candidates
   (6) Expediting and monitoring recruiting performance
c. Centralized, assigned recruitment responsibilities to individual personnel staff members.

2. Establish that personnel has formal procedures and programs effected through specifically designated persons for the processing and orientation of new employees. Review the procedures and establish that controls (instructions, formal policies, check lists, forms, etc.) assure:
   a. The orientation will cover specific major company personnel policies, pension plans, group insurance, medical service, employee loans, other assistance, safety, security (including confidentiality of company information), vacation, holidays, sick pay allowances, company stores and cafeterias, and company ethics.
   b. All newly hired personnel will complete, as applicable and at the time of orientation:
      (1) Patent agreements
      (2) Employment agreement
      (3) Fidelity bond application
      (4) Covenant against disclosure agreement
      (5) Payroll authorization and deduction forms
      (6) Documents signed by the employee acknowledging receipt of returnable items, for example, orientation material, badges/identification cards, tools, manuals, and so on.

Terminations

1. Establish that the personnel department has a formal process for the effective and timely discharge of terminated employees. The process should ensure that:
   a. Documentation exists to support the decision to terminate.
   b. A formal policy is in effect so final paychecks are released only with or after an exit interview clearance (state law may require

that the employee be paid all monies due and payable on the last day worked).

c. Exit interviews are formally documented, preferably on standard forms, for inclusion in the terminated employee's files, which are maintained in accordance with the company's records retention policy.

d. Administration/personnel written instructions or guidelines on the objectives and procedures to be followed, and the reporting of results of exit interviews, are available to those supervisors/managers needing them.

e. Exit interviews are conducted by the employee's supervisor or department manager/director first, and by the assigned personnel manager last. Both interviewers sign and date their reports.

f. Exit interviews are conducted using a checklist that is initialled by the person(s) responsible for verifying that company property has been returned. This should include manuals, instruments, tools, identification badges, company credit cards, clothing, loans, advances, and so on, as well as security debriefings.

g. Payroll will not release a final paycheck or separation allowance without receiving an approved release.

h. Information developed from an exit interview is communicated to management, as appropriate; and is combined with other exit interview data to yield statistical information on the stated reasons for voluntary and involuntary separation.

Management Practices/Data Validation

1. Verify that management at all levels has, through practice and as authorized in written policies, the mechanism and capability of effectively controlling (toward minimizing) disciplinary situations, for example, chronic lateness, absenteeism, and unusually or chronically low performance.

2. Verify that the company formally recognizes the necessity of motivating employees through recognition of superior achievement and granting commendations, prizes, awards, and bonuses, in accord with written policies that assure fair and equitable treatment of employees in specified function, grade levels, or work categories.

3. The company should establish a merit increase policy that rewards and differentiates above average employees.

4. To ensure the merit increase policy is properly executed, personnel should provide guidance on the handling of appraisal interviews and the monitoring of employee performance. Such

education should stress the documentation of substandard (as well as superior) performance.

5. Establish that designated managerial and supervisory personnel, including a responsible person in the personnel/administration department, have been instructed on the actions to be taken if an employee were to suddenly be stricken with an illness or to suffer an accident, including: doctor or hospital to be contacted, means of transfer thereto, first-aid measures to be taken, and so on.

   a. Determine the degree of knowledge and preparedness of the unit's employees for dealing with accidents and sudden illnesses, for example, heart attacks, fits, seizures, and so on.

   b. Establish that all prescription drugs and medicines are maintained in a secure, locked cabinet or closet within a secure room, which is locked whenever staff personnel are absent.

CHAPTER 9

Advertising

GENERAL CONSIDERATIONS

Nature of Advertising

Advertising has been defined as "mass, paid communication, the ultimate purpose of which is to impart information, develop attitude and induce action beneficial to the advertiser (generally the sale of a product or service)."*

The results of advertising are often difficult to measure in definite terms. In a direct mail business, or in a promotional department store advertisement for a specific item, it may be possible to determine the benefits of advertising quite accurately. In the more common situations, mass advertising is but one element of the general marketing plan. If this plan results in increased business, it is difficult to credit any precise portion of the increase to advertising.

Measurement of results is not only difficult, but it is also hard to determine the best form and media for advertising use. Advertising planning calls for specialized creative talent to think of new and effective ways of using the media of advertising communication. The one certain element in advertising is change—a fresh approach, an unusual appeal that will induce a more favorable customer attitude.

*Association of National Advertisers. *Defining Advertising Goals.* 1961, p. 51.

The atmosphere of constant change and new plans that characterizes advertising is apt to give an impression that advertising is a unique phase of business operation to which few of the systems and controls that are normal in other phases of the business can be applied. This impression is incorrect. Good advertising programs are planned to meet specified requirements. Studies and surveys are made to determine the effectiveness of various advertising media; these may be likened to the value analysis programs that assist in effective procurement of materials and supplies.

The internal auditor auditing the advertising activities of the company should not be misled or preoccupied by the atmosphere of continual change, the large amounts of money spent, or the glamour associated with some phases of the advertising operation. Reduced to essentials, the acquisition of advertising may be considered as a specialized form of procurement. While the results may be hard to measure, the products that are purchased—television and radio programs, magazine and newspaper advertisements, and similar items—are concrete and definite. The internal auditor is concerned, as in any procurement, with whether the purchase was properly authorized and in accordance with plans, whether adequate controls exist over the price to be paid, whether what was ordered was received, whether final payment was made, the manner in which the transaction was recorded, and when the transaction (liability) was recorded in company accounts.

Nature of Sales Promotion

Sales promotion may be defined as the application and use of material or plans that have the objective of furthering the marketing activities of the company. Probably the best way to draw the line between advertising and sales promotion is to consider that sales promotion activity is designed to carry on after advertising has done its job of communicating an awareness of company products. Media advertising communicates with a general group (such as a television audience) in the expectation that the advertising message will impress itself on a reasonable proportion of that group. Sales promotion is then directed to inducing more specific action (usually in the form of the purchase of company products) on the part of those who have been impressed.

Much of sales promotion activity and expenditure is concerned with the development, purchase, and distribution of specific materials and sales aids. Included among these are:

Point of purchase (POP) material:
    Counter cards

Display racks
Signs and posters
Dealer and salesperson material:
Catalogs
Circulars
Films
Shows and exhibits

When a company deals in consumer goods, sales promotion activities include various direct means of promoting interest in the distribution of products by dealers and the purchase by consumers. Examples include:

Distributor sales promotion:
Premiums
Special discounts or allowances
Free goods
Contracts for special display or promotion
Consumer sales promotion:
Coupons
Samples
Premiums
Contests

In sales promotion activities, novel and unusual plans and materials are helpful in attracting a favorable response from distributors and consumers. The novelty often extends to methods of distribution and other promotion. These factors increase the problem of effective control, since the control plans applicable to one sales promotion may be unsuitable for another.

Activities relating to acquisition of sales promotion materials are subject to the customary controls that apply to the procurement of advertising and to the purchase of materials and services. Beyond this, the distribution and use of these materials and such special activities as coupons and free goods create special problems for which controls are more difficult to establish and enforce.

The internal auditor auditing sales promotion activities in a company selling consumer products must recognize that close control over many of these activities is difficult. The auditor must be satisfied that the controls maintained reveal the out-of-the-ordinary situation and that reports show final costs of the activities in relation to the originally authorized plans.

Responsibility for Advertising and Sales Promotion Activities

Organizationally, the responsibility for both advertising and sales promotion activities is often assigned to an advertising manager. In other cases, only advertising is handled by the advertising manager, with sales promotion responsibility assigned to a marketing or sales manager. Whether the responsibility is single or divided is not particularly significant to the internal auditor, but it is important to ascertain the effective coordination between advertising, sales promotion, distribution, and selling responsibilities, and that those responsible receive adequate and timely reports of activities. (To illustrate the dangers of poor coordination, the sales promotion department in one company ordered floor display stands too large to be carried in the cars of the salespeople who were to make distribution.)

Definitions

In this section, the term *advertising* applies to general communication through such media as radio, television, magazines, newspapers, and billboards. *Sales promotion* applies to materials, plans, and activities that are designed to follow through on advertising, to induce customers to purchase or dealers to give special attention to the company's products or services.

To distinguish advertising and sales promotion from direct sales efforts, advertising and sales promotion activities are confined to plans, materials, and campaigns designed to influence customers and dealers; such promotional efforts as sales contests between salespersons are consequently not included.

This section is based upon study and discussion of practices in the United States. While there are undoubtedly both similarities and differences in advertising and trade practices between the United States and other countries, the suggestions and recommendations are general enough to be applicable to advertising and sales promotion activities in most countries.

THE ADVERTISING DEPARTMENT

Organizational Setup

Because of the importance of advertising in the marketing plans of most companies, the director of advertising usually reports to the senior officer who has general marketing responsibility.

The advertising department organization varies widely among companies. For example, one company with a $100 million advertising budget has a large advertising organization able to do all of its preparation and production work. Supplementing the technical personnel (artists, copy-writers, and layout experts) are employees who specialize in media and placement of advertising. In effect, this company provides for itself most of the services that are available through an advertising agency.

At the other extreme is a company whose detailed study of overall requirements for the development and execution of its advertising plans indicated that its relationships with advertising media could be best handled by the agency, since the agency has to deal with media in the actual placement of advertising. In this company, technical advertising matters are considered to be the responsibility of the agency and general planning and control functions are the responsibility of the company advertising department.

Whatever the organizational plan, you should recognize that the function of the advertising department is to represent the company and the products that are to be sold. The function of the agency is to apply the knowledge of the agency specialists in advertising presentation and consumer viewpoint to the company situation.

Financial Control

In many companies, the financial phases of advertising operations are important enough to require a separate financial control group. In smaller companies, such a financial control group may be maintained as a section of the advertising department. For example, in one company with an extensive advertising program, a separate creative manager has responsibility for the advertising of each of the major sales divisions. These creative managers, who report to the director of advertising, work with the sales divisions in the development and application of advertising and sales promotion activities. The financial control is handled by an advertising controller, who is organizationally on a level with the creative managers, and also reports to the director of advertising. The advertising controller is responsible for financial matters pertaining to advertising, such as:

1. Developing and maintaining budgets
2. Recording commitments
3. Approving billings
4. Preparing and interpreting reports

In companies where advertising expenditures are greater, the financial control function should be in the controller's department (also the *preferred* method with smaller firms).

Record keeping and report preparation should be handled by the mechanical facilities of the accounting department. This is a sound arrangement, since it should assure the advertising department that records are well maintained and in agreement with the general accounting records.

Duplication of Functions

There is often a tendency toward duplication of functions between the advertising department, other company operating departments, and the company's advertising agency. Some examples:

1. In one company, media billing charges, insertions, and similar data were verified by:
   a. The advertising agency (100 percent)
   b. The company advertising department (100 percent)
   c. The company marketing accounting department (100 percent)
   d. The company internal auditors (test checked)
2. In another company, the advertising department kept complete records of commitments and payments that are duplicates of regular accounting records and reports.

The records maintained and the functions performed in (1) the advertising agency, (2) the company advertising department, and (3) the company accounting department should be organized with the objective of maintaining an effective and simple control structure with minimum duplication.

Role of the Advertising Agency

Since advertising department organizational and other control can be effectively appraised only when the functions of the advertising agency are included as an element of the appraisal, we next deal with the role of the advertising agency.

RELATIONSHIP WITH ADVERTISING AGENCY

Function of Agency

The advertising agency plays an important role (especially with smaller firms) in planning and placing advertising for a number of reasons:

1. The agency is familiar with the entire range of advertising media and can give expert advice as to media that will best accomplish the objectives of the advertising program.
2. The agency is experienced in the production of advertising, and can assist in the development of advertising that will have maximum appeal to prospective customers.
3. The agency can help coordinate advertising campaigns with sales objectives and sales promotion plans.
4. The agency can assume responsibility for determining that the advertising contracted was actually delivered (received).

Compensation of Agency

Media 15 Percent Discount

In the past (and currently), most companies compensated their agencies through the infamous 15 percent discount granted by the advertising media. The discount is retained by the agency, with media charges billed by the agency to the company at the gross amount.

In addition to media discounts, the agencies add the equivalent of the 15 percent commission to charges for advertising services purchased or rendered by the agency where no discount is granted to the agency by the supplier of the services.

The following case is an illustration involving a space charge of $10,000 and a production cost of $2000:

Item	Paid by Agency*	Commission (15 Percent of Billing to Company)**	Billed to Company
Media cost	$8,500	$1,500	$10,000
Production	2,000	353	2,353

While the principal compensation of the agency comes from the 15 percent commission granted (or charged), the agency may perform other services that it charges for on an agreed-upon basis. For example, the agency may undertake a market survey of a specific area that will be charged for on a cost-plus basis.

The commission basis of compensation introduces a degree of conflict of interest, as is also the case with architects, insurance brokers, and travel agents. Since the agency commission depends on the amount of company money spent, the agency's interest is to handle as much as possible of a client's advertising and sales promotion expenditures. Company personnel (including the internal auditor) have the responsibility for determining that the service rendered by the agency in matters that could be handled either by the agency or the company (such as design and purchase of sales promotion materials) justifies the cost of the agency commission.

Compensation of Agency

Fee Basis

The current trend is to compensate agencies on a cost-plus basis. The agency submits a budget by line item for current-year expenditures.

*No allowance is made for any cash discount passed along to company.
**Computed by agency at 17.65 percent to equal 15 percent of billing to company.

Separate budgets are presented for creative, media, production, and other costs, plus an explanation for what costs are contained in overhead (secretarial support, accounting, etc.) and general and administrative (officer salaries, fringes, etc.), plus a profit factor.

Agreement with Agency

The understanding between the advertising agency and the company should be embodied in a written contract or other form of agreement that clearly states what will be handled by the agency, how it will be handled, and the nature of the agency's compensation. It is particularly important that the agreement specify those agency services to be covered by either the 15 percent media discount or the negotiated fee.

Typical points to be included in agreements are:

1. Provisions for duration and cancellation
2. Basis of allocation of direct or indirect agency costs, such as administrative salaries, traveling, entertaining, telephone, and so on
3. Extent of contribution by the company to research and special investigations by the agency relating to markets, competition, and so on
4. Requirement for preparation of estimate sheets for all advertising, showing media, estimated cost, description of advertising, and date of appearance. Estimate sheets should be approved by the company, and thus serve as the means of authorizing commitments and expenditures.

Different types of agreements may be in effect in various companies; for example:

1. In Company *A,* the agency considers the advertising budget too low to provide enough income to the agency through the application of the 15 percent media discount. Consequently, the company guarantees a minimum compensation to the agency, with supplementary payment made when earned media discounts are below the minimum.
2. Company *B* advertises largely in higher-cost media. Most of the production of advertising is handled by the company staff, and the agency compensation is limited to the 15 percent media discount.
3. Company *C* advertises largely in specialized (and lower cost) media. The agency handles and bills separately for all production costs.
4. In Company *D,* the contract with the agency provides for a fixed retainer to be paid by the company, plus charges for definite services

on bases specified in the contract. In this case, all discounts granted by media are allowed to the company in agency billing.

5. In Company *E,* the company uses a specialized buying service to purchase network and spot buys. The fee basis is the net cost for the time plus 10 percent and 2 percent, respectfully.

One survey by the Association of National Advertisers shows that only about half of the companies participating in a survey had a formal contract with their advertising agencies. From the control and audit standpoint, this is totally unacceptable. The lack of a contract can only hurt your organization. More than likely, the auditor will end up spending an inordinate amount of time trying to get recommendations past company management. Through experience, most agencies will only do what the companies allow. The more latitude they are given, the more they will take.

If questioned by the auditor, management will downplay the lack of a properly executed contract. The lack of a contract may not be particularly important where the entire compensation is derived from the standard media discount—until a misunderstanding occurs. The lack of a contract can also be meaningless on a cost-plus fee basis—until someone asks, "Why are we being charged for their accounting department?"

When the agency is charging separately for such items as production costs, special services, and purchase of materials, effective control requires a specific written agreement. The agreement should include a provision that the company's internal auditor or other authorized representative shall have access to all agency records forming the bases for charges to the company. Such records include:

1. Vouchers covering payments for services and materials rebilled to the company. (Many companies require that copies or originals of vendor invoices accompany the rebilling.)
2. Time reports, payroll records, and other internal agency records forming the bases for specific labor costs and labor overhead billed to the company.
3. Authorizations for revisions, overtime, and any other abnormal items specially billed.
4. Copies of contracts.
5. Inventory records of company property supplied to the agency.
6. Disposition of props purchased on the company's behalf.

Agency Responsibility for Payments to Media

As mentioned, billing for the appearance of advertising is rendered to the agency by the advertising medium. Accompanying this billing is evidence of the appearance of advertising in such forms as:

1. Tear sheets from magazines, newspapers, and classified directories
2. Performance affidavits from radio and television stations or networks
3. Location lists for outdoor advertising

In addition to checking for appearance and date of advertising, the agency should assume responsibility for:

1. Making claims for unsatisfactory items, such as:
   a. Wrong position in publication
   b. Poor printing
   c. Radio or television station interruption or incorrect run times
   d. Torn billboard posters or lack of illumination at night
   e. Billing for advertising that did not appear
2. Checking space or time rates with original contracts
3. Verifying that discounts applying to quantity space and time rates are granted where earned
4. Payment of invoices rendered by media
5. Checking that cancellations are made as scheduled
6. Test checking performance through an outside service, such as Broadcast Advertisers Reports (BAR), Arbitron, or Nielsen

Where the business of a company is divided among several agencies, all should receive reports of media usage from the other agencies serving the company or, better yet, assign one company employee to consolidate their media usage. The media buying agency should combine media usage figures and modify the quantity rates of the other agencies and the company advertising department that are applicable to overall company usage.

Agency Responsibility for Direct Costs

When direct costs (such as charges for artwork or photography) are incurred for the company's account, the agency is responsible for verifying that the charges are correct. Payment is then made by the agency and rebilled to the company with supporting charges specified and with the agency fee added where applicable.

Reliability of Agency Financial Operations

A number of different companies were questioned as to their opinion of the agency verification, payment, and billing operations. They generally agreed the agency financial work was reliable. However, a healthy degree of skepticism can be helpful. Recent articles describe many problems with agencies maintaining banks of time for spot and syndication time. Other concerns include the use of barter—whether it be direct (with your own products) or indirect (using other products but affecting your account).

For additional research, review the 8-K filings of the H.J. Heinz Corporation and the McCormick Corporation, as well as the articles published on the problems alleged in the J.W. Thompson Agency and Tanner Broadcasting.

Although the great majority of agencies are 100 percent honest, a bad agency and/or a bad person in an impeccable agency still can emerge from time to time. Sometimes honorable intentions get out of hand. Each audit should be approached with a degree of skepticism and from a control viewpoint. Review your own advertising department and marketing department as well as your agency for their degree of control consciousness. Watch for changes from product to product, from one part of the country to another. Familiarize yourself with the quarterly and four-year cycles of media advertising—that is, costs are higher in the fourth quarter (new season introductions and the holidays and every four years during presidential campaigns and the Olympics).

CONTROL THROUGH BUDGET AND ACCOUNTS

Establishment of Budget

Control over advertising and sales promotion expenditures begins with the establishment of an advertising and sales promotion budget. In some cases, separate budgets are prepared for each function; in others, they are combined.

Budgeting of advertising in some companies presents an interesting variation from customary operating budget preparation procedures in that the total amount of the budget is first determined, after which a decision is made as to the manner in which detailed expenditures will be incurred. These companies plan to use a certain proportion of sales revenues for advertising, and the total advertising budget will be a ratio of projected sales. After the total budget is established, the advertising department develops its plans to allocate the total in the manner that will best promote the fulfillment of the sales objectives.

Regardless of the basis used to determine the total and the details of the advertising budget, a definite budget is the first, and basic, step in control. Since much advertising is contracted for on a long-term basis, records of future commitments must be maintained as an integral part of budget control. Budgets for sales promotion activities are similar to departmental expense budgets. Plans for specific activities are made and budgeted, and appropriate accounts are charged as the activities occur.

Account Classification

For effective control, budgets and related accounts should be established according to the nature of the expenditure and the manner in which control will be exercised. The large item of media costs is customarily controlled through such means as insertion schedules and time and space contracts. Some companies provide separate media accounts for control and reporting purposes, for example, network television, spot television, syndication, magazines, newspapers, and cable. Once media contracts have been made, further control steps are concerned principally with assuring that the company receives the media contracted for. Many years ago, rates and total charges were readily verifiable in standard rate books; today, however, rates are very competitive and negotiable, and additional audit work must be done to verify *actual* rates paid.

Production costs are very difficult to verify and control. For example, because of a revision in merchandising plans, someone may decide to secure additional artwork, or to revise a layout, or to incur overtime charges. Such changes will have no effect on media expense but can be major factors in increasing production costs. The stars in a commercial are paid every time the commercial is shown, so these costs can continue for the life of the commercial. Consultants specialize in auditing production billings. Courses are also available on how to audit production costs.

Looking at advertising costs in total can lead to an attitude expressed by one company's advertising vice president, who agreed to an audit finding, but stated that "the amount is only $1 million, and my budget is $75 million." This attitude is very different than that expressed in manufacturing operations, where plant managers look for savings from any element that contributes to cost.

Revisions in Budget

Such factors are revised sales plans or the introduction of new products often lead to decisions to transfer advertising expenses between products or media, or to revise the overall budget. However, transfers between amounts allotted to specific products sometimes are made with the objective of concealing overexpenditures that were not anticipated or authorized. From the control standpoint, the reasons for transfers or revisions of substantial amounts should be documented and approved by executives above the level of those who administer the sections of the budget affected by the revisions. Unless this requirement is met, the control provided by the budget will be seriously weakened.

Justifiable reasons for revisions in budgets can include:

1. To meet competition (competition's unanticipated increased marketing expenditures).

2. To (re)introduce a product.
3. To create a marketing blitz.
4. To take advantage of a competitor's negative press, in an attempt to gain share of market.

PROCUREMENT OF ADVERTISING

Development of Plans

After the general advertising budget has been approved, the next step is the development of plans for detailed programs and specific campaigns. This is accomplished by dividing the budgeted totals allocated to each activity or product into the detailed expense classifications to which actual expenses will be charged as incurred. For example, a total budget for a product might be divided into the following classifications, with appropriate subclassifications as required for reporting and effective control:

Television	Network, syndication, regional, spot, production
Radio	Network, syndication, regional, spot, production
Magazines	Space, photographs and artwork, other production
Newspaper	Space, distribution, production

Where specific campaigns are a feature of advertising plans, a separate group of accounts for each major campaign is desirable. This facilitates the accumulation and comparison of the direct cost of the campaign with sales results.

Insertion Schedules

The actual procurement of advertising begins with the preparation of tentative insertion schedules (or buying platform) within the annual marketing plan. These schedules, usually prepared by the advertising agency (or the planning department of the company's marketing services department), list the media for which definite commitments are to be made. Each schedule shows:

Medium
Dates of insertion or usage
Details such as:
    Amount of space
    Color

Amount of time
  Time of day
  Day of week
Cost of use of medium
Volume discounts

The tentative insertion schedule is submitted by the agency to the company for approval. When approved, this constitutes the company's purchase order and authorizes the agency to contract with the media for time or space. The total amounts contracted for are noted on the budget and commitment records of the advertising department, thereby showing at all times the net amount available for further planning or contracting.

Production Costs

Under the general classification of production costs is included the cost of preparing advertising for use in the selected media. Typical items classified as production costs are:

Copywriting
Photography
Artwork
Layout and typography
Preparation of radio and television shows and commercials
Paper and printing (for outdoor billboards)
Freight for transportation of paper and other materials

A certain portion of these costs will usually be assumed to be covered by the agency commission, but there should be a very specific agreement as to what is, and what is not, included in the service to be rendered by the agency for the commission received.

Because the commission income varies with the gross media cost, the proportion of production costs that the agency can be reasonably expected to assume will vary with the gross media billing. For example, if a single advertisement were to appear simultaneously in several mass-circulation magazines, the media cost would be large and the agency commission would be a considerable amount. In such a situation, the entire production cost might be assumed by the agency. At the opposite extreme, a single advertisement (which might cost almost as much to produce as the mass-circulation advertisement) appearing in several technical journals would generate a low commission to the agency. Here the agency should not assume the entire production cost.

Production cost is one of the principal items of advertising expense that is controllable in many of its aspects, although one can argue that the creative, semiartistic nature of advertising development makes the application of any effective controls difficult. Another reason given for comparative uncontrollability is the atmosphere of flexibility and constant change in marketing plans. Both of these reasons may be valid on occasion. On the other hand, they may be used to excuse ineffective planning, coordination, or operation.

From a control standpoint, the causes and the cost of unexpected changes in plans should be correctly and completely revealed in reports of advertising operations. Effective control requires that production costs paid by the company be separated in budgeting and accounting records, although they are grouped in accounts with the corresponding media costs. Media and production costs are then combined to show the total expense for each medium and product. Production costs of larger amounts should be separately budgeted (or estimated) by major expense classifications (such as artwork, typography, engraving, etc.) so that a detailed comparison of estimates with actual expenses will be available on completion of the production job.

One cost often not anticipated in advance planning is overtime expense incurred when new or revised ideas must be rushed to completion. Such deviations from the original program may result in considerable extra cost. For example, in one case a delay in the release of marketing plans resulted in nonbudgeted overtime expense incurred by the advertising agency amounting to 15 percent of the total production cost.

Assessing responsibility in such a situation may be difficult. For effective control, additional overtime (or other unanticipated) expense should be properly approved before incurred—and should be clearly revealed in reports to management.

Verification of Receipt

Since no tangible goods are received in many phases of advertising procurement, strict controls must be maintained to eliminate the risk of duplicate payment. Duplicate invoices for advertising charges should never be accepted as proof of insertion. As with other purchases, those responsible for checking appearance, rates, and discounts in the agency or the advertising department should not be also responsible for placing orders for the material or services billed.

The requirement for proof of receipt of materials or services as a condition of payment is quite easily met for media advertising. Newspapers and magazines supply this proof by means of a tear sheet (a copy of the advertisement as it appears in the finished publication), which is either forwarded to the advertiser or kept on file in the advertising agency, usually for a minimum of three months. After this period of time, the records may be put into storage. For radio and television advertising, station affidavits or reports from independent agencies should attest that the advertising actually appeared. For outside billboards and advertising signs, the appearance of the advertising can be certified by an independent agency or by your own sales force.

The agency should have complete responsibility for verification of appearance. In checking proofs of receipt with related billings, the agency verifies such items as insertion date, quality of production, position in publication, rates, and applicable discounts. In case of variations, the agency enters a claim with the medium. Typical variations include:

1. Charging for space that does not agree with the measured size of the advertisement
2. Advertisement appeared in a less favorable location (or time period) than was contracted for
3. Poor printing
4. Interruption of telecasts due to technical difficulties
5. Substitution of programs by local stations
6. Torn posters on billboards

Reimbursement for claims will often take the form of allowances to be made on future advertising or free reinsertion of correct material. Here, controls must be maintained to insure that such allowances are obtained and actually used.

Receipt of materials and services billed as production costs is first verified before payment is made, and is finally attested to by the appearance of the advertising to which the production costs apply. Do not forget to audit the IS system of agencies, including spot buying agencies and so on. Review their controls and edits over initial input, schedule changes, input of actual times aired (both Gross Rating Points (GRPs) and dollars), and review changes that can take place from the first day to what may read 90 or 180 days later! Schedules can be established six to nine months in advance. Changes to that schedule may occur from the date established to the actual date commercials are run.

Verification of Price—Media Advertising

The initial verification of media price is made by the agency against the insertion schedule. Beyond this, verification may be made with scheduled rates that are available from individual publishers. Many publications exist but their reliability may be subject to question. The data fed to them may not be accurate, and no one—the stations or the advertisers—is motivated to tell the truth (to a company publishing "actual" rates). No agency wants its client to believe it is paying more than the market. You may therefore assume that the published rates are probably higher than the average rate paid for a market. In addition, the prices charged by independent stations are usually lower than for comparable time and daypart on an affiliate station in master markets. Buyer beware!

Pricing is complicated by the existence of volume discounts that apply to usage of individual media or to combinations of media—such as newspaper or television affiliates or groups. Sometimes the volume discount is applied to give a net price when a contract is made. In other cases, the media usage is accumulated and the discount is applied retroactively when the quantity discount point is reached. Other cases exist, where an agency buys (or is sold) a block of time encompassing many dayparts—some that an advertiser wants and other less desirable times. If purchased in this fashion, substantial discounts can be had for the agency. Usually these transactions go through a third party (agency subsidiary), and the billings are not direct from the stations. The auditor should be extremely cautious in these cases and, if a subsidiary, insist on seeing the original station affidavit.

For newspapers and magazines, if multiple agencies are used, the media usage should be accumulated (by one agency or the company) to ensure that the company gets its quantity discount. Media discounts can be substantial, and control procedures should be adequate to assure that such discounts are not overlooked.

The application of volume discounts can lead to some interesting possibilities. For example:

1. It may be less expensive to advertise on an entire television network at the network rate than on desired stations or markets at spot rates, even though this involves using some stations in regions where company products are not distributed.
2. If the volume used is not quite up to the discount breaking point, it may be possible to secure broader advertising coverage at little additional cost by using enough space to reach the breakeven point.

Verification of Price—Production Costs

The verification of charges for production costs is usually more straightforward than for media. The simplest situation exists where there is a definite agreement or contract for a specific item, such as a television commercial.

Invoices from the agency that itemize charges for outside materials or services (such as artwork or engraving) should be supported by copies of invoices that the agency has paid for the advertiser's account.

Where charges are made for agency services, verification of the reasonableness of the charge should rest with the company advertising (creative) department. For example, charges by outside artists for drawings and artwork should be approved by an advertising department executive familiar with the cost of such work. Expenses of outdoor advertising should be tested with approved charges and with supporting vouchers.

Whatever the source of the charge, invoices should show sufficient detail to permit analysis and question prior to payment (and verification at the time of internal audit). Particular attention is required in the case of additional charges for unforeseen contingencies; these should be duly authorized by a responsible executive.

Cooperative Advertising

The marketing plans of some companies provide for sharing the cost of local advertising with retail or wholesale distributors of the company products. Common forms of such cooperative advertising are newspaper ads and local spot radio or television announcements and on-pack couponing. Usually the company will provide basic advertising materials, such as newspaper mats or copy for spot announcements, and will contract to pay an agreed percentage of the cost. When the advertising appears, the distributor presents the proof of performance (appearance) and bills the company for its share.

In general, the requirements for checking such items before payment are the same as for the company's national advertising. The proof of performance and the price should be verified and the proportion to be paid checked with the written agreement with the coadvertiser. In the case of newspaper advertising, large local advertisers often have special quantity rate contracts with local media that are lower than the generally published rate schedules. While it may not be easy to learn of such contracts, an effort should be made to see that the company is charged at the rate actually paid by the distributor (unless the company has agreed to pay at published rates).

Payment for Media Charges

Payments to some media are required in advance of the date of appearance, while payments to other media may not be required until the advertising has appeared. Company payments to agencies should be coordinated with these requirements.

Trade practice usually requires the agency to receive payment from the company in advance of the agency payment to media. On the other hand, company payments should not be made so far in advance of the agency's payments to media that the related funds are equivalent to a financing of the agency. The agency usually renders to the company a pro-forma billing for media usage, with a final billing including debit or credit adjustments after the appearance of the advertising.

The auditor may wish to inquire as to how an agency pays bills. How do you know they are paying the bills on time? Are they using your company's money for 30 to 90 days before paying? To alleviate the problem, verify payments with the media; or better yet, establish a joint bank account to pay the bills, and/or have the agency mail the bills and checks to someone in your corporation, and have your corporation release the checks the same day the company wires the funds into the joint account.

AUDIT OF ADVERTISING ACTIVITIES

General Approach

The internal audit of advertising activities follows the approach used in the audit of other operating departments. As stated previously, procurement of advertising is similar in many respects to other procurement operations. For example, when an agency charges for certain services or materials on a cost-plus agency commission basis, the transactions and controls resemble those of a cost-plus construction contract (see Chapter 7, Fixed Assets). With such similarities and background, the auditor can focus attention on the special controls pertaining to the acquisition of advertising.

The Audit Team

The auditor assigned to the advertising audit should coordinate closely with the company's advertising employees and those responsible for the financial control of advertising operations. One or more of these people might accompany the audit team when auditing an advertising agency. These employees' knowledge of the day-to-day problems and activities could be of help in the agency audit.

Auditors should not have a merely critical approach. They should be concerned with the overall effectiveness of the controls over the program. One of the controls of particular interest to the auditor are the reports that show costs in relation to budget plans.

Auditors are in an ideal position to contribute ideas that will improve operations through such means as more effective interdepartmental coordination or actual savings. A principal objective of the audit is to appraise the adequacy and effectiveness of established controls and to help find ways for better control so that the company and the advertising department may gain maximum results from the advertising expenditure.

The Audit Program

Because of the specialized nature of advertising activities, and because of the division of responsibility between the company advertising department and the advertising agency, a tailored audit program is essential.

Tailored audit programs are also essential if your company's advertising department is so large that you must segment your audit program. The program designed should define the general approach to the audit and outline the steps to be taken in the verification phase of the auditor's work.

The audit program at the end of the chapter is divided into many categories of advertising activities that can be performed inside as well as outside the company.

Beginning the Audit

The audit should begin with a study of reference and background material such as this chapter, data from the Association of National Advertisers, media books and magazines, as well as your company's policies, guidelines, and relationships. Thereby, the auditor will be generally familiar with the objectives of the company's advertising and marketing activities and with the means by which these activities are controlled.

The next step is discussion of the audit with appropriate company personnel. In these discussions, the objective is to learn from operating personnel how they work to attain the planned results, what their problems are, how they maintain control over their operations, and if any changes occurred in controls or activities since a preceding audit. Specifically, in discussing the audit with the advertising manager, the auditor should:

1. Outline the scope of the audit, and invite suggestion as to specific items to be investigated. (For example, poor coordination of distribution activities during a sales drive.)
2. Learn the general manner in which the overall marketing budget and its specific parts is developed, approved, reviewed, revised, and controlled.
3. Inquire into relationships between the advertising department and the agencies.
4. Inquire into internal communications between the advertising department and the product mangers and any other marketing departments.

Relationship with Agencies

The auditor must have a clear understanding of the relationship with the advertising agency (see Relationship with the Advertising Agency, above). By far, the preferable relationship exists when a written contract or agreement defines (1) the areas of responsibility of the agency, (2) the services that will be separately charged for and those that will be provided by the agency without direct charge (included in overhead or G&A), (3) the nature of items subject to added commission charges, and similar matters. If no written agreement exists, the auditor should ascertain how a decision is made and the reasonableness of charges made by the agency.

Budgets

The advertising budget is the principal control used by management and the advertising department. The auditor should learn how the budget is developed, how commitments and expenditures are approved and controlled, and how effectively the budget and related accounts and reports serve as controls over expenditures. Transfers between budget subgroups should be reviewed to see that they are approved at adequate levels of the marketing organization (including program management as well as advertising services) to insure they are bona fide—and not manipulations to conceal overexpenditures, or unanticipated or unauthorized charges; or that they do not use up unexpended balances to forestall a budget reduction in an ensuing period.

Organization and Procedures

In appraising the organizational and procedural controls of the advertising department, particular attention should be given to the possibility of duplication in personnel or operations between the advertising agency, the advertising department, and other company activities.

Verification of Payments

Wherever feasible, the auditor should perform at the agency a verification of advertising expenditures that the agency has rebilled to the company. Charges for the time of agency personnel and other specific items should be checked with the agency records on which the charges are based. Verification at the agency has two advantages:

1. Records are checked at the source.
2. The auditor can decide how much reliance can be placed on the agency financial controls.

When the auditor is satisfied that reliance can be placed on the agency's financial controls, the auditor may wish to modify the audit program and expand into more operational areas at the agency.

The agency should be requested in advance of the auditor's visit to furnish a listing of current year's billings separated between media advertising and nonmedia expenditures. Agencies usually maintain adequate files and records of paid invoices, job costs, contracts, films, artwork, and similar items. Advance notification of the projects that are planned to be reviewed will enable the agency to have data ready for the auditor's visit. As an alternative, the auditor may prepare his own listing of advertising payments from the company records for verification at the agency (if that is where the *original* records are maintained).

Controllable Costs

Attention should be given to the amounts paid for such items as overtime costs, revisions in production plans, and other controllable expenditures. Payments should be questioned as to the reasons and the authorization for the additional expenditure. Significant extra costs should be brought to the attention of, and approved by, those who have general responsibility for advertising management.

Records of Advertising Properties

The creation of advertising often involves various items, such as:

1. Artwork
2. Furniture and other items used for photographic sets
3. Company products
4. Props rented or purchased to complement the artwork

The internal audit program should provide for review of the method of accounting for use, disposition, or current location of such items. Where there is possible future use or disposition, records should be maintained so the nature of the item and the responsibility for physical storage may be readily determined. (One company retains a copy of the advertisement in which the item was used as a part of their inventory record.)

Inquiry should be made as to the control over items with value and that are desirable to employees or others. (Advertising employees have been known to appropriate a number of pieces of china or furniture used in a photographic set.) The usual tendency is to regard such items and company products used by the advertising agency as expense items of no value. Therefore, possible salvage value or storage for subsequent use should be considered and provided for. For those properties where no further use is anticipated, the goods should be sold and the proceeds returned to the company.

SALES PROMOTION

Nature of Sales Promotion Activities

The general heading of sales promotion is used to designate a wide range of activities and materials that have the general objective of inducing

(1) distributors to give extra attention to the sales of company products, and (2) ultimate customers to buy company products.

The control and internal audit features pertaining to the acquisition of advertising are similar to those applying to other procurement. By contrast, the unusual approaches used in sales promotion activities often require correspondingly unusual approaches in control and audit, which is best illustrated by some examples of typical sales promotion activities:

1. Coupons having a definite cash value toward the purchase of a company product are widely distributed to potential customers.
2. Sales literature is imprinted with a dealer's name and is sent directly by the printer to the dealer with the company paying the bill.
3. A sales drive calls for giving salable products free to distributors in a certain ratio; for example, one case free with each eight cases purchased.
4. A sales drive is based on a temporary price reduction to distributors. Distributors are given credit for the reduction applying to stock on hand at the beginning of the deal plus all goods ordered for the duration of the deal.

Each of these comparatively common forms of sales promotion requires distinct and separate control procedures and internal audit techniques.

Sales promotion activities are discussed in three separate sections:

1. Sales promotion—purchased materials
   a. Material for general distribution
      Point of purchase materials
      Catalogs
      Circulars
      Direct mail material
   b. Special sales promotion materials
      Exhibits
      Sales meeting material
      Films
2. Sales promotion—distributors
   Free goods deals
   Special discount deals
   Contracts for special promotions
   Premiums
   Samples
   Contests

3. Sales promotion—retail customers
   Coupons
   Combination sales
   Samples
   Premiums
   Contests

Because of the wide variety of materials and activities classified as sales promotions, it is not practicable to present a general internal audit program for sales promotion. Instead, the special controls and related internal audit procedures are included in the description of the individual activities. From this, an internal audit program may be developed to meet a particular situation.

General Control Requirements

The following controls and techniques apply generally to all sales promotion activities and should be tested and utilized in all sales promotion audits:

1. Organizational responsibility for each sales promotion campaign or activity should be completely and specifically assigned; for example, to a section of the marketing services department.
2. Accountability controls should be established over the storage and distribution of free goods, premiums, samples, coupons, and other items having monetary value.
3. Coordination of sales promotion, sales, production, and advertising activities must be rigidly enforced. Lack of coordination can be very costly to a company and result in actual loss of goodwill on the part of distributors and consumers. For example, a coupon campaign is useless unless distributors have adequate merchandise to cover coupon redemptions.
4. During each promotion and at its conclusion, reports to management should show direct costs and results. Costs include such items as the value of merchandise, allowances, promotion materials, coupon distribution, and any other direct and specific items. Results will include such items as increased sales in comparison with previous periods, number of inquiries, new accounts opened, and so on. Only with complete reporting will management be able to evaluate the results of the promotion and use these results in planning and estimating the cost of future activities.
5. Prior to internal audit, the auditor should arrange with the sales department to visit some distributors and customers with a representative of the sales department. The objective in these visits is to

gain an understanding of the problems in conducting and controlling sales promotion.

SALES PROMOTION—PURCHASED MATERIALS

Material for General Distribution

Control over Acquisition

Controls over acquisition of sales promotion materials are similar to those pertaining to any procurement operation. Before purchase is negotiated, there should be an appropriately approved requisition or other authorization showing quantity required and estimated cost.

In making purchases outside of the sales promotion field, a number of qualified suppliers will usually be asked to bid on definitely specified items. As long as the vendor is reputable, financially responsible, and can meet specifications, the purchase can be awarded to the lowest bidder with confidence that the delivered materials will be satisfactory.

By contrast, in negotiations for purchasing sales promotion materials, potential vendors will often be furnished only general specifications and will be asked to suggest design, typography, or other features that they believe will best meet the requirements. Each vendor will develop its plan; the final purchase decision will be based on an aggregate of design, price, and production capability. The purchase contract may not necessarily be awarded to the lowest bidder, since those responsible for the purchase may decide that a more expensive item will be justified by its greater appeal or effectiveness. This decision logically should be made by those responsible for sales promotion. However, the records of purchase should show the bids received and the reason for the award to the successful vendor.

An interesting question arises as to whether a vendor developing an original design for company use should be entitled to subsequent reorders without competition. While the original order should go to the vendor responsible for the original design, a stated policy on reorders should be approved by the company purchasing group. To guard against possible legal action, this policy should be embodied in contracts or purchase orders.

Responsibility for Acquisition

In the majority of companies, responsibility for acquisition of sales promotion material is split between marketing and/or the purchasing department. Because of technical knowledge in the advertising department, purchasing may have little say. In some cases, acquisition is assigned to the advertising agency. Such assignment has the advantage of fostering coordination of advertising and sales promotion plans by agency personnel assigned to the company account. Moreover, agency purchasing personnel often have better knowledge of the printing requirements of such items as display material and of the vendors who can best meet these requirements. Offsetting these advantages are possible additional costs resulting from agency commission charges on these purchases; the possibility of less effective purchasing because of the failure to use know-how available within the company purchasing department; and the agency may be less interested in holding costs to a minimum than is the company purchasing department.

Some companies have circulars and price lists printed in a company printing department. Here the usual controls over department work should be supplemented by occasional comparison of company printing costs with the cost of using outside printers.

Audit of Acquisition

The audit of the acquisition of sales promotion materials should be approached in the manner of a regular purchasing audit. Where deviations occur—for example, when an order is placed with a bidder at a higher price because of design or other claimed advantages—the auditor should be satisfied that the higher price was properly approved.

Because of the close relationship (or poor planning) between advertising campaigns and related sales promotions, rush orders for tie-in material are a common occurrence. The auditor should be sure overtime or other unusual costs have been brought to the attention of and are approved by the appropriate level of authority, and that items such as overruns are within specified limits.

Where the advertising agency orders the material, the auditor should examine the agency's procedures in placing the orders. In addition, the agency procedures should be reviewed with the company purchasing department to ascertain that the purchase of material is being handled effectively from an overall company standpoint. Deviations from usual purchasing control procedures should be discussed with agency and company personnel.

Controls over Shipment and Receipt of Material

To save handling costs and the expense of duplicate packing and shipping, arrangements are often made to ship sales promotion material directly from the suppliers to a distributor or user and to produce the material simultaneously in several widely separated locations. When shipment is made directly, every effort should be made to secure a direct report of receipt from the distributor or user that may be checked with supplier's notices of shipment. Control is seriously weakened if such reports are not obtained. For example, in one company, product circulars, imprinted with a distributor's name, were sent directly to the distributor by the printer. An auditor's request for verification of receipt from the distributors disclosed that the printer charged the company for about 20 percent more circulars than were actually sent.

One method of verifying receipt is to have the agreement state that the distributor check the quantity received and then sign and return the packing slip enclosed with the shipment to the company. While this indicates the shipment was received, it may not report the quantity received, since the consignee may not verify the quantity of items sent to them on a no-charge basis. The degree of reporting accuracy possible in usual company operations may be unattainable in this situation. Where a receiving report is not required from the consignee, confirmation letters to selected distributors or physical test-checks arranged with specific distributors/salespersonnel are possible techniques for the auditor.

When materials are distributed on a rush basis, shipment will be made by such higher cost methods as courier, Express Mail, or Federal Express. When bulky material, such as a trade show exhibit, is involved, the cost of premium transportation may be quite high. Whatever the material, the auditor should question the reason and need for premium-rate shipments and ascertain that such premium transportation was approved.

Audit of Controls Over Storage and Usage

Since many sales promotion materials, such as circulars and catalogs, are designed for wide gratis distribution by other than company employees, those handling the distribution will probably have little interest in economical procedure. While the ultimate use in this situation is beyond the company's control, storage and usage controls within the company (and outside the warehouse) should be maintained to minimize spoilage. The auditor should examine receiving and shipping controls, and also the existing facilities for storage and handling. They should also review inventories periodically for obsolete and unused items.

Billing for Sales Promotion Materials

Certain sales promotion materials may be billed to a distributor on a basis under which part of the cost is charged to the company. For example, a special magazine that has articles describing uses of company products may be imprinted with a distributor's name and mailed to the customers. The charge to the distributor may be set at a rate designed to cover printing and mailing costs. Whatever the basis, the auditor should ascertain that adequate billing and collection controls are applied. As another example, if a special cookbook is authorized for printing, on the basis that the cost would be recovered through sales of the book to consumers, the actual revenue and net cost should be compared and verified by the auditor.

Special Sales Promotion Materials

A wide variety of sales promotion material may be produced for:

1. Exhibits for trade shows
2. Exhibits for sales meetings
3. Films describing company products
4. Product samples

With the possible exception of samples, these items are usually characterized by low unit production and high unit cost. A film or trade show exhibit may cost many thousands of dollars.

Audit of Controls over Production

The audit of controls over production of special materials should begin with examination of the authorization for production. This is then related to the final cost, with particular attention to unusual or special charges such as overtime and alterations. When materials are produced with company facilities, the auditor should appraise the basis on which sales promotion expense was charged for the items produced.

When vendors produce materials, the auditor should verify the approval for original production on the contract or purchase order. Such revisions and last-minute changes may result in the final transaction being more like a cost-plus construction contract than a fixed price purchase order.

Audit of Related Items

When examining transactions relating to special materials, the auditor should be satisfied with answers to:

1. Are materials stored and handled in a manner that guards against loss and damage?
2. Are materials shipped to point of usage by economical methods?
3. Are charges for materials distributed to proper budget and expense accounts?
4. How does actual cost of materials compare with original estimates? What approval was secured for overexpenditures?

5. What control exists over revenues derived from exhibit sales?
6. How are expenses of employees at exhibits authorized and controlled?
7. What controls are maintained to guard against loss or misappropriation of company products or other valuable items used in sales promotion activities?

The audit of sales promotion materials and related activities calls for both curiosity and ingenuity on the auditor's behalf. As previously mentioned, variety and new approaches are normal, and the auditor must be prepared to be adaptable to each plan and situation.

SALES PROMOTION—DISTRIBUTORS

Nature of Activities

A wide variety of activities having the general objective of increasing interest in and sales of company products is focused on distributors and other large quantity buyers. Many plans fall under the general classification of distributor sales promotion.

Because these plans approach the basic objectives of influencing the distributor in many different ways, it is hard to prescribe any general standards of control or methods of approach for the internal auditor. In some types of promotion, such as demonstrations, it is customary to have a signed agreement between the company and the distributor that specifies the terms and dates of the promotion. In other promotions, such as free goods deals, the terms of the deal apply to all distributors alike, and any agreements with individual distributors should be executed considering fair trade and practice (pricing) laws. The auditor should be looking for an annual contract indicating proof of performance and so on. The initial step in most promotions is usually a notice to distributors outlining the general nature of the activity.

In the following pages, the control and audit features of some of the more common varieties of sales promotion plans for distributors are treated individually:

Free goods deals
Coupons
Combination sales
Samples
Premiums
Contests

Legal Requirements

Whenever any sales promotion activity is being considered, the legal department should review and approve the general features of the proposed plan before announcing the details to customers. Watch for ambiguous wording, which, if interpreted in another way, could cost the company many times what it intended.

Many sales promotion plans take the form of temporary price reductions. The auditor should be assured that such reductions are applicable on an equitable basis to all distributors. Otherwise, legal action against the company for discriminatory pricing practices is possible.

In regard to contests, the legal and tax departments should determine (1) if the prizes awarded to distributors should be reported for income tax purposes, and (2) that the company is adequately protected against possible legal action from a dissatisfied contestant.

Free Goods Deals

The customary free goods deal provides that salable merchandise will be given to distributors in proportion to their purchases during the period of a sales drive. In a typical deal, one case is given free with each 10 cases purchased during the promotion period (eight weeks). This in effect amounts to a price reduction of about 10 percent during the sales promotion period. The purpose of the deal is to have the distributor pass the lower cost on to the customer through lower prices. Such a deal may also serve to move an overstock or seasonal glut of merchandise out of warehouses or packing plants, thus saving storage costs for the producer. However, some companies run their deals like clockwork (for two months **every quarter**); the customers plan accordingly and end up purchasing very little at regular prices. The auditor may want to test what percentage of product is sold at deal prices. Ratio analysis can be performed to see if there is value-added for deals. Where the product spoils (food), check for returns and the price credited for those returns. See if the distributor or store is overstocking and creating out-of-code-date problems for the manufacturer.

Control over free goods deals is relatively simple, since the free merchandise will bear a definite ratio to quantities billed. In most instances, billing summaries should show quantities billed and free goods allowed. The auditor should verify that free goods were shipped in the proper ratio, and that shipment was made according to specified terms of the deal.

Free goods deals have the effect of concentrating sales during the period of the promotion, with an abrupt drop in sales after the deal is terminated. Where future orders are permitted under the terms of the deal, distributors (with the cooperation of company salespersonnel) may take advantage of the promotion by entering orders that will be delivered after the deal.

SALES PROMOTION—RETAIL CUSTOMERS

Nature of Activities

A variety of incentives may be offered to prospective customers as inducements to purchase the products of a company. The primary objective of such sales promotions is usually to broaden distribution by securing new customers for the promoted product—or to introduce a new product.

In this section, five types of customer sales promotion are considered:

Coupons
Combination sales
Samples
Premiums
Contests

Legal Requirements

Some states and countries have legal restrictions against giving allowances to customers in such forms as coupons, premiums, free samples, or prizes for winning contests. Therefore, it is essential that the company legal department approve the legal and tax phases of promotional plans before they are put into effect.

Announcement of Promotion

The initial step in sales promotion at the retail customer level is the notice to the customer. This will usually take the form of an intensive advertising campaign that may use a number of approaches. For example, promotion of a new item might involve any, or all, of the following:

Magazine and newspaper advertising (with or without coupons)
Television and radio advertising
General mailing describing the product and enclosing coupons or samples
Premiums
Contests

Coupons

Coupons usually have the objective of offering a product at a reduced price. The reduction may take the form of a direct allowance—for example, 20 cents toward the purchase of an item. Other coupon offers might include an item free for each two or three purchased, free coupons, and additional coupons for repeat purchases. Couponing has evolved into a very sophisticated business. Redemption is tabulated by cents-off market, and region. Misredemption is tracked also.

Whatever the offer may be, the auditor must recognize that the coupon has a definite value when redeemed through proper channels. In fact, many coupons are designed to give the impression of value through the elaborate printing of serial numbering or the showing of an expiration date.

The ultimate redemption of coupons represents an out-of-pocket expense to the company, and is subject to many abuses. For example, a friendly cashier at a chain store may accept coupons from a customer even though the coupon is for a product that was not purchased. Company employees or outsiders may purchase a supply of newspapers containing coupons, cut the coupons and clear them for redemption at stated values, even though no products were purchased. Bona fide coupons turned in by distributors for a cash allowance may be abstracted and reused by a company employee. Coupons have been counterfeited, phony grocery stores have been established to process fraudulent coupons, and families have been known to gather coupons and get them processed through stores. Coupons have spawned state and local coupon clubs, national newsletters, and coupon swap clubs. All of these practices help increase the legitimate and fraudulent processing of coupons.

Where coupons are printed for separate distribution (not as part of media advertising), control begins with the original printing. The quantity printed should be certified by the printer and subsequently accounted for either through distribution or destruction of undistributed coupons.

In the redemption of coupons, the following control features apply:

1. Employees or outside agencies handling redemption should have no responsibility for coupon distribution.
2. Coupons presented for redemption should be examined for signs of fraud; for example, a group of clean, fresh coupons in consecutive numerical order may have been fraudulently included for redemption.
3. Coupons should be destroyed by the company immediately upon redemption.
4. The printers' premises should be toured and the custody over the printing plates should be determined.

5. The coupon redemption house(s) should be visited, and audited on site.

Coupons may be precoded to indicate the territory of distribution. If precoded, redeemed coupons may be sorted to show the rate of redemption by area. A comparatively high rate in a specific territory may be an indication of misredemption or fraud.

Controls over the redemption of coupons that should be covered in the audit program include the five items mentioned above plus:

1. The determination of the ratio of coupon redemptions to the sales of the product the coupon applies. Gross abuses are indicated by coupon redemptions in excess of sales. This ratio should be developed in total and on a test check basis for individual retail outlets (if possible).
2. The examination and appraisal of the procedures applying to the distribution and redemption of coupons. For example:
   a. Employees handling cash should not have access to undistributed coupons to guard against substitution of coupons for cash.
   b. Redeemed coupons should be counted and immediately canceled to prevent reuse.
   c. Undistributed coupons should be safeguarded against possible misappropriation by company employees or others.

Where coupons are redeemable for cash or products, effective safeguards over coupons and redemption must be established and enforced. (The program for control of coupon operations of one company is given below.)

Combination Sales

Combination sales usually offer the customer an opportunity to purchase a combination of units of product at a reduced price. For example:

1. Two units may be banded together with the covering band announcing that the two combined are sold at a price less than that of the separate units.
2. A large and a small package of a new product may be tried first. If the product is unsatisfactory, the large package may be returned for full credit.
3. To introduce a new product, a package of the new product may be banded with a package of an established product.

The principal possibility of abuse in combination sales centers around the separation of the combined packages by an unscrupulous dealer and the sale to the customer of the separated packages at full price. The principal controls against this are:

1. Stressing the combination offer in advertising campaigns so the customer will expect to receive the combination.
2. Marking trial packages as "free samples" so that they cannot be sold individually for cash.

When auditing combination sales, the auditor should investigate such matters as:

1. Coordination of advertising with sales plans
2. Adequacy of products to meet demands from customers
3. Disposition of combination products at the conclusion of the promotion

Samples

A common method of introducing a product to consumers is the distribution of samples. This may be effected by such means as:

1. Mailing
2. House to house distribution
3. Special distribution—for example, cigarette samples on street corners in major cities

Since samples, like coupons, are intended for wide distribution, complete control over the original distribution is usually not feasible. However, the auditor should examine the procedures by which samples are handled in company channels and should ascertain that opportunity for misappropriations and unauthorized use by company employees and outsiders is minimized. Controls over acquisition, storage, and shipment should ensure that the samples actually reach the point of distribution. The customary safeguard against abuse through sale of samples is the imprinting of samples packages "Not to be Sold."

Mailing of samples is commonly handled by outside mailing agencies. The general reliability of the agency should be established and controls over the mailing and the samples should be examined.

Where samples or other sales promotion materials are distributed on a house-to-house basis, the auditor should inquire into how the house-to-house distribution is handled. Such work is usually undertaken by crews of comparatively low-paid employees. The danger is, of course, that crew members may not make the house-to-house calls for which they are being paid. Samples, coupons, and advertising material may be misappropriated, sold to salvage operations, or destroyed. House-to-house operation requires close control by supervisors, and the auditor should determine how this control is exercised.

Premiums

Premium offers are a common form of customer sales promotion. To receive the premium, the customer is required to send proof of product purchase, such as a box top or a label (usually with a stipulated amount in cash or postage stamps) to a designated office where premiums are handled.

The majority of premium offers are designed to be self-liquidating; that is, the cash sent in is sufficient to cover the cost of the premium and its handling and shipment to the customer. Premium orders from customers may run into very large volume on a widely distributed product that offers an attractive premium.

Where large volume is anticipated, common practice is to employ an outside firm to handle premium orders. (In the case of a self-liquidating premium, the payments to the firm for its services plus the cost of premiums and handling should approximately offset the cash received with premium orders.) Before arrangements are concluded, there should be investigation into the general financial responsibility of the firm, and the internal auditor should examine and approve the controls that will be maintained over cash received and premiums purchased and shipped.

Where there is an agreement with an outside agency to process orders for a fixed charge per premium handled, the audit should relate the incoming payments to the units shipped. (Usually there will be a slight excess of units shipped because of claims by customers for nonreceipt of premiums.)

Where the amounts received for premiums more than cover the out-of-pocket costs, the auditor should verify that the appropriate profit is received by the company.

Whether premiums are handled by company personnel or by an outside agency, the auditor should inspect and appraise:

1. Controls over the handling of cash received with premium orders
2. Controls over premiums ordered and shipped
3. Controls over claims of nonshipment
4. Basis of charging cost of premium operations to sales promotion expenses

The auditor should also inspect correspondence covering complaints about nonreceipt of premiums, delays, and similar difficulties to ascertain that the promotion is properly handled and that controls are adequate. A surprise visit is also suggested. The auditors may wish to use individuals from the company's local sales force to assist them. The company may also request performance bonds from lesser established (or new) firms.

Contests

Consumer contests may offer prizes varying from those of small value to such large-value prizes as a car, extended travel, a house, or an income for life. Evidence of the purchase of a company product is a customary prerequisite for entry in the contest.

Receipt of contest entries and judging handled by specific arrangement with a reputable outside agency is customary. This relieves the company of a large volume of work and permits the checking of eligibility and judging to be handled by those most familiar with it. Moreover, the use of an outside agency minimizes the suspicion of possible collusion by company employees in the determination of the winners.

The control and audit procedures depend on the exact nature of the contest. In general, the agreement with the judging agency should be reviewed and the terms checked with the services provided and charges made to the company. Where merchandise prizes are offered, the controls over purchase and distribution and receipt should be examined and appraised.

INTERNAL AUDIT PROGRAM ADVERTISING & MARKETING SERVICES

This program is used in one company for a review of the internal advertising and marketing services departments.

Scope and Objectives

The audit of the advertising department covers the examination and appraisal of the controls established and administered by the department responsible for the advertising program. (The audit program concerned with the operations, records, and controls administered by the company's advertising agency is contained in audit program for advertising agency operations, below. Depending upon the company's and the agency's contract, some mix of the two programs may be necessary to meet a specific organization's requirements.)

The audit includes:

1. Advertising budget and planning
2. Contracts (or relationships) with advertising agencies

3. Purchase and control of
   a. Artwork
   b. Sales promotion materials
4. Cooperative advertising

The objectives of the audit are (1) to determine whether effective controls are established and maintained over advertising expenditures, and (2) to identify situations and make constructive recommendations in areas where improvement or cost-saving opportunities appear to be possible.

Analysis of the Advertising Budget

1. Review the appropriate company and division policies and procedures relating to advertising and marketing.
2. Obtain a copy of the budget, review for approval, and determine if the budget elements are classified for direct comparison to accounting reports.
3. Review the delegation of authority. Determine if it is adequate or too low.
4. Examine the method of original determination of budget amounts. Is the total dollar amount requested based on planned advertising expenditures, and are subcategories in sufficient detail for measuring performance?
5. Examine budget revisions for management approval. Ascertain that the amounts budgeted for advertising programs that are later deferred, abandoned, or curtailed, have not been diverted to unauthorized projects, but have been used to reduce the budget—or to advertise other company products with the appropriate approvals.
6. Analyze significant over- or underexpenditures and ascertain reasons therefor.
7. Question expenditures appearing to be exorbitant or disproportionate to total amounts budgeted. (Good judgment must be exercised in challenging these expenditures because of the intangible nature of advertising results.) Examples of items that can be properly challenged include:
   a. Any large or significant advertising expenditure where it appears questionable that the benefits derived are commensurate with the advertising dollar investment. An example is contests or prizes limited to a single key market that run for a relatively short period of time.
   b. Situations where proportionately large expenditures are made for such items as overtime, production costs, or high-cost shipment.

8. Ascertain if any prepaid and deferred amounts are proper charges to future operations and that these items are consistently treated.

9. Examine the method used in allocating advertising and promotional costs to the various divisions and subdivisions of the company. Is it equitable and easy to administer?

10. Examine advertising expenditures for home office and divisions by months to determine whether large expenditures are being made at year-end to use up budget balances. Conversely, determine that advertising expenditures do not phase out prior to the year-end because of budget limitations—indicating weakness in budget planning and administration of expenditures. In this regard, examine evidence of project cancelation and prepare a schedule of expenses on projects that were subsequently canceled because of budget limitations.

11. Determine if consideration is given to omitting certain recurring advertising programs during periods when the promotion of other specialized merchandise lines is more prominent. (As an example, many retail auto supply organizations run continuous ads promoting their auto accessories in certain key publications. At Christmas, Easter, and other holidays, these ads are canceled and funds are channeled to promote seasonal merchandise.)

Agency Relationships

1. Examine the advertising agency contract, noting all provisions for payment and compensation for later comparison with billings. In connection with examination of billings, determine whether all charges billed to the company are in accordance with the agreement and that none are of the type that should be borne in part or in total by the agency.

2. Check dates of payment of billing by the agency for media advertising to see these are coordinated with dates on which payments are made by agency to media. (If not coordinated, the agency may have the use of large sums of company money.)

3. The agency contract will normally specify the commissions to be added to the cost of outside materials purchased. Examples of such materials are: artwork, typesetting, engravings, mats, television production costs, and so on. Examine billings to determine whether the correct application, per the contract, is made. (Be careful; some agencies bill on a cost-plus basis but have a ceiling at which they may stop billing the company.)

4. Examination of agency relationships should include a comprehensive review of the controls exercised by the advertising department

to ensure that (a) advertising billed was actually run, (b) proper rate applications were made, (c) due consideration was given to discounts and special rates and the savings passed to the company (watch out for forgeries), (d) a proper control was established over artwork and advertising props (and their rental), thereby eliminating the necessity of duplicate costs, (e) the agency utilized proper purchasing techniques (such as competitive bids) where applicable, and (f) proof of receipt was a prerequisite to the payment of invoices. In addition, costs of agency staff work billed to the company should be accumulated by the agency for each job and should be related reasonably to the kind and quality of work required.

5. In connection with agency relationships, inquire into possible duplication of planning and operations between the agency and the advertising department. For example, verification of insertion may be unnecessarily double checked, or there may be duplicate specialists in such areas as media selection and artwork.

6. Request Dun and Bradstreet reports, or review incorporation papers of smaller agencies. Determine if vendors are relatives, in-laws, cousins, and so on, of anyone in a responsible position (conflict of interest). Also look for competition and documentation of competitive bids.

Outside Purchases

1. Examine the provisions of contracts with suppliers of signs and display material and art studios, for later comparison with invoices.

2. Determine whether competitive bids for advertising materials are secured from suppliers, and review them to ascertain if:

   a. Terms, conditions, and exceptions in the bids are clear, are sufficiently specific to eliminate any additional costs not provided for in the contract, are submitted on identical specifications, and that the costs for extras or additions and deletions are stipulated.

   b. Approval levels (not just one approval) of appropriate company management are obtained before work is started by suppliers.

3. Examine payment arrangements with various supply sources and determine whether payments are made accordingly. (Printing and display materials are normally paid for on completion of the run, while it is not unusual for sign manufacturers to be paid upon shipment.)

4. Select a representative number of invoices for outside artwork and compare the layout, composition, artwork, and so on, with the finished advertising to verify the work was performed and

the material was used as intended. Determine reasons why unused materials were not used.

5. Determine if the quantity of advertising materials ordered is based on needs established by field requests or on a reasonable experience basis.

6. If a supplier contract has an overrun provision, determine that materials in excess of the overrun are (a) accepted only with proper management approval, and/or (b) a reduced fee is charged for such overruns.

7. Usually, suppliers maintain material in their warehouses awaiting shipping instructions. In this case, examine the control over the accountability for this inventory and verify that proper evidence is received prior to payment of charges.

8. Examine destroy orders issued to suppliers for unused materials, and relate to original order to determine reasons for destruction. (Be alert for destroy orders issued because the field offices are reluctant to request materials due to budget constraints or due to improper planning by the advertising department when ordering.) Be alert for destroy orders issued for good material shipped to friends or to a salvage company where proceeds may not be directed back to the company.

9. Is any advertising material shipped from suppliers to the home office (or to a storage facility) and then to field locations? (If so, consideration should be given to having this material shipped direct by the supplier to the field.)

10. Does the supplier charge for storage? If so, are some items stored for extended periods of time, thereby creating unnecessary charges?

11. Is recurring artwork allocated to the same studio year after year, or are competitive bids occasionally requested as the basis for a possible change? (In reviewing art purchases, the auditor should be alert for favoritism in making purchases; this may indicate collusion or fraud.)

12. Question outside purchases of artwork, photostats, and printing and inquire if this work can be done within the company. (If the company does not have an art staff and artwork costs are significant, consideration should be given by the advertising department to hiring an artist or establishing an art staff.)

13. Examine payments made to dealers or received from manufacturers for cooperative advertising. Are they in accord with company policy? Are the ads placed in the proper media and are they of the type specified in original agreements for this advertising? Do tear sheets or media affidavits accompany invoices for cooperative advertising?

Test actual payments and relate amounts paid to the performance of the dealer, the quality of the advertising, the space frequency, and the size or kind of audience.

14. Examine transactions involving advertising and promotional materials chargeable to dealers. Is there an effective system of control over these materials? What control assures such materials are charged to the dealer?

15. Don't forget to review the system of internal controls. Be alert for controls whenever interfaces occur between the company and the vendor and back into the company again. Controls may be missing or duplicated.

INTERNAL AUDIT PROGRAM—ADVERTISING AGENCY OPERATIONS

This program is used by another company to review controls at and over outside agency activities.

Objectives

The general objectives of the advertising agency audit are to:

1. Establish that billings rendered to the company are in order.
2. Examine and evaluate the agency's system of internal control over financial and other transactions for the account of the company.
3. Identify and present for consideration possible cost-saving opportunities in such areas as (a) purchases of materials and services, or (b) duplication of work between the agency and the company advertising department, and (c) if the technical competence is on staff, determine if the process is giving the company the best return for the dollars expended.

General Approach

The accomplishment of these objectives requires verification and review of the following types of transactions and controls:

1. Verification of the propriety of payments made to the agency by establishing that:
   a. Billings are supported by agency payments for the company account (a joint account may also exist, in which case the auditor will want to review the co-release of checks and verify the receipt of wire transfers).
   b. Time charges for agency personnel are at approved rates as defined in the contract.

    c. Billings are legitimately billable and not properly an agency expense.

    d. Billings are charged to the proper product (or project estimate) and period.

    e. Prebillings are not made under any circumstances.

    f. Computation and application of commission and other agency charges are accurate and in accordance with the billing agreement or service contract.

2. Review and evaluate the agency's system of internal control to assure:

    a. Rates, insertions, reproductions, and performances are adequately checked by the agency.

    b. Credits for better earned rates, cash discounts, omissions, interruptions, and other credit adjustments or other guarantees are obtained in the proper amounts and, where applicable, are turned over to the company within a reasonable period of time.*

    c. Agency records covering artwork, merchandise, props, films, asset disposal, and so on are adequate.

    d. Legal releases for use of names, pictures, music, copyrights, and so on have been obtained.

    e. Insertions are planned realistically to obtain maximum discounts.

    f. Estimates are sufficiently detailed to enable the company to compare significant actual costs in detail as well as in total.

    g. Adequate preplanning time is allowed by both agency and company to avoid extra cost.

    h. The company agency agreement is kept up to date to meet changing situations. The agreement should also be reviewed to determine what components are charged to overhead, general and administrative charges versus direct charges.

Magazine, Newspaper, and Trade Paper—Production

Make a review of advertisements that have appeared, and select specific advertisements in representative publications. Secure from the agency the job cost jackets on the selected advertisements.

*Some agencies do not allow their clients' internal auditors access to the agency general ledger. In these cases, the internal auditor may wish to accept a direct certification from the agency's public accountants (or maybe hire another public accountant) attesting that the agency billing records reflect all allowances received by the agency during the audit period.

1. Check agency billings with supporting invoices from vendors, noting:
   a. Supporting invoices are for the company's account.
   b. Correct product, expense account, and period is charged. (Has the agency used progress billing, billing at completion of the job; have they prebilled?)
   c. Charges apply to the advertisement checked.
   d. Agency commission is correctly computed. (Postage, telegrams, duty, packaging, and shipping charges may be billable at net cost with no commission, depending upon agency contract.)
   e. Billable time agency personnel is at approved rates and in accordance with billing policy or contract.
   f. Charges should be billed to the company rather than an agency expense. Review and list all unusual charges, such as overtime and apparent inefficiencies, and determine whether they were approved by the agency production people and the company, and whether the company or agency caused them.
   g. Compare the total actual cost to the agency estimate. In cases where the agency supplies detailed cost estimates, compare the variances between major categories of expense, and obtain reasons for such variances. Determine that total billings do not exceed reasonable variations from approved estimates.
2. Check the ads selected for detailed testing to the media insertion schedule, and examine tear sheets.
3. Determine the method employed by the agency in selecting artists, vendors, and so on. Are bids secured prior to the placing of the purchase orders?
4. Are copies of vendors' invoices submitted for review by the company to justify billings of production costs?
5. Review and evaluate the agency's system of internal control over production costs.

Magazine, Newspaper, and Trade Paper—Space

Select a representative group of advertisements and publications.

1. Secure media estimates for magazines, newspapers, and trade papers.
2. Using the estimate and the master schedule of insertions, check each invoice for insertion date, lineage ordered, and total lineage for the particular estimate.

3. Verify cost of insertion or line rates with space contracts and Standard Rate and Data Service (SRDS) for rate, quantity, and cycle discounts. (Other standards also exist, especially in the top 10 markets.)

4. Select a number of insertions (newspaper and magazine) and check against lineage and rates that appear on the invoice. (This step can be accomplished when reviewing the agency's procedure for checking tear sheets and verifying that present controls in effect are adequate.)

5. Check billings to supporting publishers' invoices, noting if:

   a. Invoices are for the account of the company.

   b. Correct period and expense account is charged.

   c. Agency commissions are correctly computed.

   d. Cash discounts accrue to the company and are correctly computed.

   e. Footings and extensions on publishers' invoices are accurate.

   f. Rebates from publishers are passed on to the company by the agency, with commission added.

6. If a master control agency is designated for magazines and Sunday supplements:

   a. Secure the latest master insertion schedule for all magazines and main Sunday supplements from the media department.

   b. Review and evaluate the agency system of control over rates and volume discounts.

   c. Determine at what volume discount levels billings are being made by major publications, for example, *National Geographic, Forbes, Time,* and so on (e.g., progressively as the rate is earned, or on the basis of planned insertions during the contract year).

   d. Verify to publishers' invoices.

7. Determine the billing and payment procedure for each publication, covering:

   Billing by publication to agency

   Billing by agency to company

   Payment by company to agency

   Payment by agency to publication

   a. Test the bill-paying sequence of the above.

   b. As a result of the tests, list and describe any financing of the agency on the company and what the amount is over the publication's contract year.

8. Determine if cancelable commitments are controlled.

9. If the company has more than one agency and no master control agency exists for newspaper space, the agency that places the initial insertion in any given contract year issues the master contract and thereby becomes the master agency for that particular publication. In this case, determine if the agencies:

   a. Communicate with each other to coordinate planned insertions to obtain the lowest and most realistic volume rates throughout the year.

   b. Select trade papers and newspapers that allow volume discounts.

   c. Tabulate lineage insertions and rates for the contract year, or year-to-date, and interchange lineage between agencies.

   d. Ascertain that the company has been billed at the same rate by each agency. (If the insertion rate was revised downward, make certain the company was credited with the applicable rebates.)

   e. Included all the company products under the same blanket contract. (If the company uses different agencies for different products and if the company is not getting full credit for all product advertising in a publication, you may want to bring the buying in-house.)

Television and Radio—Network

Prior to the audit of the agency, determine the number of shows for each network, the time period covered, and the applicable discount structure in effect.

1. Determine that the discount is in accordance with each network's discount structure and that the company is securing the highest discount available based on the number of shows and so on. During the agency audit, verify that the discount, as determined above, agrees with the network's billing and the estimate prepared by the agency.

   a. Select for review at least one radio and television show for each major network and only those for which the agency acts as the master agency (where two or more agencies are involved.)

   b. Verify that the approved media estimate agrees with the network station listing at the beginning of the 13-week cycle, that is, in number of stations and in aggregate dollar amounts.

   c. Trace subsequent additions and deletions of stations or changes in rates during the 13-week cycle as shown on network invoices, to estimate revisions and network notices of rate changes. Note that the rate increases are effected subsequently to any rate protection period stipulated in the contract.

d. On a test basis, verify station rates on the estimate to the "SDRS-Network Rates and Data" booklet (or whatever is used by your media department) for the applicable period.

e. Note that the billings to company have been correctly allocated to participating products; that they have been billed in the proper month, and charged to the correct expense classification.

f. Ascertain that the network invoices are for the account of the company and that they are certified by the network positively or negatively, by a certificate or affidavit of performance.

g. Determine whether the agency commissions have been correctly computed and whether they exclude taxes. Check the bases upon which commissions are applied, and check also the agency procedure for billing and paying the taxes.

h. Check billing and payment procedure for transactions with each network as follows:

> Network billing to agency
>
> Agency billing to company
>
> Company payment to agency
>
> Agency payment to network

i. Test the bill-paying sequence of the above and ascertain if delayed or prebilling to the company does not exist.

2. Determine that adjustments for interruptions or nonperformance are supported by credit memoranda and that computation is in accord with each network's billing policy. Also, develop from actual billings how the networks render their credits to the agency, that is, with or without commissions; whether the agency, in turn, credits your company with or without commissions. In each case, make certain the agency obtains, for your company's account, the highest credit available.

3. Test check the performance of individual stations by reference to Broadcast Advertisers Reports (BAR), noting agreement of performance time with the estimate.

a. For any cases of nonperformance or interruption, or if the show was rescheduled per a change order, or credit was passed on to the company.

b. Review procedure to makeup time.

c. Ascertain the extent to which the agency uses BARs (or Arbitron or Nielsen rating) to check station performance.

4. Review all shows with the agency media personnel to determine if there are any unsettled matters or any outstanding commitments for which the company has not yet been billed: major interruptions, switch in product insertions, and so on.

5. Select a time period and product and/or programs for the audit of production and media time costs.

   a. Determine which agency charges are subject to commission, which are not, and which are properly absorbed by the agency. Verify that the billable time of agency personnel is in accordance with the contract and that the agency time charges are properly approved by agency supervisory personnel.

   b. Check charges per the agency billings to supporting billings from the networks, noting:

      (1) Supporting invoices are for the account of the company.

      (2) The correct product, expense, and period are charged.

      (3) Agency commission is correctly computed.

      (4) Credits and discounts are given to the company.

      (5) Allocation (if any) of costs to participating division or sponsors is accurately computed. (Comparison should be made with any other company agencies.)

      (6) The pay-bill sequence (see the next section) is proper.

   c. Determine that talent costs billed are in agreement with prevailing union scales. How are taxes reported and paid? How is commission computed?

   d. Review the network billing for studio rental, time, and so on. (Note: Each network publishes a booklet showing all necessary billing data. Secure a copy from the agency media department.)

   e. Review and evaluate the agency system of internal control over talent payments, including price payments and other production charges. On package shows, check the contract and determine:

      (1) Whether the agency is billing the company in accordance with contractual terms, including the computation of commissions.

      (2) If the show includes both originals and reruns, how does the agency bill: separately for each, or at an average of the two?

   f. Prepare a listing of charges that appear to be unusual or extraordinary. Review with agency personnel, or if this is not advisable, then review the charges with the corporate advertising department. Determine whether they are proper and whether they should be described in detail in your billing policy.

Television and Radio Commercial Production

Select several commercial announcements for audit.

1. Check charges per agency billings to supporting invoices, noting:

   a. Supporting invoices are for the account of the company and have been billed under the proper estimate.

b. They have been approved by responsible agency personnel.

c. Invoice charges are for the correct commercial and product.

d. Agency commission is correctly computed according to contract or policy.

e. Billable time or finished work, such as story boards and jingles, is at approved rates or amounts as outlined in billing policy. Determine whether charges should be billed to the company rather than agency expense. List all unusual charges for review with agency and company advertising personnel or product managers.

f. All credits and discounts received are passed on to the company.

2. Determine if competitive bids are secured from producers by the agency, noting that:

a. Specifications of the bids are clear and sufficient to eliminate any additional costs not provided for in the contract.

b. Approval of appropriate company personnel is obtained before work is started by the producer.

3. Determine when the producer is to be paid—after the completion and acceptance of the commercial, or in partial payments.

4. If no competitive bids are requested, determine how producers are selected.

5. Does the agency submit detailed estimates by major categories or expense? Is there an effective comparison of actual costs with detailed estimates?

6. Review the listing of props used in the production of film commercials, verifying their physical existence on a test basis.

7. Review and evaluate the agency's system of internal control over:
Props duplicated
Stored props used
Rental and disposal of props
Overtime
Payroll and taxes
Actors, models, and so on—their use, going rates, release statements, payment of union dues, reuse payments
Preplanning—Producing three commercials at one time instead of one, and so on

Television and Radio—Regional Syndication, and Local (Spot) Time

Select several television and radio spot announcement estimates for a calendar quarter.

1. Verify billings to the company are in agreement with the approved estimates by checking selected stations, related rates, and number of spot announcements.
2. Check actual billings rendered to the company that refer to the selected station invoices and note whether:
   a. Charges are for the account of the company and that the correct product, expense, and period is charged.
   b. Agency commission is correctly computed and excludes all noncommission items such as taxes, postage, shipping, and packaging charges.
   c. Performance is certified by the stations by a certificate or affidavit of performance.
3. Select a representative number of invoices checked in Step 2, and:
   a. Verify that station rates listed against master contracts are located in the media department and the Standard Rate and Data book.
   b. Determine that the time of performance as per the invoice agrees with the time ordered as shown on the estimate.
   c. Secure related BAR reports and check the time of actual shown on the invoice. Review reports for possible triple spotting. Where BAR reports are not available for the stations listed, trace available BAR reports to station invoices on a test basis.
4. Review and test the agency's control system to determine if there is an effective reporting procedure on spot announcements used and to assure that the lowest possible rates are obtained. Determine if the agency refunds commissions on rebates earned on volume discounts.
5. Determine the method followed by the agency in obtaining frequency discounts, that is, progressively from the beginning of the contract year; quarterly; or at a planned insertion level for the entire contract year.
6. Determine if there are any commitments outstanding for which the company has not yet been billed.
7. Review and describe the procedure for obtaining rebates for interruptions, preempted time, and cancelations. Determine who is responsible for acceptance of makeups submitted by the station. Does the agency negotiate to obtain highest credit for the company?

Outdoor Advertising

1. Determine whether the agency belongs to the National Outdoor Advertising Bureau. If so, does the agency use the bureau services? If not, should it consider joining?

2. If the agency purchases space directly from outdoor plants (companies making the billboards), check and trace the poster contract to the estimate to see that such information as product, city, posting dates, cost per month, and total cost is accurate.

3. Ascertain that all contracts have been accepted and any exceptions or charges are covered in revised estimates.

4. Check vendors' invoices to the approved space contract.

5. Review the billing arrangements the agency follows and ascertain that no prepayment exists.

6. Ascertain that the lithography on outdoor posters has been ordered directly by the company.

7. In addition to reviewing affidavits or performance from outdoor plants, inquire as to what additional verification of performance and appearance is made by the agency or company sales force.

8. Check allowances granted for such items as torn posters and lack of illumination. Are allowances passed on to the company? How is the agency commission affected?

INTERNAL CONTROL OF COUPON OPERATIONS

Printing

1. Employees responsible for procurement should satisfy themselves that the coupon printers are reputable and financially responsible, and that their employees are bonded.

2. Before placing the order, the printer's system internal control over printed materials should be reviewed by a company representative to ensure that the coupons will be effectively controlled. The printer should have controls such as:

   a. Presses equipped with locked counting registers

   b. Production control through issuance of paper stock and determination of material usage variances from standard

   c. Perpetual inventory control and physical safeguarding of finished production and plates, with procedures calling for supervised destruction of plates and nonbillable overruns at conclusion of job

3. Agreements with printers should provide for access by the company to the printer's production and shipping records to ensure that the printing and shipment are effectively controlled.

4. Procurement of coupons should be governed by the usual company controls over ordering, receiving, and payment.

Distribution of Coupons in—or on—Package

1. Storage and custody of coupons should be centralized at the location where the coupons will be inserted or used. Storage facilities should give physical security; the custodian should be a responsible employee.
2. Perpetual inventory records should be maintained by an employee other than the custodian.
3. Physical inventory should be taken and checked with perpetual inventory records on a regular basis.
4. Determine what happened to coupons for product destroyed or rendered unsalable due to damage in carton, on shelf, and so on.
5. As soon as coupons become obsolete, stocks on hand should be verified by physical inventory and destroyed under supervision.
6. Daily approved requisitions for coupons should equal the approximate production requirements. Unused coupons should be returned each day and a credit receipt issued by the custodian.
7. If finished goods are produced by an outside processor (toll packer), agreement with the packer should provide that the toll packer maintain controls over coupons similar to those maintained by the company over its own coupon consumption. The processor should return unused coupons to the company.

Distribution of Coupons by a Mailing House

1. Employees responsible for contracting should satisfy themselves that mailing houses are reputable and financially responsible.
2. A company representative should review the system of internal control used by the mailing house for such features as:
   a. Verification of quantities received
   b. Physical facilities for safeguarding coupons
   c. Perpetual inventory records
   d. Issuance of coupons on approved requisitions to cover the requirements of each shift
   e. Supervision of mailing house employees
   f. Inspection by supervisors
   g. Credit to coupon inventory records based on statements prepared by the mailing house and verified by the post office
   h. Verified mailing statements supporting billings to the company
   i. Control and verification of unused and spoiled coupons by test check

    j. Verification of perpetual inventory records by physical count

    k. Disposition of unused coupons by:

        Shredding or burning under company supervision

        Return to the company

        Destruction with certification to company

    l. Bonding of mailing house employees

    m. Bonding of the printer's employees

3. If the mailing house prints the coupons, the controls over printing should be the same as for the purchase of coupons from an outside printer.

4. The company should maintain inventory records covering coupons delivered to and used by the mailing house. Receipts should be verified with printer's invoices and consumption with verified mailing statements.

5. Agreement with the mailing house should provide for audit by a company representative covering such items as checking of mailing statements against mailing lists and postal receipts and verification of inventories of company-owned materials.

Redemption

1. Centralized redemption of coupons has the following advantages:
   a. Effective control of redemption payments (or credits) to customers
   b. Increased customer goodwill through prompt and expert handling
   c. Freeing sales personnel from redemption duties
   d. Development of statistical information that might otherwise be difficult to secure, for example, redemptions by area and class of customer. Central office data processing equipment may be effectively utilized to develop this information.

2. Envelopes in which coupons are received should be retained with payment vouchers, or the postmarked envelope may be used as the voucher. This will guard against substitution of payees.

3. Coupons received should be reviewed for mixed denominations and for coupons of other companies. Coupons received in quantity from salespersonnel, retailers, or direct accounts should be counted on a test basis or measured against precounted standard stacks. Accounts with a pattern of unreasonable differences should be subject to constant verification.

4. Coupons redeemed should be promptly and effectively canceled (for example, by perforation) to avoid subsequent misuse.

Redeemed coupons should not be destroyed until there has been adequate time for audit.

5. In making payments for coupon redemption, company checks (or drafts) are normally issued. These accounts should be reconciled monthly.

6. If payment is made by draft/wire:

   a. Unused drafts should be subject to the same physical safeguards as cash.

   b. Numerical control of drafts/wires should be maintained by the employee responsible for custody.

   c. Drafts should be issued in numerical order in quantity equal to about one day's requirements, with a record maintained of first and last numbers issued.

   d. At the close of each day, all financial instruments should be accounted for as used, voided, or unused. Unused forms should be returned to custody.

CHAPTER 10

Insurance

GENERAL CONSIDERATIONS

Definition

Insurance, as used in this chapter, is defined as the method or methods through which an organization transfers the risk of potential losses from casualty, property (business interruption/net income), theft, personnel, catastrophe, or legal liability to others. This definition is very broad, and is not limited to insurance in the form of policies purchased from insurance carriers. Although it is possible to purchase insurance policies to provide indemnity against almost any conceivable risk, no company or individual ever maintains such complete coverage. This is primarily because the known or perceived exposure can be assumed by the risk-taker to the extent that any loss or series of losses will not impair the asset levels of the organization, or the cost of insurance is prohibitive.

Insurance Versus Risk-Taking

In the development and structuring of insurance programs, a distinction must be made between insurance and risk-taking. Insurance is the applicable term when risk is transferred by such means as (1) purchase of a policy from an insurance company or other source, or (2) provision against possible loss through a self-insurance program. Risk-taking normally occurs when the hazard or exposure to loss is considered to be so small or remote that it is not a probable source of major loss, or where the potential hazard may be highly predictable and, therefore, manageable or unknown and unintentionally assumed. For example, in the mail order business, the customary practice is not to carry insurance against parcels lost in transit. Individual values are comparatively small, and shipments are numerous. The small number of losses can be readily assumed by the business without appreciable hazard to its profits. Conversely, a company in which shipments are very few in number and very high in unit value would probably insure against loss on shipments up to the point that title passed to the customer.

A form of risk-taking found in almost every insurance program is the maintenance of insurance policies with a specified deductible provision. Losses below the deductible, or self-insured retention, are assumed or proportionately shared by the insured, with the carrier liable for covered losses in excess of the retained limit up to the limits set by the insurance policy. Where the retained limit is high, provision against possible loss may be funded through the use of a reserve account maintained by the insured for payment of losses in the retained limit or funded by current cash balances.

Nature of Potential Risks

Insurance hazards that are covered by an insurance program may be separated into two general classes:

1. Risks involving potential loss or damage to various company exposures or impairment of assets. This covers such hazards as:
   a. Fire and extended coverage, including windstorm, earthquake, and explosion
   b. Vehicle collision
   c. Employee fidelity bond
   d. Plate glass breakage
   e. Business interruption/net income (sometimes called time element coverage)
   f. Machinery breakdown
   g. Officer, director, and fiduciaries liability
   h. Kidnap insurance
   i. Key-man life insurance
   j. Excess liability coverage

   To a large degree, a characteristic of these hazards is that the exposure to possible loss is definite in terms of valuation. For hazards such as vehicle collision and fire, the maximum exposure to loss is the value of the insured property based on a current appraisal or replacement cost. The determination of the amount of exposure to loss is less determinable with defalcation, forgery, and time element. In these cases, study of previous experience, loss control, and existing internal controls indicate within certain probabilities where the amount of loss may fall. The 1974 ERISA provisions require a guarantee that the administrator of the programs will give *personal* indemnification of performance as long as they are acting prudently

2. Risks involving potential liability to others for which a company may be held legally responsible. Types of insurance against such risks include:

   a. Comprehensive general liability, including products/completed operations, third-party liability under lease obligations, and special risks such as vessel charters and advertising

   b. Workers' compensation and employers' liability

   c. Boiler and machinery explosion

   d. Automobile liability

   e. Aircraft liability insurance (with guest passenger voluntary settlement waiver for a $500,000 policy)

   f. Marine (hull and personnel) insurance

A characteristic of these hazards is that it is difficult and often impossible to determine what the exposure to potential loss may be. For example, a proven claim that a defective product has caused permanent injury or loss of life to a user may result in a very large award for damages.

Some hazards may involve the possibility of loss or personal injury to both company property and personnel and to noncompany property and personnel. Examples include (1) an explosion that causes extensive damage to both company property and a surrounding area, and (2) automobile accidents, which cause damage to the property of others, personal injuries, and damage to company property.

The potential hazard and the indefinite limits of exposure and loss because of possible liability to others result in the customary practice of carrying outside insurance protection against excessive loss from these sources. In addition to protection against liability for covered occurrences, such insurance gives a company the benefit of the legal counsel of the insurance carrier in defending any court actions.

An exception is often found in insurance for workers' compensation. In the United States, its' territories, or possessions, compensation liability is limited by law and is administered by local governmental boards. In many instances, however, governmental units permit a company to operate as a qualified self-insured with a guarantee deposit, usually required by the state governmental unit, in the form of a surety bond to insure the fulfillment of the liability of the company to its employees. In addition, the self-insurer can purchase specific excess and aggregate excess coverage (where not prohibited by law) to limit its liability on a per-loss and annual aggregate basis.

Exclusions

Certain specialized coverages are not included in this chapter—either because of restricted applicability or because of factors that tend to place the responsibility outside of those customarily included in a program administered by a company insurance department.

Group (medical, dental, life) insurance
Insured pension plans
Marine (hull and personnel) insurance
Executive (key-man) life insurance
Expropriation insurance
Insurance levied by governmental authorities (i.e., unemployment)

Fire and Related Coverages

Fire is a peril customarily covered by insurance. Provisions for certain other perils, such as those from windstorm, earthquake, riot, and falling objects are possible and usual to include in fire policies. Where assets to be covered fluctuate in quantity and value, as in the case of inventories, policies usually provide for complete coverage with periodic reporting of values to the insurance carrier as the basis for the determination of premium.

Many fire policies contain a coinsurance feature that stipulates that insurance must be carried up to a prescribed percentage (usually 80 percent or 90 percent) of the present-day insurable value. This means if a partial loss is incurred—and the insurance coverage is below the prescribed percentage—the insurance carrier will pay for the loss only in the proportion that the amount of insurance carried bears to the actual cash value of the property insured. As an example, assume $4000 in insurance is carried in a property with an insurable cash value of $10,000. The policy contains an 80 percent coinsurance clause. If a partial loss of $4000 is sustained, the insurance carrier will be liable for payment of only 50 percent—$2000—of the loss of $4000, even though the face amount of the policy is $4000. If $8000 in insurance (at 80 percent of the actual cash value) had been carried, the entire loss of $4000 would have been paid.

Insurable values of material and supply inventories are usually on a basis of current cost and are readily determinable from accounting or market records; finished goods are usually insurable on a basis of selling price. Insurable values of buildings, equipment, and other fixed assets are much more difficult to determine. Such assets have often been acquired over many years, and accounting book values may have no relation to the present insurable values that are the basis for insurance. Failure to establish proper insurable values may lead to unrecognized assumption of risk on the part of a company. Moreover, if the difference between insurable and insured values is great, a partial loss may subject a company to the operation of the coinsurance feature just described.

Determination of insurable values of fixed assets may be made by periodic appraisal by outside appraisers, appraisers employed by insurance carriers, or qualified company personnel who are familiar with equipment, construction, and costs. Other methods of arriving at insurable values is by applying costs of various classifications of construction and costs, or by applying index factors to original costs. These indices show the ratio of costs of various classifications of construction and equipment between previous years and the current year. Most appraisals or index calculations result in a present-day gross replacement value, to which is applied a depreciation factor that reduces the gross value to a net insurable value. Customarily, companies limit the depreciation factor so the assets are valued at a figure representing their usefulness to the company as operating facilities. For example, one company limits the depreciation on buildings and machinery to 35 percent—regardless of the age of the assets. Where an appraisal has been made, it is possible to buy full replacement insurance that will cover the entire cost of replacing damaged or destroyed property, regardless of depreciation.

Specialized policies are available that provide broad coverage for movement of inventories and materials. For example, a blanket floater contract can be purchased to provide complete coverage against loss of practically any nature to products, materials, and supplies in any location or in transit between locations. One company carries such insurance to cover consigned merchandise in the hands of customers. Another company, which has extensive incoming shipments of large value by truck, carries coverage against the possibility that the trucking company might not be able to pay the full amount of a loss.

The principal problems in fire and related coverages are (1) the recognition of the risks, and (2) the determination of insurable values. Values that are too low may lead to unanticipated or unwarranted risk-taking; values that are too high result in excessive insurance premium costs.

Motor Vehicle Coverage

The common exposures in the operation of company-owned motor vehicles are losses through fire, theft, windstorm, water, or collision, and liability for injury to other persons or damage to the property of others.

Where a motor fleet of any size is in operation over a widespread area, it is common to find that losses through fire, theft, and collision will be covered by a company self-insurance program or by assumption of any loss as a current operating expense. The reasons for this are:

1. Risk is spread.
2. The maximum foreseeable loss exposure is the value of the vehicles.
3. Actual losses in a sizable motor fleet tend to follow normal ratios.
4. Adjusting losses with claimants outside the company poses few problems.
5. The company supports proper loss control.

The potential liability for injury to others or damage to property is usually covered by insurance purchased from outside carriers. The reasons for this include:

1. The loss exposure for a single accident may be very large.
2. Insurance company adjusters provide expert service in settling claims with outside claimants.
3. Insurance company legal forces provide experience and talent in handling litigation.
4. Insurance carriers offer nationwide service for such activities as safety campaigns.

Employee Fidelity Bond

Insurance against the dishonest acts of employees is carried by virtually all larger companies in the United States and Canada, but is less common in many other countries. Fraud is one form of potential loss to a company where it is difficult to anticipate just how great a loss may be. Many cases have occurred in small business and small financial institutions where a fraud loss has been so great as to impair the financial future of a business. The potential for loss is further increased with the onset of EDP systems. The first line of defense against fraud is the internal control plans established by the business and appraised by the internal auditor. Fidelity coverage operates to protect against the losses that occur when the control plans fail to protect. This coverage is becoming harder to get with deductibles and premiums increasing dramatically.

In reviewing fidelity insurance coverage, the company might self-insure part of the deductible. For example, the primary deductible may be stated as $25,000 when, in fact, the company policy may be $150,000—with a captive insurance company insuring the amount between $25,000 and $150,000.

In one company, the insurance broker interviewed various corporate individuals about internal controls. One individual interviewed was the general auditor. The internal control systems, both manual and system, were discussed annually. The insurance manager was asked to sign a statement on the adequacy of internal controls as a prerequisite for obtaining a fidelity bond.

Business Interruption

Business interruption is a form of insurance that acts to preserve the business from the time a disastrous loss occurs until the business is reestablished on an operational basis. Many different forms of business interruption policies exist. In general, such policies provide for expenses necessary to maintain the business organization—such as salary payments to key personnel and a skeleton working force—and for reimbursing the policyholder for profits that would have been made during the period of the loss. If desired, ordinary payroll can also be insured for a limited period.

The decision to carry business interruption insurance is usually governed by consideration of the effect that a disastrous loss at one location would have on the business as a whole. For example, a company whose entire operations were in one building would be seriously crippled if a disastrous fire or explosion occurred in that building—and accordingly should carry business interruption insurance. A similar situation exists in a multiproduct company where all of the facilities for one product were in one plant or building. Where a number of decentralized plants make the same product, business interruption insurance is probably not required. Business interruption may also be carried to qualify a company under state financial responsibility laws.

Holdup, Burglary, Forgery, Plate Glass

These are examples of specialized coverages that may or may not be found in a company. Often an analysis of the risk and the possible maximum amount of loss indicate that these hazards may be assumed on a self-insurance or risk-taking basis. For example, a factory in which the only cash is a small petty cash fund and all financial transactions are handled by check would probably not be the victim of a holdup or burglary. If it were, checks are usually traceable and replaceable, so the loss would be minimal. A factor in considering insurance against a hazard such as check forgery is consideration of the third-party liability of the bank in relation to any possible loss to the company.

Workers' Compensation and Employers Liability

Workers' compensation, which covers company employees against injury and loss of life because of the hazards of their work, is required by law in many countries. Some companies give full salary for a set time period under a special salary category (fringe benefit), rather than having the employee go on workman's compensation (a duplicate coverage).

In the United States, each state stipulates the requirements of this insurance and regulates the liability of the company to employees because of claims. In some states—termed *monopolistic*—a company must carry its compensation insurance through a state-administered fund. These states include: Washington, West Virginia, Wyoming, Ohio, North Dakota, and Nevada. Some states permit employers to self-insure under specific regulations, which usually require the maintenance of a guarantee fund on deposit with the state. Other states specify the rates for classifications of employees; these rates vary widely according to the type of work performed.

Sundry Liability Coverage

Policies insuring against the legal liability of a company for loss or damage to the persons or property of noncompany individuals take many forms. Some of the more common ones are described below.

General Liability

General liability insurance covers the liability of a company to outside persons for occurrences on its premises or in connection with its operations. An example of the need for such coverage is an award against a company because of an outsider's accident—such as slipping on the floor—on the company premises. Since it is virtually impossible to specify every sort of hazard that might be the subject of a liability lawsuit, general liability policies should be written to provide broad coverage (to protect against third-party liability and special risks).

Products Liability

Products liability insurance is carried by companies—such as food, drug, beverage, and machinery—that manufacture and distribute products used or consumed by individuals. The purpose is to protect against possible liability for damage to health or loss of life to a user because of some claimed defect in the company's products. For example, a defect in a pharmaceutical product might result in serious harm to users and the assessment of very heavy damages against the manufacturer. Similarly, a defect in a machine might cause extensive injury and property damage. The losses charged to a company not covered against such occurrences by products liability insurance might be great enough to seriously affect a company's financial viability.

In addition, the companion coverage to products liability insurance for contractors providing a wide spectrum of services is Completed

Operations Insurance. This coverage provides indemnification for covered losses after the particular job has been completed and the contractor has vacated the premises.

EDP Coverage

Some companies insure computer equipment separately under the blanket business interruption coverage. The property is covered under direct damage and the corporate data under the time element coverage of business interruption. Industries that usually have specific and separate coverage under error and omission coverage include broadcasting, insurance, and banking/financial institutions.

Contingent Liability

A company may suffer financial loss from many happenings over which it has little or no direct control, but for which the company can legally be held financially responsible. For example, a contractor may have an accident in the course of construction of a building for a company. The contractor's own insurance should cover any damages assessed because of the accident. If it does not, the cost of the damage may—and usually will—be assessed to the company. Similarly, a company is often held responsible for injury and property damage caused by an employee driving his own car on company business, or by trucking companies hauling materials under contract.

Contingent liability may be insured or guarded against in four ways:

1. By specific insurance taken out by the company against such liability.
2. By examination of policies held by outside contractors—or the securing of certificates of insurance—to verify that they carry adequate limits of coverage. (One company's purchase order specifies the limits of insurance for workers' compensation, auto liability, and general liability to be covered by a contractor.)
3. By showing the company is insured on policies of others—and examination by the company to verify this is done and that limits of coverage are adequate. This plan is often followed with employee-owned cars used on company business.
4. By contract or performance bond policies that guard against the assessment of liability for failure to perform the terms of a contract.

Deductible Loss Coverage

For many types of coverage, a company may be willing to assume the risk of loss up to a certain amount—but consider that a loss beyond that amount would be so great as to be an unjustifiable risk-taking. Where the first part of the loss is assumed by the company, the premium for outside coverage will usually be much less than that for full coverage. In effect, the company takes the risk (or provides for it by self-insurance) up to the limit for which it has assumed responsibility, and the insurance carrier takes over the risk from that point on. Examples of such protection are:

1. A chain store may decide to self-insure against fire loss in any individual unit up to $10,000—with coverage purchased beyond that amount.
2. An airline may carry insurance against liability for loss of life or injury to passengers in accidents, with the airline assuming the initial $100,000 of loss on each accident.
3. A petroleum company may self-insure against refinery fires up to $500,000 and purchase coverage against losses over that limit.
4. A company may decide to assume the first $500 of any loss on automobile collision.

Broad Coverages

Originally and up to relatively recent years, the majority of insurance policies were written to cover risks that were limited and very definitely specified in the policies. The result was that broad coverage in an insurance program required the maintenance and servicing of a large number of policies by the insured and the insurance carriers. There was a further problem in that occasional losses would occur where a claim revealed no coverage existed against the specific hazard that brought about the loss. For example, a company might carry a position schedule bond against fraud that specified the exact job positions of the employees who were covered by the bond. A fraud committed by an employee in an unspecified job position would not be insured.

To guard against such situations, insurance carriers have tended to broaden the coverages of their policies. In the case described, a blanket position bond—at probably very little additional premium—might have covered all employees of the company instead of just those specified. A floater policy may be purchased giving much broader coverage in terms of values and locations than policies restricted to specified values and locations. Liability policies are available to provide protection in a single policy against a variety of direct and contingent liabilities. For example, insurance carriers in the United States offer (in most states) a single manufacturer's output policy, which covers loss against fire, burglary, windstorm, liability, and certain other risks to a business at a rate appreciably lower than the cost of the same coverage in individual policies. Any gaps in liability coverage may be protected against by an umbrella policy, which covers uninsured risks and provides excess coverage on liability hazards that are already included in the insurance program. The problem for the executives determining company policy on insurance is to decide whether the possible risks are sufficient to justify the costs of such coverage.

Remember, insurance coverage is not static. Insurance carriers are constantly changing and improving their policies. In fact, the availability of insurance to a specific insured sometimes has little bearing on the individual exposure facing the insurer. Like any industry, the insurance industry is driven by present day economic conditions, and short-term financial results. The ability of the insurance industry to provide the necessary products to its consumers is largely contingent upon the insurers' ability to proficiently spread their risk. Unfortunately, when the necessary support cannot be ascertained, many insured become self-insured and are forced to fund internally for this uncertainty, which can sometimes impair growth. These areas of exposure are of concern to the auditor and should be appropriately disclosed.

Foreign Operations in the United States

Europeans consider the legal system in the United States to be too lenient, but usually insure themselves similar to most U.S. companies. European operations usually are insured separately from United States operations because of the differences in U.S. liability laws. The Japanese do not care for the U.S. litigious society and obtain first dollar coverage, therefore assuming no risk; they prefer to pay the known insurance premium cost.

ACQUISITION OF COVERAGE

Insurance Carriers

Insurance carriers are principally comprised of capital stock companies, mutual companies, and various kinds of syndicates. Capital stock companies underwrite insurance on a profit-making basis. Mutual companies are controlled by the policyholders, who may share in any surplus remaining after provision for losses, expenses, and reserves. Syndicates are combinations of individuals or companies that underwrite insurance—usually in larger amounts—on a cooperative basis. The best known of these is Lloyds of London, which is composed of individuals who combine to write insurance on almost any conceivable risk. Other syndicates specialize in a particular class of risk—for example, fireproof factory buildings that are protected by sprinkler systems. Still another form of insurance carrier is the reciprocal underwriter syndicate, formed by a combination of companies, usually operating in the same industry.

Determination of Premium Rates

Since insurance is essentially the spreading of risk against a possible loss over a number of insureds, the determination of premium rates by insurance company actuaries depends on such factors as previous experience and the anticipated risk. To simplify this determination, carriers may participate in joint rating bureaus, which handle the accumulation of experience and the establishment of rates for customary risks. Large and specialized risks may in some instances be rated by an insurance carrier's own underwriters.

An important factor in rating in the United States is the variation in the degree of control exercised by the individual states over the premium rates. In the individual states, rates on certain coverages must be approved by a state insurance regulatory board. Thus, a corporation operating in a number of states may find that a single policy covering locations in several states will be billed at a number of different rates.

For certain types of coverage—workers' compensation, for example—the policyholder's rate may be markedly influenced by experience. If accident frequency is low and claims are small over a period, an eventual reduction in cost may occur through the application of an experience credit to rates, or the effect of a retrospective rating plan. If experience is poor, costs will be increased. The net effect will be that from a long-term standpoint, such insurance is on a cost-plus basis, with the final cost sufficient to recover losses, plus the allocable amounts covering service, administration, overhead, and profit to the insurance carrier. Experience rating plans have the great advantage of providing the company an incentive to minimize claims and losses. The result will be the conduct of such activities as campaigns to reduce industrial accidents (zero defects campaign) and contests to recognize and reward safe drivers of company auto equipment.

In general, premium rates are relatively inflexible where coverage is restricted in scope or policy amount. Even where experience is favorable, it is not feasible for an insurance carrier to keep the records and make the calculations necessary to give an experience rating in such situations.

As policies become large in scope and amount, it becomes increasingly possible to purchase insurance in forms that give credit for good experience or other factors. More latitude exists for variation and negotiation—with resulting benefit in terms of more complete coverage and lower rates.

Function of Insurance Broker

A principal part of insurance coverage placed with outside carriers is done through insurance brokers or agents, who receive their remuneration in the form of a commission paid to them by the carriers. The rates obtained by placing insurance through a broker or agent are generally the same as would be quoted for direct purchase from an insurance carrier where direct purchase is possible.

The insurance broker's relationship with a company and the insurance carriers is similar to the relationship an advertising agency has with a company and the advertising media. The broker has the expert knowledge of insurance carriers and risks that will enable the broker to recommend the carriers that will provide the most effective coverage at minimum cost. Moreover, the broker is in close touch with the constantly changing picture of risks and coverages. From this knowledge—and the knowledge of the client company through constant dealing—the broker can keep its client informed of the latest developments in the insurance field.

In some companies and for certain types of insurance, coverage may be acquired through direct dealing with insurance carriers, rather than through the use of brokers. In fields where the services of a broker are utilized, the determination of general policies and the administration of the program must be centered in the company. The broker can then best fulfill the function of serving as an expert adviser and critic in the optimum application of the insurance program to company operations and in the development of markets in which insurance may be purchased. Since the compensation of the broker (commission or fee) is dependent on the amount of premiums on insurance placed with outside carriers, do not expect a broker working on a commission basis to ordinarily take the initiative in a project to develop or broaden a self-insurance program that could reduce premiums.

In addition to rendering valuable services in the acquisition of insurance coverage, the broker serves as the intermediary between the company and the insurance carrier during the life of the policy. For example, large brokers have separate groups that specialize in such fields as engineering, fire protection, and claims—and can provide advice and assistance in reporting and negotiating settlements and other matters with the insurance carriers. In these cases, a fee arrangement can be maintained on a time and expense basis.

Another service of brokers is the maintenance of continuing records of policy coverages and expirations. These records insure that policies are brought up for consideration and possible revision in time to prevent any lapse in coverage.

Function of Insurance Consultant or Advisor

Insurance consultants provide a means for appraisal and advice on the adequacy of company insurance programs. These consultants should operate independently of any insurance company or broker. Their independence—and their professional knowledge of the whole insurance field—permits them to render valuable advice and assistance in the development and application of a company program.

Insurance Policies

The insurance policy is the binding contract between the insurance carrier and the insured. While some policies are simple in form, the majority are rather long documents containing declarations, agreements, definitions, exclusions, and conditions. Many of the policy provisions in the United States are governed by the requirements of state insurance departments. Often the exclusions or restrictions printed in the policy are canceled or modified by special amendments or endorsements attached to the policy.

The result is that the analysis of coverages and other provisions of insurance policies is primarily a matter for experts in the insurance field. The company employee responsible for insurance (and the insurance broker where insurance is placed) is responsible for seeing that each purchased insurance policy contains the coverages desired and that no provision of the policy entails unanticipated risk-taking on the company's behalf.

CLAIMS

Reporting and Settlement

The real test of the protection provided by the insurance program comes when a loss occurs and a claim is filed with an insurance carrier. It is not an unusual experience for operating executives to find that coverage is not in the exact form they thought. For example, a fraud occurs in a storeroom, and an inventory reconciliation discloses the value of the physical inventory is $25,000 less than the amount of the book inventory. An operating department head is then sometimes shocked to learn the bonding company will not automatically settle the claim for the amount of the shortage. Instead, it will be necessary to develop reasonably complete proof that a specific defaulting employee actually abstracted (and converted to his own benefit) materials to the value of $25,000.

The first requirement for satisfactory handling of claims is a prompt report to the company insurance department and, by it, to the insurance carrier. Instructions to company operating units should be specific and complete to assure that every loss is reported promptly and as completely as possible. Instructions used by one company for product liability claims are shown at the end of the chapter. The first report is preliminary, sometimes with little or no idea of what the final claimed loss will be.

Once the claim is reported, adjusters for the insurance carrier work with company representatives until a final settlement of the claim is made.

Some claims are simple and straightforward; others may be highly complicated and take many months for final settlement. Some examples follow:

1. A claim for destruction of finished products is usually simple. The basis of valuation (e.g., lowest wholesale selling price) are specified in the policy, and the quantity and the amount of loss is definite.

2. A claim for fire loss in a building can be quite complicated. The question of exact present-day valuation is sure to arise, along with factors such as the cost of rebuilding or repairs and the proportion of such costs that are chargeable to insurance coverage.

3. A fidelity bond claim in an ingeniously contrived fraud can carry on for many months. Almost certainly, the original items discovered, and any items confessed to by the defaulter, will be much less than the actual shortage. Further investigations usually uncover more manipulation, which must be reviewed and proved to the satisfaction of the adjuster.

4. Public liability claims are invariably exaggerated by claimants and their attorneys, and awards are often large. This highlights the importance of carrying adequate limits on public liability coverage both to cover the company against possible loss and to gain maximum benefit from the services of the insurance carrier's facilities for settlement. Usually the settlement of these claims are handled almost completely by the insurance adjuster and the insurance carrier's law department, with the company furnishing factual evidence and other material, and the services of company attorneys to assist in making final settlement.

5. The settlement of business interruption claims is invariably protracted and involved, since the basis of the claim hinges on what is contended would have happened under certain specified (and theoretical) conditions. The adjustment of these theoretical figures to a specific value entails long negotiation.

Legal Liability

When a claim involves an apparent wrongful act committed by an individual against the company, it is essential that no legal action be taken against the individual without the approval of legal counsel. Instructions to company locations should be very specific that *under no conditions* are arrests to be made or complaints filed against individuals by company employees without the definite approval of the company's legal counsel.

For example, if a defrauder is arrested and then subsequently acquitted, the company is immediately open to a suit against it for false arrest, defamation of character, and similar charges. Jury awards in such cases are often generous.

SELF-INSURANCE

Requirements of Self-Insurance

In the general description of insurance above, a distinction was made between insurance placed with outside carriers, risk-taking, and self-insurance. Before consideration is given to administration of the insurance program, there should be an understanding of the characteristics of true self-insurance.

In a conservative program of self-insurance, a company in effect acts as its own insurance carrier. If self-insurance is to be on a sound basis, certain requirements should be met. Principal among these are:

1. The risk should be spread on a physical basis so exposure to loss is reasonably evenly distributed over a number of locations.
2. A study should be made of the maximum foreseeable exposure to loss.
3. Consideration should be given to the possibility of unfavorable loss experience, and to the decision reached as to whether this contingency should be covered by provision for self-insurance reserves.
4. Servicing requirements should be evaluated.

Most large companies self-insure for losses up to specified limits. Losses over these limits are covered by either purchasing insurance from outside insurance carriers or spreading the company's risk through the reinsurance market.

The examples that follow illustrate how self-insurance may be applied:

Tank Cars

One company had about 200 tank cars used in shipping raw materials, with a cost of $100,000 each. Insurance was purchased to cover these cars. Study of the possibility of self-insurance developed the following factors:

1. The cars were spread out on many railroads—there was little chance of loss or damage to more than one or two cars at any one time.

2. In many cases, damage or loss would be the responsibility of a railroad or another third party and could be recovered from it.

3. The materials hauled were not explosive, inflammable, or dangerous in any way.

These factors led to the adoption of a program of self-insurance that was implemented by an arbitrarily set premium charge against operations considerably less than the previous cost.

Warehoused Inventories

One company has a large number of branches and distribution warehouses, with inventories ranging in value from $50,000 to $1 million in a single location. The company decided to self-insure against inventory losses up to $25,000—with coverage for losses over that amount purchased from an outside insurance carrier.

Spreading of Charges for Losses

Self-insurance may be regarded as risk-taking on a companywide basis. Where premiums for self-insurance are charged to operations, there is the advantage that losses that are sustained will in effect be spread over all company units. This has the advantage of guarding against the uncontrollable factor of an actual loss distorting the profits of a single operating unit—which would be the usual result if no provision existed for self-insurance premium charges to all units.

Accounting for Self-Insurance

The accounting features of a self-insurance program are summarized as follows:

1. Operating units should be charged with a premium amount that takes into consideration a combination of the following factors, which are based on previous experience and estimates for the future:
   a. Estimated losses
   b. Cost of comparable coverage purchased outside
   c. Adequacy of reserves

2. Losses should be separately accounted for so that loss experience in relation to premium charges is regularly reported. In the United States, losses must be kept separate for income tax purposes, since only sustained losses are deductible on tax returns as a business expense.

3. Reserves for losses should be periodically appraised for adequacy. Excessive reserves should not be accumulated, and inadequate reserves should be increased. In one company, reserves are set at an amount based primarily on total losses during the three preceding years.

An effective method of accounting for self-insurance transactions is to establish separate groups of nominal accounts for premiums charged to operating units, claims paid, and expenses for each type of self-insurance. These accounts could well be carried under the general classification of miscellaneous income. Where reserves are carried, related reserve accounts are shown on the balance sheet.

The nominal accounts are credited with premiums charged to operating units and charged with losses and expenses. At the close of each year, the reserve accounts are appraised for adequacy. Any adjustments made in reserve accounts are charged or credited to the self-insurance accounts. The resulting net balance of the nominal accounts in effect represent the underwriting profit (or loss) from self-insurance operations during the year.

Effective control of self-insurance requires that insurance carriers be asked to survey and bid on the cost of outside coverage at periodic intervals. Otherwise, the possibility exists that profits shown for self-insurance operations might be misleading and fictitious in comparison with the up-to-date cost of coverage by an outside carrier.

Captive Insurance Companies

The objective of risk management is to eliminate the risk of important impairment to the capital or earnings capacity (worldwide) using the most flexible and efficient combination of risk management techniques available. Accordingly, most major companies have considered or established some form of captive insurance company.

The advantages of having a captive insurance company include:

1. It permits concentration of worldwide funds into a central location for volume purchase of catastrophe insurance and attendant services at lower cost while still protecting the tax deductibility of local insurance premiums; and
2. It permits the utilization of excess cash flow into other areas of the business.

One company insured their (1) domestic property risks through a fronting company and reinsured 100 percent with their captive, (2) primary liability risks, and (3) international property risks (separated for tax purposes). The captive retains the first $100,000 to $200,000 per loss, and reinsure the excess with other participating captive and through a clearing house into the general reinsurance market.

Reasons for Establishing Captives

The reasons why captives are established by companies include:

1. The inability to obtain coverages in the required scope in conventional market
2. Unavailability of excess coverages in the amounts required to protect assets

The advantages of a captive operation can be expressed in two ways—insurance and financial, as follows.

Insurance

1. The captive insurance company, as an insurance operation, has access to the worldwide reinsurance market (rather than just having access to the more limited primary market only). The reinsurance market tends to be more flexible in its coverage, grants, and pricing techniques than the primary markets, which must comply with state regulations and more limiting underwriting policies.
2. The captive provides the only means for a company to be individually rated as one risk (rather than individual plants) to gain the credits for individual performance on loss control. In other words, the corporation gains credibility to its own results and does not have to be area-rated with other local high-risk operations.
3. The captive provides U.S. standards of loss control worldwide, through fire prevention engineering inspections worldwide and claims-settlement services.

Financial

1. Lower net cost is obtained by realization of reinsurance commissions and profit sharing arrangements not available if insured commercially. (Some savings must be accrued since the company does not have to pay for an insurance company's overhead and profits. This can approximate 30 to 40 percent of the premium.)
2. The opportunity to obtain and utilize excess cash flow, including claim reserves, is available to generate additional earnings, either by direct investment, or by means of intercompany loans to the corporation or any affiliates.

3. Lower service charges for claims handling and loss control inspection services are incurred.

4. By writing insurance with a captive insurance company, lower deductible limits for liability insurances are available to the company than when directly writing insurance in the commercial insurance market—with no increase in premiums.

Controlling Values

For property damage insurance, property values should be updated annually by engineering personnel. This is sometimes done more frequently in countries with high inflation, such as Brazil and Argentina.

During the course of the year, the management company for the captive operation should furnish loss control engineering service to all major worldwide locations. Local problems other than engineering should be discussed with plant personnel and, if deemed significant, should be brought to the attention of the corporate risk manager. (The possibility that values may exceed policy limits is typical of the type of problem referred to.)

Liability Limits

One company carries its basic liability coverage (via a U.S. blanket policy covering all locations worldwide) to a limit of $2 million. This is in excess to any other local coverage. Liability risks covered under this policy include general liability, products liability, and third-party liability under lease obligation and other contractual agreements where local coverage is not available for purchase or where there is no local coverage.

In addition, for certain risks, the company carries $100 million of coverage in excess of this basic policy. For domestic risks, this $100 million excess coverage includes automobile, general (including product) liability, and certain special risks such as vessel charters and advertising. By including the latter, the company obtains both protection and legal expertise in the event of suit for false advertising or other suits arising out of any consumer products advertising activity. This excess coverage is also extended to foreign operations but only in the area of products liability.

Excess coverage this large is not written by one insurance company. Typically, coverage is purchased in layers (each layer is effectively a deductible to the insurance company that agrees to contract for the next level of risk). To reach $100 million in coverage, one company found it necessary to negotiate separate agreements with over 15 insurance companies.

Obviously, the insurance companies writing the top layers with the largest deductible are confronted with great difficulty in determining the extent of their exposure, and many would prefer simply not to assume this type of liability at all.

Coverage Terms and Conditions

In the recent past, due to large losses experienced by underwriters in the general market, many frills and negotiated fringe benefits popular over the years are being canceled, and policies are being restructured to only basic coverage.

The underwriters for one company issued their standard form of coverage on a take it or leave it basis. They instituted a $100,000 deductible where before there had been none, and doubled the premium. Several competitive quotations were obtained, but none matched the above offer. Other quotes involved a $500,000 deductible, and others outrightly refused to quote on the business.

Most companies cannot place this risk through their captives because most franchises exclude fidelity insurance as part of operations. This is based upon the highly technical and legal liability aspects inherent in the claims handling process.

ADMINISTRATION OF THE INSURANCE PROGRAM

Definition of Company Policy

The administration of the insurance program starts with the defining of company policy in insurance matters. General policy should be determined by a company's management after consideration of the hazards inherent in the business, the cost of insurance coverage, and the effect losses would have upon the company's operations. Policy should be specific on such matters as:

1. Providing for business interruption
2. Areas where insurance is to be purchased
3. Areas to be covered by self-insurance
4. Areas where risks will be assumed
5. Basis on which coverage is to be carried—for example, lowest wholesale selling price on inventories; replacement value on buildings

If company policy is not specific, and the decision as to specific areas and nature of coverage is left to lower responsibility, there may be a trend to overinsure to provide for all possible risks and losses.

The Insurance Administrator

The responsibility for administering the insurance program usually is—and should be—definitely assigned. In a smaller business, this may be a full- or part-time duty for one employee; in a larger business, an insurance department is formed. Sometimes company policy gives complete responsibility to an insurance broker with perfunctory control by some company executive. This is seldom a good plan, since the broker usually does not have the intimate knowledge of company problems and operations necessary to provide an adequate insurance program at the most favorable cost to the company.

In general, the insurance administrator is responsible for seeing that prescribed company policies are applied effectively and economically. This involves:

1. Keeping informed of coverages offered by insurance carriers and studying their possible applicability
2. Keeping informed of changes in company operations so related risks may be realized and provided for in the insurance program
3. Studying and recommending any changes in company policy necessary to meet current conditions
4. Analyzing and keeping informed of the experience and financial condition of insurance carriers
5. Supervising and maintaining the reports and records of the insurance program
6. Seeing that adequate instructions are issued to company operating units on insurance matters. For example, instructions should be complete and definite on such matters as:
   Reporting of losses
   Basis on which insurable values are to be determined and reported
   Periodic reports of values for insurance purposes
7. Periodic interviews or other interface with the general auditor to review the current status of internal controls

Over the long term, the company's loss experience will have a decided influence on insurance costs. For this reason, the insurance administrator should take an active interest in the promotion of any plans designed to minimize losses. These plans include the following types of safety campaigns:

1. Safety campaigns to reduce industrial accidents
2. Safe-driver campaigns to reduce automotive accidents

3. Cleanup campaigns to reduce automotive accidents
4. Installation and periodic testing of fire prevention, alarm, and fire-fighting equipment (a safety inspection check list is shown at the end of the chapter)
5. Follow-up to see that safety recommendations made by inspectors for insurance carriers are put into effect
6. Regular fire drills in larger plants and buildings

In most instances, the actual responsibility for safety activities is assigned to operating units that have direct control or contact with property and personnel—for example, the plant maintenance, personnel, and distribution departments. In this circumstance, the insurance administrator is responsible for seeing that the operating units are fulfilling their assigned part in the safety program.

Records of Insurance Coverage

If the insurance program is to be effectively administered, adequate and up-to-date records of values and coverage should be maintained. These records include:

1. Policies with insurance carriers
2. Tickler files showing policies by expiration date and reports to be rendered to insurance carriers
3. Reports of insurable values in company operating locations
4. Copies of reports to insurance carriers on policies where values are reported periodically—for example, inventories
5. Records of premiums and losses on each policy
6. Reports to management

Records of Claims

As soon as a loss or possible claim is reported to the insurance administrator, a separate claim file should be opened. This file is used to segregate all correspondence, reports, and other material pertaining to the claim until final settlement is made. The final gross amount of the settlement should be entered on a record of losses, which is maintained for each policy (or each class of self-insurance coverage). Any recovery or salvage that has the effect of reducing the loss should be entered as an offsetting item. Thus an actual experience record on each coverage will be available. This is essential in indicating situations where experience is poor and attention may be required. For example, a poor loss experience on fidelity bonds indicates the need for study of internal controls in the affected areas. The records of loss experience are also valuable as background information when policies are up for negotiation at the time of renewal.

Claim records should be reviewed by staff departments where applicable. For example, major industrial accident claims should be reviewed by company safety engineers, and major or unusual frauds should be reviewed by internal auditors. (Many companies refer all fraud claims to the internal audit department.) This practice brings to attention situations where study or revision of policies and controls may be necessary.

Distribution of Premium Expense

In the customary accounting treatment of spreading the cost of insurance over the term of the policy, certain complications may arise. Particularly if a large number of operating units are involved in a single premium payment, the distribution to individual units on an exact basis may be quite burdensome and sometimes inequitable.

One such situation in the United States is where specified coverage is carried in a number of various states. Because of the requirements of some state insurance administrative agencies, coverage billed at an individual rate for one state is different from that in other states. An equitable method of equalizing these differences is to develop an average rate for the entire policy, regardless of location. This rate is then applied on an overall basis. Probably the majority of companies prefer to charge premiums to local operations on a local (actual) basis with each operation absorbing actual costs. There is no right or wrong in the decision as to an equitable method of distribution; the company policy should be determined on a basis consistent with the policy for distribution of other similar expenses to operating units.

Another situation arises when a policy calls for a deposit premium, which is then adjusted to an experience or other basis at the expiration of the policy. In some cases, the deposit premium may be several times higher than the anticipated final cost. Here an equitable solution is to charge current operations with the estimated cost rather than with the amount of the deposit premium.

The basis of charging insurance cost is usually examined as a part of the audit of the distribution of expenses to operations. In such examination, it is important to see that distribution is on a basis representative of reasonable costs—and not just an arithmetical exercise.

Report to Management

Insurance operations are a collateral activity apt to receive little attention or recognition from management except as losses occur or new hazards arise. For this reason, it is highly desirable that the insurance administrator render a periodic report to management, summarizing the operation of the insurance program and the insurance department.

As an example, one company with 20 comparatively large plants in the United States and nine in other countries, prepares an annual report. This report begins with an outline of insurance policies and responsibilities, followed by separate sections on:

Property insurance
Casualty insurance
Employee insurance
International division insurance
Miscellaneous insurance
Major unprotected risks

Each section describes such essentials as company policy on coverage, premium cost, losses, and recommendations and plans for the coming year. On property insurance, the status of appraisals is described. Where self-insurance is applied, a cumulative record of coverage, premium charges, reserves, losses, and savings through self-insurance is given for a five-year period. Brief descriptions are given of major unprotected risks, together with the cost of insurance coverage and the reasons that purchase of coverage is not considered advisable.

As a whole, the report gives management a summary of insurance, calling attention to the operation of company policy during the period of the report, together with recommendations for future activities and revisions of the policy. Such a report is a valuable means of providing reasonable assurance that complete and specific determinations of company policy are made and are understood by management and by the insurance administrator.

DEVELOPMENT OF INTERNAL AUDIT PROGRAM

Approach to Internal Audit

In development of the program for internal audit, several points are worthy of particular attention:

1. Although the internal auditor should not be expected to be a technical expert in insurance, the auditor should have a knowledge of insurance essentials and their application.
2. The existence of definite company policies established by management is essential for the insurance department. Such policies must be specific and complete, giving recognition to areas of possible

hazard and prescribing the form of insurance protection—or lack of protection—that is company policy.

3. The ultimate test of an insurance program comes when loss occurs. Consequently, the review of claims, uninsured losses, and collection of claims is an important feature in the appraisal of policy and procedures.

The internal audit program that forms the following section comprises six major areas: (1) coverage, (2) insurable values, (3) accounting for premiums, (4) losses, claims, and incoming payments, (5) self-insurance, and (6) the audit report. Each section begins with a General Information description, which gives the background applicable to the audit of the area.

The program that follows is a composite and general one developed from programs used in various companies. The presentation of a specimen program requires certain assumptions as to general policy and assignment of responsibility that may vary considerably from the situation in any specific company. Thus the specimen program is intended only to be a guide to the internal auditor in developing a tailored program. For example, the program assumes that an authoritative and comprehensive statement of company policy in insurance matters exists, and that responsibility for the insurance program is assigned to a specific corporate insurance department. Where no such statement or assignment exists, it then becomes necessary for the internal auditor to modify the examination. A normal outcome of this particular situation may be a recommendation in the audit report, drawn from the audit findings, that a statement of company policy or more definite assignment of responsibility is necessary for effective administration of the insurance program.

THE INTERNAL AUDIT PROGRAM—COVERAGE

General Information

The risk manager is assigned the responsibility for procuring and maintaining coverage to protect the company against risks and hazards against which company policy prescribes that insurance be carried.

In the fulfillment of this responsibility, the risk manager is required to develop and administer procedures to provide:

1. Procurement and maintenance of coverage in accordance with company policy
2. Up-to-date information on risks or hazards to which the company is or may be exposed
3. Knowledge of coverages currently available from insurance carriers
4. Assistance to all company units in matters of insurance coverage

5. Written policies and procedures necessary to coordinate insurance matters
6. Advice (in the form of written procedures) to personnel dealing with suppliers or contractors to assure adequate coverage is maintained by the company and by outside contractors or vendors against possible liability or hazard
7. Consultation with and reference to outside insurance counsel to assist in the optimum application of the company insurance program

Purpose of Audit

The audit objectives are:

1. To determine how company policies on insurance coverage (risk avoidance) are fulfilled through procedures established by the insurance department
2. To determine the compliance with procedures by employees in the insurance department and other company units
3. To report on how the controls are operating in relation to company policy

The audit does not attempt to cover such matters as the technical provisions of insurance policies or the adequacy of limits of liability, since the auditor may not be qualified to give an opinion in these matters. The extent of coverage should be generally defined in company policy and specifically applied by the risk manager in consultation with any necessary outside counsel.

Audit Program

Maintenance of Coverage

1. Secure and examine statements of company policy covering insurance, and discuss with the risk manager.
2. Review written procedures, memoranda, and other material to determine that:
   a. Instructions are in force covering the procurement and maintenance of coverage in accordance with company policy
   b. Procedures are adequate for both insurance department personnel and for personnel of operating units reporting on insurance matters to the insurance department
3. Review contract files, lease files, and pertinent correspondence files in the insurance and other departments (such as real estate,

construction, sales, and purchasing) to determine if the insurance department is informed of risks to which the company may be exposed—so adequate coverage may be maintained in accordance with company policy. (Coordinate this work into such other audits as purchasing, accounts payable, cost accounting, and facilities.)

4. Determine requirements for company insurance coverage under loan agreements, sales contracts, and similar items. Verify that requirements are met.

5. Determine that responsibility for informing the insurance department of contracts and contract revisions is definitely assigned and endorsed, so adequate coverage may be maintained.

Policies with Insurance Carriers

1. Prepare (or ask the insurance department to prepare) a schedule (inventory) of policies in force with outside carriers, showing:

     Carrier

     Coverage

     Exposure

     Locations

     Premium

     Term of policy including start and end dates

     Other pertinent data

   (In a large company with an insurance department, the preparation of such a schedule might be unduly burdensome. In such a case, the internal auditor works with the records of the insurance department.)

2. Review to see that types and limits of coverage are maintained in general accordance with company policy.

3. Examine policies and related correspondence to verify that:

    a. Policies on file are listed in the schedule and policies listed on the schedule are on file.

    b. Policies are adequately safeguarded.

    c. All significant data are shown on the schedule.

    d. The company is shown as the insured.

    e. Where applicable, subsidiary divisions, locations, and companies are specified.

    f. Endorsements are physically attached to policies and are properly applicable.

    g. Required premiums or deposits were appraised by the insurance department for reasonableness and accuracy.

    h. Risks and exclusions or restrictions are definitely specified and are applicable.

4. Review and test the procedures followed by the insurance department to assure that:

    a. When orders for insurance are placed, binders and policies are received.

    b. Renewal of policies is adequately controlled.

    c. Policies are considered for renewal in sufficient time to permit considerations of changes.

    d. Invoices for premiums and deposits are reviewed and approved by the insurance department before forwarding to accounts payable unit for payment.

    e. Financial position of insurance carriers is checked periodically.

5. Secure a copy of any reports rendered to management on general insurance department operations.

    a. Test check any financial figures shown on reports—such as premium cost, insurable values, claims paid, and savings made—with appropriate original records.

General

1. Discuss uninsured losses with risk manager to determine whether losses arose because of a risk assumed under company policy or through failure in the application of established procedures.

2. From your general knowledge of company operations and background, discuss with the risk manager any risks that may not seem to be covered by insurance to determine whether these risks are realized in the determination of company policy. Discuss also any situation where there is any question in your mind regarding the necessity of insurance presently being carried.

3. From observation and discussion, determine situations in which insurance department control and operations appear to be handicapped because of poor interdepartmental coordination.

4. Test check premium charges, as derived from insurance department records, with entries on company accounting records. Determine that the allocation of charges to profit centers is appropriate.

INSURANCE VALUES

General Information

In addition to specifying the types of insurance coverage to be carried, statements of company policy should specify the method of valuation for insurance purposes, for example, current replacement cost less depreciation, cash value, lowest wholesale selling price, and so on.

The responsibilities of the insurance department include (1) determining the form, contents, and frequency of reports from company units necessary for the compilation of insurable values, and (2) reporting values at risk to insurance carriers where periodic reporting is required.

Certain policies—usually those covering fluctuating quantities of materials—are carried on a floater basis under which the company is completely covered at all times. These policies provide for premium on an estimated basis, which is adjusted to an actual earned premium figure based on periodic reports of values rendered to the insurance carriers.

Policies covering such risks as business interruption, liability, and fixed assets are usually written at fixed face amounts. Through periodic reviews of reported values or reconsideration of risks, the insurance department determines whether a change in the face amount should be negotiated.

Purpose of Audit

The insurable values audit objectives are:

1. To examine the procedures to determine if values are properly reported by company units to the insurance department
2. To examine for adequacy the procedures covering summarization of reports of values in the insurance department, and reporting of values to insurance carriers
3. To examine the procedures under which insurance coverage in such areas as fixed assets, business interruption, and liability is appraised for adequacy

Audit Program

1. Discuss company policy on determination of insurable values with the risk manager.
2. Examine procedures and forms used to secure reports of insurable values from company operating units. (The basis of preparation and the accuracy of reports of insurable value from detached operating units may be included as a part of the internal audit of these units—for example, in the audits of facilities and inventories.)
3. Test reports submitted to insurance carriers:
   a. Determine how original cost of assets are related to insurable values.
   b. Determine how changes in insurable values are handled by revisions in face amounts of insurance policies.

    c. Determine whether proper allowance is made in insurable values for such items as:

       (1) Facilities written off accounting records but kept in active use

       (2) Facilities (dies, patterns, tools, drawings, technical libraries, etc.) that may have considerable value but are charged to expense when acquired

       (3) Uninsurable values, for example, foundations

       (4) Construction-in-progress (i.e., amounts shown as construction-in-progress on insurable values report could be checked with corresponding balance sheet item or with progress reports to engineering department)

       (5) Operation of coinsurance features specified in policies

       (6) Assets, such as rented buildings, that are insured by others. As another example, construction contracts may provide for carrying insurance on work-in-progress by the contractor.

       (7) Off-premises property, such as patterns and dies

    d. Determine the basis of selection of the appraisal company.

    e. Determine whether reports are submitted on dates due.

    f. When outside appraisal services are used, determine whether values and price trend factors are properly applied.

4. Compare reports of total insurable values with amounts of coverage.

5. Examine and appraise the effectiveness of controls designed to assure that property additions and retirements are reported to the insurance department.

6. Determine how the risk manager is informed of changes in risk or of general business conditions that might require revision of face amounts of policies on liability or business interruption.

ACCOUNTING FOR PREMIUMS

General Information

The initial payments made to insurance carriers for premiums are often on some basis other than that which will be the final cost of the insurance at the expiration of the policy. Variations between initial payment and final cost may arise because of:

1. Variations in insurable values. The rate is usually the same throughout the life of the policy.

2. Variations due to experience—either of the policyholder or of the

insurance company itself. Here, a deposit premium will be the initial payment, with an adjusting credit (or charge) made by the insurance carrier if experience is favorable (or unfavorable).

Accounting for insurance premiums has two phases: (1) entry of insurance premium payments on accounting records and distribution to applicable accounting periods, and (2) equitable distribution of insurance cost to operating units.

This second factor presents the principal problem. For example, an insurance policy may require the payment of a comparatively large deposit premium, with reasonable expectation from past experience that a considerable portion of the premium will be credited to the company at the termination of the policy. Here the problem to be settled by company policy decision is whether:

1. Operating units should be currently charged on the basis of the deposit premium with a compensating (and possibly distorting) adjustment when the final premium settlement is made, or
2. Operating units should be currently charged on the basis of an estimated actual premium cost, with the final adjustment either distributed to units or absorbed as a home office item.

A somewhat similar situation arises when identical overall coverage is—because of regulatory requirements—billed at different rates for different geographical locations. Here the question to be settled by policy decision is whether:

1. Each location is to be charged at the billed rate for that location, or
2. All locations are to be charged at an average overall rate.

Premium payments and related accruals and charges are usually recorded in an insurance register by individual insurance policy. Distribution of accrued charges is then made to operating units by journal voucher.

Purpose of Audit

The purpose of the audit of insurance premiums is to determine if:

1. Company policies and procedures provide for the accurate and timely recording of insurance premiums over the financial periods concerned
2. Company policies and procedures provide for the equitable charging of insurance premium costs to operating expenses

3. Company policies and procedures are being followed in a satisfactory manner

Audit Program

1. Verify through test checking that premiums covering policies in force have been charged to appropriate accounts in the general ledger and are recorded in records of insurance.
2. Determine policy and procedures that cover the distribution of insurance expense to operating units.
    a. Review journal entries for accuracy of distribution and compliance with policy.
    b. For one accounting period, test check entries covering distribution of insurance cost through the referenced journal entries to originating documents.
3. Discuss with the risk manager (and others as appropriate) the policies and procedures applicable to the allocation of premium costs to operating units in the following situations:
    a. Where initial charge for premium may be adjusted by application of experience or other charge or credit at termination of policy
    b. Where premium rates for identical types of coverage vary between locations
    c. Where premium amount varies because of fluctuating values (e.g., inventories).
4. Verify application of policy and procedures in situations described in (3) and consider their reasonableness from an accounting and overall company standpoint.
5. Test check the basis for reporting and calculation of premium for such coverages as:
    a. Compensation. Check reasonableness of employee classifications and how total payroll is reported. For example, overtime premium payments should usually be eliminated in reporting payroll for compensation purposes.
    b. Product liability. Premiums are often based on total sales. Here, the basis of reporting sales should be verified to insure that such items as inter- and intracompany sales are eliminated.
6. Review (or test) all premium credits and other adjustments affecting the insurance cost to determine basis and correctness.
    a. Appraise the reasonableness of the basis on which credits and other adjustments are distributed to company operating units.
7. Test control of premiums by verifying total prepaid and accrued

premiums as recorded in the insurance department records, with general ledger control account.

LOSSES, CLAIMS, AND INCOMING PAYMENTS

General Information

The insurance department responsibilities in connection with claims for insurable losses include:

1. Developing and issuing to all company units published statements of policies and procedures relating to substantiation, filing, and collection of claims for insured losses
2. Maintaining contact and coordination with company units to assist in claims preparation and processing and to insure that policies and procedures are enforced
3. Filing and collecting claims for insured losses as specified by general policy (for example, compensation claims of small value might be filed and collected by a local operating unit, with a report of closed claims to the insurance department)
4. Maintaining contact and dealing with insurance company adjusters, company legal department, and others affected on all major claims until final settlement
5. Maintaining records of losses and salvage by policy so a record of premiums and net losses on each coverage is continually available
6. Working with all company units in their efforts to prevent losses and minimize the cost of losses occurred.

Purpose of Audit

The audit of losses and claims has the general objective of examining and determining that policies and procedures covering claims and losses are established and enforced so (1) proper recovery of insured losses is made from insurance carriers, and (2) losses and claims are minimized through accident and loss campaigns.

Audit Program

1. Select for test check a number of open and completed claim files, including some from each of the following classes of coverage (in some instances, no claims may have been filed, or may be pending):
    Fire
    Fidelity

Products liability

General liability

Automobile property damage

Workmen's compensation

Automobile liability

2. Examine each claim file, beginning with original reports of loss and following through to final settlement of closed claims. Give particular attention to compliance with policies and procedures in such matters as:

a. Promptness in reporting loss by company unit

b. Completeness and accuracy of documentation

c. Values claimed in relation to terms of insurance policies

d. Reduction of losses through recovery or other salvage

e. Entry of payment of claim in cash records

f. Accounting treatment of pending and closed claims

g. Entry of amount received on closed claims to insurance department records of losses by policy

h. Timely follow-up action on pending claims

i. Where applicable, comparison of losses claimed with the cost of replacing or repairing the damaged property

3. Review accident reporting procedures and records covering handling of claims and related reserves.

4. Examine and appraise the effectiveness of instructions for reporting losses by operating departments to the insurance department.

5. Check to see that provisions of insurance policies regarding the reporting of losses to insurance carriers are being complied with. For example, if a defalcation by an employee occurs, the insurance company is usually not liable for any further loss caused by the employee, whether or not the defalcation is reported.

6. Verify and test the application of policies and procedures relating to loss prevention in such matters as:

a. Referring accident claims to industrial relations or plant safety departments

b. Referring fidelity bond claims to the internal audit department

c. Promotion and assistance by the insurance department in safety and loss prevention campaigns carried on by company units. This may be handled as a feature of the audit of these units

d. Action taken on reports rendered by insurance carriers or other inspectors on fire and safety hazards

7. Request insurers or brokers to furnish list of all payments made to

company during a selected period (e.g., three months) for premium adjustments, claims, or other reasons.

   a. Check records for proper entry.

8. Discuss policies and procedures relating to reporting of losses and filing of claims by company units with the risk manager.

SELF-INSURANCE

General Information

The risk manager is usually assigned the responsibility for administering the company self-insurance program, according to general policies prescribed by management. (Self-insurance may be considered to exist only when the company has a formal program that includes charging premiums or spreading losses over operating units. (Where these requirements are not met, the applicable term is risk-taking, and the self-insurance program should not be considered as such.)

In fulfilling this responsibility, the risk manager is responsible for the performance of the following functions:

1. Periodic analysis at suitable intervals of specific risks, and making proposals to management or the board of directors regarding areas in which self-insurance might be considered, areas in which insurance might be purchased from outside carriers, and areas in which no insurance applies

2. Establishment of premium rates or other means of spreading the cost of self-insurance over company units

3. Maintaining loss records as a basis for determination of experience and premium charges on self-insurance and for recommendations regarding changes in the self-insurance program

4. Analysis of reserves for losses, where these are maintained, to determine that they are adequate but not excessive

5. Recommendation for any changes in reserve accounts

Purpose of Audit

The audit of the phases of self-insurance relating to coverage, insurable values, accounting for premiums, and losses and claims may be readily developed from the outline of the audits of those functions. In addition, the audit of self-insurance will be concerned with the application of policy and procedures relating to charges for self-insurance, the recording and treatment of losses, and the maintenance of reserves.

Audit Program

1. Discuss policy and procedures relating to the company self-insurance program with the risk manager. Give particular attention to:
   a. Basis of charging self-insurance costs to company units
   b. Reporting and settlement of losses
   c. Policy on reserves
   d. Policy on purchase of excess coverage against catastrophic losses
2. Verify insurance department reports or records showing self-insurance experience during the latest year. These reports should show, according to type of risk:
   a. Charges to company units for self-insurance premiums
   b. Losses incurred (including estimated reserves for pending losses unsettled at year-end)
   c. Transactions in related reserve accounts during the year
3. Examine claim files to verify that losses were settled in accordance with policy and procedures and on a reasonable basis.
4. Verify that all costs of settlement of losses and other costs of self-insurance, such as payments to adjusters, costs of bonds, and legal fees are charged against the self-insurance program.
5. Review records of the self-insurance program for the latest five-year period, test checking, for each type of risk, by year:
   Premium or other charges to company units
   Losses
   Related reserve accounts at close of year
   Cost of excess coverage purchased from outside insurance carriers
6. Examine and test check any reports prepared by the insurance department on the operation of the self-insurance program.
7. Determine policy on treating any excess of charges to company units over incurred losses and verify the application of this policy over the five-year period. Similarly, determine and verify the application of policy where losses exceed charges.

THE AUDIT REPORT

In preparing the report of the audit of the insurance program, the internal auditor should remember that the risk manager and general management are concerned with the effectiveness of control and the applicability of established policy, and not in a recital of financial details.

As a general matter, the auditor should expect that the risk manager and management will be principally interested in the auditor's appraisal of the controls over:

Procurement and maintenance of insurance coverage
Intracompany coordination in insurance matters
Handling of claims
Operation of self-insurance program
Uninsured risks

The general nature of the audit scope should be described to obviate any possible misunderstanding that the internal auditor is posing as an expert in technical insurance matters—such as adequacy of coverage, premium costs, evaluation of self-insurance and similar items.

The auditor's work—and the report—should be concerned with examining, testing, and appraising the controls over the insurance program. This includes how company policy is promulgated and applied, the effectiveness of cooperation and coordination between company units in insurance matters, the correctness and completeness of reports on insurance administration, and other insurance matters. The audit report should also contain constructive recommendations in areas where policies or controls appear ineffective or inoperative.

CHAPTER 11

Information Systems

INTRODUCTION

Although many books address preinstallation/acquisition controls, many corporations do not. As is true with all operational auditing, the best approach is still to develop a rapport with management (this takes time) and become part of the management team. Let management get to know that you are there to learn as well as to participate in the system development process.

The information systems (IS) department usually processes data for a number of departments and must be able to deal objectively with these departments. To do this effectively and to be able to maintain its independence, the IS department must be well managed and have the necessary degree of support and authority from top management. Frequently this requires that the department be headed by an executive of at least equal rank to the managers of the departments for which it processes data.

An effective organization structure is needed to ensure the primary responsibilities of the IS function—processing of user department data and development, maintenance of systems—are performed accurately, in a timely manner, and on a cost-effective basis. Accordingly, an IS organization is often structured into three major areas:

1. *Operations* includes the computer room with the central processor(s) and all peripheral equipment, the program and media library; computer operations personnel, data entry operators, data control group, librarian, and job scheduling.

2. *Systems development* (systems and programming) normally includes the activities of systems analysts and programmers in planning, developing, and maintaining business application systems that will meet the information processing requirements of the users.

3. *Systems programming* (technical support) provides advice to data processing management on the acquisition of new hardware, software, data bases, and telecommunications; implements supporting software (for the operating system); monitors and coordinates equipment capacity planning with the corporate planning group.

The best approach in beginning to interface with system development is to phase in one project at a time, and to build a departmental information base in this area, including:

Knowledge of the department and the power brokers

Knowledge of activities

Getting to know the people

Developing self confidence in the audit approach

Modifying the approach used if need be (one project at a time is easier and will cause minimal embarrassment if the initial approach is not successful)

Trying to develop one-on-one relationships, and the individual's trust, support, and integrity (this makes it easier to interface with other staff members if you have internal departmental support)

AUDITOR INVOLVEMENT IN INFORMATION SYSTEMS

With management demanding more data on a more timely basis and with larger and relational on-line data base systems, the auditor involvement is or will be mandated in the development of information systems. If the auditor does not get involved, someone else will—to the detriment of the audit group.

Most, if not all, auditors should have a background in IS. Auditors without such knowledge will see their ability to perform in an in-charge or supervisory capacity severely diminished if they lack a good understanding of system hardware and software and their ramifications on the control environment.

Management will also want assurance that proper controls exist in the system programming function, which *may* require the establishment of a super technical IS audit function or the use of consultants.

The areas in IS that an auditor may wish to review include:

1. Organization, administration, and control
2. The data center installation:
     Media program library
     Data control
3. Applications
4. Use of IS resources to increase auditor productivity and efficiency
5. Computers used in the engineering and manufacturing areas (i.e., CAE/CAD/CAM), shop floor data collection, automated time-keeping (also an assist to industrial engineers in establishing, verifying, and modifying and monitoring standards), MRP II, Computer Integrated Manufacturing (CIM), Just in Time (JIT) manufacturing systems

Input controls:	IS should have this responsibility only through data control; otherwise, this is now a user responsibility, except for Input/Output daily totals
Processing controls:	Run to run and edit (rejects) controls should exist; fatal and nonfatal errors should be flagged
Output controls:	Control distribution to appropriate users only; dispose of waste properly
	Centralization of data gathering, storing, processing, and reporting functions should be in one department

Four Major Areas for Audit Involvement in Information Systems

1. Administration/organization
2. Data center installations
3. System development/application systems
4. Microcomputers (a specialized fixed asset—including intelligent terminals, personal computers, special-purpose computers, such as word processing, CAD, CAM, CAE, etc.)

Automation is so prevalent in the financial arena that the logical migration for IS is to other areas with much data and paperwork (the manufacturing floor), and to engineering documentation.

Information systems installations have a joint responsibility and participate with accounting and operating personnel in the processing and maintenance of financial data and related records. Separation of the following functions is a basic control procedure:

Authorization of transactions
Recording transactions
Custody of assets

The IS department is a service department, and its role should be limited to the processing of data. Source documents should originate in and be authorized only by departments outside of IS.

Information Systems Organization

This section is divided into IS organization, administration, and staffing; operations and information system application controls. The first section discusses IS administration and staffing, and the placement of IS within the company organization structure.

Traditionally, IS was part of the controller's organization; however, with the increased processing power devoted to engineering and manufacturing applications, this may no longer be the best placement for the IS function. In some companies where manufacturing systems or the engineering applications far outweigh the importance of accounting systems, the IS director reports directly to the president.

The section on operation controls encompasses the systems development process and computer room operations. The final section discusses information systems that can be used to control and evaluate hardware utilization and data entry productivity.

In a minicomputer environment, many of the control functions described are performed with fewer people than in a traditional computer environment. However, they should be considered in an evaluation of a minicomputer system.

Management should also be concerned with the quantity and quality of staff and the stability of employment within the data processing department. More IS problems can be traced to an imbalance between quantity/quality of staff and the quantity/complexity of work than to any other cause. Staff inadequacies not only create a series of direct and obvious problems but also contribute to frequent systems changes, disruptions in schedules, and severe morale problems that accompany long crises.

The data base administrator within the data processing installation sets up the discipline for how data are to be used. The major functions of the data base administrator are to establish and administer procedural measures designed to protect the integrity of various data resources against accidental or willful penetration, modification, and/or disclosure.

Development of a multifaceted application system that interfaces with other processing systems requires a large number of skilled people from many departments, and often takes several man-years to complete. These projects are frequently characterized by uncertainties and require careful planning to achieve successful operating results. The following methods should be used during the systems development life cycle process.

An IS planning board/steering committee should exist to establish and monitor the major long-range strategic goals and objectives of the IS systems planned or in process. The committee should be made up of senior management, user department, and senior IS and internal audit representatives.

General

The following computer processing internal control standards consider the various operating systems currently available. The following sections are structured for ease of selecting only those areas needed in a specific environment. Audit need only test those sections that apply to the specific installation being tested.

The *Administrative/Organization Standards (1.00 series)* apply to the overall administration and organization of a data processing department. The objective is to assess the environment relating to all data processing activities. These general controls should identify major strengths and weaknesses to be considered in the evaluation of installation and application controls. These standards apply to all installations, but can be modified for minicomputer installations.

The *Installation Standards (2.00 series)* apply to each computer installation used in processing records or transactions. This includes computer installations owned and operated by the company as well as any outside computer service centers or computer processing companies used. These standards can also be used to review computer installations used for other applications such as manufacturing process control systems. These standards apply to all large and medium-sized installations with information system staffs.

The *Application Standards (3.00 series)* apply to each application that is processed, in whole or in part, by a computer installation. An application is any sequence of steps or tasks involved in processing transactions or records.

To assist the auditor in reviewing this series of standards, a flowchart (Exhibit 11–1) is provided. Depending upon the size and complexity of the computer facility, some standards (sections) may not apply. The flowchart also serves as a quick method to locate a specific group of standards.

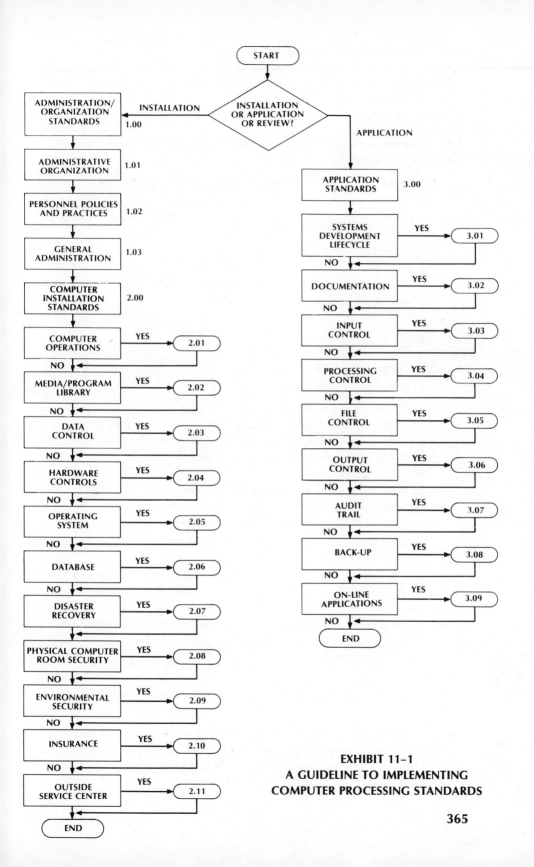

START

INSTALLATION OR APPLICATION OR REVIEW?

INSTALLATION

APPLICATION

ADMINISTRATION/ ORGANIZATION STANDARDS — 1.00

ADMINISTRATIVE ORGANIZATION — 1.01

PERSONNEL POLICIES AND PRACTICES — 1.02

GENERAL ADMINISTRATION — 1.03

COMPUTER INSTALLATION STANDARDS — 2.00

COMPUTER OPERATIONS — YES → 2.01 / NO

MEDIA/PROGRAM LIBRARY — YES → 2.02 / NO

DATA CONTROL — YES → 2.03 / NO

HARDWARE CONTROLS — YES → 2.04 / NO

OPERATING SYSTEM — YES → 2.05 / NO

DATABASE — YES → 2.06 / NO

DISASTER RECOVERY — YES → 2.07 / NO

PHYSICAL COMPUTER ROOM SECURITY — YES → 2.08 / NO

ENVIRONMENTAL SECURITY — YES → 2.09 / NO

INSURANCE — YES → 2.10 / NO

OUTSIDE SERVICE CENTER — YES → 2.11 / NO

END

APPLICATION STANDARDS — 3.00

SYSTEMS DEVELOPMENT LIFECYCLE — YES → 3.01 / NO

DOCUMENTATION — YES → 3.02 / NO

INPUT CONTROL — YES → 3.03 / NO

PROCESSING CONTROL — YES → 3.04 / NO

FILE CONTROL — YES → 3.05 / NO

OUTPUT CONTROL — YES → 3.06 / NO

AUDIT TRAIL — YES → 3.07 / NO

BACK-UP — YES → 3.08 / NO

ON-LINE APPLICATIONS — YES → 3.09 / NO

END

**EXHIBIT 11–1
A GUIDELINE TO IMPLEMENTING
COMPUTER PROCESSING STANDARDS**

1.00 Administration/Organization Standards

These standards apply to all environments.

1.01 Administrative Organization Provides Effective Controls over the IS Department

1. The IS department should be organizationally and functionally independent of operating user departments. The IS department should report directly to a designated member of local senior management with sufficient authority to provide adequate support and independence for the department.
2. An IS steering committee, or local management group comprised of members of senior management, should guide the overall direction of IS in the company.
3. The following functions should be segregated within the IS department:

   Applications programming

   Systems programming

   Database administration

   Computer operations
4. IS personnel should not have any authority to initiate or authorize transactions, except for transactions directly related to the administration and operation of the IS department (such as the purchase of supplies).
5. IS personnel should not have any authority to correct, or cause to be corrected, errors in application processing unless the error originates in the IS department.
6. IS personnel should not have any authority to initiate changes to master file contents.
7. IS personnel should not be responsible for preparing initial records of transactions (such as sales orders, order forms, check requests, etc.).
8. IS personnel should not have responsibility for the custody of any assets except computer equipment and other fixed assets used in the IS department.

1.02 Personnel, Policies, and Practices Adequately Provide Suitable Controls

1. A terminated IS employee should be immediately released. Procedures should exist to promptly notify appropriate personnel (security and personnel departments, other IS employees) and to immediately prevent access to the facility by the terminated employee.

2. Employees should be aware of their responsibilities in safeguarding sensitive information through written procedure statements from management.

3. Employees should be prevented from consistently processing the same applications through a program of job rotation, shift rotation, and vacations.

1.03 General Administration Procedures Provide Effective Controls over the Department

1. IS management should maintain a current organization chart and written job descriptions for all IS employees, which clearly establish individual responsibilities for each function.

2. IS management should maintain written policies and procedures for:

   Applications programming
   Systems programming
   Computer operations
   Media librarian
   Security
   Disaster recovery
   Personnel

3. IS management should formulate suitable written short- and long-range plans for the IS department in accordance with the company's IS steering committee recommendations.

4. Records of computer processing should be maintained so the computer center accounts for all computer time. Records should be reviewed by an IS manager familiar with the operation.

5. The IS department should have a formal record retention policy in accordance with company guidelines, systems requirements and generally accepted backup procedures.

6. IS management should maintain contracts for all hardware/software in use, including all maintenance agreements, rental agreements, warranties, and service center agreements. Copies of pertinent contracts are to be maintained at a remote location.

7. All hardware/software or service center agreements should specify:

   Cost
   Vendor responsibility
   Buyer responsibility
   Insurance coverage, where applicable
   Contract life

8. The IS department should effectively utilize all hardware and

software. All equipment and software not in current use should be brought to the attention of the designated employee in 1.01-1.

9. IS management should maintain communication with local internal auditors to inform them of significant problems or changes in equipment or systems.

2.00 Computer Installation

A sample audit program for use in a data center installation is included later in the chapter.

2.01 Computer Operations Procedures include Effective Controls

1. Local management should establish written procedures to prohibit personnel responsible for systems design and program writing from operating the computer without specific prior approval.

2. All operator intervention should be identified, controlled, and reviewed by management. The use of any sensitive utilities or privileged instructions should be identified, logged, and reviewed by management.

3. Computer operators should run nonproduction jobs only on the basis of properly authorized run requests.

4. Data center personnel should maintain a log of all operating system, software, and hardware problems.

5. Computer operations should be functionally independent of the data control, scheduling, librarian, and programming areas.

6. Computer schedule preparation should be based on a formal job priority.

7. Computer operations personnel should sign off on scheduled jobs when completed. Jobs not completed should be reentered on the next processing schedule.

2.02 Media/Program Library Procedures include Adequate Controls

1. Labels on data media (tapes, disks, diskettes, etc.) should contain an identifying name, number, creation date, and program/system.

2. The librarian should maintain a log of all data media in the IS library.

3. Periodic physical inventories should be conducted by an employee independent of the librarian function, and compared to a media log.

4. Sensitive information (payroll, product formulas, research and development data, company classified information, etc.) should be adequately protected from theft or unauthorized access.

5. Procedures should exist to control data media lent out by, or received by, the IS department.

6. The IS department should have established uniform naming standards for all data and program files.

7. An employee should periodically review all libraries to identify their accuracy, and to look for obsolete or duplicate data/programs at least every six months.

8. Unauthorized personnel should be denied access to data and program libraries by means of appropriate physical or password controls.

9. Intermediate work files (i.e., tapes or disk packs used in sorts) containing confidential data should be controlled to prevent improper use.

10. Prior generations of confidential data files beyond the last retention cycle should be placed under an appropriate level of control.

11. A log of all program versions should be maintained.

12. All program changes should be made at the source level and recompiled and tested.

2.03 Data Control Procedures Are Effective over Computer Operations

If a data control function exists, these standards apply.

1. An employee independent of computer operations is assigned to log all input forwarded to the data center.

2. An employee independent of computer operations is assigned to record all output and to review output for general acceptability and completeness.

3. Logs are maintained indicating at what time and to whom tapes, disk packs, and other data processing media containing confidential data were signed in and out.

4. A distribution list is maintained that identifies the individuals authorized to receive confidential reports; this list is kept secure. Users, so authorized, sign for the receipt of confidential reports.

5. In all larger computer centers (IBM 4341 or equivalent), breakdowns of computer time are reviewed to detect deviations from normal patterns.

6. Written procedures exist to insure periodic checks are performed to determine if:

   a. Specific jobs were actually run by checking output.

   b. Individual run durations conform to the schedule, if work is scheduled.

   c. Number or frequency of runs of specific program conforms to schedule, if work is scheduled.

    d. Total time charged to a specific program over a given time period conforms to schedule, if work is scheduled.

    e. An unusual number of runs or amount of time is charged to reruns.

    f. The causes of reruns are analyzed and corrective action is taken.

    g. Programs being run are authorized versions.

7. Console sheets are examined to detect unauthorized use of the computer.

8. Meter hours are correlated with elapsed time. End meter readings are compared with begin meter readings each day for unexplained gaps.

9. A detailed schedule of a shift is prepared by authorized personnel.

10. Shift performance is compared with the schedule to detect deviations.

11. Usage statistics are periodically reported to unit management.

2.04 Hardware Controls Provide for Adequate Maintenance

These standards apply to all installations.

1. Current adequate documentation is maintained for all hardware in the data center.

2. Written procedures are established to assure that hardware is kept in good working order according to the manufacturer's maintenance guidelines. Maintenance is performed as recommended.

2.05 Operating System—System Programming Controls

These standards apply to all major operating systems.

1. Documentation is adequate and current on all operating systems maintained in the IS department.

2. In a multiprocessing environment, the operating system allows only one program at a time to modify a given file record.

3. Changes to operational programs are subject to a control procedure (such as rejection of sensitive jobs executed with a patch) to ensure the integrity of program changes prior to entry into the library.

4. Safeguards exist to prohibit application programs from modifying the operating system.

5. System programmers are prohibited from accessing object and source program libraries.

6. All changes to the operating system programs are properly authorized and approved prior to implementation.

7. Detailed specifications and schedules are prepared and approved by managers of system programming, operations, and application programming prior to working on any major operating system change.

8. Memory protection features are used to prevent an application program from reading or writing outside the memory area assigned to that program.

9. Memory areas used by sensitive programs are cleared prior to their release for use by other programs.

10. When spooling systems are used, runs that process confidential data are scheduled so authorized information systems personnel can be present to insure that files are not improperly retained or misused.

2.06 Data Base Administration Is Properly Assigned

These standards apply where a data base management system (DBMS) is in operation.

1. A data base administrator should be assigned responsibilities, which include:

    Naming and defining the data structure(s)

    Monitoring security, privacy, and integrity controls

    Establishing recovery and backup procedures

    Performance measurement.

2. The data dictionary contains sufficient control information to restrict access to authorized users only.

3. All usage of restricted data base instructions is controlled, recorded, and reviewed.

4. All changes to the data base(s) are authorized, adequately documented, tested, and approved prior to implementation.

5. Current documentation is maintained for all DBMS, that is:

    Data structures

    Data descriptions

    Transaction matrices

    Data/program relationships

    Storage structures

    Security rules

    Data sources

    Edit and validation criteria

2.07 Disaster Recovery—Adequate Controls Exist to Provide for the Continued Running of the Business in Case of a Breakdown or Destruction of the Computer Installation

These standards apply to all major installations.

1. The data center should maintain an up-to-date disaster recovery manual that specifies current hardware/software inventories, key contacts, backup procedures, and task assignments in the event of a data center disaster.

2. The data center should maintain a current copy of the disaster recovery manual in an off-site location.

3. A current copy of the operating system software should be maintained at an off-site location.

4. Data center personnel should have the ability to identify and locate all data media in the event the primary media log is destroyed, lost, and so on.

5. The data center should have written procedures for recovery from failure of power, water, and air conditioning systems.

6. To provide backup for critical responsibilities within the data center, employees should be cross-trained to perform another function outside their normal duties.

7. Employees and outside emergency people (police, fire, ambulance, insurance, etc.) are periodically briefed on emergency and disaster recovery procedures.

8. Written procedures are established to reconcile file control totals before and after a system recovery.

9. Periodic inventories of all backup storage (data, programs, documentation, forms) are compared to backup inventory logs, and all differences are reconciled.

10. Formal arrangements are made for the use of alternate computer facilities, which are fully tested and documented annually. The IS representative should be notified of any change (hardware, software, computer time availability) at the backup installation.

11. Adequate physical/environmental security should be maintained at the alternate computer facility when company application programs are being processed.

12. All user identifying passwords are required to be changed after recovery to continue using computer resources.

13. Access is restricted to the data center at the off-site location.

14. Off-site storage facility is of sturdy construction, and is under lock and key protection with access restricted to authorized personnel.

15. The accuracy and currentness of program and data files is maintained at the off-site storage facility by processing them at the designated backup installation at least once a year.
16. Compatibility has been established by successfully running some company programs on the backup system.
17. For confidential applications, the company has provided for security of confidential data files and programs while operating at the backup installation.
18. The contingency plan has identified by program all data files, run instructions, forms, and so on necessary, and indicates where they can be located and how they are accessed.
19. The contingency plan identifies the priority of applications, the changes in run and print frequency, and other load reduction techniques.
20. For teleprocessing systems, written alternative backup procedures are defined, such as using direct input instead of telecommunications, or resorting to manual procedures.

2.08 Physical Computer Room Security Is Adequate

These standards apply to all installations.

1. Access to the data center is limited via physical controls (keys, card identification, etc.).
2. All employees must receive authorization prior to entry to the data center at times other than their scheduled working hours.
3. The data center maintains a log of all visitors, maintenance personnel, and other employees who enter the data center.
4. Visitors are never left unaccompanied in the data center.
5. IS personnel are periodically briefed on security and instructed to report all suspected security violations to an appropriate level of management.
6. Physical security is maintained at all backup locations.
7. Adequate fire detection devices (heat and/or smoke) are installed and working at the installation.
   The devices should alert employees prior to automatically turning on any fire extinguishing systems.
   The devices should have been tested in the past year.
   Portable fire extinguishers of carbon dioxide, halon, or similar type should be provided for electrical fires.
8. The floor of the computer room should be equipped with a gravity feed drain or a pump system that prevents deep water accumulation.

9. Paper waste (printouts, carbons, etc.) should be properly controlled to prevent unauthorized access or disposal.

10. Programmers and systems analysts are excluded from the computer room except for critical operating conditions, and then only under personal supervision of authorized personnel.

11. Access to the computer center is controlled for the vendor's maintenance and support personnel.

12. The computer center is adequately protected whenever the center is not in operation, either by a manned guard station on or off premises, or by security guards on a scheduled basis.

13. Doors are controlled by electronic locks and badge readers. These can be operated in the event of a public utility power failure.

14. If there is more than one entrance to the computer room, the secondary entrance(s) are appropriately protected.

15. If there is only one entrance to the computer room, there is at least one secure additional one-way fire/safety exit.

16. The walls separating the computer center (including input/output section, data entry rooms, etc.) from internal corridors are made of solid construction (not glass or window).

2.09 Environmental Security Is Adequate

These standards apply to all major installations.

1. Good housekeeping practices and a system of protection/detection devices provide adequate security from fire, water, or smoke damage in the data center.

2. Temperature and humidity controls are monitored and maintained within the manufacturer's equipment and media guidelines.

3. Fire alarms, smoke detectors, and so on are properly maintained, and are tested periodically.

4. The data center power distribution panel/switch is not accessible to unauthorized persons. Safeguards are in place to prevent an accidental shutdown of power.

2.10 Insurance Coverage Adequately Protects the Company

1. The company has an insurance policy that provides adequate coverage for replacement of:

    Computer equipment

    Media and software

    Microcomputer equipment, media, and software in the event of damage due to fire, water, air conditioning breakdown, building collapse, faulty sprinkler system, vandalism, rioting aircraft, theft, explosion, and so on

2. Procedures exist to inform the insurance agent of any hardware/software changes in the data center that may affect coverage.

2.11 Outside Service Center Controls Are Adequate

These standards apply when the company uses an outside service bureau only.

1. Written agreements with the service center are maintained and include:
   Type and amount of services
   Price of services
   Term of agreement
   Ownership/custody of programs and files
   Insurance coverage (if provided by service center)
   Performance of third-party or internal audit review.
2. The IS department or the user maintain copies of, or have procedures to recreate, all documents sent to the service center for processing.
3. The service center provides appropriate security/access controls over company data and programs at the service location.
4. The service center provides backup of files and programs to ensure continuity of processing.
5. Output is received from the service center in a timely and secure manner.
6. The financial condition of the vendor has been reviewed to determine its ability to continue in business and provide satisfactory service.
7. Data, programs, and so on are afforded appropriate protection while in transit.
8. All programs, files, and documentation that were specifically developed for the company by the vendor are contractually defined as company property.
9. The service bureau contract specifies that all vendor program errors, operational errors, and machine malfunctions will be corrected without charge.

Computer Acquisition and Systems Development

The internal auditors' responsibility for and involvement in decisions about computerized systems begins with the feasibility study and continues with periodic audits of the function and related controls.

Preinstallation (Preacquisition) Controls

Controls should ensure that a new or replacement computer is acquired only when the benefits from doing so exceed the benefits of the present or other system's alternatives. Also, the capacity of the machine may exceed an efficient percentage and may need to be upgraded. The benefits may be faster response time and satisfied users. Controls that the auditor would be interested in include:

1. Feasibility study. Management appoints a committee that analyzes all feasible alternatives and makes recommendations to management. After reviewing the study and recommendations, management chooses a path of action from various alternatives. Factors relating to the committee and the decision process of its members include:
   a. Representation should be from all affected user departments.
   b. The committee should have a member who is thoroughly knowledgeable about computer systems, including hardware and software.
   c. The in-place system should be examined to determine if improvements to it might delay the need for any change. When examining the current system, the committee should be particularly concerned that all past internal audit recommendations were properly implemented.
   d. Careful consideration should be given to the equipment specifications so they do not limit the available choices of equipment to one vendor.
2. Equipment specifications should consider present and future needs.
3. Bids and presentations of equipment and software vendors should be sought.
4. Preinstallation plans should include a list of all activities to be affected and all tasks to be performed.

CONTROL OF SYSTEMS DEVELOPMENT

These controls should ensure that applications are converted only in areas where computers will provide equal or greater benefits than the existing system. Senior management should review all proposals for change and determine their acceptability.

Documentation is the key to a good system. The documentation that directly relates to the computer-based information system and its operation is made up of three types:

1. General systems documentation provides guidance and operating rules for users when interfacing with the system. The documentation for each system should include:
   a. Problem statement that provides an adequate definition of the purpose of the application and how it complements other systems
   b. Systems flowchart
   c. Input and output requirements and specifications
   d. Methods of processing
   e. Equipment requirements
   f. Needed controls

2. Procedural documentation acquaints operating, programming, and systems staff with the master plan of the system; computer operating standards, controls, and procedures; and programming standards and procedures.

3. Program documentation consists of all documents, diagrams, and layouts that explain aspects of the program supporting a particular system's design. The documentation file for each program should include:
   a. Problem statement that identifies the function of the particular program in the total system
   b. Program flowchart
   c. Transaction and activity codes used
   d. Record layout specifying the characteristics of the data and fields on the computer file
   e. Operations instructions
   f. Program listing
   g. Details and approvals of program changes
   h. Description of input and output forms.

APPLICATION CONTROLS

Application controls are specific to each individual IS system. They include controls over the input, processing, and output functions of the system.

1. Input controls include preventive controls for the prevention of mishandling and resubmission of input data. Examples include:
   a. Batch controls
   b. Document counts
   c. Hash totals.

2. Detective controls determine the validity of input records by searching for:
   a. Invalid characters in a field
   b. Computational agreement with a self-checking digit
   c. Invalid transactions
   d. Missing data
   e. Matching data between transactions and the master file
3. Processing controls that assure the proper updating of the master files include:
   a. Reasonableness or limit tests on data
   b. Crossfooting of output arrays
   c. Control figures designed to assure that all records are processed and that a file is updated
   d. Comparison of transaction file records with master file records
   e. Maintenance of a suspense file for error messages and unprocessed records caused by out-of-sequence conditions

Auditing around the computer is insufficient and inadequate in today's environment for most sophisticated systems.

Auditing through the computer is auditing the entire system. A system is defined as all software, communications, security, people, documentation, procedures, and other controls involved in its execution, whether automated or manual.

Methods used to audit through the computer include test decking, integrated test facility, embedded audit routines, parallel simulation, and the use of audit software and system utilities (such as code comparisons).

3.00 APPLICATION STANDARDS

The following questions apply to in-house development of new systems only (they do not apply to purchased packages).

3.01 System Development Life Cycle (SDLC) and System Changes Are Adequately Controlled

These standards apply to all applications.

1. Formal requests are prepared and properly authorized for development of new systems and changes to old systems.
2. User departments are suitably involved in the appropriate phases of system development.

3. A feasibility study is prepared for all new system development and major modifications to existing systems.

4. Detailed specifications and schedules are prepared for all new systems and major changes to existing systems; they are approved by IS management and the user prior to program development.

5. Programming changes and code development are performed only in the test environment.

6. All new systems and changes are adequately tested and formally approved by IS and user management prior to implementation.

7. A conversion plan (parallel, phased, direct cutover, etc.) is established, and procedures are maintained for a suitable period to monitor system changes.

8. Adequate backup of the old system data and programs is maintained in case of conversion problems.

9. Documentation is revised immediately after every system change; users and operators are trained as required.

10. Program patches are recorded when instituted, and replaced via normal change procedures as soon as practical.

11. A group or person within the IS department, not part of the project team, formally approves each new system for sufficiency of controls, division of responsibilities, totals, and other internal control features.

12. Internal auditors formally approve financial and other sensitive systems at the design stage for adequacy and determination of controls, division of responsibilities, and other internal control features.

13. The following reviews are performed by the internal audit function on a periodic basis:
    a. Random checks of control totals
    b. Unannounced checks of master file record printouts to ensure the integrity of the data
    c. Test of operating programs by tracing transactions from input to output
    d. Test of operating programs using test decks or test transactions

14. Internal or external auditors periodically review the procedures of the users and the control group to determine their adequacy.

3.02 Documentation Procedures Provide Adequate Controls

These standards apply to all applications.

1. Up-to-date documentation is maintained, including flowcharts, record layouts, program listings, code descriptions, description of test data, and a historical record of modifications.

2. User documentation is adequate and includes input preparation, description of available output, and control and error correction procedures.

3. Operator-run instructions are current and contain only information necessary to assure proper running of the application (i.e., input data, job setup, output format, halt condition procedures, etc.).

4. Operators do not have access to program documentation.

5. The systems design and programming function have written guidelines for the development of procedures and programmed controls necessary for the detection and correction of errors.

6. Users compare computer-generated control totals with their own control totals and initiate corrective action when necessary.

7. Systems generate control totals and are checked by the control function.

8. The control group at the mainframe or host computer center can review console logs, error listings, or other evidence of error detection to insure that all detected errors are reported, corrected, and reprocessed.

9. If master files are kept on disk at the mainframe or host computer center, adequate controls exist to ensure the completeness and accuracy of processing and that records are not lost during file reorganization or file backup.

3.03 Input Control Procedures Are Adequate

These standards apply to all applications.

1. Data center personnel review source documents for accuracy, completeness, and proper approval prior to data entry.

2. Written procedures are established to ensure data input is complete via record counts, batch totals, and so on.

3. Input data are checked for validity, completeness, and reasonableness as appropriate to the application via terminal edits, limits, table look-ups, check digits, and so on.

4. Unprocessed input data are listed and monitored for follow-up.

5. Procedures exist to verify that the correct files/versions are being accessed by an application.

3.04 Processing Control Procedures Are Adequate

These standards apply to an on-line or batch environment.

1. Written procedures exist to detect any loss or alteration of data or processing errors during an application run.

2. Processing errors are listed and monitored for follow-up.
3. All system overrides during processing are automatically logged and reviewed.
4. Old versions of program code are deleted from source/object libraries.
5. Program patches are only allowed in emergency situations and only with supervisory approval.
6. Checkpoint and restart procedures are followed whenever a processing error occurs.
7. Operations personnel are not permitted to make changes to, or gain access to, program libraries.

3.05 File Control Procedures Are Adequate

These standards apply to all media (disk, tape, paper, etc.).

1. Changes are made to master files only on the basis of written user authorization.
2. File maintenance transactions create before and after records to permit users to trace all changes made.
3. An employee of the user department, independent of the initiator of the change, verifies all changes to master files via a maintenance routine prepared by data operations.
4. File maintenance records have a retention period appropriate to the application.

3.06 Output Control Procedures Are Adequate

These standards apply to all applications.

1. The data center maintains a listing of all application system output reports, the number of copies per report, and the distribution.
2. Written procedures are established to assure any alteration, loss, or nonprocessing of output data is promptly detected and corrected.
3. Special procedures exist to safeguard sensitive output.
4. Written procedures exist to control the security over, and ordering of, critical forms.
5. Output is reconciled to input by user or the data control group.

3.07 Audit Trail Is Adequately Maintained

These standards apply to all applications.

1. All activity on an application can be identified on the console log or activity report.

2. An established audit trail can enable a user to trace individual transactions forward to final totals, and final totals back to individual transactions.

3. Individual transactions are identified to enable a user to trace a transaction to a source document.

3.08 Back-Up Documentation Is Adequate

These standards apply to all applications.

1. A copy of the current application programs and job control language is maintained off-site.

2. Copies of current master files required to run the application are maintained off-site.

3. A copy of the current documentation (system, operator, and user) is maintained off-site.

4. A sufficient supply of critical forms for the application system is maintained off-site.

5. A plan for alternative processing of the application has been established and is maintained off-site.

6. A log is maintained of all media stored off-site and is periodically reconciled to the physical media.

3.09 On-Line Applications Are Properly Controlled

These standards apply to all on-line environments. These are broadly defined as interactive and inquiry systems having one or more terminals linked to a central computer, and include timesharing services and systems where the central computer is not in-house. A remote batch terminal treated as an in-house computer does not qualify as an on-line system.

1. A log of all data transmissions is maintained and reviewed, and includes:

    Messages sent/received

    Communications failures/problems

2. All users are assigned unique identification codes for terminal access.

3. The final message of a transmission contains an end-of-transmission communication.

4. Terminal access to the computer system is adequately controlled via passwords, permissions, locks, and so on.

5. System passwords, permissions, locks, and so on are appropriately assigned and controlled to ensure that only authorized users

requiring continual access can perform tasks necessary in their jobs.

6. Passwords are periodically changed.

7. The dial-up/redial message is validated and identifies the user and the specific terminal.

8. Appropriate edits or verifications are performed prior to transmission on an intelligent terminal.

9. An inventory of data communication equipment is maintained specifying lines, terminals, modems, and so on.

10. Terminals automatically log-off, after no usage for several minutes, to prevent unauthorized users from entering, accessing, or modifying data.

11. A procedure is in effect to lock-out a terminal user after several unsuccessful attempts at signing on, to prevent unauthorized access.

12. A procedure exists to remove an employee's ID and password upon termination of employment or internal transfer.

13. After a system failure, users must re-enter identifying passwords to continue using computer resources.

14. Where files are maintained in common with other users, adequate safeguards exist to prevent other users from accessing your files.

15. If any of the data files contain restricted or confidential data, a written statement from the person responsible for its use should state under what conditions a restricted or confidential file can be accessed.

16. If on-line systems exist that maintain and update on-line master files, adequate controls should be built into the system to restrict on-line file updating to authorized individuals only.

17. Daily control reports should be produced from journal and master file statistics to insure operational integrity of the system.

18. The procedures for restoring data files should be established in writing and tested.

19. A centralized authority should be established that is responsible for monitoring the network performance.

20. All network configuration changes should be documented on the control terminal.

21. System controls should ensure that all messages received are processed.

22. A procedure exists for immediate investigation of all unauthorized intrusions into the terminal system.

23. Message content is validated for accuracy by means such as character checking (vertical redundancy) and message content (longitudinal redundancy).

MICROCOMPUTER APPROACH

The auditor uses a different approach due to:

1. The software is multipurpose, and the company has a potential liability if software licenses are violated.
2. Software is being used to input and manipulate data for significant decision making, which could potentially impact the financial viability of the firm.
3. The ability to store a significant amount of data potentially without proper segregation of duties controls, and without proper backup, disaster recovery, or security.
4. The capability to access mainframe data and download and upload data.
5. Maintenance and purchasing decisions may be different than those for the larger mainframes.

The auditor should review controls, not establish them. The auditor should ensure that an information center and other controls are in place.

Problems that an auditor may encounter in the mini- and micro- (personal) computer area include:

Lack of segregation of duties
Inadequate software processing controls
Ready access to data files and/or programs
Inadequate file and program backup procedures
Lack of control over program changes

MINICOMPUTER ENVIRONMENT

Adequate general controls may not be feasible in smaller computer installations (limited staffs may preclude proper segregation of duties). In a minicomputer environment, added weight must be given to secondary and tertiary controls. Some particulars to be considered when reviewing a minicomputer environment include the following. Minicomputers:

Operate in less stringent environmental conditions
Are normally dedicated to one system
Are in a separate geographical location from the main data processing location, and
Do not usually have technical operations support.

Higher reliance must therefore be placed on user and application controls.

Internal Auditor Approach

The internal auditor should review hardware and software controls over personal (micro) computers. Hardware should be reviewed against what has been assigned to an individual. The Central Processing Unit (CPU), extra internal boards, the monitor, printer, and any other equipment should be periodically checked. Serial numbers should agree to a master list kept in an information center or in the fixed asset ledger. Modems should be well controlled. The company should also have a policy or position statement regarding the use of personally-owned equipment on company premises. One does not want to have to control or be liable for personal property on company premises. Also, we do not want to have employees using company telephone lines (via modems) for personal use.

The auditor should review software to ensure there is no bootlegged or otherwise illegal software on company premises. An appropriate inventory of software (including version and serial numbers, if applicable) should be centrally maintained. This will also be needed when the vendor offers updates to authorized users at a reduced cost.

IBM and other vendors have utilities built into their systems which will define system configuration information to the user. Other utilities can be used to display file contents and size; hidden files will also be identified.

The auditor should also review physical security over the microcomputers, hardware maintenance, and software back-up procedures employed by the users.

EXHIBITS

Exhibits 11-2 and 11-3 are presented as help aids to the internal auditor and IS and internal audit management. Exhibit 11-2 is a reference sheet outlining all hardware and software within the IS environment. Exhibit 11-3 is one company's complete program/checklist for reviewing software systems being developed in-house.

EXHIBIT 11–2
COMPUTER INSTALLATION INFORMATION

Location _____

Computer Installation _____

Installation Information—Equipment:

Please indicate equipment currently in use:
(Fill out a separate form for each data center or for each engineering computer installation reviewed.)

Manufacturer _____ Series/Model _____ Memory Size _____

External Storage Devices:
(List type and quantity)

Tape Drives _____ Disk Drives _____

Cassette Readers _____ Floppy Disk Drives _____

Other (describe) _____

Input and Output Devices:
(List type and quantity)

Card Punch/Readers _____ Printers _____

Key/Data Entry Devices _____

On-Line Equipment:

TYPE	QUANTITY	LOCAL/REMOTE
_____	_____	_____
_____	_____	_____
_____	_____	_____
_____	_____	_____

Describe the number of shifts per day and days per week the installation operates
_____

Indicate when the operators are usually on duty within the computer installation
_____

Is computer time used by anyone outside the organization? _____

Are there timesharing capabilities on the system? _____

Are any major changes to equipment planned within the next 12 months? If so, please describe:
_____
_____
_____

Indicate the name of systems software used in this installation:

Operating System(s) [Version/Release] _____

Compilers _____

Job Scheduler/Spooler _____

Job Accounting System _____

Disk Management System _____

Tape Library Management _____

Program Library Management _____

Data Base Management System _____

Data Communications Support _____

Teleprocessing _____

Programming Language(s) Used _____

Discuss any major changes planned to systems software within the next 12 months:
_____
_____
_____

Attach a copy of a current organization chart of the information systems function. Highlight the key IS personnel.

Provide a schematic of your communication network:

Computerized Application Systems

(Prepare a list as follows):

Application Name/Description	Cycle # Freq. of Programs (Dly, Wkly)	Cycle Processing Statistics		Input/Output Resources	
		Avg. Transactions Volume	Avg. Run Time	Master File Storage Devices (Tape, Disk)	Advanced Sys Tech Employed (DBMS, Teleproc, etc.)

EXHIBIT 11-3
PREAUDIT QUESTIONNAIRE
FOR SYSTEMS BEING DEVELOPED

Permanent Audit File Data

PROJECT NAME _____ PROJECT LEADER _____
AUDITOR-IN-CHARGE _____ DATE: _____

Scope of Project

1. Obtain a copy of the original and subsequent systems requests describing the project and other items available concerning the project (i.e., steering committee minutes, memos, system flowcharts, etc.).
2. Identify the primary users of the system.
3. Indicate what effect project completion will have on the users.
4. Determine if and how this project will interface with any other system.
5. Determine what, if any, impact the project will have on staffing, hardware, or facilities.
6. Get definition for any government regulations that should be considered in developing this project.
7. Obtain a sample of all forms or documents used by the system.
8. Prepare or obtain a brief overview of the project, including the basic functions to be performed by the system, all inputs and outputs, and other items you believe are basic to the project.

Feasibility Study

1. Verify compliance with the procedures for submitting proposals as outlined in the Corporate Policy and Procedure Manual.
2. Obtain documentation on system cost justification. Compare costs of the proposed system versus the benefits derived. Determine if other alternatives should have been reviewed.
3. Evaluate, if appropriate, the make-or-buy analysis documenting the decision to develop or purchase software.
4. Verify if the hardware and software acquisition requirements include documentation on lead times, and cost of new hardware and software items or enhancements to installed items.

Project Schedule

1. Obtain a copy of the performance measurement system being used to monitor the progress of the project.

If a performance tool is not being used, outline all the major milestones in the project, including such items as the given start and completion dates, final date for changes, and so on.

2. Indicate the total number of hours estimated to complete the project.
3. Determine the frequency of the project's reporting status, and to whom it is reported.
4. Determine the current status of the project.

Documentation

1. Obtain or generate a listing of all available documentation, describing the characteristics of the system and a documentation distribution list.
2. Determine the status or degree of implementation of all available documentation.
3. Obtain copies of signed-off project definition documents.
4. Verify that the project definition phase starts after management and the user approves.
5. Verify completeness of input requirements documentation.
6. Verify that input requirements include:
   Appropriate input validation requirements
   Appropriate security/privacy protection controls
   Provisions for needed administrative controls
7. Verify completeness of output requirements documentation.
8. Obtain or prepare a system flowchart showing input, flow of documents, work queues, manual controls, data entry, data control, processing (major programs) steps, output, and interfaces with other systems.
9. Verify, using the system flowchart, that the system does not merely automate inefficiencies of the prior system.
10. Verify that output requirements include:
    Appropriate security and retention considerations
    Allowance for delivery lead times and system response times
11. Verify that data base documentation includes:
    Clear definition of structural data relationships
    Definition of data set dependencies
    Identification of any special protection requirements for sensitive data and vital records
    Provisions for audit trails
    Required access level controls

System Controls

1. Review procedural and administrative controls over preparation and conversion of input data.
   a. Verify that each transaction is initially recorded on a source document that bears an identification code and is filed so that it may be referenced. Individuals responsible for input preparation or having access to unused source documents should not be responsible for the reconciliation, approval, or disbursement of the output.
   b. Verify that input data are batched, and that batch control totals are taken at point of preparation. Batch header forms should be used with an identification code and a record of the batch control total. The total number of batches submitted should be recorded and verified as being processed.
   c. Verify that output control totals are reconciled back to input control totals by an independent control group. Overall control totals should be reconciled from output to input by the source or user departments. Where appropriate, output should be listed and visually checked in detail to input documents.
   d. Insure that a well defined procedure will exist for identifying and correcting errors and re-entering corrections with a fixed responsibility for this function.
   e. Verify that procedures governing the preparation of source documents are described in user manuals. Adequate training and supervision should be given to all persons preparing data. Information on source documents should be preprinted and/or precoded and screen formats set up the same way.
   f. Verify that adequate procedures are established to insure all output is properly distributed. User departments should employ procedures that anticipate the return of output.
   g. Verify that adequate measures will exist to insure only authorized data is processed. Input documents bear evidence of authorization and should be reviewed accordingly.
2. For on-line systems, assess whether adequate controls necessitated by the on-line or real-time environment have been implemented as follows:
   a. Input controls
      (1) Programmed self-checking digits, existence checks, logic checks, completeness checks, and reasonableness checks are performed before the transaction is used in processing.

(2) For invalid data or clerical data entry error, the terminal operator is immediately notified by an error message, a video, or audio tone, and can correct the transaction at that point.

(3) Where the system itself generates a transaction, the system should document the existence of the machine-generated transaction by producing a hard copy memorandum to be verified by an independent check of the activity. Review the criteria by which such transactions are generated.

(4) The log of messages entered from each terminal is periodically reviewed by a supervisor.

b. Processing controls

(1) The system has been designed (by buffering) to handle and cue randomly occurring peak loads in an acceptable period of time without loss of any transactions. Describe the procedures followed.

(2) Procedures are used to identify and recognize priorities within these transactions besides first in, first out. Describe the procedures used.

(3) If multiprogramming and/or multiprocessing is used, techniques are employed to prevent simultaneous accessing and updating of a single master record by two or more transactions.

c. File access controls

(1) Controls are used to identify legitimate users and to prevent unauthorized access to data files.

(2) Conduct attempts at unauthorized access through a terminal and document system behavior.

(3) Terminal operators are given a key, code, or password badge that unlocks the terminal and can be read by the terminal or computer for identification.

(4) Evaluate the controls used to protect the identity of operator passwords on terminals. Are the passwords suppressed (not printed), or does the terminal itself immediately backspace and type over the password characters, making the password illegible?

(5) Appraise existing procedures for password assignment, updating, and discontinuance.

(6) Insure that the system provides regular notification to management of attempts to make unauthorized access to data files or to enter unauthorized transactions.

12. Systems reliability controls
    a. Describe the hardware and software controls used to detect system malfunctions.
    b. Describe any programming routines designed to search the data files to determine the exact status of the processing previous to a system malfunction and to reposition all the various elements of the system.
    c. Describe the approach to recovery from an error condition, such as switching to a standby system. Describe the procedure used for verifying the accuracy of the data base and for reconstructing any file information adversely affected by a system failure.
    d. Describe the procedure used for:
       (1) Reconstructing the data base in the event of a failure, such as simultaneous updating of a duplicate file.
       (2) Dumping the data file onto another device on a regularly scheduled basis.
       (3) Recording all transactions that occur as well as the contents of each master record, both before and after updating by a specific transaction.
    e. Appraise the adequacy of written alternate manual procedures or disaster/backup plans in the event of system unavailability.
13. Verify that adequate file retention is observed.
14. Verify that sufficient file security is maintained to comply with privacy legislation.
15. Insure that any transaction can be traced back and forth throughout the system (an audit trail).
16. Ascertain that management receives adequate system information to accurately appraise what is occurring in their organizational units:
    a. Activity reports to monitor resources used (labor, equipment, utilities, etc.) and output (orders, batches, etc.). The comparison of input and output data that reflects activity with predetermined standards, such as budgets or schedules, provides a manager with useful information allowing him/her to determine the organizational unit's efficiency during a specific period of time.
    b. Status reports are needed to indicate the state of a particular element or group of elements at a given point in time. Comparing the level of a particular element at the present time with its level at various past times is a common method of identifying trends.
    c. Exception reports are needed to define conditions requiring remedial action. Identify operational policies relating to the application. Verifying system design includes reports that alert management to the enforcement of these policies.

Other

17. Verify, using the system flowchart, that the system does not merely automate inefficiencies of a manual system.

Programming Definition Phase

General

18. Identify the critical programs and list who will write each one. Briefly explain why each is considered critical.
19. Appraise the completeness of the program narratives using the Procedures Manual as a guide.

Controls

Review program specifications for processing accuracy, auditability, control, and integrity. This function should use, but not be limited to:

20. In the original entry processing:
   Accumulate debits
   Accumulate credits
   Accumulate hash total of account or ID numbers
   Accumulate record count
   Balance debit and credit accumulators against the input control
   Create a control record consisting of record count, hash total, and debit and credit accumulators
   Print all totals at end of transaction listing
   If any difference exists after balancing routine—print input control totals, accumulated totals and difference.
21. For the posting programs:
   Accumulate debits (transactions)
   Accumulate credits (transactions)
   Accumulate opening balances (master)
   Accumulate record count (master and transactions)
   Accumulate delete record count
   Accumulate closing balances after posting
   Accumulate output record counts
   Apply debit and credit accumulators against the opening balance accumulator and balance against the closing balance accumulator

Apply auto-generated and delete accumulators against the master input-record count and balance to the master output-record count

Balance all input accumulators to the input control records

Write output control records. (Total closing balances, output record counts, and other principal dollar and hash fields.)

When a string of programs is run, the output file of each run must contain control records for balancing in each succeeding run using the file as input.

Programming Phase

22. Verify that programming is being conducted using an established computer librarian package.
23. Verify that a stop point for program changes has been established and is observed.
24. Select the computer programs that could be an area for fraud and review for any suspicious coding.

Test and Acceptance Phase

25. Identify the individuals responsible for preparing the testing plan, executing the testing, and evaluating the test results.
26. Review the test plan to ascertain that it contains:
    a. Instructions indicating what is to be done, by whom, when to do it, what to look for, and what to record, and listing all actions required of human operators at each piece of equipment involved in the test.
    b. Simulated input data prepared beforehand for the purpose of exercising the system during a given test.
    c. Live input to provide processing environments difficult to get from prepared, simulated input data (i.e., randomness and a likelihood of a certain amount of garbage).
    d. Predicted output (written forecasts of the exact data that should result from a given test case, where such forecasting is possible).
    e. Built-in restart points for resuming in the event of unexpected aborts during the test.
    f. Procedures for documenting each test to show clearly what the inputs were, what the results were predicted to be, and what the actual results were.
    g. Provisions for isolating the test environment from the production environment.

28. Review the adequacy of the detailed test specifications for each specific functional area of the system with respect to:

    a. The extent to which the simulated input data exercises the system: Are all valid transaction types processed, and is the processing reviewed for accuracy?

    b. Are controls tested at all levels? Are debits and credits accumulated properly; is cross-footing of reports accurate; are run-to-run totals in balance, and so on?

    c. Are all editing and error checking routines invoked and are error messages properly displayed on entry logs, exception reports, and so on?

    d. Special processing required at various time intervals (e.g., daily, weekly, monthly, quarterly, annually, on request reports).

    e. Attempts to make the system fail:

        (1) Use of invalid transactions (e.g., incorrect transaction codes, invalid combinations of transaction codes, substitution of alpha for numeric, numeric for alpha, blanks for zeroes, zeroes for blanks).

        (2) Use of transactions with incomplete or missing fields.

        (3) Attempts to update against nonexistent accounts.

        (4) Set-ups of new accounts against an account already on the master file.

        (5) Operator error.

        (6) Invocation of recovery and restart procedure.

        (7) Test of backup capability.

        (8) Off-line control and other clerical procedures.

29. As appropriate, observe the execution of the various test plans and verify that testing is executed in accordance with the plan, and that test results are adequately documented. Determine that documentation of each test is available so it can be shown clearly what the inputs were, what the results were predicted to be, and what the actual results were.

30. Follow up in areas where the test results seem to be weak to insure that any potential problem areas are identified and corrected.

Installation and Operation Phase

31. Ensure documentation has been kept up to date. Ensure missing data have been completed.

32. Review the system's controls covered in the System Definition and Design Phase to determine if they are still in effect and complete.

33. Ensure that the conversion plan includes tests and criteria for judging completeness of conversion.

34. Ensure that the conversion plan includes provisions for computer-performed editing and validation of data entered into master files.

35. Verify that controls over changes to master files exist between the time of initial conversion and the final acceptance testing prior to production.

36. Verify that the conversion plan includes provisions for appropriate user and management sign-off's initiating cutover to the new system.

37. Verify that an adequate training program exists for user and data processing personnel.

38. Appraise the arrangements for monitoring system performance after implementation.

Post Implementation Phase

39. Obtain and review an analysis of original estimated costs and return on investment versus actual operating costs and the benefits of the system. Appraise reasons for significant variances.

40. Document any differences between expected and actual system performance.

41. Evaluate user satisfaction with the system versus original user requirements.

42. Obtain description of problems with or shortcomings of the system from project members and users.

43. Examine system information for items that might indicate system problems, for example, extraordinarily high programmer maintenance costs indicating system problems; high number of abends/reruns; input/output and balancing problems.

Specialized Questions Pertinent to the Audit

Add questions as needed and indicate to which phase of the project they concern.

CHAPTER 12

The Future of Operational Auditing

The preceding chapters have described operational auditing in theory and practice, based on the experiences of a broad range of businesses. Many companies have been performing operational auditing for many more functions than those described; for example, such functions as administrative services, travel, engineering, sales, and research and development are commonly included in the annual audit plan. In many businesses, no specific limits are placed on the audit group. The audit group is expected to appraise controls in all areas of the company.

This closing chapter describes the general manner in which the operational auditing approach can be applied to any area of business, and gives particular attention to the need for a well qualified internal audit staff, since the effectiveness of operational auditing depends almost entirely on having a capable, enthusiastic audit staff with the unstinting support of management.

The functional chapters described how the internal auditor can make a constructive, management-oriented appraisal of a considerable range of operating departments in the company. In each case, the auditor follows the basic steps of:

1. Familiarization with the primary objectives and physical operations of the function being audited

397

2. Examination of the mechanisms used to control the operations and attain the objectives

3. Appraisal and evaluation of the adequacy and effectiveness of the control mechanisms

4. Reporting of findings and constructive recommendations

I cannot overemphasize the importance of familiarization as the vital *first* step in the operational audit. The process of familiarization educates the auditor in the audit area—and at the same time helps establish a rapport with those responsible for the operation to be audited. The auditor learns to speak their language and to see the day-to-day business operations through their eyes. During the familiarization stage, the auditor learns what the audited organization considers to be its problems and can hold these in mind as the audit proceeds. A problem understood and well defined is well on the road to solution.

Please note that little emphasis has been placed on accounting as a major factor in operational audits; other books discuss accounting far more thoroughly. Accounting is but one of the tools of management control. While accounting and other records may provide one point of departure for the work of the auditor, it is always necessary to remember that the ultimate, and the only, objective of the operational audit is the welfare of the business. If accounting and other management controls help the business operate more effectively and profitably, they are doing their job. If they do not make a definitely constructive contribution, the auditor's responsibility is to recommend improvement.

Broader Scope

As previously stated, the analytical, problem-solving approach of the internal auditor permits constructive audits to be made in any operating area of a business. The decision as to the areas to be covered depends on management's confidence in the internal audit department and its understanding of the possibilities of operational audits. To a large degree, this confidence and understanding is based on what the internal auditors have demonstrated in their work. Probably the broadest company applications of internal auditing to business operations have developed from capable work by internal auditors in more limited areas. This is well expressed in the saying "The reward of work well done is more work."

In addition to the areas covered in the preceding chapters, operational audits are being made of such functions as:

Treasury: cash and cash management lines of credit, bank usage and fees, minimum balances, offsets company to company

Administrative services: travel services, corporate contracts, air transportation, hotels, limousine service, plant and office cleaning, grounds maintenance, word processing, cafeteria, graphic arts

Corporate communications: the integration of duplication services, facsimile, telecommunications, telephone, telex, microcomputers

Compensation Audits: review bonus programs, commission programs

Vehicle Administration: corporate vehicles, including reviewing the ratio of mileage to gasoline usage, proper titles and registrations, repairs, disposal of vehicles, and so on

Quality Control: reviewing documentation for tests performed, and reviewing compliance to departmental standards and corporate policies and procedures

Research and Development: reviewing the department's plans, objectives and charter, cost accumulation procedures, project approvals, and methods of controlling project costs to performance progress

Plant and Data Security: access to data (via transmission lines) and physical access to the building(s), including after hours and on non-workdays

The possibilities for constructive audit are as broad as the range of business activity. In addition to the areas covered in the preceding chapters, other examples of audits being conducted in several companies follow.

Acquisitions and Mergers

The internal audit department conducted a complete audit of companies proposed for acquisition. This was far more than a financial audit. Operational auditing was necessary to analyze the operations in a very short time period. The auditors brought to bear their broad background of company operations as members of the team that determines how well the proposed acquisition would fit the company scheme of things.

Research and Development

Review coordination and cooperation among the various vice presidents and various departments in the organization. Review the minutes of the board of directors meetings of the corporation and its shell companies, divisions, and subsidiaries.

How is the research and development (R&D) department measured as far as productivity, performance, and yield? Determine if they effectively use CAE/CAD technology and other equipment utilized within their industry. Examine the flow of information from research and development through engineering into manufacturing. Determine if transferability of technology exists from one unrelated product discipline for possible use/application in related fields.

The auditor should review R&D's accountability: How is its performance measured? Is it devoting resources to indirect processes, direct process applications, or to reducing energy consumption? Review the organization structure and management methods, people skills, computer support; determine that they are consistent with the corporate goals and good internal control.

Determine how researchers maintain their skills, methodology, and education. Determine how project priorities are assigned, what job costing methodologies are used for R&D charges to production, application engineering, cost reduction programs, quality control, and so on.

Determine how marketing strategies are communicated to the R&D group. Changing customer needs/desires must be communicated continually.

Business Policy Auditing

This type of audit critiques the overall corporate structure—similar in approach to an MBA-level business policy course. The auditor critiques the major organization of the company, including a review of the board of directors committee structure as well as the major company departments, such as: quality control/quality assurance, research and development, information systems, finance, engineering, manufacturing, sales, marketing, public and community relations, advertising, personnel, accounting, purchasing, distribution, legal, production development, business development, international operations, facilities and process engineering, corporate secretary, and security, all in concert with the current external environment.

In the detailed examination, the auditor also correlates and analyzes employee statistics (by department), such as: age, years with the company, years of total experience, education, technical training, courses, seminars, and conferences taken, papers presented, and so on. The auditor looks for a balance within the department and the company.

Operations and Controls

While the auditor can perform a constructive job in any operating area, this does not mean that the auditor is an expert in all areas. The auditors' expertise is in the field of control—and every operating area has controls of some description. The auditor's authoritative recommendations are in the area of control, except in cases where previous experience may qualify him or her to give a broader perspective.

At the same time, remember that the auditor is a curious, persistent analyst who first learns about the operations being audited. In a larger company, these observations cover many similar areas—and often ideas will develop that have possible application to other locations or operating areas. Some of these may be communicated as no more than informal questions or suggestions; others may form the basis for further special study.

For example, in one large company, an auditor's suggestion on materials storage, which arose from observation in one location, resulted in a major savings when applied to other locations throughout the company. Such suggestions must be tactfully made, so as not to create an impression that the auditor assumes himself to be an expert in every sort of operating problem. However, the capable auditor has a sense and a feeling for problem areas. The auditor is enough of a diagnostician to realize when a problem exists; often the realization comes in the examination and appraisal of controls; in another situation, this comes during the process of familiarization.

The constructive recommendation to solve the problem may be within the responsibility and capability of the auditor. When it is not, the auditor may serve as a catalyst whose efforts have helped to bring about the recognition, analysis, and solution of the problem in the best interests of the whole business.

The auditors' abilities and experience as analysts, and their familiarity with the operations of the company at the grassroots level, qualify them for an important role on the management team. In addition to the examples given, internal auditors work closely with operations research staff; they can be familiar with and may help in applying these management techniques. They are members of teams that can work with outside management consultants and with teams that develop plans for the application and installation of data processing equipment and software.

Communications

In Chapter 1, the importance of reporting was stressed. This, and the auditors' other communications with management and operating personnel, must be superlatively handled if the auditors' work is to be understandable to and accepted by operating and senior managers.

Auditors should make increasing use of the communication techniques that have proved effective in other areas. Sales personnel are accustomed to presentations via charts and other visual aids; a 10-page written report on sales operations will not have the effect that a formal video presentation would produce. Pictures illustrating poor or good situations are more apt to make an impression and to produce results than will a description of conditions. With computers, storyboards can be used; overhead acetates and 35mm slide presentations are also within the scope of most audit department budgets.

One chief auditor conducts a rehearsal before each audit closing conference. In this rehearsal, the chief auditor takes the role of the auditee, and is direct, pointed, and somewhat antagonistic in his questioning of the senior auditor's presentation, the visual aids used, and the recommendations made.

The Attitude of the Auditor

Important among the requirements for working with operating executives are a liking for people, an understanding of their problems and a degree of flexibility in thought and approach that is at least as great as that which the auditors expect to find in those who are managing the functions that are to be audited. In the opening chapter, we stated that effective operational auditing depends on the auditor, not on the program. The auditor must develop a program to meet the needs of any operating department within the company where the auditor works.

Since the value of operational auditing depends on the auditor, it is necessary that the auditor be carefully selected. Chapter 1 gave brief consideration to the qualifications of the auditor. These characteristics were cited: curiosity, persistence, constructive approach, business sense, empathy, and cooperation. Together, these add up to the qualifications of a broad-minded, analytical businessperson—and that precisely is what the auditor should be.

It is vital that the internal auditor be selected, educated, and trained potentially as a business (or operations) analyst, not as a routine accountant. Probably the most ineffective type of auditor is the one who approaches an assignment with a combination of preconceived ideas, principles, and prejudices. Unfortunately, many auditors, whose principal background has been routine accounting and auditing work, are the same auditors who attempt to apply the rigorous standards of accuracy of routine accounting to operating problems.

All too often, unimaginative auditors take the position that there are principles of control that would conform to the dictionary definition and have the force of law or axiom (i.e., self-evident truth). In this situation, minimum thought and judgment are necessary, since the facts in comparison with the principle permit an immediate right or wrong evaluation. The big error is that the auditor takes the position that what is self-evident and axiomatic to him is similarly accepted by those whose operations are being audited. To them, some of the auditor's principles may seem entirely unwarranted and even against good business practice—yet because they are principles, the auditees are expected to accept them without question.

When the auditor forgets about principles, which he should, and thinks and talks of standards, then he is on much sounder ground and in a position where business judgment can apply. Standards define what is desirable, but deviation from standard is not prima-facie evidence of a crime. Such deviation is only a signal for examination and analysis. The auditor's judgment and recommendation is then based on what is best for the protection and profit of the business.

This approach requires far more thought and analysis from the auditor. When a deviation from standards is found, the auditor must decide whether the deviation is good business. If not, the auditor must sell the recommendation to operating management on the basis of talking about the protection and profits of the business, not on the basis of principles of which the auditor may be the only advocate.

The auditor who lives by principles will be looked on as an umpire; the auditor who works with standards that are adaptable to meet specific situations will gain acceptance as a member of the management team.

The Future of the Auditor

The progress of the internal auditor in business depends almost entirely on the auditor's abilities and attitude. It is difficult to imagine a position that offers any better opportunity to learn the business than that of internal auditor. To summarize:

1. In the course of work, the auditor first learns the objectives of the sections of the business being audited and how these objectives are being accomplished. The auditor comes to know actual operations and operating personnel at the working level.
2. The auditor has an excellent opportunity to see management in action. The auditor is educated in management skills, by seeing how good operations are managed, and by deciding just what seems to be wrong with ineffective operating units.
3. The auditor's work and reporting bring her into direct contact with operating executives. The auditor can see and observe them, and they see and observe the auditor in action.
4. The auditor gains a broad perspective of various management styles and reporting techniques. He sees how all the pieces (of the company) are orchestrated.

However, employment on the audit staff is like attendance at college; it can do no more than provide the environment and the opportunity. The unimaginative auditor who has little or no interest in what makes things run, who likes to evaluate people and operations on a black or white basis, will make little progress.

The imaginative auditor is truly interested in the welfare of the business and is consciously endeavoring to improve his own knowledge and skills. The auditor keeps up-to-date by studying management tools and techniques and by observing theory in relation to practice. Auditors can show their expertise by taking and passing the certified internal auditor examination. A person with this attitude progresses in business and in the profession of internal audit. An increasing number of businesses recognize these factors by using the internal audit department as a testing and training ground for potential company executives.

The auditor who bases his development and work on helping the business toward better operation and greater profitability may, or may not, become the company's president. A number of auditors have. Regardless, a true concern with the operational auditing approach is understood and appreciated by management, is much more interesting from the standpoint of work and accomplishment, and cannot but be a vital element in the advancement of the auditor, whose future depends in large measure upon himself.

The growth in recognition and stature of a profession depends in large measure upon the growth of its practitioners. The operational approach, attitude and accomplishments of individual auditors will benefit them and thus the whole profession of internal auditing.

APPENDIX A

Statement of Responsibilities of the Internal Auditor

NATURE

Internal Auditing is an independent appraisal activity within an organization for the review of operations as a service to management. It is a managerial control which functions by measuring and evaluating the effectiveness of other controls.

OBJECTIVE AND SCOPE

The objective of internal auditing is to assist all members of management in the effective discharge of their responsibilities, by furnishing them with analyses, appraisals, recommendations and pertinent comments concerning the activities reviewed. The internal auditor is concerned with any phase of business activity where he can be of service to management. This involves going beyond the accounting and financial records to obtain a full understanding of the operations under review. The attainment of this overall objective involves such activities as:

- Reviewing and appraising the soundness, adequacy, and application of accounting, financial, and other operating controls, and promoting effective control at reasonable cost.

- Ascertaining the extent of compliance with established policies, plans, and procedures.
- Ascertaining the extent to which company assets are accounted for and safeguarded from losses of all kinds.
- Ascertaining the reliability of management data developed within the organization.
- Appraising the quality of performance in carrying out assigned responsibilities.
- Recommending operating improvements.

RESPONSIBILITY AND AUTHORITY

The responsibilities of internal auditing in the organization should be clearly established by management policy. The related authority should provide the internal auditor full access to all of the organization's records, properties, and personnel relevant to the subject under review. The internal auditor should be free to review and appraise policies, plans, procedures, and records.

The internal auditor's responsibilities should be:

- To inform and advise management, and to discharge this responsibility in a manner that is consistent with the Code of Ethics of The Institute of Internal Auditors.
- To coordinate his activities with others so as to best achieve his audit objectives and the objectives of the organization.

In performing his functions, an internal auditor has no direct responsibility for nor authority over any of the activities which he reviews. Therefore, the internal audit review and appraisal does not in any way relieve other persons in the organization of the responsibilities assigned to them.

INDEPENDENCE

Independence is essential to the effectiveness of internal auditing. This independence is obtained primarily through organizational status and objectivity:

- The organizational status of the internal auditing function and the support accorded to it by management are major determinants of its range and value. The head of the internal auditing function, therefore, should be responsible to an officer whose authority is sufficient to assure both a broad range of audit coverage and the adequate consideration of and effective action on the audit findings and recommendations.

- Objectivity is essential to the audit function. Therefore, an internal auditor should not develop and install procedures, prepare records, or engage in any other activity which he would normally review and appraise and which could reasonably be construed to compromise his independence. His objectivity need not be adversely affected, however, by his determination and recommendation of the standards of control to be applied in the development of systems and procedures under his review.

*   *   *

The Statement of Responsibilities of the Internal Auditor was originally issued by The Institute of Internal Auditors in 1947. The continuing development of the profession has resulted in two revisions, in 1957 and 1971. The current statement embodies the concepts previously established and includes such changes as are deemed advisable in light of the present status of the profession.

APPENDIX B

Certified Internal Auditor Code of Ethics

The Certified Internal Auditor has an obligation to his profession, management, stockholders and the general public to maintain high standards of professional conduct in the performance of his profession. In recognition of these obligations the Board of Regents has adopted the following Code of Ethics.

Adherence to this Code, which is based on the Code of Ethics of The Institute of Internal Auditors, Inc., is a prerequisite to maintaining the designation Certified Internal Auditor. A Certified Internal Auditor who is judged in violation of the provisions of the Code by the Ethics Committee of the Board of Regents shall forfeit the CIA designation.

PREAMBLE

The provisions of this Code of Ethics cover basic principles in the various disciplines of internal auditing practice. A Certified Internal Auditor shall realize that individual judgment is required in the application of these principles. He has a responsibility to conduct himself so that his good faith and integrity should not be open to question. While having due regard for the limit of his technical skills, he will promote the highest possible internal auditing standards to the end of advancing the interest of his company or organization.

ARTICLES

   I. A Certified Internal Auditor shall have an obligation to exercise honesty, objectivity and diligence in the performance of his duties and responsibilities.
  II. A Certified Internal Auditor, in holding the trust of his employer, shall exhibit loyalty in all matters pertaining to the affairs of the employer or to whomever he may be rendering a service. However, a Certified Internal Auditor shall not knowingly be a party to any illegal or improper activity.
 III. A Certified Internal Auditor shall refrain from entering into any activity which may be in conflict with the interest of his employer or which would prejudice his ability to carry out objectively his duties and responsibilities.
  IV. A Certified Internal Auditor shall not accept a fee or a gift from an employee, a client, a customer or a business associate of his employer without the knowledge and consent of his senior management.
   V. A Certified Internal Auditor shall be prudent in the use of information acquired in the course of his duties. He shall not use confidential information for any personal gain or in a manner which would be detrimental to the welfare of his employer.
  VI. A Certified Internal Auditor, in expressing an opinion, shall use all reasonable care to obtain sufficient factual evidence to warrant such expression. In his reporting, a Certified Internal Auditor shall reveal such material facts known to him which, if not revealed, could either distort the report of the results of operations under review or conceal unlawful practice.
 VII. A Certified Internal Auditor shall continually strive for improvement in the proficiency and effectiveness of his service.

Index